The Cinema Alone

, 2001

Dear Jim,

Happy New Year to you.
Hope all is well and that
you'll enjoy reading this
effort from James and
myself.

Best, Michael

(M. James)

Film Culture in Transition

Thomas Elsaesser: General Editor

Double Trouble
Chiem van Houweninge on Writing and Filming
Thomas Elsaesser, Robert Kievit and Jan Simons (eds.)

Writing for the Medium: Television in Transition
Thomas Elsaesser, Jan Simons and Lucette Bronk (eds.)

Between Stage and Screen
Ingmar Bergman Directs
Egil Törnqvist

The Film Spectator: From Sign to Mind
Warren Buckland (ed.)

Film and the First World War
Karel Dibbets and Bert Hogenkamp (eds.)

A Second Life
German Cinema's First Decades
Thomas Elsaesser (ed.)

Fassbinder's Germany
History Identity Subject
Thomas Elsaesser

Cinema Futures: Cain, Abel or Cable?
The Screen Arts in the Digital Age
Thomas Elsaesser and Kay Hoffmann (eds.)

Audiovisions
Cinema and Television as Entr'Actes in History
Siegfried Zielinski

Joris Ivens and the Documentary Context
Kees Bakker (ed.)

The Cinema Alone

Essays on the Work of Jean-Luc Godard 1985-2000

Edited by

Michael Temple and James S. Williams

Amsterdam University Press

Cover illustration: Still from JLG/JLG: AUTOPORTRAIT DE DÉCEMBRE (1994).
Courtesy of the British Film Institute.
Cover design: Korpershoek Ontwerpen, Amsterdam
Lay-out: JAPES, Amsterdam

NUGI 922
ISBN 90 5356 456 x (hardcover)
ISBN 90 5356 455 1 (paperback)

© Amsterdam University Press, Amsterdam, 2000

All rights reserved. Without limiting the rights under copyright reserved above, no part of this book may be reproduced, stored in or introduced into a retrieval system, or transmitted, in any form or by any means (electronic, mechanical, photocopying, recording, or otherwise), without the written permission of both the copyright owner and the authors of this book.

Contents

Acknowledgements

We would like to thank Patrick ffrench, Roland-François Lack and Nigel Saint for their help and expertise in translating from French into English Chapters 6, 10 and 11. We would also like to thank Agnès Calatayud, Fabienne Reymondet and Michael Witt for alerting us to new material and sources, Burhan Tufail for his help in preparing the Index, and Birkbeck College London for its generous financial assistance. Finally, we would like to express our deep appreciation to Wardy Poelstra at Amsterdam University Press for his reassuring calm and efficiency, and to Thomas Elsaesser for his immediate enthusiasm for the project and excellent support throughout.

1 Introduction to the Mysteries of Cinema, 1985-2000

Michael Temple and James S. Williams

The work, not the name

The year 2000 marks Jean-Luc Godard's seventieth birthday. He will have been active in cinema for the best part of fifty years. Like no other film-maker, he has constantly challenged the practice and understanding of cinema as the art form and cultural phenomenon that uniquely defined the twentieth century. In the simplest of terms, we would like this book, *The Cinema Alone: Essays on the work of Jean-Luc Godard 1985-2000*, to express a certain cinephilia, a certain respect and admiration for Godard's work. The work, not the name. In film mythology, the name 'Godard' probably does represent something like 'the last of the great auteurs'. But as Godard likes to remind us, the important word in the phrase 'la politique des auteurs' was 'politique' rather than 'auteur'. In other words, it was less a cult of artistic personality than a policy or strategy designed to gain for films, and for cinema in general, the same artistic status accorded to painting, literature and music. Fifty years on, this is the lesson he wishes to retain: 'That's what the New Wave was about: the auteur-policy, not the authors, the works.'[1] It is in a similar spirit that we have approached this collection, our primary concern being to foreground Godard's work of the last fifteen years, in particular the recently completed HISTOIRE(S) DU CINÉMA. In our opinion, this videographic experiment in film-history not only gives a clearly defined shape and purpose to Godard's multifarious film and video activities since 1985, but also marks a new phase in a complex and shifting career that will now require a thorough reassessment from critics and film culture at large.

It would, of course, be futile to deny that, in France especially, there exists a curious cultural paradox whereby 'Godard' the media icon (i.e. name plus face) is universally recognisable and yet totally unknown. Such hyper-visibility obscures the fact that the real Jean-Luc Godard has never stopped working and has patiently elaborated a body of work that is truly rich and strange, and as ambitious, diverse and inspiring as anything he produced in his supposed 1960s heyday. This paradox was acknowledged long ago: 'We live in a society of names, where the name counts far more than the object or the person. A name is a form of capital. So I do with it what I can.'[2] The name allows Godard to carry on working, but at a heavy personal price: 'The phrase "I am Godard" is a philosophical problem. My current formula is "I am [*suis*] a dog and the dog follows [*suit*] Godard".'[3] In other words, his actual film and video production increasingly exists and evolves in a rather empty atmosphere, parallel to the media-world in which the 'Godard-effect', as one rather uninspired volume from 1989 chose to call it,[4] continues to flourish and circulate as never before. The legend, the myth, the name-of-the-artist – in the last decade, these signs have never been more available or prominent.[5] Yet if the film and video works signed by that name are rarely seen and virtually invisible, together they constitute one of the most innovative and promising audio-visual projects in contemporary world cinema. This is just one of the many paradoxes that we wish to bring to wider critical attention in *The Cinema Alone*, the essential aims of which are to bring Godard's latest work into critical focus and generate vital debate. In the English-speaking world, several studies of Godard's films have been published over the last five years, by Josefa Loshitzky, Wheeler Winston Dixon and David Sterritt, yet they are concerned essentially with early and middle Godard (i.e. Godard's work up until 1985), and provide at best only a summary of the corpus since 1985. Similarly, the most recent film considered by Kaja Silverman and Harun Farocki in their series of engaged dialogues entitled *Speaking about Godard* (1998) is NOUVELLE VAGUE, which dates from 1990.[6] All these volumes fail by a long way to acknowledge that Godard is a presently active film-maker who, over the last fifteen years, has found the time and energy to make not only the monumental HISTOIRE(S) DU CINÉMA, but also twenty-three discrete works. These include five feature films in 35 millimetre intended for cinema release: SOIGNE TA DROITE, KING LEAR, NOUVELLE VAGUE, HÉLAS POUR MOI and FOR EVER MOZART. In addition, Godard has produced seven substantial film essays (including collaborations with Anne-Marie Miéville). These are 35 mm or video pieces made mainly for television: SOFT AND HARD, GRANDEUR ET DÉCADENCE D'UN PETIT COMMERCE DE CINÉMA, LE RAPPORT DARTY, ALLEMAGNE ANNÉE 90 NEUF ZÉRO, LES ENFANTS JOUENT À LA RUSSIE, JLG/JLG: AUTOPORTRAIT DE DÉCEMBRE, and 2X50 ANS DE CINÉMA FRANÇAIS. To this substantial corpus one must also add eleven shorts and sketches, i.e. commissions, experiments, and occasional pieces in a variety of forms and formats: MEETIN' W.A., ARMIDE (a sequence from the compilation film ARIA), Marithé et François Girbaud commercials, ON S'EST TOUS DÉFILÉ, PUISSANCE DE LA PAROLE, LE DERNIER MOT, L'ENFANCE DE L'ART, CONTRE L'OUBLI, JE VOUS SALUE SARAJEVO, ADIEU AU TNS and the video clip PLUS OH!.

Despite such manifest evidence of creative vitality, however, Godard would probably have done better not to have survived his famous motorbike crash of 1971. This would surely have been a kinder fate than to see himself represented in the year 2000 as a radical sixties film-maker who appears rather selfishly not yet to have died. The story is well known: something political happened around 1968 which led to a series of unwatchable films, before Godard then headed for the French provinces to make TV, returning to cinema only in the late 1970s with SAUVE QUI PEUT (LA VIE). This produced in the early 1980s some late masterpieces by an Old Master, after which the old fool isolated in his Swiss retreat appeared to lose the plot. This crude digest of images and stereotypes purveyed by much contemporary Godard scholarship may appear over-reductive, but with some notable exceptions it is also depressingly accurate.[7] By publishing *The Cinema Alone*, we are seeking to change that deathly perspective and introduce a new agenda, one which orients the Godard corpus towards the future. Rather than start with the glorious New Wave and descend towards a preconceived and rather flat ending, we want to initiate an open and improvisatory process based in an uncertain present, whereby the past components of the Godardian œuvre can be continually redefined according to future changes. As the last fifteen years have confirmed, the work pursued by Godard has always proceeded by trial and error, fits and starts, in a consistent digression rather than a steady progress, and even those amongst us who have tried to keep pace are frequently astonished by where it has taken us. The vast array of themes and approaches explored at length during this period include autobiography and memory in film; age and melancholia; twentieth-century history and historiography; the fate of European art and culture; the relations between aesthetics and national identity; ethics and philosophy; the nature and status of authorship and literature; the evolution of the visual image from painting to film and video; speed and technology; and videographic montage as a new poetics.

It was the final completion in 1998 of HISTOIRE(S) DU CINÉMA, to many a surprise and to some even a revelation, that served to clarify the nature and ambition of much of Godard's recent work and to cast it in a new light. Many of the films, essays and short pieces since 1985 were revealed in varying degrees as works in parallel with HISTOIRE(S) DU CINÉMA, contributing indirectly yet significantly to it, and vice versa. The appearance of HISTOIRE(S) DU CINÉMA thus provides the prime motivation for *The Cinema Alone* as well as the focal point for many of the individual chapters. In what now follows we shall present a clear outline of that work's shape and evolution and an overview of its main themes and concerns.[8] We will then consider the challenges that HISTOIRE(S) DU CINÉMA poses to film-history and criticism, and the extent to which it redefines both our understanding of Godard's activities since 1985 and our conception of the entire corpus since 1950. Finally, we shall indicate the strategy and rationale of *The Cinema Alone* and introduce briefly the diverse essays which it brings together.

From words to work

What is HISTOIRE(S) DU CINÉMA? Very simply, it is a boxed set of four video cassettes totalling 265 minutes and comprising eight episodes or 'chapters'.[9] Significantly re-edited in 1998, this is what the final version looks like:

    1A   TOUTES LES HISTOIRES, 51 minutes
    1B   UNE HISTOIRE SEULE, 42 minutes
    2A   SEUL LE CINÉMA, 26 minutes
    2B   FATALE BEAUTÉ, 28 minutes
    3A   LA MONNAIE DE L'ABSOLU, 26 minutes
    3B   UNE VAGUE NOUVELLE, 27 minutes
    4A   LE CONTRÔLE DE L'UNIVERS, 27 minutes
    4B   LES SIGNES PARMI NOUS, 38 minutes[10]

The set of videos is accompanied by matching sets of four CDs and four art books, the latter reproducing some of the images from the video work as well as textual extracts from the spoken soundtrack.[11] Yet the art books cannot be said to constitute a source book. The text is presented in a quasi-poetic layout similar to that employed by Godard in analogous books or *'phrases'* produced to accompany several of his other recent works.[12] The sober and imageless nature of these *'phrases'* may be contrasted directly with the colourful, high-fidelity, and frequently stunning quality of the images in the book of HISTOIRE(S) DU CINÉMA. Here, the collage of word and image recalls, and no doubt surpasses, the various attempts by Godard over the years to find a text-based means of thinking about cinema that could avoid merely surrendering film's sacred specificity to the deadly evils of logocentrism. 'For me, texts are death, images are life', as he once memorably expressed it.[13] Indeed, one could speculate *ad hominem* that these experiments in literary-artistic fusion are the signs of a long-running struggle between Godard the film-maker and Godard the would-be writer, between the exorbitantly gifted visual artist and 'my royal enemy, my number one enemy, the text'.[14] This has been an ill-matched fight, however, in which the Word has always carried the heavier punch and ultimately succeeded in cutting the *cinéaste maudit* down to size.[15] What is more certain is that the completion of HISTOIRE(S) DU CINÉMA confirms one critical hypothesis that Godard had been working on the project throughout his entire career by performing the dual role of film-historian and film-maker.[16] After all, did he not start his film-life in a Museum? Was he not the most evangelically brilliant of Henri Langlois's child-messengers? Did he not first engage creatively with cinema as a critic, reviving and reviling the living and the dead, comparing and contesting the present and the past? Yes, all this is true, and certainly one could now revise in depth the general perception of Godard as a double-headed critical force: before cinema, as both critic and genealogist; during cinema, as both film-historical artist and social commentator; and most crucially, after cinema, when TV and video, assassins of the cinematograph, became the very instruments with which to investigate that death, to measure and decide exactly what it was that cinema no longer is.[17]

In 1985, towards the end of a 'biographical' interview that served as an introduction to the collected texts of *Jean-Luc Godard par Jean-Luc Godard*, vol. 1, Godard stated very simply that 'video taught me to see cinema and to rethink the working of cinema in another way'.[18] He might have added that video had also begun to teach him how to rethink the workings of the history of cinema, since in our view the real invention and elaboration of HISTOIRE(S) DU CINÉMA begins when the film historian decides to abandon the traditionally logocentric tools of the trade (that is, text-with-illustrations, narrative-plus-clips, scholarship, chronology, objectivity) and accepts instead the idea that only on video and through the logic of montage will cinema be empowered to speak its own language, relate its own story, and perform the mystery play of its birth, life, and death. Several years earlier, in a conventional pedagogical setting, Godard tried unsuccessfully to conceive and realise 'the veritable history of film and television' by employing a fairly standard methodology of talking, narrating and explaining such a history with the help of exemplary extracts from great films (including his own). The following statement by Godard remains the most lucid and enlightening account of the abandoned enterprise:

> In the autumn of 1978, having invited Henri Langlois the previous year, Serge Losique, the director of the Conservatoire d'art cinématographique in Montreal, asked me to carry on the work already undertaken. Rather than giving lectures in the way they are given in universities the world over, I suggested to Losique that he consider the affair... as an 'affair'... a kind of co-production, that would be a sort of scenario for an eventual film series entitled 'introduction to a veritable history of cinema and television', veritable in the sense that it would be made from images and sounds rather than texts, even illustrated ones [...] It was decided that the scenario should be divided into several (ten) chapters or voyages, with a budget of 10,000 Canadian dol-

lars per chapter, to be shared between the Conservatory and the film company of which I am a partner, Sonimage. So for each trip I brought with me a little of my personal history [*mon histoire*], and plunged myself back into it at a rate of two films per month. But this dipping into my past often revealed something different from what my memory had recorded, and this is no doubt explained by the fact that in the morning sessions there were projected extracts of films from the history of cinema, films which were related to what I was doing at that time. And I gave a running commentary on all this to three or four Canadians who were as lost as I was in the whole business [*histoire*]. Then everything came to a stop [...] But 'nobody's perfect'. Jean-Luc Godard.[19]

It should be noted that this statement served as a preface to the published version of Godard's improvised talks or lectures which had been faithfully transcribed and reconstituted by the Montreal Film School. Far from underwriting the text published as *Introduction à une véritable histoire du cinéma* (1980), Godard's signature serves to write it off and disavow it as a well-meaning but ill-conceived failure.

Retrospectively, one can see that the Montreal experiment in fact contains quite a number of the principles and theses of HISTOIRE(S) DU CINÉMA, but as Godard discovered several years later at the FEMIS (Fondation Européenne des Métiers de l'Image et du Son), the real problem does not lie with the country, the people, the institution or the budget. No amount of money or transatlantic crossings can conceal the truth from an artist when the problem is formal and the basic set-up is flawed. If you really want to make a history of cinema, then first you must select the proper tools. Before any thesis or theory is conceived, before any method or material is deployed, Godard the film historian makes a fundamental and irrevocable commitment to allow the story of cinema to relate its own story through its own means, and most notably through *montage*, its one true, formal invention and secret weapon. Film formally delivers its past, present, and future into the careful and thoughtful hands of the videographic artist-historian. From that critical moment, HISTOIRE(S) DU CINÉMA becomes a real, live project. It does not really matter exactly when this happened, but our own particular view is that around 1985 one begins to see material evidence of a major shift towards the new manner and method. This is marked crucially by the generally ignored television piece SOFT AND HARD, whose dialogic format, 'a soft conversation on a hard subject' between Godard and Miéville, introduces a whole new spirit of conference and exchange: between two friends and collaborators, between cinema's past and present, between personal stories and impersonal histories, and above all, between the formerly fratricidal duo of film and video who will now no longer re-enact the legend of Cain and Abel.[20] Thus, in SOFT AND HARD there appear the first sequences that actually look and sound like HISTOIRE(S) DU CINÉMA and begin to utilise its distinctive historical idiom.[21] This hypothesis appears to be confirmed by anecdotal evidence from Freddy Buache and Alain Bergala that early video drafts of HISTOIRE(S) DU CINÉMA exist from 1985 and 1986.[22] As early as 1983, in an interview relating to PRÉNOM CARMEN, Godard casually mentions that he is 'preparing a history of cinema in collaboration with Canal Plus in France, in which I will be trying to show that cinema, with all the cultural forces it brought into play, was something quite unique'.[23] Moreover, by 1986, Godard is happily answering questions regarding the formal dimensions and difficulties of what is clearly at this stage an active project in the historical and archeological style of Fernand Braudel and Michel Foucault. He explains then that cinema is literally 'an image of the world in which we live', but it is also 'the only place where you can sleep with your eyes open, in the dark. Hence, cinema is the world of dreams'.[24] We can detect in this interview a sense of urgency reminiscent of his remark in LETTRE À FREDDY BUACHE that 'cinema's going to die soon, it's an emergency', since he relates there a series of fundamental problems: the urgency and lack of time, the excess and specificity of materials, the logocentric temptation, the fact of working through complexity and difficulty, and the value and status of subjectivity. By 1988, having completed the first two episodes, Godard gave what is undoubtedly the best-known and still most informative interview relating to HISTOIRE(S) DU CINÉMA. It took the form of a filmed conversation between Godard and Serge Daney, a few years before Daney's death. This mortal fact lends a particular poignancy to their exchange which subsequently became part of the work's audio-visual fabric, notably Chapters 2A, SEUL LE CINÉMA, and 4B, LES SIGNES PARMI NOUS.[25]

Looking back today at this interview, which was intended as a pedagogical guide to HISTOIRE(S) DU CINÉMA to be broadcast on television alongside it, we are struck by the fact that most of the key themes and theses announced by Godard still form the basic intellectual material of the finalised video work. Yet equally, an important distinction must be drawn between the ideas as they might be discursively conveyed and the dynamic flux of sound, image, voice, text and music that has emerged from the intervening process of videographic elaboration. Moreover, Godard is impressively lucid about the inevitable discrepancy between 'this super-ambitious idea of mine, a thesis that even Michelet did not have when he wrote the *History of France*', and the limitations imposed by his talent, life's contingencies, and no doubt the intrinsic impossibility of realising even an introduction to 'a veritable history of cinema, the only one, the true one'. Bearing those points in mind, let us look at some key extracts from that Daney interview as well as related material from other recent interviews, arranged around the major themes:

> *Projection of history.* The greatest story is the history of the cinema. It belongs to the
> nineteenth century but was resolved in the twentieth. It's greater than the rest be-
> cause it projects itself whereas the others reduce themselves. [...] When Langlois pro-
> jected NOSFERATU and you could already see the ruins of Berlin in 1944 in the little
> town where Nosferatu lives, that's what I call a projection. Thus, a little naively, I say
> that it's the greatest story because it can project itself [...] My aim, alas, is like in the lit-
> tle poem by Brecht: 'I examine my project with care: it's unrealisable'. Because it can
> only be made on TV, which reduces. Or which projects you as the viewer, but then
> you lose consciousness and you're rejected. Whereas with cinema, the viewer was at-
> tracted. It is possible, however, to make a souvenir of this projectable history. Cinema
> was unique, and that's all we can do with it. It's the greatest story, and it's never been
> told.

Cinema's 'big picture' uniquely engages the public's subjectivity, and therefore its history will contain, combine, and maybe confuse 'the big story in
the little one, the little one in the big' ('la grande dans la petite, la petite dans
la grande'). It records and recomposes the personal and the impersonal, the
individual's insignificant story entering an egalitarian dialogue with the
meaning-laden mass of History. This is a democratic project of identity insofar as each subject can find a voice and not just a vote. But cinema's social
potential is fatally compromised by the twin evils of savage capitalism and
brutal totalitarianism. Thus, Lenin and Hitler convert the dream-machine
into factories for perpetual murder while the moneymen pervert the promise of justice with 'a girl and a gun', the sex-and-violence formula that releases the commercial genius of Hollywood and founds the new empire of
fiction. The documentary virtues of cinema were soon ignored in favour of
its powers of persuasion and spectacle. But the Real was merely biding its
time, and from 1940 to 1945 it exacted a terrible revenge. When the crisis
came, cinema failed in its duties:

> *Historic betrayal.* I realised after a certain number of years that the concentration
> camps had never been shown. They had been spoken about generally but were not
> shown. I was interested in this probably because of what you were saying about my
> own feelings of guilt, my social class, etc.. But the camps were the first things that
> ought to have been shown, in the sense that the way we walk was shown by Marey's
> chronophotographic gun. We didn't want to see the camps. Things stopped at that
> point, and, as a consequence, I thought that the Nouvelle Vague was not a beginning
> but an end.

Better than most, Godard knows that cinema's birth and death, its origins and ending, have been mythologically inseparable ever since the Lumière brothers declared that the cinematograph was 'an invention without a future', the first in a long series of cinematic fake deaths. But here the French false dawn of the 1950s, the New Wave that was barely a faint rumour, is explicitly linked to the successive waves of feeble resistance that European national cinemas momentarily opposed to the post-war invasion or occupation of visual culture by the North-American allies:

> *Identity and Resistance.* There's a desire for images, to the extent that they're the only things that satisfied the notion of *identity* which must have become fundamental towards the end of the nineteenth century. [...] There is, I think, a need for identity, a need to be *recognised* [...] We are grateful to the world for recognising us and for allowing us to recognise ourselves, and I think that, precisely, until the camps, cinema constituted the identities of nations and peoples (who were more or less organised into nations), and then afterwards this feeling faded away. I'll examine this in a programme, 3B, called LA RÉPONSE DES TÉNÈBRES[26] [...] How is it that in 1940-5 there was no Resistance cinema? Not that there weren't some resistance films, on the right and on the left, here and there, but the only properly cinematic resistance film that resisted the American occupation of cinema, or a certain standardised way of making films, was an Italian film. Italy is the country that fought the least, suffered greatly, lost its identity and then started up again with ROME, OPEN CITY. It's the only time this happened. The Russians made propaganda films or films about martyrs, the Americans made publicity films, the English did their usual thing, the Germans didn't know what to do for themselves, and the French made only prisoner-of-war films. The Poles are the only ones to have tried twice in a row to make films about the camps: Munk's PASSENGER (which was never finished) and Wanda Jakubowska's THE LAST STAGE... For a long time, cinema represented the possibility of belonging to a nation, yet remaining oneself within that nation. All that has disappeared.

Most important, however, amongst these questions of content is undoubtedly 'this thing that remains strictly within cinema, i.e. *montage*':

> *In search of montage.* The idea I'm defending with the history of cinema that I'm preparing, QUELQUES HISTOIRES À PROPOS DU CINÉMA, is that montage is what made cinema unique and different as compared to painting and the novel. Cinema as it was originally conceived is going to disappear quite quickly, within a lifetime, and something else will take its place. But what made it original, and what will never really have existed, like a plant that has never really left the ground, is montage. The silent film world felt it very strongly, and talked about it a lot. No-one found it. Griffith was looking for something like montage, he discovered the close-up. Eisenstein naturally thought that he had found montage... But by montage I mean something much more vast.[27]

As Michael Witt will argue later in this collection, the term 'montage' in Godard's discourse covers a wide and extravagant range of different ideas, from the humanist corporeality of 'thinking with your hands' to the irredeemably transcendental vision of an editorial hand-of-God. Although a common figure in film-mythology, this collocation of the artisanal and the spiritual is expressed by Godard in especially heartfelt terms during his talk at the FEMIS in 1989:

> *Montage and me.* In montage you finally feel safe. It's the moment that to me seems unique in the world, which I don't find in video because with video you can't cut. In montage, you have physically – it's what I said in KING LEAR with a shot of Woody Allen splicing together film with the aid of a safety pin – physically you have a moment, like an object, like this ashtray. You have the present, past and future. Mothers do not have this in relation to their children, lovers don't have this in relation to their love, and politicians, you can see it from their faces, are truly a long way from having it. No-one has it. I don't have it in relation to my own life, but in montage I have an object, which has a beginning, middle and end, which is there, in front of me [...] At that moment, there is an arrangement of things which is closer to architecture, or to an art which I have never really understood and which I am only beginning to understand: sculpture. There are sculptors who start off with the side of the nose, and sculpt everything from there. Michelangelo, it seems, started off from the toes then did the rest. Others proceed via successive essays, and that's more or less what I do. It's this feeling of essay, of essaying, and working through a subject, which seems to me difficult to obtain from a technician, judging from the experience I've had.[28]

As this passage should illustrate, Godard is at times capable of 'doing montage' with mere words, as if on rare occasions his famous stutter and literary impotence were magically transformed into a simple oral poetry.[29] But generally we must remember to bear in mind the distinction between videographic performance and straightforward intellectual themes and theses. After all, many of Godard's 'ideas' about cinema and film history are, as he says himself, quite standard fare: the purity of origins, the infinite promise of invention, the compact between Méliès and Lumière, document and fiction, the betrayal of cinema's popular mission and scientific vocation by Hollywood and spectacle, the death of the silents at the hands of the talkies, the ethical irresponsibility of cinema at critical moments of contemporary history (Auschwitz, Hiroshima, Vietnam, Bosnia), the cancerous spread of global television, the slowly successive deaths of distinct national cinemas, and so on. Yet it is also true that even discursively Godard gives some of these common motifs a powerful and idiosyncratic twist, as in the following extract from a 1995 interview:

Cinema has failed in its duties. It's a tool that we've misused. In the beginning, it was thought that cinema would impose itself as a new instrument of knowledge, like a microscope or a telescope, but very quickly it was prevented from playing its role and was turned into a toy. Cinema has not played its role as an instrument of thought [...] Almost from the beginning, with the arrival of Thalberg as head of MGM. There were certainly individuals, especially in France, who rose up against this but they were not big enough. In the end, cinema failed in its mission [...] Naively, we thought that the Nouvelle Vague would be a new beginning, a revolution. However, it was already too late. It was all over. The final blow had come when the concentration camps were not filmed. At that moment, cinema totally failed in its duty. Six million people, principally Jews, were killed or gassed, and cinema wasn't there. And yet, from THE GREAT DICTATOR to THE RULES OF THE GAME, it had announced the major events. By not filming the concentration camps, cinema threw in the towel completely.[30]

In the considerable number of interviews he has given during the last ten years, Godard has rehearsed these historical motifs so frequently that to some extent they have a life of their own. Intellectually, one could engage with them according to their own conceptual merits or factual shortcomings. In the definitive HISTOIRE(S) DU CINÉMA, as if to pre-empt such responses, Godard has liberally confessed to numerous 'errors' in his work, even going so far as to flash the term 'ERREUR' across the screen accompanied by an appropriate 'correction'.[31] In a similar vein, his public pronouncements since 1998 have tended to defend the line that his video work is less a scholarly or properly historical enterprise than an experiment in 'visual criticism' (a term he used, in fact, in the Daney interview), whose value should thus be discussed in the kind of terms usually reserved for music, architecture, painting, and sculpture. This move is apparent in the first major interview to have appeared since the commercial release of the video tapes and accompanying art books. After the conference on 'Godard et le métier d'artiste' held at Cerisy-la-Salle in August 1998, Godard requested an interview with the philosopher Youssef Ishaghpour whose interventions in the plenary debate had been recorded by Godard's assistant, Gilbert Guichardière. The resulting dialogue was published the following year in two successive issues of Trafic. Faced with a philosophical interlocutor, Godard is respectful of Ishaghpour's commentary and analysis but is also keen to underline those elements and aspects of HISTOIRE(S) DU CINÉMA which he thinks would be neglected or undervalued by such an approach. Therefore, when Ishaghpour compares Godard's project to Walter Benjamin's Paris, capital of the 19th century, the film-maker responds: 'Certainly, it was a feeling like that, it's not very clear, it was very unconscious... But when you, or others like you, quote an author or talk about a book, you've really read it, whereas I just hear a sound and think it should go in a particular place, and then there's a mixture with all the other elements.'[32] As the conversation extends from Benjamin to Charles Péguy, another major literary presence in HISTOIRE(S) DU CINÉMA, Godard again intervenes to defend his own work from this kind of bookish or 'meaningful' analysis: 'It's cinema, it's not like literature, which is more closely linked to meaning. In the film there's rhythm, it's closer to music. That's why I used the black screen, it's for the rhythm.'[33] Finally, again in relation to Benjamin, Godard picks up on the French term *entendement* because it can signify both 'understanding' in the sense of comprehension and 'hearing' in the sense of listening and paying attention to what something sounds like: 'There's the French word *entendement*, which means two things. It means that you hear, but also that you understand. One says: "I hear what you're saying", but also: "I see what you're saying". For me hearing and seeing are two different things but which go together and are indissociable.' What is interesting for our purposes is not just the fact that Godard is here reaffirming his belief in what one might paraphrase as 'equality and fraternity between sound and image' (although this is still extremely important in the context of HISTOIRE(S) DU CINÉMA), but also the suggestion that a proper approach to HISTOIRE(S) DU CINÉMA would need to be sensitive both to questions of comprehension, i.e. that which can be logically or discursively paraphrased, and to questions of rhythm, i.e. those formal or structural features that require a very different type of attention and sensitivity altogether.

The second strong message which Godard wishes to convey in this interview with Ishaghpour is that he does not consider HISTOIRE(S) DU CINÉMA to be complete, even though it is clearly finished: 'It's eight chapters of a film that could have contained hundreds more, especially the annexes, which are like footnotes, that is to say, they're often more interesting to read than the text itself [...] There would be many other things one could do on cinema. The main work hasn't been done [...] it would have required a whole team working together for five or six years, at least a hundred annexes, but I couldn't do them all on my own, I'd have had to have been paid a salary by the CNRS [National Centre for Scientific Research] in order to do that'.[34] Regular Godard-watchers will recognise here the disingenuous velleity for teamwork and state subsidy, but more important is the notion that the work itself is open-ended and 'to be continued'. In our opinion this gesture indicates the futility of a strictly hermeneutic approach to HISTOIRE(S) DU CINÉMA, and it also points the way forward to similar forms of experimentation by other artists and, crucially perhaps, by other technological means. Unlike Chris Marker, for example, Godard will not engage with 'digital' or anything related to computers, arguing somewhat unconvincingly that the effects used in HISTOIRE(S) DU CINÉMA 'are the same trick-shots that Méliès used to employ [...] It's cinema, technically it's manual, it's very simple things. I only used two or three of the forty or so options that the editing suite made available to me. Above all I used superimposition, which allowed me to retain the original film image [...] It was an act of painting.'[35] This appeal to technical primitivism should be taken with a pinch of salt. In real terms, there are very few film-makers who have shown themselves to be as technologically curious and inventive as Godard, even though his cultural critique of televisual imperialism or digital fakery could hardly appear more virulent.[36] Reading between the lines, it seems fairly clear that HISTOIRE(S) DU CINÉMA could just as easily have been a digital project, both in terms of its fabrication (digital editing rather than video-montage) and in terms of its distribution (CD-ROM rather than video-cassettes). For strategic reasons, however, it is vital that Godard be seen to respect the great mythology of film-culture, i.e. that just as sound killed silents, so digital is killing the already severely lacerated corpse of analogical cinema. But as Godard reveals towards the close of the *Trafic* interview, he is much more open and clear about these questions of shift and mutation than he often likes to pretend. He claims that, in one sense, film and video were part of the same spiritual family, that 'video was one of the avatars of cinema [and that] there wasn't a great difference between them, one could use them interchangeably, or get one to do what the other couldn't'.[37] While rationally there is plenty of evidence to suggest that video was technically and aesthetically a very different entity from its sibling rival, for Godard what matters most is that ever since the invention of the magic lantern, something called 'cinema' has continued to exist, metempsychotically speaking, in a whole succession of different hardwares and mortal coils. And Godard knows that what comes next may well not correspond to his own 'certain idea of cinema', but, as day follows night, cinema will certainly invent a new image of its own for a world as yet unseen and unknown:

> For me, HISTOIRE(S) DU CINÉMA was historical, it wasn't desperate. It may show things that could make you despair. But life can't afford to despair. Basically, one can say that a certain idea of cinema, which wasn't that of Lumière but a little of Feuillade and continued with Delluc, Vigo and me to a certain extent, that idea of cinema has passed [...] One can say that a certain cinema is over. As Hegel said, an era is finished; afterwards it's different. One feels sad because one's childhood is lost. But it's perfectly normal. Now there's a new cinema; a different art form, whose history will be made in fifty or one hundred years time. Now there's a new chapter of humanity, and perhaps even the very idea of History will change.[38]

Analysis terminal and indeterminable

As will be clear by now, the story of HISTOIRE(S) DU CINÉMA has itself
reached a turning point. The first phase of critical interest in the work was
marked by a curiosity for a project that did not yet exist, and which indeed
might never have come to fruition. With the appearance of the finished
work, that time is over and we have entered a second phase in which commentary, interpretation, contestation, and, one hopes, inspiration, will each
find their voice. So what are these new paths of enquiry to which research-
ers might wish to commit themselves? Very schematically, we can identify
two general tendencies: the search for meanings and the study of models. In
the first group are to be found positivism, source criticism, and hermeneutics. In the second, the examination of formal, cultural and historical models. Practically speaking, these approaches will all be mixed and matched by
every critic and viewer, including the contributors to this volume, but let us
present them now separately nonetheless.

A positivist approach would start from the very reasonable premiss that,
whatever the technical novelty or artistic bravura of HISTOIRE(S) DU CINÉMA,
one still has the right to analyse what Godard claims to be telling us about
the history of film and television, and to evaluate what his work contributes
to existing knowledge and current debates. Such an expectation is encouraged by Godard's own wish to enter into direct dialogue with general historians, notably the contemporary French historian, François Furet.[39] Yet
clearly, this desire for truth might soon become frustrated by Godard's evident disregard for scholarly method, an attitude reflected in his rapid but re-
laxed correction of apparent factual errors. In a similar vein, one might well
protest that Godard's 'veritable history of cinema, the only one, the true one'
is not only riddled with inaccuracies, but also presents a fundamentally nar-
row-minded and Eurocentric film history that does little more than reproduce the familiar topics and the same old names, places, moments and
movements: France, the mother of invention; Hollywood, the corruptor of
her child; Russia, in revolution and terror; Germany, in the shadow of Hitler; and a few post-war flickerings of Italian resistance and French renaissance. With such terms of reference, one could hardly recommend Godard's
history as an introduction to world cinema, a fact that would equally punc-
ture his somewhat hubristic claims to know and show 'all the histories' of
cinema (including those films which were lost, destroyed, abandoned or
never even made!). In Godard's defence, one could, of course, respond that
such extremist claims to exhaustivity and veracity ('It's all true!', as Welles
would have said) are rhetorical gestures rather than verifiable guarantees.

They pre-empt such literal-minded critiques and serve to expose the ratio-nalistic pretensions and totalitarian desires of historical discourse *per se*, with its terrible yearning for meaning and order and its phobic exclusion of that which it cannot control. Indeed, HISTOIRE(S) DU CINÉMA reveals power-fully the enormous transformations in the sense and representation of his-tory since the beginning of the twentieth century, in particular the status of historical matter as a significant or discrete 'event'. As Hayden White has rightly observed, the historical event has 'dissolved as an object of a respect-ably scientific *knowledge*', there being no limits on what can be legitimately said about it. The traumatic events unique to the twentieth century, argues White, can only find their appropriately tenuous representation in the 'de-realisation' effected by modern media and modernist forms of collage and fragmentation, forms that entail a need to 'mourn' the loss of full historical explanation and comprehension.[40] From this perspective, the vices of error and omission in HISTOIRE(S) DU CINÉMA, along with its recourse to poetic knowledge (for instance, Godard's imaginary tale of the discovery of the mathematical principle of projection in Chapter 2A), seem more like virtues of modesty and exchange.

If the verification of HISTOIRE(S) DU CINÉMA is justified in principle but awkward in practice, then what about source criticism? The dazzling intertextual surfaces of the video work would surely reveal to us their his-torical, philosophical, or artistic signification, if only one could identify and examine the myriad source texts which Godard manipulates, collocates and remotivates with such energy and brilliance. Given that almost everything we see, hear and read in HISTOIRE(S) DU CINÉMA seems to be a quotation or extract from somewhere else, one could, in fact, divide each episode into distinct sequences, proceed systematically to identify the sources of the dis-parate materials brought together in each sequence, and then formulate an interpretative judgment regarding the possible meanings provoked by each specific moment of collocation, each 'violent yoking together of heteroge-neous elements' as Dr. Johnson said of the metaphysical conceit. If one then had the heart and patience to work through a whole series of such moments and sequences, eventually one would accumulate enough sense and mean-ing to form a critical mass that could then reasonably stand as an interpreta-tive paraphrase of an entire chapter. This quasi-exegetical method would tend towards situating HISTOIRE(S) DU CINÉMA in the predominantly liter-ary canon of great modernist hyper-texts like Joyce's *Finnegans Wake* or Pound's *Cantos*.[41] Although such a move certainly has the merit of taking the work seriously, it poses genuine practical difficulties as well as a major stra-tegic threat to the kind of *entendement* evoked by Godard in his discussion with Ishaghpour. The problems of identification are real and even intimidating since one would need to be able to recognise many distorted and decontextualised sounds and images from a wide variety of audiovisual sources, as well as paintings, drawings, photographs, voices, texts, and music. Such practical difficulties are compounded by the perhaps more significant danger that an interpretative method of this kind, whatever its good intentions, may perversely reduce HISTOIRE(S) DU CINÉMA to little more than a film buff's guessing-game, and stifle at birth the extraordinary richness and movement of Godard's fluid and polymorphous composition. One could rather disappointingly end up with a series of explanatory notes and captions severely disempowering and essentially misrepresenting the specific film forms and underlying historical forces that are summoned and deployed throughout the work.

As with the issue of verification, the desire to interpret through textual sources is perfectly natural but far from clear cut. One could develop this observation into a general critique of hermeneutics, whose presumption of personal intentionality would at first sight seem just as suspect in film analysis as it does in literary studies. To the question 'What does it mean?' the response would rightly be: 'Go figure!'. But such a position would still need to recognise that HISTOIRE(S) DU CINÉMA also represents a form of personal testament placing Godard's own life and work within the story of cinema's century. The unmistakable voice of the artist does announce a presence to the spectator. It speaks, reminisces, narrates, confesses, digresses, condemns, and generally communicates with the audience in a direct manner which, paradoxically, no literary word could ever emulate. This set-up recalls some of the earliest film shows when an announcer would often stand by the screen and comment upon the projected action. Equally, Godard's physical presence, a striking component of his recent work, is displayed for all to see as never before in a variety of poses and personae and with a range of stills and photographs taking us right back to life before the cinema, to the 'little photo' used in JLG/JLG showing an otherwise anonymous boy 'with a slightly stunned look [...] already in mourning for myself, my own unique companion'.[42] In this sense, what could be more insistently and personally meaningful than the very body of the artist himself? The whole question of self-portraiture would oblige us to reconfigure our expectations of what we mean by meaning in a cinematic context. It is an issue that Jacques Aumont highlights at the start of *Amnésies: fictions du cinéma d'après Jean-Luc Godard* (1999), the first serious study of HISTOIRE(S) DU CINÉMA to appear since its completion. Aumont acknowledges that to write about this work, he has been obliged to talk about 'a certain Jean-Luc Godard [...] Like every essay since Montaigne invented the format, HISTOIRE(S) DU CINÉMA is more a sampling of experiences and opinions than a confrontation of scientific facts.

And like every essayist, this particular one, a famous if supposedly obscure film-maker, could not avoid saying "I". It is this *I*, the simple shifter of enunciation, who is Jean-Luc Godard for me: the little image, soberly, carelessly crafted, of someone who puts himself on show within his private world, like Balzac in his dressing-gown or Proust amidst his scraps of paper, the only difference being that here it is firstly a voice that reaches us, a timbre that changes everything and colours the whole image with its inimitable texture.'[43] Along with the authorial fiction and the bodily document, Aumont also recognises a strange projection of these familiar elements into a personification of cinema itself: 'This is not just a confession, it is also a personification: I, the cinema, am speaking; or more exactly: I, Jean-Luc Godard, who for the moment and for the needs of the cause incorporate the cinema, am speaking. So I express myself in the language of cinema, through moving images and sounds, and my phrasing is that of cinema, i.e. configurations of time, successions, encounters, and concomitances. In order to remind itself of itself, the cinema must utilise its own modes of memory, and therefore above all its invention, the only one perhaps that at the end of a century it has ever proposed, montage.'[44] Prosopopoeically speaking, this certain Godard will personally figure as the cinema's memory and montage will be his signature. It is a figure in the rhetorical sense but equally a figural act of self-exposure and artistic commitment. So whatever the evident complexity and polyvalence of HISTOIRE(S) DU CINÉMA's magnificent textures, we can, as critics, legitimately isolate and respond to what must also be seen as the sincerest expression of responsible subjectivity since Cocteau's LE TESTA-MENT D'ORPHÉE. It is difficult to imagine, after all, a more explicit promise of authorial meaning than the final image (a recent picture of Godard) and the final words ('I was that man') spoken by the video master's own voice.

The search for meaning may well be a legitimate critical pursuit, but even the most severe exegete could hardly ignore the raw power and sheer excess of Godard's late videographic style. Putting aside all matters of content and signification, one might openly pursue a formal enquiry into the material issues of rhythm, texture, sound, colour, and movement, as well as the more technical aspects of this 'manual' labour that Méliès supposedly could have performed. One might, for example, categorise and analyse the different kinds of materials redeployed in HISTOIRE(S) DU CINÉMA rather than fixate on the source as a site of meaning. In that way, one could eventually establish a material inventory of musical styles (classical/contemporary), vocal performances (speech/song), radio broadcasts, film soundtracks, televisual images, newsreels, cartoons, film sequences (silent/sound, colour/black-and-white, Hollywood/European, etc.), textual citations (performed/inscribed, literary/philosophical, French/translated, classic/modern, etc.), and, of course, the whole range of other visual media such as painting, sculpture, drawing, engraving, sketches, photography. This may seem like a massive and thankless task but it would enable critics to gain a sense of proportion and balance regarding the Heraclitean flow of heterogeneous resources. It would also provide a substantive approach to the tricky but inviting question of rhythm, for one could analyse and engage with the relative deployment of diverse materials according to measures of frequency, speed, intensity, alternation and repetition. In a similar but more technical vein, one could begin to categorise the kinds of process that Godard administers to these prime resources, first in isolation (transforming, distorting, or suppressing either sound or image; acceleration, slow motion, freezing; recutting montage sequences, editing *plan-séquence*, etc.), and then in combination (juxtaposition, superimposition, cross-cutting; fading, *fondu enchaîné*, irisation, black screen; spotting, flashing, etc.). Etymologically linked to mountains, ascensions, and sublime elevations, the high concept of montage would certainly be demystified to some degree, and this would serve to remind us that as well as haute couture, the editorial act entails the simple art of 'cutting', as Hitchcock's East End/West Coast vowels express it in Chapter 4A, LE CONTRÔLE DE L'UNIVERS.[45] It is the artisanal prestidigitation of 'making beautiful images do beautiful things', to paraphrase Jean George Auriol, as well as a parade of the world's robes and corporeality.[46] One could thereby bring HISTOIRE(S) DU CINÉMA genuinely closer to the musical and painterly or sculptural models that Godard has long claimed for his videographic manner, and perhaps more broadly for his essayistic idiom during the last fifty years. Such a materialist analysis could only strengthen those claims and would help to bolster the more elevated and meaningful spins on the arcane *métier* of metamorphosis or image transformation.

Despite this evident appeal to extra-linguistic models for legitimacy and comprehension, it is clear that a work entitled 'Hi/stories of cinema' will invite comparison with verbal and indeed textual precursors. Leaving aside the strictly historiographical aspects of such a comparison, e.g. with previous French film-makers such as Louis Delluc and René Clair who also doubled up as historians of cinema, one could therefore approach HISTOIRE(S) DU CINÉMA via a study of the literary-philosophical paradigms which Godard invokes as sympathetic antecedents. The most visible genealogical line to emerge thus far is the so-called 'Diderot to Daney' series of French critical writers, that is, Denis Diderot, Charles Baudelaire, Élie Faure, André Malraux, André Bazin, François Truffaut, and Serge Daney.[47] With typical extremism, Godard will blithely claim in interviews that only the French have produced genuine art-history or film-criticism. By this he means high-quality writing of intrinsic literary value which interrogates the art form in a subjective, informed, intimate, and judgmental manner, but also always opens up the analysis or criticism of the specific object towards a broader and ever more ambitiously speculative sphere of thought. This is neither theory, in the institutionalised or terrorist sense, nor expertise, in the buffish or connoisseurial acceptation. Indeed, it is worth underlining that of the seven names in the series only two are properly film critics (Bazin, Daney), one is an idiosyncratic and visionary art historian (Faure), and the others are better known for philosophy (Diderot), poetry (Baudelaire), fiction (Malraux), and film-making (Truffaut). The choice of Bazin and Daney in preference, say, to Jean Mitry confirms a philosophical bias against systema- tisation and specialism in favour of curiosity, performance, provisionality and experimentation. In the French cultural tradition, to name such values is to invoke Michel de Montaigne, whose inventive, citational, free-flowing, self-contradictory and self-portraying 'essays' might arguably provide the deepest structural and spiritual model for HISTOIRE(S) DU CINÉMA. If only the walls of his famous Bordelaisian library-cum-sanctuary had been lined with films, videos, and art books rather than the classic texts of Greek and Latin culture! It could be argued that 'Essays in film history' would be just as appropriate a title as 'Hi/stories of cinema', and perhaps even 'Essays in film-thinking', given the predominantly non-narrative drive and bric-à- brac dynamic of the work. Or just *Essays* plain and simple, thus allowing the scientific connotations of test, trial, attempt and experiment gradually to emerge and evolve alongside the literary sense of improvised miscegena- tion and infinite reworking of self and world.[48] It is worth noting on this score that as early as 1962, in an astonishingly prescient interview with *Cahiers du Cinéma*, Godard identified himself as essentially an 'essayist', thereby accurately predicting the rest of his film work as a headily impure blend of critical cinema, documentary enquiry and fictional play, as well as a personal engagement with the vital risks and errors intrinsic to a con- stantly changing medium. 'As a critic', he declared then, 'I already thought of myself as a film-maker. Today I still think of myself as a critic, and in a sense more so than ever. Instead of a critique I make a film, but I introduce a critical element into it. I think of myself as an essayist. I make essays in the form of novels or novels in the form of essays. I just film them rather than write them. If cinema were to disappear, I'd get used to it. I'd go over to tele- vision, and if television were to disappear I'd go back to pen and paper.'[49] The ghost of Montaigne, armed with plume and parchment, would not only approve of such a credo, he might also point out the Godardian pertinence of his proto-cinematographic axiom: 'I do not portray the Being of the world, I portray its movement.'[50] That is what might be called a 'deep pre- cursor'.

Turning finally to the question of historical models, it should be obvious by now that HISTOIRE(S) DU CINÉMA is far from conventional film history, and indeed may not be 'history' at all in the recognisable sense. No doubt it is closer to inventing some original form of film thinking that would have an impact on what is understood by cinema itself, and thereby inform the general conception and practice of film history. We can, however, identify on Godard's part several quasi-historiographical presumptions and promises which he effectively summarises in the titles of Chapters 1A, 1B, and 2A: TOUTES LES HISTOIRES, UNE HISTOIRE SEULE, and SEUL LE CINÉMA. The first makes a rash and vainglorious promise to tell 'all the stories of cinema', a hostage to positivist misfortune if ever there was one. But the title implicitly acknowledges the pre-programmed impossibility of the historian's task and, more significantly, the evidential diversity that the historian must sacrifice in order to inscribe a coherent fiction upon that random mass of lives and voices known as the Past. In stark contrast, the title UNE HISTOIRE SEULE appears to remove from history all marks of fabrication or human agency and surrenders time and destiny to a metaphysical, incomprehensible force: 'My idea is that History is alone, distanced from man, and that's it.'[51] Together, these programmatic titles suggest a Godardian sense of history torn between extreme aesthetic humanism (we are what we make) and pragmatic spiritual determinism (God only knows). The resultant mystique of cinema ('neither an art nor a technique, but a mystery') is most clearly expressed in the title of Chapter 2A, SEUL LE CINÉMA. Metaphysically alone, because of its unique vocation as high art and mass entertainment, as spectacular delusion and new exploration of the world. Aesthetically alone, because of its famous tripartite specificity: the recording of the real, the image in process, and the projection into the dark. Historically alone, too, because of its unrivalled credibility as witness and unfulfilled duty as judge. Or as Charles Péguy's Clio, the Muse of History, disarmingly reflected: 'You ask me to play the judge, but I'm just the court stenographer.'[52] In Péguy's *Clio*, of course, the higher judicial power is an irrefragable, unknowable divinity, but mere mortal history should also heed her remark, whether it is seeking to construct some laughable hypothesis or just maintaining its records and facts. For on the human level, Péguy reminds us that history is one fairly minor mode of recollection, and that Memory, the Muse of all the Arts, recruits a whole host of private aids and collective forces. All our thoughts, forms, stories, images, coincidences, slips and lies combine in a common cause or question: What did happen then? What sign is left? How do I remember it now? One can call that sign 'mneme', in which case amnesia or forgetting is less an aberration than a natural state of mind. If amnesia is required to make the sheer accumulation of lived experience quantitatively tolerable, it also enforces those principles of selection, order, and emphasis that allow us to give form, and thereby meaning, to our otherwise chaotic lives. In *Amnésies*, Aumont considers cinema's mnemonic status in relation to this concept of amnesia as a necessary forgetting and editing of the past. Like no other instrument of thought, the cinematograph records the world in motion and our movement in the world. But fiction must also have its say, cutting the mnemic material into narrative shape and relegating to oblivion the unpresentable and the insignificant. The forms it creates are some of art's most marvellous illusions, but they perish and fade even as we admire them. Hence the mortal beauty of cinema and its mournful preoccupation with the fatal instant, when the shutter enacts Death's snap twenty-four times per second. But if that is cinema's double loss, remembering Eurydice as she disappears, then what is the memorial function of Godard's videographic enterprise? An extension of Aumont's argument would lead us to *anamnesis*, the attempted restoration of cinema's negated memories, as if the video retrieval and recasting of film's triumphs and defeats could somehow restore to screen life both the faded forms which cinema invented, and the inchoate matter it had chosen to forget. Here one could be tempted to superimpose the sequence of remembrance (mneme, amnesia, anamnesis) over the three fundamentals of cinema (record, process, project), leading to the suggestion that anamnesis and projection are jointly the real objectives of HISTOIRE(S) DU CINÉMA.

But what is all this about projection? How can there be projection through a videographic history of cinema? For, to return to the Daney interview, Godard's grand scheme is only feasible as 'a souvenir of this projectable history', as ultimately a set of video tapes destined for private replay and domestic recollection. But what is truly mysterious about HISTOIRE(S) DU CINÉMA is precisely the power with which cinema does return from the dead and succeeds in reprojecting itself even from the meanest square screen of the smallest little box. How many times have we seen Nosferatu, or some other cinematic undead, arising from the grave and scaring the life out of our spectatorial selves? How many times have we seen Jean Marais, or some other Orphic avatar, passing through a mirror to the other side and drawing us with him into the Zone? It has been so many times that we do not remember. Or rather, so many times that we can only remember. For a curious side-effect of watching HISTOIRE(S) DU CINÉMA is that we even remember those films we have never seen before. It is as if the viewer were a monstrous, impossible cinephile who had always already seen every single film that was ever made. Then amnesia cut in and wrote film history. But now with HISTOIRE(S) DU CINÉMA it is all coming back, in another form, another time, another place. As for the format, it is true that it is film returning as 'digital video', but this, in turn, will become something else. Whether it is DVD, CD-ROM, interactive web site, or a technique as yet undiscovered, each form renders its precursor immortal even as the fangs sink into the throat. Godard's sometimes reactionary, though never stable, discourse on technological change should therefore not be confused with the living example of his endlessly adaptive and inventive works. They show uniquely that change is the only immutable essence which cinema can know. Ontologically, as Bazin would say, cinema is 'the mummy of change'. That paradox cuts to the very quick of HISTOIRE(S) DU CINÉMA whose mourning is always invention, and whose video-eye indeed records the death of cinema but in Cocteau's sense of filming 'Death at work'.[53] Of course, for all its mysterious powers, Godard's anamnesis against – or in the face of – oblivion could never be anything more than a temporary flicker of resistance, an illusion of survival or revival. That said, two thousand years of western art have hardly been less evanescent. Only in such a context can we start to appreciate the value and efficacity of these *mysteries of cinema* that are histoire(s) du cinéma – a series or serial work, potentially infinite but actually curtailed, whose hero Cinema would be some indestructible Fantômas, death-defying and always promising more adventures 'to be continued...'.

The Cinema Alone: a book of essays

The Cinema Alone does not pretend to cover or exhaust all aspects of Godard's production in the last fifteen years, if only because we have no idea what will come next and how it might change our perception both of the work and of cinema in general. By the time this collection is published, THE OLD PLACE, a collaborative video piece with Miéville, as well as a video short entitled L'ORIGINE DU VINGT ET UNIÈME SIÈCLE, will have become available. In addition, a brand-new feature film, ÉLOGE DE L'AMOUR, will have been released. Yet while it is still far too early to say whether the end of HISTOIRE(S) DU CINÉMA marks the end of a phase in Godard's evolution, or a a potential new beginning, it is abundantly clear that a major critical task now lies ahead: to reconceive Godard as a contemporary visual artist and to reconsider his whole career from the fresh perspective that HISTOIRE(S) DU CINÉMA provides for neophytes and apostles alike. *The Cinema Alone* will help set that process in motion, most obviously by making available for the first time to a non-francophone audience some essential critical material, including important recent texts and interviews by Godard. More specifically, the aesthetic, philosophical, ethical and political implications of Godard's later work are explored in three distinctive types of essay. Firstly, those that provide an overview of the œuvre and attempt to assess how Godard's work since 1985, especially HISTOIRE(S) DU CINÉMA, alters key aspects of the larger picture: montage in Michael Witt's 'Montage, my beautiful care, or Histories of the Cinematograph', and Alan Wright's 'Elizabeth Taylor at Auschwitz: JLG and the Real Object of Montage'; documentary in Jonathan Dronsfield's '"The present never exists there": the temporality of decision in Godard's later film and video essays'; and cultural precursors in Michael Temple's 'Big rhythm and the power of metamorphosis: some models and precursors for HISTOIRE(S) DU CINÉMA', a chapter that contextualises and questions Godard's grand historiographical manner. The second type of essays featured in *The Cinema Alone* are those that engage directly with HISTOIRE(S) DU CINÉMA by focusing on a particular episode or theme: death in Jacques Aumont's 'Mortal beauty' (a reading of Chapter 2B, FATALE BEAUTÉ); resistance in James Williams's 'European culture and artistic resistance' (a reading of Chapter 3A, LA MONNAIE DE L'ABSOLU); and early cinema in Vicki Callahan's 'The evidence and uncertainty of silent film in HISTOIRE(S) DU CINÉMA'. Finally, three essays examine important related works of the recent period: KING LEAR in Timothy Murray's 'The Crisis of Cinema in the Age of New World Memory: the Baroque performance of KING LEAR'; the shorts PUISSANCE DE LA PAROLE, LE DERNIER MOT, and ON S'EST TOUS DÉFILÉ in Jean-Louis Leutrat's 'The Power of Language'; and HÉLAS POUR MOI in Lætitia Fieschi-Vivet's 'Investigation of a mystery: cinema and the sacred in HÉLAS POUR MOI'.

Although the ten individual chapters cover various disciplines (film, literature, art history, philosophy, theology) and pursue a range of critical approaches, they share common themes and points of theoretical focus, notably the film philosophy of Gilles Deleuze, Godard's experiments in television during the 1970s, Wittgenstein's analysis of language games and doubt, the Surrealist poetics of Pierre Reverdy, Heidegger's writings on poetry and the human condition, and theories of beauty and the sublime. The result is an interweaving critical dialogue around Godard's later work that generates new and far-reaching questions about his cinematic practice. For example, how exactly do the feature films of this period, such as SOIGNE TA DROITE, NOUVELLE VAGUE and FOR EVER MOZART, inform our understanding of HISTOIRE(S) DU CINÉMA, and vice versa? Could one talk perhaps of SOFT AND HARD, LE RAPPORT DARTY and 2X50 ANS DE CINÉMA FRANÇAIS as 'preparatory sketches', and even of certain films as 'ancillary studies', e.g. the 'German chapter' that is ALLEMAGNE ANNÉE 90 NEUF ZÉRO, the 'Russian chapter' that is LES ENFANTS JOUENT À LA RUSSIE, and the 'portrait of the artist' that is

JLG/JLG? Moreover, what is the particular significance of the book *Histoire(s) du cinéma*, which Godard himself describes as an 'anti-art book'. Do the four lavishly coloured volumes of hybrid images represent a separate artistic venture, or perhaps even an attempted transcendence of the transient audiovisual flux?[54] Looking at the corpus as a whole, what could one now say, too, about the collaborative nature of so much of Godard's enterprise if one were to approach his working partnership with Miéville as paradigmatic of a whole series of technical and creative partnerships that date back to the original 'Langlois gang'? Is the late solitary genius and totem of auteuristic integrity in fact an exemplary colleague and born team-player? Similarly, how might one now speak of art, memory, autobiography, the sacred, science and new technologies in Godard's work if one reconsidered these themes as long-standing motifs whose status and potential concerned the pre-cinematic journalist as much as the digital Old Master?

But all of this, as Méliès once wrote, is merely *l'enfance de l'art*, a phrase that suggests both child's play and the infancy of artistic growth.[55] Watching late Godard may at first seem far from simple care-free play, yet the late video work is really no more complex than the early films now that we think about it. There's sound and there's image, and it all moves around a lot. It is simple enough if we keep an open mind and stick to first principles: what is cinema? How does it change? What can it yet become? On such a basis it seems clear that cinema is barely emerging from 'the infancy of the art', and while the end of cinema's first century may offer a perfect occasion for stock-taking, Godard's project remains live and direct, unpredictably changing and always in search of fresh subjects and forms. His is an ingenuity of vision, a curiosity for the world. Isn't that also what cinema is, from before the cinematograph to those digital means and motifs which the future will soon outwit? In which case, critics like ourselves can scarcely afford to sit on our vantage points devising cool assessments. There is a long way to go. And Godard is still one of cinema's brightest hopes and promises for the new century.

2   Montage, My Beautiful Care, or Histories of the Cinematograph

Michael Witt

'The cinema is montage.' (J.-L. Godard)[1]

Introduction: Godard's theorem

Could it be that coming years will see the addition of a further 'Godard' to those currently in circulation, a 'Godard, montage artist/theoretician'? In view of the centrality and high visibility of the term 'montage' in Godard's theory and practice of recent decades, this unexpected turn of events now seems a distinct possibility. But omnipresence is accompanied by polysemy: if at first glance the equation of cinema with montage appears to suggest a bizarre alignment with early theoreticians such as Lev Kuleshov for the absolute pre-eminence of montage in cinema, then Godard's dialogue in HISTOIRE(S) DU CINÉMA with his 1956 critical article, 'Montage, mon beau souci' ('Montage, my beautiful care'), quickly reminds us that his take on the subject has always transcended any localised sense of 'editing'.[2] Besides setting in place a productive tension between successive 'Godards' across five decades, the presence of the 'Montage, mon beau souci' title in HISTOIRE(S) DU CINÉMA – adapted by the young Godard from a François de Malherbe love poem – marks the realisation of a belated date with a long-standing passion: montage.[3] There is abundant material to fuel an extended study of Godard and montage. The term provides both a convenient gateway into his later work and a highly suggestive perspective within which to situate a critical reappraisal of his wider œuvre.[4] This hypothetical study would certainly not lack material, and it would need to focus on conceptual and practical issues in equal measure. After all, montage's provision of a source of constant inspiration for Godard is paralleled by his accumulation of probably incomparable film and video editing skills. In view of his insistence on systematically assuming the role of editor of his own work since the 1970s, there is a real sense in which Godardian thought has been consciously channelled through a physical, sculptural engagement with his material ('To think with ones hands', as Godard suggests through reference to Denis de Rougement in FATALE BEAUTÉ[5]). More than this, he came to cinema through editing: across the 1950s, his apprenticeship as critic and as dialogue writer for other film-makers was complemented by work as a professional editor on documentary films for Jean-Pierre Braunberger, and on silent travel films for the Arthauld company.[6] More generally, there is a strong sense in which his cinema has perpetually pushed found footage around on the editing table, both literally (as in his irreverent 1958 remix of material shot by Truffaut, UNE HISTOIRE D'EAU) and as an underlying strategic principle (the wayward semiotician's combination of people and objects as quotable material). Godard is, as he has often characterised himself, above all a 'combiner' who positions himself between disparate worlds, and 'puts Raymond Chandler in contact with Fyodor Dostoevsky in a restaurant on a particular day with well- and lesser-known actors'.[7] A thorough study of Godard and montage would need to address Godard's debt to antecedent montage theorists and practitioners, the intervallic conception and structure of his video work of the 1980s and 1990s, and his substantial production as a graphic photomontage artist. In particular, an examination of the evolution of his editing practice from the 1950s to the present would need to consider how the combination of ideas played out at the plastic level of shot linkage in his films of the 1960s has nourished his subsequent exploration of videographic juxtaposition and superimposition.

These issues will be set aside here in favour of an analysis of Godard's understanding and use of 'montage' in the context of his discourse on cinema, history and cinema history. A genealogy of the meanings collapsed by Godard into 'montage' in and around HISTOIRE(S) DU CINÉMA leads us quickly to his lectures on cinema history at the Conservatoire d'Art Cinématographique in Montreal in the late 1970s.[8] Here, Godard took over from his mentor and friend, Henri Langlois, whose eclectic collage-based programming style at the Cinémathèque Française looms large over the montage-based conception and structure of HISTOIRE(S) DU CINÉMA. For Godard, we recall, Langlois was not just a programmer but an auteur who assembled great experimental macro-films, 'shot' through projectors rather than cameras.[9] In Montreal Godard expressly declared his intention to devote the remainder of his life and work to an exploration of 'the geology and geography' of montage.[10] As Serge Daney pointed out, in the transition from the Montreal lectures to HISTOIRE(S) DU CINÉMA, the 'founding hypothesis' that the cinema somehow 'is' montage has been retained.[11] The series, as Godard himself semi-jokingly claimed in 1998, is based on a montage 'theorem':

I'm a bit upset that it's only cinema people who talk to me about it [HISTOIRE(S) DU CINÉMA] and that the word 'history' is forgotten. I feel like a mathematician who sets out a theorem and to whom people just say 'your theorem's lovely', or 'it's lousy'... It's as if people had said to Pythagoras (and I'm not comparing myself to Pythagoras), 'your theorem's great!'... Yes, but how is it useful? [...] Freud and Feuillade recount something, and this came at more or less the same time as set theory, fluid mechanics, and Stravinsky... These rapprochements aren't made. The only thing capable of providing an account of them – not because it tried to do it, but because it was made for it – is the cinematograph. Let's call it 'cinematograph' so as to differentiate it from what's called 'cinema' today, and which only ever designates the regular weekly releases and the cinema listings in the papers. At a given moment in time, History became incarnate – or arranged itself like a tired virus – in cinema's very substance. And then the cinematograph was no longer used.[12]

Cinema is a privileged visual witness to the past, video a fluid space in which a neo-cinematic form of montage can offer a glimpse of History. The following quotation, taken from Godard's lecture on montage at the French National Film School (the FEMIS) in 1989, indicates the diversity and opacity of ideas with which this discussion will have to engage:

The idea that I'm defending in the history of cinema that I'm preparing, QUELQUES HISTOIRES À PROPOS DU CINÉMA, is that montage is what made cinema unique and different as compared to painting and the novel. Cinema as it was originally conceived is going to disappear quite quickly, within a lifetime, and something else will take its place. But what made it original, and what will never really have existed, like a plant that has never really left the ground, is montage. The silent movie world felt it very strongly and talked about it a lot. No-one found it. Griffith was looking for something like montage, he discovered the close-up. Eisenstein naturally thought that he had found montage... But by montage I mean something much more vast [...] To return to what I said at the beginning: the idea of cinema as art or the technique of montage. Novels are something else, painting is something else, music is something else. Cinema was the art of montage, and that art was going to be born, it was popular. Mozart worked for princes, Michelangelo for the Pope... Some novelists sold in huge quantities, but even Malraux, even Proust didn't sell immediately in the same quantities as Sulitzer. Nor does Marguerite [Duras]. Suddenly, very quickly, cinema rose in popularity, much faster than Le Pen. In three years it went from thirty spectators to thirty million. Painting has never been popular. If Van Gogh were popular his paintings would go on tour. But cinema was popular, it developed a technique, a style or a way of doing things, something that I believe was essentially montage. Which for me means seeing, seeing life. You take life, you take power, but in order to revise it, and see it, and make a judgment. To see two things and to choose between them in completely good faith.[13]

As is clear here, Godard's theorem relies on a very specific view of cinema history: cinema is reduced to the cinematograph, which in turn exemplifies a series of fairly distinct processes conflated in the term 'montage'. By thinking Godard's 'theorem' in the context of his critical discourse of the past fifty years, this chapter seeks to unpack the series of elliptical equivalences outlined here, to retrieve and position the cinematograph at the heart of Godard's discourse on cinema and history, and to throw into relief what we might understand by its 'montages'.

Vertov/Eisenstein/Godard

As founding figures of the left-wing intellectual cinematic adventure, and as names that recur regularly in Godardian discourse generally, it comes as little surprise that Sergei Eisenstein and Dziga Vertov should have become key points of reference in work on Godard. The key task here is to move debates around the conjunction of these three cinematic projects beyond bygone discussions of Godard as a militant political film-maker. Taking their cue from the hostile critiques of Eisenstein inscribed in Godard's work of the late 1960s and 1970s (VENT D'EST, LEÇONS DE CHOSES (episode 2A of SIX FOIS DEUX), FRANCE/TOUR/DÉTOUR/DEUX/ENFANTS), commentators have habitually allied Godard with Vertov. This position now requires revision, or at least moderation: the legacy of both film-maker/theorists, and of their respective mathematical and musical montage theories, is felt powerfully in Godard's recent work in terms of a broad climate of influence and of specific points of detail. Vertov's quest to perfect an extra-linguistic, visual, symphonic-cinematic form, and Eisenstein's claims for film's unique power to articulate thought outside language, pave the way for the flux and flow of HISTOIRE(S) DU CINÉMA. The adoption of the Dziga Vertov name by Godard and his collaborators in the early 1970s signalled an allegiance with a form of political cinema rooted in the present instant and the everyday, while also serving as an intervention against the widespread deification of Eisenstein as unchallenged paradigm of the revolutionary film-maker. But it is now clear that this also announced an engagement with central strands of Vertovian theory whose effects continue to resonate across Godard's current practice: an unshakeable faith in the camera as a scientific 'scope' through which to penetrate the surface of reality; the dream of a quasi-scientific research 'laboratory' in which to conduct audio-visual experiments; a deep-rooted mistrust of any semblance of literary narrative, combined with contempt for the conventional written script; the expansion of the idea of montage to include every stage of the film-making process; and finally, the crucial theorisation and application of 'interval' theory (according to which film poems are composed around the movements and transitions between the visual stimuli carried by individual shots).[14] Eisenstein's favouring of stylised recreations of the past over an urgent engagement with the present once earned him disdain from Godard and Jean-Pierre Gorin. Eisenstein quietly re-entered Godard's work in a far more positive light at the end of the 1970s, and by the time the early versions of the first two chapters of HISTOIRE(S) DU CINÉMA were complete in 1988, Eisenstein had come to occupy a prime position in Godard's schema.[15] In view of the recurrent critique of THE BATTLESHIP POTEMKIN in Godard's earlier work, the inclusion of the Odessa steps sequence in TOUTES LES HISTOIRES signals the closing of a circle. Similarly, the position adopted by Godard at his editing table in HISTOIRE(S) DU CINÉMA as he speeds the film back and forth through the gates of the Steenbeck self-consciously reprises Eisenstein's posture – scissors in hands, celluloid draped around his neck, scrutinising a strip of celluloid against the light in his editing studio – in the photograph frequently redeployed by Godard since the early 1980s.[16] This identification with Eisenstein signals a partial rapprochement with Eisensteinian theory which, as with Vertov, is most fruitfully read in terms of the appropriation of a handful of key ideas. For Godard's engagement with Eisenstein's theories has been fairly loose and avoided any elaborate dialogue with the constituent specificities of the fivefold montage typology (metric, rhythmic, tonal, overtonal, intellectual). His interest lies primarily in Eisenstein's status as a philosopher of art who sought tirelessly to chart and redefine what 'montage' might mean.[17] Godard's long-standing critique of the 'visual' (Serge Daney), that is to say, the floods of representations generated by the media machine, draws on the Eisensteinian distinction between 'image' ('*obraz*', related in Eisensteinian theory to montage) and 'depiction' ('*izobrazhenie*', sometimes translated as 'representation' and related to the individual shot), which is mapped on to the opposition between 'image' and 'picture' in English.[18] But the importance of Eisenstein to late Godard runs far deeper than this, and takes the form of intellectual liberation. On the one hand, Godard and Eisenstein both pursue cinematic montage with an exceptional and almost transcendent intensity, one that is directly related to filmic materiality: montage is integral to the cinema, not just as the grammatical basis to filmic expression (the combination of shots) but also at the micro-level of the interstice separating photogrammes on the celluloid. Thus 'all cinema is montage cinema, for the simple reason that the most fundamental cinematic phenomenon – the fact that the picture moves – is a montage phenomenon'.[19] On the other, the respective theorisations of montage by Eisenstein and Godard set aside 'the limited business of the gluing bits of film together'[20] to focus on the larger picture of montage as a productive principle accompanying the combination or juxtaposition of two or more events, facts, or objects across the arts (architecture, music, painting, theatre, the novel, poetry, and so on). The freedom with which Eisenstein's later discussions of montage range across Maupassant, Milton and Mayakovsky – he goes so far as to label both Leonardo da Vinci and Pushkin 'montage artists', and to read the painting *Deluge* and narrative poem *Poltava* as cinematic 'montage scripts' – thoroughly prepares the way for Godard's projection of the term in every direction in and around HISTOIRE(S) DU CINÉMA.[21]

The importance of Eisenstein and Vertov to late Godard, and to HISTOIRE(S) DU CINÉMA in particular, should not obscure the limits of their contribution. As Godard has consistently argued since the time of TOUT VA BIEN, although Eisenstein considered himself to have been on the trail of montage, hindsight reveals him to have formulated a unique means of articulating his vision through a self-reflexive fusion of cinematic and political 'angles' on contemporary events. This argument culminates in Chapter 3B of HISTOIRE(S) DU CINÉMA, UNE VAGUE NOUVELLE, where Godard suggests through a dissection of the sequence in which the three stone lions 'rise up' in OCTOBER that Eisenstein's experimentation with the combination of camera angles gives the mere *impression* of montage:

> All Eisenstein ever talked about was montage, but he was a calculator rather than an editor. He discovered the angle. It's because he found extraordinary angles – like Welles a little later – that his work necessarily suggests the beginnings of montage, and you hear people say: 'It's a wonderfully edited film.' But that's still not what montage is about. It's something else. We don't know what... We don't know.[22]

Similarly, Vertov's attempts at montage are scorned as 'completely flat'; he may have had good ideas for individual rapprochements but he failed to inject cinematic life into them.[23] In this way, Godard is able to cut Eisenstein and Vertov down to size and recuperate them as just two of the film-makers of the silent era who were collectively feeling their way across a vast uncharted 'continent', montage. The list of favoured cinematic explorers of the silent era is usually short – Eisenstein, Vertov, Vigo, Griffith, Lang, Gance, von Stroheim, Murnau – and none is deemed to have ultimately realised montage. This apparently paradoxical treatment of Eisenstein and Vertov, whereby they are promoted and criticised in virtually the same breath, leads us to our central concern. Their theories and practices – especially in the combined form of Vertovian interval theory and Eisenstein's enlarged concept of montage – underpin Godard's project. But in the process of surveying the history of cinema, Godard opens up the concept of 'montage' to areas far beyond anything envisaged by Eisenstein:

> Cinema was the true art of montage that began five or six centuries B.C., in the West. It's the entire history of the West. It's not the history of the East, nor that of Mexico and the Indians. Nobody knows what the history of black Africa is, and we're not even close to knowing. It's the history of the West, the history of a view of the world, of art coming to an end, and which can be seen today through cinema. Now we're entering another history. It was montage, the relationship between things, between people, by means of a relationship to things viewed in the form of a reproduction of these things.[24]

Throughout HISTOIRE(S) DU CINÉMA, cinema is positioned and read as modern painting, inheritor and extension of a representational tradition indicative of western art. 'Montage' comes to designate the relationships internal to a given art form, as well as those established through art between the world and its inhabitants. In the domain of cinema, it comes to signify not merely a common formal idiom or singularly potent expressive tool, but the power and specificity of silent cinema as an historical force.

The intelligence of the cinematograph

'Cinema projected, and people saw that the world was there.'

On what is the conflation of montage with the cinematograph based, and what critical positions in relation to film history does it generate and demarcate? More precisely, how is this equation conceptualised and played out at the micro-level of the 'montages' internal to the cinematic apparatus, and at the macro-level of the cinematograph as a whole? Godard's reading of the relationships and tensions internal to cinema as 'montage' is reasonably straightforward. The idea of montage has entered popular discussions of cinema as a byword for inter-image relationships, but theoretical work of early film semioticians such as Yuri Tynyanov in the 1920s, not to mention that of Eisenstein, reminds us that the application of 'montage' to intra-image relations also has a well-established history.[25] For Maurice Merleau-Ponty, whose ideas on cinema foresee and inspire Godard's films of the 1960s, the unique and unprecedented power of cinema lay in its astonishingly direct capacity for laying bare 'the link of the subject to the world, of the subject to others' through its ability to frame and project vast moving images.[26] Malraux's claim for cinema as an art in his 1946 *Esquisse d'une psychologie du cinéma* is strongly reminiscent of Merleau-Ponty and Bazin, and prefigures Godard's reading of cinema and art as 'montage': 'I call art here the articulation of unknown yet suddenly convincing relationships between people, or between people and things.'[27] Godard's argument in 'Montage, mon beau souci' (1956) that montage and *mise-en-scène* enact identical processes in time and space respectively therefore forms part of an ongoing debate within film theory rather than a significant new insight.[28] In the context of Godard's recent work, it is the irreversible blurring of categorical boundaries between editing (temporality, traditionally identified with poetry) and *mise-en-scène* (spatial representation, usually allied to painting) that should be retained from his feisty riposte to Bazinian realism. In spite of superficial appearances to the contrary, Godard's essay borrows as much from Bazin as it does from Eisenstein and retrieves the dual sense of the subject-world relations caught *within* the image (for Bazin, generally those articulated through the uncut take and deep focus) and those expressed by the *combination* of shots as the basis of an already expanding concept of montage. In line with the openness implicit in the positions of Merleau-Ponty and Bazin, Godard's discourse operates on a double register and oscillates constantly. If the cinema materially fixes and foregrounds the interspace, so at the level of narrative representation it throws into relief human behaviour and social relations and makes them available for criticism:

> Montage allowed one to see things and no longer to say them, that's what was new. You could see that the boss was robbing the workers, it wasn't sufficient to say it. By managing to show that the bosses were robbing the workers... it became obvious that the boss was a nasty bloke or whatever.[29]

From the outset, and long before it is grafted on to emergent hypotheses regarding the history of cinema, 'montage' is therefore already highly charged. Applied to both plastic and social inter- and intra-image relations, it is extended to the viewer/world relationship mediated through cinema.

Making sense of Godard's elision of the cinematograph with montage requires a detour through a number of antecedent positions inscribed in his critical discourse, and notably the theorisation of cinema as art and science. First, clarification of Godard's exploitation of the term 'cinematograph' as a vehicle for two reasonably distinct sets of meanings is required. Its use by Jean Cocteau and Robert Bresson as a gesture of defiance to the homogenising momentum of the forms and codes of the Hollywood-derived mainstream has obvious attractions for Godard.[30] Although forever tinged with this wider sense of cultural resistance, the term primarily designates the extension of the neo-scientific project of the Lumière brothers. One can barely exaggerate the centrality of silent cinema to Godard's work. As films such as VIVRE SA VIE and LES CARABINIERS remind us, of all the forms fed pell-mell into the generic remix machine of his 1960s films it is often the silent cinema whose undiluted presence is most powerfully felt. He has reiterated in countless interviews over the course of preparations for HISTOIRE(S) DU CINÉMA that a 'true' history of cinema should brush aside diversions such as box-office hit orchestration by the entertainment multi-nationals to focus on what he identifies as the true history of cinema, that of the 'invisible' films lost, disintegrating, destroyed, or seldom shown, precisely, Langlois's treasured illicit cinema, much of it silent and absorbed in awe by the emergent Nouvelle Vague during the 1950s. In this respect, the Montreal lectures provide not only a rehearsal space for the substance of HISTOIRE(S) DU CINÉMA but a structural prototype. It would clearly be an oversimplification to claim that HISTOIRE(S) DU CINÉMA is 'about' silent cinema in any straightforward sense, not least because of the presence of chapters devoted to topics such as Hitchcock, Neorealism, and the Nouvelle Vague, the presence of enormous quantities of extracts of sound films, and the sheer sonic density of the soundtrack. In Montreal, Godard systematically projected a silent film at the beginning of each session as a benchmark against which to evaluate an assortment of sound films (his own included). If here the overarching significance of the silent era remains clearly signalled, it assumes the role of structuring subjacent armature in HISTOIRE(S) DU CINÉMA, determining the parameters of the loosely grouped subject areas into which the respective chapters are bracketed off. Despite initial appearances, Godard's histories are less 'histoire(s) du cinéma' than 'histoire(s) du cinématographe', a fact signified by the shift in intertitles in TOUTES LES HISTOIRES. Forays into the sound era are primarily driven by a quest to follow the residual trail – flashes of resistance on the part of a handful of figures, films and movements in the face of widespread homogenisation – of the cinematograph and 'what it became in the age of the talkies'.[31]

Complementing this use of the cinematograph as a point of entry into cinema history is a wider conceptual engagement on Godard's part with the films, critical discourses, and socio-cultural context of the cinematograph, an engagement that has had a powerful influence on his later practice. In Montreal, he explicitly set himself the brief of integrating a rediscovery of the cinematograph into his ongoing project: 'if I look at my own trajectory, I get the impression that I'm trying to retraverse the silent era, but so as to be able to find my own form of the talkies'.[32] The optimism and vitality of the scientific-philosophical impetus to early intellectual cinema has provided a source of strength and inspiration for Godard and Godard/Miéville in their attempts to negotiate a post-television form of cinema. In this respect, experimentation with slow- and stop-start motion is exemplary, its use as technique and effect symptomatic of a wider conceptual solidarity with the proto-cinematographic work of pioneers such as Étienne-Jules Marey and Eadweard J. Muybridge. At the same time, it signals an alignment with commentators such as Walter Benjamin and Élie Faure for whom slow-motion's ability to penetrate the temporal continuum announced nothing less than a revolutionary 'deepening of apperception' and 'unconscious optics' (Benjamin), 'a whole world of hitherto unknown and even unsuspected harmonies' (Faure).[33] First systematically employed in FRANCE/TOUR/DÉTOUR/DEUX/ENFANTS, slow motion punctuates Godard and Godard/Miéville's work to the present and culminates explosively in HISTOIRE(S) DU CINÉMA. The cinema, of course, rapidly contributed to the natural sciences through the camera's role as a 'temporal microscope' (Jean Painlevé) capable of the revelation of previously invisible realities.[34] If Godard's early films overflow with urgent news from the 1960s, his work of the past two decades – so often dismissed as impenetrably obscure – might rather be approached as a sustained and measured combination of the inclusive address and fresh, perplexing forms characteristic of the best of the cinema of the silent era. In this perspective – and this is a reading that Godard would probably be keen for us to pursue – it is not Godard's work but the rest of cinema that has somehow lost its way and been sidelined to the margins.

Just how does Godard equate the cinematograph with art? Setting aside transitory, factional in-fighting, political affiliation, or the divisions of national boundaries, Godard identifies widespread unanimity on the part of contemporaneous commentators: the world has unexpectedly acquired an extraordinarily precise machine capable of intensifying perception, jolting us out of our routine complacencies, and reinstating a sense of astonishment at a world still poorly understood. René Clair's collation of testimonies to the power of the cinematograph (those of Pierre Albert-Birot, Jean Cocteau, Fernand Léger, Pierre Mac Orlan, Paul Valéry, and Philippe Soupault) reminds us of the vivacious enthusiasm felt by so many for a young art form being carried along on the wings of optimism and curiosity.[35] Godard is therefore far from being alone in viewing silent cinema in terms of its capacity for the casual generation of constant streams of highly charged, vibrant images of the present. Godard's view of the cinematograph is entirely in keeping here with his polemics of the past five decades generally, where priority is always accorded representations in any art form born of a quest for expression outside the regulatory constraints of accumulated aesthetic formulae. In other words, Godard is ultimately interested in Art, and the cinematograph is a singularly fresh art form. As Jean Epstein insisted long before, the impact of radical formal novelty far outweighs questions of localised narratives or representations: every metre of film serves to reveal and inform, to directly communicate a savage reality 'before names and before the law of words'.[36] The birth of the cinematograph not only echoed that of art, but *produced* a sudden and unexpected, short-lived period of renewed childhood for art ('the childhood of art', as suggested in an intertitle in FA-TALE BEAUTÉ). Astonishingly, fresh form and technical/aesthetic innovation was matched by mass appeal, and Art was suddenly in real demand. Recognition of the significance of the cinematograph's instant and massive popularity pervades the critical work of commentators such as Clair, Cocteau and Louis Delluc in the 1910s and 1920s: the cinematograph is simply the first truly popular art form ever.[37] This reading of the cinematograph as Art impacts decisively on the choice of films and film-makers to be included in HISTOIRE(S) DU CINÉMA. Those who have been content to run through inherited forms and formulae are set aside, making room for those who sought to represent the world honestly and directly through a simultaneous interrogation of the technical means at their disposal. This logic provides the rationale for the unparalleled esteem for Alfred Hitchcock – 'a visionary', 'as unique as a star' – that has accompanied the evolution of the HISTOIRE(S) DU CINÉMA project, culminating in Chapter 4A, LE CONTRÔLE DE L'UNIVERS.[38] Hitchcock achieved his immense popular success on the back of ambitious, technically difficult, formally inventive, non-formulaic and visually-driven narratives: 'Hitchcock is one of the century's great artists. He made difficult, sensitive, mysterious and successful films that didn't follow a recipe. That's extremely rare.'[39] Uniquely, in the moving interview he gave to Serge July at the time of Hitchcock's death, Godard goes so far as to credit Hitchcock – the exception who proves the rule – for having *achieved* 'montage'.[40] Here we see the slippage from 'cinematograph' to 'cinema': it is Hitchcock's *sound* films – forever rooted in a resolutely visual logic intimately linked to the cinematograph and painting – that serve as an illustrious but all too solitary example of what full-scale cinematographic montage might have become. This pervasive investment in a vision of the silent era clears the way for a potentially vast reassessment of the period, and indeed the conjunction of HISTOIRE(S) DU CINÉMA with recent scholarly interest in montage as a composite idiom and radically new, post-industrial, kaleidoscopic form of vision opens up a rich area of future research.[41]

   Accompanying this reading of the cinematograph as art is a parallel theorisation of the image as scientific document, and cinema generally – positioned in the context of the nineteenth-century scientific project – as an immensely powerful social X-ray machine capable of the revelation of hitherto imperceptible physical realities and the injuries of social inequality. Fiction films, as Godard has suggested in a neat image, have always operated as 'Jean Painlevé plus actors'.[42] If the narratives inscribed in individual films provide a reflection of the world that made them, so fiction films carry a record of the past in their form. The shifting fortunes of film 'language' provide a concise echogram of social structures: social and formal innovation go hand in hand, just as the regurgitation of pre-existing forms indicates social stagnation. At the other end of the scale, neither documentary nor newsreel footage is valued for any spurious objective truth value. On the contrary, it is fed into HISTOIRE(S) DU CINÉMA and scrutinised for traces of rehearsal and control. In documentaries, as Godard suggested recently, it is the otherwise imperceptible processes of socio-political '*mise-en-scène*' that are recorded and revealed.[43] Caught in the Lumière brothers' celebrated film of workers leaving their Lyon factory are multiple layers of mediations and manipulations: not only do the workers, schooled in the process of moving images, know they are being filmed and act accordingly for the camera, but they rehearse the gestures and stage directions mapped out for them by the factory management. The documentary root and duty of cinema comes through very powerfully in HISTOIRE(S) DU CINÉMA. Like Malraux, Godard is careful to counterbalance his reading of cinema's role as true art and purveyor of myth with an insistence on its inherently and properly *journalistic* function.[44] Malraux's L'ESPOIR recurs in HISTOIRE(S) DU CINÉMA as a privileged example of cinema as real 'news' through its frantic attempt to trace the outline of an instant image worthy of the horrors of the Spanish Civil War. At the same time, the film's formal ambition and invention served simultaneously to revitalise cinema itself as an art form. No matter if any given film has presented itself as 'news' or as the height of the fantastic – all true cinema for Godard delivers up-to-the-minute news bulletins:

> It's said that Lumière is documentary and Méliès the fantastic. But when we see their films today, what do we see? We see Méliès filming the reception of the King of Yugoslavia by the president of the Republic. In other words, news. And at the same time, we see Lumière filming his family playing belote in a style reminiscent of *Bouvard and Pécuchet*. In other words, fiction.[45]

In a position held unswervingly by Godard from the 1950s to the present, fiction films are deemed to carry an intrinsically high documentary charge. 'I think all the great films', as he put it as early as 1958, 'tend at their profoundest level towards the documentary.'[46] On the one hand, momentous moments of social instability and conflict are crystallised immediately in cinematic form and given an image which is then distributed and subject to criticism and discussion. Fiction films can therefore be read as the real 'news' of the century ('news of history, history of the news', as Godard formalises it in TOUTES LES HISTOIRES). On the other, in a critique that recalls

Kracauer's survey of the traces of an embryonic fascism in the German cinema of the 1920s, Godard ascribes to cinema the power to effect a visionary ethnology of imminent social mutation by *foreseeing* emergent political turbulance and social upheaval. In this perspective, the cinema is a kind of clairvoyant gossipmonger (*'colporteur'*, as suggested in LES SIGNES PARMI NOUS), peddling rumours about what the future might hold:

> I've always thought that the cinema represents today what music was in the past a little: it communicates in advance, it communicates in advance great shifts that are going to occur. And it's in this sense that it shows illnesses before they become visible. It's an external sign that shows things. It's a bit abnormal. It's something that's going to happen, like an irruption.[47]

TOUTES LES HISTOIRES and LES SIGNES PARMI NOUS underscore this view: Renoir's LA GRANDE ILLUSION and LA RÈGLE DU JEU foresaw the imminent disintegration of Europe into war and Murnau's NOSFERATU depicted a Berlin reduced to rubble in the aftermath of war from a vantage point long before the events had taken place.

Godard's entire theory and practice constitutes a sustained reflection on *vision*, a relentless critique of the homogeneities inscribed in visual imagery and subjectivity complemented by a constant search for fresh expressive forms. In the context of his theorisation of the cinema as art and science, he reads silent cinema as an eye- and mind-opening vision machine, and the silent era as an explosive moment of 'great popular cultural revolution' driven by the cinematographic revelation of the physical world and social relations.[48] Godard's histories are audience-based and set aside issues such as the drift towards narrativisation or the chronological intricacies of technological change. The foregrounding of the human eye and the act of looking (the magnified eye from Orson Welles's MR. ARKADIN in SEUL LE CINÉMA and UNE VAGUE NOUVELLE, and James Stewart wielding his telephoto lens in REAR WINDOW in TOUTES LES HISTOIRES and UNE VAGUE NOUVELLE) serve as a shorthand for the visual education set in motion by the cinematograph. Inherently all-inclusive in its extra-linguistic mode of address and drawing social classes together physically in the movie theatre, the popular, nascent art/science is endowed with a pedagogical function and contagious democratising effect. By simply re-presenting the physical and social world to vast numbers of individuals in instantly accessible form, it encouraged – indeed, made almost inevitable – a profound renegotiation of one's place in the world. The novelty, difference and danger of the cinematograph is located in its latent power effortlessly to unleash a mass of popular energy through the revelation of how the world might be perceived and inhabited differently. In a passage again strongly reminiscent of Malraux, Godard conflates the successive 'montages' effected by the cinematograph (within the image, between images, between the viewer and the screen, between the subject and society, and between the individual and the world) as follows:

> When people saw a film, there was something that was at least double, and since someone was watching, it became triple. In other words, there was something, something else, which in its technical form became gradually known as montage. It was something that filmed not things, but the relationships between things. In other words, people saw relationships, and first of all they saw a relationship with themselves.[49]

It is through this concept of 'social montage' that the cinematograph is associated closely with questions of national identity. The logical consequence of an inherently montage-based art is social and/or existential 'montage'. Less a question of adhesive than of social *cohesion*, cinema 'represented the possibility of belonging to a nation, and of being oneself within that nation'.[50] Although surprising in view of Godard's roots in Langlois's unconventional trans-national film education programme at the Cinémathèque, a sustained reading of film history in terms of national cinemas is thereby established in HISTOIRE(S) DU CINÉMA.[51]

Godard's reading of how western society has represented and 'projected' the world around it, and of the ensuing interpretative process (of negotiation, agreement, astonishment or rejection) set in motion when audiences in turn 'project' themselves into those representations, feeds into a favoured metaphor: the cinema theatre as a popular courtroom, films as evidence, and the audience as judge and jury. To view films is to participate in a process of judicial review: 'Cinema is made for spreading things out, for flattening them. I always compare it to justice. It's a file that you open, that's cinema (*he opens a file*). And then you weigh it.'[52] Films representing pressing contemporary concerns are made, projected, viewed and discussed in the same way that evidence is brought into a courtroom and laid before a jury. The representation can be accepted or refused but it is there for discussion and awaits a verdict: is this a just reality represented on the screen, and does the representation itself accurately reflect one's personal experience? In this context, courtroom dramas, and films in which questions of guilt and innocence hang in the balance, inevitably acquire particular resonance (whence a further reason for the importance of Hitchcock). This identification of cinema with the scales of justice not only underscores the idea of popular empowerment, but also relates neatly and self-reflexively back to the underlying model of the rapprochement/montage of two or more photogrammes (or images, or ideas) that returns endlessly in HISTOIRE(S) DU CINÉMA:

There's a shot before, and another one after. And between the two, there's a physical support. That's cinema. You see a rich person and a poor person and there's a rapprochement. And you say: it's not fair. Justice comes from a rapprochement. And from then weighing it in the scales. The very idea of montage is the scales of justice.[53]

HISTOIRE(S) DU CINÉMA was always intended as the history not only of cinema's revelatory power but also of 'the blindness to which it gave rise'.[54] The series recounts a narrative of rise and fall, of splendour and poverty. Where the cinematograph is equated with the drawing together of peoples and nations, the talkies are identified with a pre-televisual process of *'démontage'* (collapse or, literally, dismantling):

> Montage is what had to be destroyed because it's what allowed people to *see*. The role of the talkies, supported by the publishing houses and bad writers, was to prevent people from *seeing* what montage allowed them to *see*. Control over what one saw had to be regained immediately. Moreover, that's what television is. A great lost battle.[55]

All that remains of the fully-fledged 'montage' that a mature cinema might have allowed are partial traces of its extraordinary emergent form, 'a blocked chrysalis that will never turn into a butterfly'.[56] As Godard has argued consistently since the early 1970s, the combination of economic recession and Roosevelt's 'New Deal' conspired with the coming of sound to produce an aesthetic mutation and the beginning of the end of cinema's status as popular, documentary-based art: 'Walter Benjamin said the same thing to Adorno: the industry's unconscious took fright and so the talkies were introduced.'[57] In the context of a century marked by the rapid proliferation of technologies, notably by television as a brief but crucial intermediary step from the chemical (photography/cinema) to the digital, cinema's capacity for 'montage' fell by the wayside. The montages of the cinematograph, taken in hand by mass production and the rhythms of consumer capital, were forever buried beneath the weight of the script-based, dialogue-ridden talkies:

> The word montage has been much used. Today people talk of montage in Welles or in Eisenstein or, on the contrary, of the absence of montage in Rossellini. What fools, as Bernanos would say. Cinema never found montage. Tobis and RCA didn't allow it the time, and something was lost along the way, its language. And it's speech, words, that took the upper hand, but of course not the speech or words of the Jeromine children, nor those of Narcissus and Goldmund.[58]

Conclusion

'Bring together things that have never yet been brought together and
did not seem predisposed to be so.' (R. Bresson)[59]

'Montage' is the central, volatile, and essentially open-ended metaphor
through which Godard has developed his evolving ideas on cinema and
history, while 'Montage, mon beau souci' is the generative formula into
which he has condensed his hypotheses. It would be easy to ignore
Godard's provocatively blunt insistence on the direct equivalence between
cinema and montage cited at the head of this chapter, or to respond dismissively that 'no, cinema is not montage'. But if we are to engage with Godard
as critic and historian of cinema, we are obliged to pass through these and
other ostensibly perverse and trenchant statements. If we take the time to reflect on what they might mean, and treat them as poetic formulae rather
than as statements of fact, the contours of an enormously rich range of debates open up before us. Godard is, of course, not a systematic theoretician
of montage, and any future 'montage theory' associated with his name will
perhaps most likely serve as shorthand for his vision of the rise and fall of
the cinematograph as Art. In its most extreme formulation, Godard's stance
leaves itself open to obvious criticism: to declare cinema the final chapter in
western art comes close to the reproduction of a flimsy discourse on technological change which can easily be brushed aside. But such statements
should always be viewed as strategic postures rather than as immutable
opinions; there are no fixed positions in Godardian discourse, but always
scope for the coexistence of a variety of conflictual points of view. His position leaves little room for optimism regarding the function of contemporary
cinema as a vibrant cultural form, but it is based on a reading of the cinematograph in the context of an artistic tradition – 'an idea of the relationship to
the world, invented by white people'[60] – whose renewal through other
forms remains open. HISTOIRE(S) DU CINÉMA is essentially poetic, and any
attempt to reduce it to a conventional historiographical narrative inevitably
mutes its power of suggestion. Weaknesses in the fissures between the various critical positions Godard traverses are more than compensated for by
the extraordinary wealth of ideas generated by contact with even a short extract of the series.

The emerging critical work on HISTOIRE(S) DU CINÉMA has tended to set
aside the issues around montage discussed here to focus on Godard's
videographic editing techniques. In the process, the tight self-reflexivity of

the series has passed without comment. The underlying rationale and textual form of HISTOIRE(S) DU CINÉMA are both rooted in an appropriation and condensed videographic re-enactment of what Godard has identified as the principal novelty and power of the cinema: montage. From the Montreal lectures onwards, the meanings of 'montage' can be divided into two broad categories, although in practice, of course, these are irreversibly blurred. On the one hand, as we have seen, cinema's essential difference as a cultural form is reduced to montage: the power of revelation rooted in a unique facility for bringing disparate ideas into the same orbit as one another and holding them in dynamic tension. On the other, historical studies ('*études*' in the dual musical and scholarly sense) are creatively composed through videographic montage: the rapprochement of ideas vehicled through the dissolution and recombination of fragments of the century's cinematographic ultrasound.[61] Godard's obsessive reworking of Pierre Reverdy's poem 'L'Image' in his work since the early 1980s therefore not only signals an alignment with a combative form of cultural resistance (surrealism), but also provides the formula and conduit for these two interrelated sets of meanings of montage:

> The image is a pure creation of the spirit.
>
> It cannot be born of a comparison, but of the rapprochement of two more or less separate realities.
>
> The more distant and just the relationships between these realities that are brought together, the stronger the image will be – and the more emotional power and poetic reality it will have.
>
> Two realities with no relationship between them cannot be usefully brought together. No image is created.
>
> Two contrary realities cannot be brought together. They oppose each other.
>
> Rarely is strength obtained from this opposition.
>
> An image is not strong because it is *brutal* or *fantastic*, but because the association of ideas is distant and just.[62]

As Gilles Deleuze noted, Godard's long-standing concern has been to examine how a genuine Image might be retrieved and preserved from the morass of media clichés.[63] But Godard's urgent drive to chart a poetics of the image in the age of neo-television has been mapped on to his parallel historiographical project: to 'do' montage is to make an Image (Eisenstein's '*obraz*') and evoke History.[64] Beneath the surface of Godard's vision of micro- and macro-montage hovers a singularly resonant model, that of metaphor theory. At the macro level, the definition of the cinematograph as Art serves to position it squarely *as* metaphor, the perpetually inventive *bricoleur* at the slippery juncture of reality and its representation.[65] At the micro-level, the

montage/rapprochement of the constituent elements of an Image reproduces the dynamic interplay activated by the productive conjunction of the
components (what I.A. Richards terms the 'tenor' and 'vehicle' of the metaphor) in the metaphorical process.[66] Reverdy's model of the 'distant and
just' association of ideas provides a quick shorthand for the process of conceptual 'stereoscopic vision' set in motion by the rapprochement of tenor
and vehicle.[67] In visual terms, this model is carried by the economical image
of the juxtaposition of two video monitors (a constant in NUMÉRO DEUX,
KING LEAR, JLG/JLG: AUTOPORTRAIT DE DÉCEMBRE, and Chapter 3B of
HISTOIRE(S) DU CINEMA, UNE VAGUE NOUVELLE, usually to the melodic ac-
companiment of variations on the Reverdy poem on the soundtrack), which
in turn serves as a schematic shorthand for the array of videographic editing
processes through which worlds, ideas and realities are combined in
HISTOIRE(S) DU CINÉMA. If metaphor provides a condensed model of the
process of rapprochement/montage inherent in cinema ('One might say
that there are laws of metaphor- and image-making in cinema, certain of
which represent univeral laws')[68], HISTOIRE(S) DU CINÉMA makes History by
making metaphors, or at least by the systematic simulation of the metaphorical process: 'The simple scientific means for this series and these books is
comparison and metaphor. For every image is metaphor.'[69] Here Godard re-
joins Eisenstein. As Geoffrey Nowell-Smith has noted, for Eisenstein the
terms 'montage', 'image', and 'metaphor' are fundamentally interchangeable.[70] Eisenstein and Godard therefore both leave us with a series of elliptical equations: cinema = image = montage = metaphor = art. To compose
images (make metaphors) is to resurrect moments of History, or, as Godard
wrote by way of a prescient subtitle to HISTOIRE(S) DU CINÉMA in his 1958 review of Léonard Keigel's film, MALRAUX: 'Art, in its own way, makes History come back to life.'[71]

3 Elizabeth Taylor at Auschwitz: JLG and the Real Object of Montage

Alan Wright

Montage=Happiness+Catastrophe

In a number of interviews conducted over the last decade, Jean-Luc Godard has insisted that cinema has yet to accomplish its true mission, the invention of montage. Painting succeeded in reproducing perspective, the novel introduced psychology to narrative. Film, too, promised a new take on reality, but the real object of cinema disappeared in the due course of historical events. Godard explains his theory with a story, and he finds a scene to represent the unattainable idea of montage. George Stevens was among the first to shoot footage of the concentration camps at Auschwitz and Ravensbrück. After the war, Stevens filmed a young Elizabeth Taylor in A PLACE IN THE SUN, a Hollywood adaptation of Theodore Dreiser's classic novel *An American Tragedy*. In HISTOIRE(S) DU CINÉMA Chapter 1A, Godard inserts a tender interlude from Stevens's film into an elegiac meditation on the Holocaust, the relationship between cinema and memory, and the crisis of documentation in the face of terror and mass murder. He superimposes pictures of stacked corpses in the ovens and the image of Taylor's peaceful smile as she cradles Montgomery Clift in her arms on the shores of a lake. A gradual dissolve reveals the lovers against a backdrop of atrocity and death. It literally appears that the beautiful film star, with a gentle stroke of her hand, might calm the horrors of the camps. Conversely, the pain of an unendurable grief, a sad portent of an unhappy fate, tempers the romantic pathos of the couple's embrace. They pledge their love in place of a death. Loon Lake holds an awful secret: Shelley Winters and her unborn child will soon find a watery grave in its depths.

Godard explained his reasons for making such an audacious juxtaposition to Serge Daney:

> In A PLACE IN THE SUN, there's a deep feeling of happiness that I've rarely encountered in other films, even much better ones. It's a simple secular feeling of happiness, one moment with Elizabeth Taylor. And when I found out that Stevens had filmed the camps and that for the occasion Kodak had given him their first rolls of 16mm color

film, that explained to me how he could do that close-up of Elizabeth Taylor that radiated a kind of shadowed happiness...[1]

In a later interview with Gavin Smith, Godard refers to the same scene of Elizabeth Taylor and the victims of the Holocaust as an example of 'historical montage'.[2] Film exposes the brutal reality of human suffering in the interval between the beauty of a smile and the hell of the Final Solution. Montage *à la* Godard constructs an image of history in the light of an extreme variation between a vision of happiness and the sense of catastrophe.

Cinema serves as the ideal instrument for representing the 'dubious' nature of historical relations. The technical procedure of montage supplies the formula for a conceptual principle. It contains the promise of a method. For Godard, the capacity of an image to project in two different directions at once, to display two distinct senses of meaning, assumes the status of a rule. His theory of montage depends upon drawing a set of connections from a relationship of looks. But, as he tells Smith, an image does not exist. It is subject to the law of 'Stereo', a conceptual figure created by Godard to describe the drama of projection and reflection that circumscribes the look: 'the image is the relation with me looking at it dreaming up a relation to someone else'.[3] In a scene from JLG/JLG: AUTOPORTRAIT DE DÉCEMBRE, he draws a diagram to illustrate the geometry of attraction and aversion that constitutes the image:

> Stereo is made for dogs and blind people. They always project like this but they should project this way. Because they project like this, because I, who listen and watch, am here, because I receive this projection as I face it, because I reflect it back, I am in the position described by this figure. This is the figure of stereo.

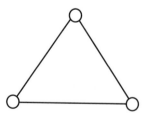

The points locate the various angles from which an image can be viewed. The 'sight lines' form a triangulated force-field of desire. But, as Pascal's revision of Euclidean geometry proves, a change in perspective turns a given formal system on its head. A second set of coordinates can be plotted on top of the original grid. Graphically, their conjunction traces the outlines of a star. History is the science of calculating the relative influence that this eternal symbol casts over the horizon of events:

> There was Euclid and then there was Pascal – this is the mystical hexagram. But in History, in the history of History, there was Germany which projected Israel. Israel reflected this projection and Israel found its cross. And the law of stereo continues. Israel projected the Palestinian people and the Palestinian people in turn bore their cross. This is the true legend of stereo.

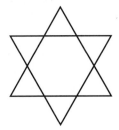

An idea of the image arises in the profound abyss that separates such contrary positions. Montage takes the measure of the unfathomable gulf which lies at the heart of historical knowledge, and cinema becomes uniquely identified with History. Elizabeth Taylor and the Holocaust, Israel and Palestine, Rimbaud and Marshal Pétain – montage entails putting the two together to tell a story, the story of History and Cinema.[4] Godard pushes this experimental strategy to its logical extreme in HISTOIRE(S) DU CINÉMA, often to stunning effect. In one instance, he mixes newsreel footage of a prisoner's death by firing squad with a dance number from AN AMERICAN IN PARIS. A guard ties the blindfold over the condemned man's eyes as Gene Kelly and Leslie Caron execute their movements with grace. The gradual inscription of a phrase on the screen punctuates the slow motion rhythm of the couple's respective actions: 'Never shall I forget/the blood/foretold by the crimson/of a kiss.' The 'montage' sequence follows the choreographed gestures of love and death. This oscillation between musical routine and war reportage remains consistent with Godard's cherished maxim that cinematic truth combines the poles of documentary and fiction: 'Cinema, Truffaut said, is spectacle – Méliès – and research – Lumière.'[5]

These wilful constructions, and others like them, suggest the rudiments of a conceptual technique. Gilles Deleuze observes in regard to Godard that 'the interaction of two images engenders or traces a frontier which belongs to neither one nor the other'.[6] That which happens *between* two images – the cut, the interstice – acquires primary value, not their reconstitution into a synthetic unity deriving from the principle of continuity or conflict, as in the Eisensteinian model of intellectual montage or the classical Hollywood style. The axiom from the days of the Dziga Vertov group and SIX FOIS DEUX – 'not a just image, just an image' – returns in JLG/JLG with the claim that an image acquires its strength when 'the association of ideas is distant, distant and just'. A visual image or mental picture composed of the most antithetical elements inspires a clinical depiction or lyrical expression of the least intelligible aspects of experience. Moreover, the contentiousness of the association enhances its critical acuity, since the customary distinction that separates the smile of Elizabeth Taylor from the disaster of the Holocaust actually attests to their unbearable proximity. Montage sees a conjunction in the discordant clash of such incongruous images without ever seeking to resolve their irreconcilable difference. Rather than oversee the production of resemblances, it orchestrates a process of radical distantiation. One does not compare school to a prison by pointing out their resemblance. A series of cuts from one site to the other would only establish, as Deleuze puts it, 'a confused relation between two clear images'.[7] In such an instance, a conservative application of the montage technique amounts to a mechanical repetition of an obvious formula. Better, therefore, to disclose the 'separate elements and relations which elude us at the heart of an unclear image'.[8] Something is missing. For Godard, a school is and is not a school. The prison appears where the gap between seeing and saying suddenly becomes evident, just as a smile bears the mark of disaster.

Elizabeth Taylor's smile is not *like* the grimacing rictus of a skull. They are terribly different, and it is the gulf between that Godard makes visible. He superimposes one upon the other to show literally how both 'realities' inhabit each other. Their true face only appears within the maw of the Real (with a capital R). The Real, as Lacan was fond of saying, is the Impossible. It founds the Symbolic Order but is also the object upon which it founders. Slavoj Žižek grants the Sublime a similar function: 'the Sublime is an object in which we can experience this very impossibility, this permanent failure of the representation to reach the Thing'.[9] Something is missing. The impossible task of montage as imagined by Godard is to make visible the abysmal structure at the heart of cinematic representation, the absence that haunts every film image, i.e. the traumatic kernel of the Real. Montage shows that which a narrowed range of vision renders imperceptible in the image, the unspeakable fact of an unrepresentable Thing. The name of that Thing is Auschwitz. Traditionally, documentary aims to record reality, to act as a witness to events. Yet Godard wishes to go further. By presenting a fleeting glimpse of happiness and the deadly grip of terror within the same frame, he attempts to document that which can only obtain expression at the extreme limits of comprehension. His version of montage produces an apparition of the Real, a sublime recognition of the impossibility of doing justice to reality.

An Art of the Encounter

It is surely objectionable to pair Elizabeth Taylor with the Holocaust in such a provocative fashion. Godard may even be said to exploit the genocide of the Jews as raw material for a wayward aesthetic exercise, an intellectual amusement, a purely formal encounter in a game of 'Truth or Dare'. Deleuze has commented on Godard's attempts to thwart the comfortable assumption of a habitual perception or predictable representation, that is to say, to wrest a real image from clichés. According to Deleuze, the image regularly functions as an alibi for an exercise in evasion or denial:

> We have schemata for turning away when it is too unpleasant, for prompting resignation when it is terrible and for assimilating when it is too beautiful [...] As Bergson says, we do not perceive the thing or image in its entirety, we always perceive less of it, we perceive only what we are interested in perceiving, or rather what it is in our interest to perceive, by virtue of our economic interests, ideological beliefs and psychological demands. We therefore normally perceive only clichés.[10]

After all, how can words or images possibly do justice to the Holocaust. Any moral response is reduced to the level of an automatic reflex. 'It means nothing', as Godard says of SCHINDLER'S LIST.[11] The standard patterns of visual representation reproduced by the media promote an attitude of cultural amnesia and critical illiteracy. They further the communication of received ideas. As a visual document, film and video offer a selective record and limited view of an already proscribed 'reality'. The spectacular assumption of the image betrays an inability to recognise the obvious fact of its artificial construction. An historical explanation or political description remains beyond the brief of film and television as long as they refuse to show what exceeds the frame. A schematic expression of understanding cannot grasp the unjustifiable existence of the world, the inexplicable character of things and events.

A cinematic description of events and actions, one that functions, in Deleuze's words, as a medium of 'criticism and compassion', demands a Copernican revolution in the politics of representation. Godard invokes Copernicus directly in a scenario which he devises to illustrate the productive effect of montage:

If you say that around 1540 Copernicus introduced the idea that the Sun no longer re-
volved around the Earth, and if you say that a few years later Vesalius published *De
humani corporis fabrica*, which shows the inside of the human body, the skeleton and
écorchés, well, then, you have Copernicus in one book and Vesalius in another... And
then four hundred years later you have François Jacob who says: 'The same year, Copernicus and Vesalius...' Well, Jacob isn't doing biology anymore, he's doing cinema.
And that's what history really is.[12]

The pragmatic results of such a speculative fancy become plain when applied to the current context of media culture. Godard sees ample evidence
for cinema's failure to 'find' montage in the imagery and commentary of
television programming:

It's obvious when you watch an anchorwoman speak about Afghanistan and the
commuter-train strike and things like that. If the cinema had been able to grow up
and become an adult – instead of remaining a child managed by adults – she would
talk about them as if they were Copernicus and Vesalius and that would be clearer.[13]

The TV screen neutralises that possibility by reducing the active pleasure of
looking to the passive indulgence of watching. 'Today in Kabul...' and 'hundreds of stranded Paris commuters...' merely affirm the indifferent statements of a homogenous discourse. The order of images corroborates the
visual logic of the system. They blindly reflect the outlook of an uncritical
vision. The real story of Afghan rebels and striking workers is more effectively told by exhibiting literally their status as images. The Mujahidin and
the French citizen may then enter into a relation of potential detente. Their
tête-à-tête takes the form of 'a visual alliance', a term Philippe Dubois uses to
describe Godard's technical manipulation of images through superimposition and dissolves. Dubois sums up Godard's method as an attempt 'to
bring together, actively, in the mixing of images, in order to be able to see'.[14]
For Godard believes that cinema allows seeing and saying to occur at one
and the same time. The power of thought – the ability to make connections
and draw conclusions – inheres in the very act of vision, and montage, as
Godard conceives it, permits the instant realisation of perception and cognition. Recognition involves thinking while you look.

A Cinematic Poetics of the Mix

Godard's reinvention of montage cannot be regarded solely in conceptual
terms. His formal and technical innovations also mobilise the powers of cin-

ema in a comprehensive engagement with major transformations in the function, composition, presentation and accessibility of images.[15] Montage – cinema's *beau souci* – does not remain untouched by the radical development of electronic media. As part of his superambitious plan to fulfil the task of montage, Godard has attempted to absorb the properties and devices of the new media in order to renew the art of cinema. HISTOIRE(S) DU CINÉMA, while mourning the death of the medium, refashions montage in the light of televisual, video and digital technology.

The mixed use of film and video inspires a great breakthrough in cinematic representation. The electronic treatment of the image unites the successive stages of production, transmission and reception. Recording, projection and viewing become part of the same interactive and instantaneous process. Godard liberates montage from the work of suture and the limited operation of 'cut and splice', with the result that editing occupies a totally integrated function within the actual film. The spasmodic rhythm and choppy action which pervades sound and image tracks in the later works imitates the rapid whir of the tape-heads, the blur of accelerated motion, as the ribbon of film speeds back and forth at the editing bench. Changes in speed and direction, no longer considered a mere accessory of the post-production process, extend, deform, condense the duration and pacing of any scene, thereby disclosing a further dimension in the filmic image – a deep, material quality of the medium. The combination of forms – video effects within the cinematic frame – produces a wondrous array of devices which alter the composition of the filmic image: rewind and fast forward, slow motion, freeze frame, double exposure and superimpositions, wipes, keying, split screen, titles and texts, strobe-like flashes, rapid-fire cuts, staccato rhythms, sudden lurches and jumps in motion, distorted and amplified sound.[16]

Armond White explains how the capacities of video editing enhance the possibilities for montage:

> One can hold images, add to them, erase them (partially or entirely), recall them and layer them ad infinitum. This ability to literally recompose and mix preexisting images to create new ones (whose meaning still resonates with those of the originals) had previously been too technically difficult or economically unfeasible over such extended stretches with standard optical printing devices.[17]

Superimposition and syncopation replace juxtaposition as the main filmic device for arranging visual information. Moreover, the decomposition of the image gains precedence over the recombination of sequences of images. The assimilation and appropriation of video techniques provides Godard with a means of 'writing directly *with* and *in* images' (Dubois).[18] In his hands, montage creates the illusion that the moment of seeing corresponds exactly with the live movement of thought.[19] It condenses action, time and vision into a single cinematic substrate. For Godard, montage orchestrates a dialectic between the process of mechanical reproduction and the simulated performance of 'liveness'. Dubois describes well the spontaneous quality with which the image 'unmakes and makes itself':

> Video slow motion is controlled *by the finger and the eye*, and the operator *discovers the effect live*, at the very moment he executes the operation, which can, moreover, be altered any time he chooses, all the while watching the result shown instantaneously on the screen. And we're aware (the spectator is here strictly in synch with Godard) that with each manœuvre, with each change in speed, we feel violently *the pleasure of a perceptual revolution*, the 'aha' effect of 'so that's what's *in* images, and what I'd never before seen *that way*'.[20]

The technical coordination of visual and manual functions (finger and eye), mental and motor capacities (seeing and doing), bestows a tactile dimension upon the image. The thrill of a eureka experience attends the discovery that an image appears to possess the properties of a material object.

In this way, Godard's cinema addresses both the senses and the intellect and appeals to the experience of thought and feeling. The 'imbrication of film and video images' (Dubois) fulfils the purposes of critical analysis and artistic creation. In practice, Godard creates the live connection between the look in action and a thought at work by breaking down, mixing up, disconnecting and recombining the various elements of disparate images in order to expose their ideological content or disclose the sublime function of their identity. These repeated exercises in decomposition often carry a pedagogical intent. Such technically manipulated constructions mount a pointed critique of the media, consumerism, work, sexual relations and historical memory in contemporary society. But Godard's analytic of the image proceeds by means of a deep identification with the materiality – the substantial body – of the cinematic medium. The deformations of time, speed and motion incite a perceptual revolution which the viewer receives after the manner of a physical sensation or emotional shock. 'The cinema screen', as Nadia Seremetakis observes in relation to HISTOIRE(S) DU CINÉMA, 'is not a flat text-like surface [...] rather it is a volume into which [Godard's] auto- and political biography is sunk; it is his Aphrodite's peach, an organ of memory made palpable'.[21] The slow motion and freeze frame effects which Godard explores open up a new dimension in the image which belongs solely to the cinematic order: an 'organic, material, physical – in other words *carnal*' experience of the visible (Dubois).[22] So, on the one hand, the reinvention of montage supports an analytic/critical practice (politics), on the other, an aesthetic/lyrical performance (poetics). Indeed, Godard speaks of 'plunging from one image to another *through an image event*',[23] as if the film embodied an elemental substance or atmospheric condition. In his later films and videos, the cinematic image replicates the elemental quality of liquid or luminous waves, seismic tremors and subterreanean echoes, 'cardiac pulsing', atomic explosions or galactic bursts, not because it discovers the wellsprings of a universal knowledge but because it communicates a sense of the materiality of language both visual and verbal.

The scene with Elizabeth Taylor and the victims of the Holocaust, in particular, manifests the visual impact of Godard's technical (re)discovery of a 'language' specific to the cinematic and videographic medium. For Godard, montage bears witness to the splendour and misery incarnated by the cinematic image. The instant that each image shares on the screen is imbued with the potency of a communion. The composite image reinforces a comment made in Chapter 1A of HISTOIRE(s) DU CINÉMA upon 'the martyrdom and resurrection of the documentary'. But Godard performs a further technical *coup de grâce* that highlights the palpable aura and apparent physicality of the scene. He slows the film down as Elizabeth Taylor bends to kiss her lover, arresting the course of her irresistible descent at unexpected moments. A pictorial image – a *Noli me tangere* representation by Giotto – absorbs her image totally and momentarily conceals the kiss. Mary Magdalene, who appears almost as an angel in a beatific vision, enframes her as she leaps back to her feet, in fits and starts, according to the impetus of the stop-action decomposition of her movements. The voice-over by Godard breathlessly declares: 'O what wonder to look at what one cannot see/O sweet wonder of our blind eyes.' Montage!

The gospel according to Jean-Luc affirms that the language of cinema, still to be invented, never to be concluded, always in process, requires 'a new form of writing, a new way of calling things by their names'.[24] The idea of montage as practised in HISTOIRE(s) DU CINÉMA challenges established discursive categories and accepted filmic conventions. Godard, as James S. Williams observes, seeks to return 'to a moment before the order of linguistic and cinematic syntax has taken over and words and images have lost their immediacy, freedom and innocence'.[25] Critical wisdom has so far privileged the religious element in the elevation of the image to the order of an illumination. Godard's belief in the testamentary powers of the cinema – 'neither an art nor a technique, but a mystery' – does not imply an attitude of mystification, however. While quite capable of attaining a moral, existential or spiritual rigour, the focus of his activity in HISTOIRE(s) DU CINÉMA is a historical and political understanding of 'montage (not one plus one, but one plus two) as the basic language of filmic thought'.[26] Philosophers and technicians since Plato often tend to think of new media in terms of the old language. The singular claim of Godard's watchword – 'the cinema alone' – asserts the resistance of montage to classification within the paradigm of literacy. Film proposes a mode of reasoning and logic quite distinct from the pattern of the written word. For this reason, the practical and theoretical implications of Godard's position can be usefully illuminated by Walter Benjamin's politically motivated engagement with the popular forms of mass culture, notably film. Benjamin's philosophy of history found its method in cinema; he harnessed the sudden shock or rush of pleasure at the associations provoked by Soviet montage for critical writing. The dialectical image achieves in the realm of thought what Eisenstein conceived in cinematic terms as the aim of intellectual montage, that is to say, the presentation of historical consciousness.

Yet the work of the dialectical image in an age dominated by the flow of electronic information, the global traffic in images and commodities, and the triumph of corporate ideology, will feel the force of History differently than in an era of mechanical reproduction and mass revolution. The condition of displacement and emergence which attends the shift from a colonial to a postcolonial perspective, as well as the move from print literacy to electronic culture, demands negotiating a response to radical developments in media practices and cultural formations. In this sense, Godard's project in HISTOIRE(S) DU CINÉMA can be viewed as a decisive new episode in the history of art and technology, aesthetics and politics. Like Benjamin, he devises both a *poesis* and a *techne*, a conceptual method and a concrete form, from within the current historical context and its different means of representation and recording. It may justifiably be argued, too, that Godard is inventing in video, with the aid of cinematic techniques and above all montage, a multimedia version of the popular, material, political, technical, and supernatural properties distilled in the dialectical image.

4 'The Present Never Exists There': The Temporality of Decision in Godard's Later Film and Video Essays

Jonathan Dronsfield

'Godard avoids the choice.'[1] With this remark Stanley Cavell expresses a worry, somewhat understandable in my view, concerning the way Godard's characters seem untouched by the problem of ending or change, and insensible to the director himself. Godard depersonalises his characters, with the result that they exist elsewhere, already in the future. Godard is indifferent towards his characters, to the question of whether their responses and actions are valid. His position towards them remains unclarified and arbitrary, and his films lack justification for showing them *that* way – 'pastless and futureless, hence presentless'.[2] 'Cinema is like that, the present never exists there, except in bad films.' This observation was made by Godard in 1982.[3] I shall take it to imply that the present is in some way absent from Godard's films but, against Cavell, not to the extent that it cannot be put into question by them, and not such that something like the present moment cannot in turn put to his films or disclose in them a question. There is in Godard an avoidance of the present, but this need not entail saying that his films inhabit a future time, or a world other than this one. On the contrary: 'The cinema, when it's well done, has a direct, total power... The cinema is live and direct...'.[4] The present is avoided not because a stigma attaches to it, but because the present is unattainable, or must not be attainable. In agreement with Cavell, I want to say that this amounts to an affirmation: that it affirms something which is *already* true of our being in the world, the way the world keeps to itself, and that moreover, the avoidance of the present moment in some sense even explains our prior distance from it.[5] But this does not mean that Godard avoids the choice; rather, he asks whether we *can* choose, whether choice is possible, and he does so by looking to see what sorts of presuppositions – both conceptual and cinematic – are embodied in the ways we are ordinarily and historically shown things. In an important way this requires of the viewer a decision as to what is shown, in that one is shown things and states of affairs in a manner which seeks to put into question both what is shown and what is showable. By 'put into question' I mean that Godard temporalises the things he shows us, giving the time for our decision about them. Cavell charges Godard with *irresponsibility* in failing to provide us with justification for his position towards what is shown on screen; he has not achieved the right to objectivity or he denies the possibility of such achievement, thereby his films 'give a sense of the ways things are only from the position of one who cannot see his responsibility in those ways'.[6] I would say that Godard's failure to synthesise (objectify) the elements of his films into a justification of a position we might call his own towards them ought not to be seen as a deficiency, for if synthesis were to succeed then its connection as a film to the viewer as individual would risk being negated, and its claim on the viewer's responsibility undone. Indeed, it could be argued that Godard's films are ethical inasmuch as he has *not* reached an achieved objectivity, for in that way the heterogeneity of their elements is maintained, not reduced to the same.

It is therefore insufficient, perhaps even incorrect, to say that the present does not exist in Godard's films. Absence of the present in fact gives a certain time in which the necessity of having to decide about the world, about the world being presented to us, becomes apparent. By removing or displacing the present, that is to say the givenness of the world decided by the present, Godard creates a space in time in which a decision is asked of the viewer as to what is given. In this sense Godard's films do demand a temporality of the now but without that ever constituting a present. The absence of the present moment is not, then, a simple absence, it is not simply not there; it is rather that the present moment is extended and indeed spatialised – it is referred to throughout Godard's later work and writings, as if in answer to Cavell, as 'time before and time after' – with the effect that the present is refused any kind of sanctity, and the viewer denied refuge in it since no longer shielded from the work of time. In having demanded of us a decision as to what is presented on screen, the viewer is being asked to endure a duration that cannot be grasped or fixed, the radical temporality of things. At the same time, the viewer is no longer oppressed by the absence of time, no longer protected from things by the absence of time.

How does Godard go about putting into question the cinematic illusion of being 'in' time, therefore lacking time, such that he permits the viewer to see what time is capable of, but at the same time constrains the viewer to respond to what is shown? In the first place by an act of violence against the medium, one which requires the medium of presentation to become *itself* materially, something which is possible only if it is encouraged to renounce its claim over time by bringing about a gap in time, by introducing an interval which displaces its present moment. It is in Godard's video essays and television series especially that the medium of the moving image becomes no longer the obstacle which separates time from itself. On the contrary, it allows the movement of time to be shown, and each time as if for the first time. We are given what is proper to the moving image: temporality. We might suppose this is especially pertinent for 'documentary' inasmuch as it seeks to reveal how what it represents becomes what it already is, before the events, objects and characters become what they are, 'before the name' as Godard puts it. But for Godard fiction is no different from documentary in this respect.

Godard has always been concerned to question, from the 1960s right through to HISTOIRE(S) DU CINÉMA, the distinction between objective/documentary and subjective/fictional approaches to film-making; it is the relation between them, invariably referred to as a 'movement', that interests him: 'the underlying movement of the film [DEUX OU TROIS CHOSES QUE JE SAIS D'ELLE]... is the attempt to describe a complex (people and things) since no distinction is made between the two [objects (things) and subjects (people)], and in order to simplify, people are spoken of as things and things as people...'.[7] Over the intertitle 'Documentaire et fiction' one of the lead characters of NUMÉRO DEUX asks: 'Why either/or? Sometimes both. *Sometimes. But when?*' And Godard has written: 'Everything divided has always profoundly moved me: documentary and fiction...';[8] 'I have always tried to make what is called documentary and what is called fiction two aspects of a single movement, it is the relation between the two which produces the true movement'.[9] Or as Godard declaims in SCÉNARIO DU FILM PASSION: 'between fiction and documentary, fiction leads back to documentary, you are there now'. As Claude Ollier puts it, documentary and fiction 'exchange their attributes' in Godard;[10] properties traditionally or normatively attributed to one are shown also to be attributable to the other. It is an articulation made possible by both fiction film and documentary sharing the same root as it were: temporality. Another way of putting this is to say that both narrative, the fictional propositions arrived at by Godard, and historicity, his more documentative propositions, *have the same history,* 'the pre-(hi)story of (hi)story', as Albert, the male presenter, puts it at the end of the first episode, or *movement* as Godard prefers, of FRANCE/TOUR/DÉTOUR/DEUX/ENFANTS.[11] And it is this which I think Godard is trying to show in his HISTOIRE(S) DU CINÉMA.

HISTOIRE(S) DU CINÉMA poses two questions concerning history, or, more precisely, performs two problems *of* history: (i) does cinema have a history? (ii) is there history at all?[12] If history really does exist – 'all alone' as Godard puts it – then cinema will have been a presentiment or a memory, the before and after, of its existence. It is important not to understand this as a claim to objectivity – or rather, if there is objectivity, then it has to be understood in a special sense of the term. Godard does not presuppose that there is or was

history, and that it has always been, and that it therefore always merely continues. Instead he attempts to think history with and through the representations *of* history and its presentation *as* history. Together with many other
essays Godard has made since the late 1960s, HISTOIRE(S) DU CINÉMA constitutes a radical questioning of history 'as such', bringing with it a transformation both of the concept of history and the medium of cinema.[13] It is a
work reviewing the entire spatial-temporal limits of its presentation by repeating history – which needs must include its own history – as if for the
first time, a cinema perpetually remade and permanently provocative. It is
not that Godard thinks history has a purpose or a teleological sense which
has to be captured by cinema; rather, he is interested in cinema becoming
what it is, in getting back to where cinema is, something which can be
achieved only by questioning its history. If there is a sense of something yet
to come for Godard it is that we have still to make history.

As is the case with each one of Godard's film and video essays,
HISTOIRE(S) DU CINÉMA presents itself to itself as the process of film-making
itself. Cinema becomes what it is by representing itself to itself, and in doing
so it becomes visible to itself in its proper form. It inscribes in its *becoming*
cinema the law of cinema itself, the law is inscribed in cinema in the process
of its becoming cinema. But this is not the presence of cinema to itself; rather,
there is something of a 'gap', a spacing, what Godard calls a 'between'. Now,
one way of describing this gap is to say, as does Gilles Deleuze, that it is the
way in which images continuously act and react on one another.[14] There is a
gap between the action undergone by these images and the reaction that is
achieved, and thus an effect of something like a suspension in time, where
time is no longer a continuous flow. An aspect of time becomes an interval
in time in the space of which something can happen. That is, time is *produced*, a temporalised structure is created. It is what I would call, diverging
from Deleuze, the structure of subjective space, because the viewer, and
Godard is no less a viewer in this respect, is asked to decide what it *is* that
happens there. In the more fictional films this structure gives us the possibility of saying 'I', in the more documentary films the possibility of saying
'we', but of course the two cannot be separated since both pose the question
of the other. Hence, Godard's concern to ask throughout HISTOIRE(S) DU
CINÉMA, for instance: 'Where do *I* come into it?...The solitude of history.' It is
a solitude which enables Godard to say: 'If I go and see a *good* film called
HÉLAS POUR MOI by, let's say, Oliveira or Cassavetes, or X or Y, if it's any
good I'll interpret the 'me' in the title as "me" the spectator.'[15] This decision
is the possibility of presenting to oneself the 'I' made possible by the spacing
in time. It is not dependent on any content – anything can happen. It is simply *that* something happens. In the gap or interval one perceives or glimpses

the possibility of oneself as a self, as an other self. This is finitude: to be exposed to the otherness of being an 'I'. Every now is absolutely other in the sense that the present is constituted by this otherness. We could not have a relation to others, and therefore ourselves, without this alterity of time.

The images that happen in Godard are accompanied by various and varying commentaries, descriptions, narrations, continuities, all of which tend towards blurring the distinction between the documentative and the fictional. Or rather, they hesitate to presuppose in what that distinction consists. In Godard's words, 'adding an objective description to the subjective should uncover certain more general forms – not a generalised overall truth but a certain "feeling of the whole"'.[16] And there is no way of telling in advance, that is to say objectively, where and when objective description begins to become something other than or opposed to it. If the *definition* of the truth of history is to be no longer abstractly objective, then any historical account, and equally any account of truth, must contain an expression of its antithesis to objectivity: we might call what Godard alludes to with his subjective description an *objective uncertainty*. Godard's commentaries tend towards this point of objective uncertainty. It is the performative aspect of giving an historical account, one that asks whether cinema has a history and whether there is history. A singular witness, Godard redoubles in himself a subjective attitude, he is both subject and object of our viewing. We see him as an object of knowledge in that he subjectively bears witness to his own subjectivity. We might say that HISTOIRE(S) DU CINÉMA begins when representation ends.[17] If cinematic representation does have a history it does not consist in the presentation of a historical present. History is not representable: it happens. Rather than presuppose the possibility of objective description, Godard's is a response to the real, and in this sense he is a witness to the happening of history just as much as is the viewer, Godard's is a response to what happens just as much as is the viewer's, giving us a cinema which as he puts it in Chapter 1B of HISTOIRE(S) DU CINÉMA 'receives before it gives'. Cinema's movement is its beginning by returning.[18] Then we might more accurately say that we cannot tell which comes first, the receiving or the giving. 'A film between the active and the passive, between actor and spectator', as an inscription in ICI ET AILLEURS has it. Neither active nor passive but this side of the distinction. A waiting directed towards, as I shall go on to say, an essential questioning of oneself. It is what enables Godard to say to Marguerite Duras, in disagreement with her, that he is a witness, but this does not imply silence.[19]

The first three parts of HISTOIRE(S) DU CINÉMA begin with the following chapter headings: 1A, TOUTES LES HISTOIRES (All the (hi)stories); 1B, UNE HISTOIRE SEULE (A lone (hi)story); 2A, SEUL LE CINÉMA (Cinema alone:

meaning something like 'Cinema alone did that' but also 'Cinema was alone').[20] Why 'alone', what is meant by 'alone' in 'cinema alone'? That this history, the history of cinema, is the only history there has ever been, it is the only history there will ever be and that there has ever been. As the director himself remarks in the first chapter: 'all the histories, with an "s", all the histories that might have been. That will be? Or that might have been? That have been!' The history of cinema is the only history – why? Because it can 'speak for itself': 'I say that [the history of cinema] is the greatest story because it can *project itself*. The others can only reduce themselves.'[21] 'My fundamental intuition was that cinema is uniquely equipped to tell its own story... Film is alone because its story can be told in its own language, through its own means of expression... unlike the rest, *cinema can tell its own story*, indeed it is only in the visual domain that one finds a history that speaks'.[22] Godard goes so far as to say that cinema can do the thinking itself,[23] and proposes that when Ingrid Bergman holds a key in her hand, for instance, that key looks at us the viewer and demands a response from us.[24] A double reflection enacted in part 2A of Godard's television series SIX FOIS DEUX, LEÇONS DE CHOSES, for instance, where what is narrated is the way in which things reflect on the character Paolo as he attempts to reflect on them. This implies that not just the viewer but the film-maker, too, is *a priori* a receiver, as much an addressee of what he films as are we the spectators; that the film-maker is as little able to overcome a certain compliance regarding what is to be shown (i.e. what we might thus call the autonomy of the image), as is the viewer.

For Godard this suggests that cinema is disclosive rather than inventive. Indeed, in this regard it is 'live and direct': 'there's no invention in cinema. All you can do is look, and then try to give some order to what you've seen... if you've managed to see properly, that is.'[25] But this ought not to presuppose that the camera is outside the world it films, that cinema can only reveal what is revealed to it. In my view Godard shares the basic intuition with Stanley Cavell that what is projected on to the screen refers to itself and reflects upon its physical origins. If something (or someone) is on screen it is because it is not here, it is absent, located in another place, but not such that it no longer participates in the re-presentation of itself; on the contrary, 'objects are essential in the making of their appearances'.[26] But, and this is the important point, this is no different from how things anyway are in the world being presented, the world referred to in the presentation of its objects, wherein *any* giving of a thing is a reproduction of it: there is no pure perception. Godard puts it like this: 'I don't make any distinction between reality and the image of it... There's no difference between shooting and the following of something when the camera isn't turning. That's something which people in the movies don't understand... To shoot is to rerun'.[27] This would be in agreement with what Derrida, for example, says about the necessarily *reproductive* work of cinema; here the consequence is that if all film, film as such, is reproductive, is linked to a structure of reproduction from the outset, then the only interesting film is one whose reproductive work transforms the entire space of its presentation rather than one which is simply reproductive of what it sees and how it sees.[28] Godard's films would succeed to the extent that they bring into question the conditions of their possibility in a way which does not just mechanically expose the rules of their production. The medium itself is structured by the absence of its objects, in which case when film strives to present its own history necessarily it will be concerned with this structural absence. What is shown in 'good' films in Godard's sense is both the world keeping to itself at the very moment it gives presence to its objects and characters, and the film's concern for this absence so essential to its own materiality.

Thus, to make history filmically is not simply to record certain events, it is not simply to represent some past or present, it is to traverse a certain boundary within its own present, and the presence of its – film's – passing: this would be cinema's movement. Godard often says cinema has a *duty to report*. He argues that with the advent of speech in cinema its spectacular side won out over the more research-based, documentative, reporting side.[29] Godard has in common with most of his commentators the tendency to provide a political or cultural explanation for this. But what I am seeking to draw attention to is what makes the loss of the documentative, the illusoriness of the objectivity of the camera eye, structurally possible. Saying that cinema has a duty to report implies that film can bring to presence something which would otherwise not be admitted were it not for film, and that film cannot assume that this is not so, at least not without potentially denying that presence. But in doing so it points to the absence or withdrawing of itself, of the film medium itself. So when Godard speaks of the cinema having a duty to report, cinema must itself be included in the realm of that which it has to report. Film has a duty to report on itself. If film brings into existence something otherwise not revealed, if film is to show something's existing for it that, were it not shown, would go unacknowledged or denied, then this necessarily must include the limits of film's *own* materiality.

Godard's films present not some particular content, or not just that, or not importantly that, but film itself, in order that the film does not just 'go along with' the effacement of its materiality in the telling of its story. In Godard's hands film's materiality is used rather than used up, it is not effaced. The possibilities of the medium of film (and it is not as if film is different from any other media in this respect) are revealed by those works which question and redefine film's necessary conditions, and in so doing change the conditions of film's possibilities by questioning the terms of those possibilities as defined prior to the event of that work. Which is to say that film's materiality cannot be said to pre-exist the film, materiality is not simply given. Film's materiality is not known in advance – why, what would it be for film to presuppose its materiality? It would be yet another form of representation, of something decided prior to the event of any particular film. Therefore its materiality must become a question for it in its presentation. One way of doing this – and Godard does it extensively and multifariously – is through the use of filmic techniques. As Cavell rightly argues, the question of what it is to utilise a technique in art, in film, can only be answered by appeal to the work of art itself. The significance or success of a certain technical device, the freeze frame say, or the slowing down of a sequence of shots, or the insertion of black leader, all of which Godard uses extensively, cannot be decided in advance of their use in a particular film, their success being neither a technical nor an ideological matter. If we are taken by a film, if we find it convincing, then we find it convincing in its being frozen or slowed. But what we mean by 'convincing' is itself informed by our being in a world which is itself frozen, slowed, or blacked out. Thus, how these 'formal' devices are utilised is subject to the same constraints as is content. It is difficult to argue that a medium is made materially specific by properties or devices reducible to it, for film's materiality consists not in its techniques or material base but in how it succeeds in reproducing the materiality revealed to us by the world or in transforming the place of that materiality. Simply put, film's realism is this: its materiality is both of the world and a response to – perhaps even symptom of – the way the world keeps to itself.

If it remains to be decided what happens in Godard's films, what does emerge is time, a space in time in which something *can* happen. However, and this is the important point, because Godard features the otherwise of events, the possibility of their being other than what they are, their becoming something else or something other, what happens has to be decided, decided by us the viewer and by Godard the director, in the face of objective uncertainty. It is not just that we have to decide between this interpretation or meaning and that one, but rather that we are presented with the necessity of the decision to decide whether it is indeed decidable or undecidable. In a sense nothing happens in Godard's films, or rather what does happen emerges from out of nothing; and it is this space for decision, this silence at the heart of Godard's films, that mainstream television seems unable to tolerate.[30] It is the silence of temporality. As the presenter in the first part of the last episode of SIX FOIS DEUX puts it: 'To go from a before to an after and backwards from an after to a before... and with this before and after there is something... there is a silence... a word. Perhaps there would be no before or after if there were no speech or silence.' This law of silence, as one of the narrators of HÉLAS POUR MOI calls it, requires us to act in order that we see and receive that which can happen, before the events, objects and characters become what they are, before the name. Godard's most explicit attempts to reveal this silence are his two television series, FRANCE/TOUR/DÉTOUR/DEUX/ENFANTS and SIX FOIS DEUX.

At the end of the second movement of FRANCE/TOUR/DÉTOUR/DEUX/ENFANTS, LUMIÈRE/PHYSIQUE, Godard says: 'we are never shown the beginning and the end'. Why are we never shown this? Because it cannot be shown. It is the beginning and the end to which, precisely, we cannot lay claim. Rather, we find ourselves already situated and placed. Causality does not govern history, since for Godard history is not a matter of causal or linear succession. His films show us images bereft of causality, the better that our relationship to them be established. In one sense the images Godard presents are autonomous – the world has withdrawn. The same images are used against different backgrounds, with different associations, are accompanied by different sounds, reshown in different films. It is instead the question of how history begins that interests Godard, how we enter it, how we find ourselves already in history. Or, as it is repeatedly posed in SIX FOIS DEUX (especially part 2A and the first section of the last episode, part 6A, AVANT ET APRÈS): *où et quand?* Where and when do you find yourself there? The interest is not in presenting the outcome or result of history, almost the opposite; it is to show how history is not the succession of events but what makes images available for representation at all, and committing this to film is for film to put itself into question, both as cinema and as history.

The central approach adopted in these two series is to question what it is we are used to seeing on the television screen. This is achieved not simply by questioning, but by putting into question what a question is, where it comes from, who poses it. The sorts of questions asked of the interviewees do not insist on an answer, are not asked narratively as a means to an answer. A comparison is made with the 'selling technique' outlined by the journalist interviewed in part 4A of SIX FOIS DEUX, PAS D'HISTOIRE: 'There's one thing you've got to do if you want to get inside people's houses, and that is to ask questions in such a way that they've got to reply.' Against this, disquisitions seemingly more interested in a lost question, in search of a missing question, the two television series pose questions in the hope that the question which best expresses the problem will emerge. It is not for nothing that one commentator, Deleuze, finds these questions direct, another, MacCabe, indirect.[31] Deleuze argues that Godard's questions tend to silence answers, whilst MacCabe argues that Godard asks questions the answers to which he does not in advance know – and it is this to which his interviewees have to submit. I would say that both these positions are captured by the thought that Godard's questions suspend themselves as questions in their asking. The work of the question is carried out as much by the person interviewed as it is by the questioner. As Godard interviews a young girl in the first movement of FRANCE/TOUR/DÉTOUR/DEUX/ENFANTS, OBSCUR/CHIMIE, a female voice cuts in: 'Sometimes I dream of a kind of society where people meet a TV reporter not to answer him but to question him... Instead of questioning the workers it would be better working on the questions.' (This is precisely what is glimpsed by the female journalist in TOUT VA BIEN after she and her partner are taken hostage. They go to interview the company boss but end up being interrogated as to their method by the workers.) Towards the end of episode 4B of SIX FOIS DEUX, NANAS, Godard's collaborator Anne-Marie Miéville (who has herself been interviewing one of the women characters) voices over: 'You know, your programme about women was a bit weak. You set them up, you question them, you more or less tell them how to reply... I wouldn't like it myself'. The way in which Godard edits sequences, and the way in which questions are posed both by him and within his films by the narrators and voices-off and his collaborator, and by characters and interviewers, is *essentially* interrogative, that is, his films question themselves as much as their putative objects.

Cavell makes it a matter of Godard's irresponsibility that he does not give us his answer *vis-à-vis* what is shown on screen. Against this I would argue that Godard, at least the later Godard, seldom loses sight of the point that answers gain their motive authority from the asking, and are only the *beginning* of a responsibility for answering.[32] An answer detached from the inquiry nullifies itself as an answer and loses what is most essential to it *as* an answer. Only by remaining in question does film, for Godard, force what is worthy of questioning to appear, in the gap between question and answer, a gap occasioned by the complicity of an answer which retains the question within it. Asking a question without insisting on an answer, posing a problem despite not being able to solve it, but to ask what it is to pose it in the right way, makes explicit a way of being different from not asking the question at all. The work done by such questions is not imperatival or commanding, but equally it is no less questioning for not insisting on an answer.

In taking up that which it questions, a question presupposes a certain responsibility. Isn't it already, in its questioning, beginning to answer for that which is questioned? We surely don't want to say that its responsibility can simply be exercised, as if it were open to the questioner to assume or leave aside his responsibility. If a question really is to question after something –

Godard's HISTOIRE(S) DU CINÉMA questioning the history of cinema and the possibility of history, Godard stating: 'I constantly ask myself questions. I watch myself filming, and you can hear me thinking. In short it's not a film, it's an attempt at a film and it presents itself as such'[33] – then the question must question after its own possibility, both as a question at all and as a question adequate to that which is questioned. Any question, then, poses the question of its responsibility for that which is questioned. We might say that responsibility is opened by the question. At the very moment the question takes up that which is questioned, and in doing so runs up against its own possibility as a question, it protects the object of its questioning from a certain determinacy. The question protects that which is questioned from the question by suspending itself in its asking. Only then will that which is questioned retain the possibility of exceeding the delimitation and finitude of the question. Hence, the autonomy of Godard's images. And this because questioning is essentially finite, essentially a matter of focusing itself by way of specific questions. Every question must succumb to its finite aspect. And, *if* it questions, the question poses the question of responsibility for its own finitude. This is the protection afforded that which is questioned, as well as the source of a possible violence done unto it. It is also the beginning of the effect of not having answered. Might one not think of this as something like giving both the right counter to the right point? After all, FRANCE/TOUR/DÉTOUR/DEUX/ENFANTS is described by its director as chamber music (and its episodes referred to as movements), even philosophy in the form of chamber music.[34] Or the charge against together with the defence – a montage of two images producing not another image but the justice of the two?[35] What the voice-over in COMMENT ÇA VA calls the beginning of thinking, of 'bringing together in order to think. Simply bringing two images together... Yes, to begin to think as you look'.

The experience of watching a film by Godard is marked by this equivocation, manifest as a definite irresolution – but this is not the same as leaving things completely open, a weakness implied by Alain Badiou, who characterises HISTOIRE(S) DU CINÉMA as 'une désarticulation thématique' between (hi)story and idea, between the assembly of all available interpretations and the murmur of principles beneath, of which we can make what we will.[36] We are given choices made then unmade, and we are given options discarded then retrieved. For Ollier it is an 'aesthetic no man's land' in which various options are given us from a field of possibilities and a quick inventory made of their descriptive and suggestive potentialities, on one of which Godard will alight before just as quickly abandoning it, then renewing his interest in it through different approaches, then undoing it, seemingly uninterested in it, and so on.[37] Serge Daney makes this 'confusion' an essential aspect of

Godard's pedagogical method: 'To what the other says, assertion, declaration, sermon, Godard always replies with what *another* other says.'[38] And for Peter Brook it is the liberation of the picture from its own consistency, 'so that at one second you are genuinely looking at a photograph of three people in a bar, then you are half alienated, then three-quarters alienated, then you are looking at it as a film, then as something made by a film-maker, then you are reminded that it is made by actors, and then you are thrown right back into believing it. This is the changing relationship that you have in Shakespeare.'[39] But doesn't all of this point to our exposure to change, to the historicity of time, the way in which heterogeneity can be shown to emerge as time? The manner in which the elements are arranged, the system of their acceptance, confers on them a sort of unity, and to that extent Godard's compositions are complete – yet they await something. This would be the musicality of Godard's style: his films await the viewer's decision. We might even say that Godard tests his own response to different subjects and situations, to see which are permanent and which contingent. There is a line in a poem by Wallace Stevens which states: 'One poem proves another and the whole'.[40] What Godard's decision is regarding one Godard film may have to wait for its confirmation until the next. This is, I think, what Godard is moving towards when he says: 'Basically, what I do is make the viewer take part in the arbitrariness of my choices and in the search for the general laws that would justify a specific choice...'.[41] And it is what Cavell himself says, of another in another place, but as if by now in chorus with Godard, when he suggests that Debussy saw what Mallarmé observed in Maeterlinck's play *Pelléas et Mélisande*, 'its texture of totality yet discreteness of juxtaposition, or irresolution without decisiveness... understanding without meaning, the complete awaiting completion, *the before and the after of saying*'.[42]

In *The World Viewed* Cavell charges Godard with avoiding the choice because of the implausible way in which he depersonalises his characters. For characters to appear to us plausibly depersonalised requires, for Cavell, two things of the viewer: (a) that we be able to respond to these persons; and (b) that we continuously fail to read their motions within the stresses of ordinary human emotion and motivation: with the consequence that we respond to them by believing they are unable to feel.[43] Concerning the events filmed, Cavell reduces our alienation to the question of *Godard's* position towards them. In Cavell's account the events do not justify or clarify Godard's position which remains arbitrary. To the answer that an artist is under no special obligation to give us his position, Cavell says then that he must instead do one of two things: either provide us with pleasure (which Godard does not) or give us knowledge of the way things are. Works that accomplish this latter do so by at the same time allowing us to see the artist's own position towards what is revealed by him, through the expression of various moods and evaluative judgments. Whilst Godard does give us a sense of how things are, in Cavell's view it is only from the position of one who fails to see his own responsibility towards them. And because he does not express his own position with respect to what is revealed, he abdicates his responsibility for so revealing. We can concede that Godard's work admits of arbitrariness, but does this open it to Cavell's charge of irresponsibility? In my view no. If, as Cavell contends, Godard regards the achievement of objectivity as impossible or unnecessary, then we *do* get a position from Godard. Taking Cavell's argument on its own terms though, if we say that film has a duty to report then must it not satisfy the requirement that it reproduce the world by enabling us to view it unseen? But to view a film that makes automatic the condition that we can no longer hope to marry our fantasies or hopes to the world takes the responsibility for it out of our hands, it naturalises this condition.[44] Yet does Godard not deny this? He shows us a world lacking our decisions about it but not our responsibility for it – in this sense we are no longer unseen, we no longer feel as if we are unseen, and we refuse to believe that the world with which we are presented is a *natural* one. We are included in the world to the extent that we are required or demanded to make a decision regarding it. Our absence *is* the requirement that we decide, my absence from the film is its awaiting my decision.[45] What could be said is that we lack Godard's decision. It is not so much that Godard rehearses the options but whether they are optional; it is this we are asked to decide. Even the characters are asked this: running throughout SIX FOIS DEUX, for example, is the question posed by the film-maker to his interlocutors. What images would best express your thoughts and opinions? Godard's characters are certainly questionable, but this does not mean that they do not stand as answers. They answer not by accounting for their actions in further acts, acts of justification, but by standing as answers for the problem of the temporality of things.

I have just said that Godard's works have a sort of unity – is there not after all a way in which Godard *does* choose, despite himself, in his capacity for thematisation? It is a capacity which at times lends itself to totalising different experiences by conferring on them a commensurable and therefore generalisable look, one that seems to generate out of their differences and mutual contradictions a kind of style, rather like the way John Cage breaks the sound barrier in his gathering of seemingly disparate sounds into a piece of music. The sheer arbitrarinesss of sounds makes them so recognisably a piece by Cage, even if we do not go as far as saying that their subsumption beneath the proper name of the composer makes that name into the measure of them, thereby reducing them to an expression of his thought.

But it is more than a tension placed over the images in their being presented to us at all. Whilst it was certainly more than that in the political totalitarianism favoured by Godard in the late 1960s, it never quite seemed to subdue the autonomy of the images. The lack of resolution ought not to be seen as negative since it puts the self into question by requiring a decision from the viewer. Godard's failure to synthesise the elements into a position we might call his own ought not to be seen as an intellectual or artistic deficiency. If synthesis were to succeed then its connection to the viewer as individual would have been negated. Godard's is less a position, more a system of doubt, his irresolution something of the nature of a characterful style, but one which is not, as the sceptic's so often is, the occasion for expressing again one's certainty.

A major example given by Cavell of Godard's indifference to the validity or otherwise of his characters' reactions concerns philosophy: Godard 'doesn't care' whether what the philosopher says (in LA CHINOISE, for example) is valid or not. He listens to philosophy in the same way his (female) characters do; he doesn't choose between philosophy as a nobler form of seduction, or philosophy as powerful because distinct and separate.[46] We might say that Godard is blind to the choice. As it happens, one of Godard's favourite sources for philosophical citation is Wittgenstein's *On Certainty*, paragraphs 121 and 125 of which, concerning the absence of *ground* for doubt, appear in at least three of Godard's works: SIX FOIS DEUX, JLG/JLG and HISTOIRE(S) DU CINÉMA (twice). Paragraph 121 asks: 'Can one say "Where there is no doubt there is no knowledge either?"' and 125 whether, 'if a blind man should ask me if I have two hands, and if I should doubt it, would I look at my hands to find out? But why should I trust my eyes more than or before my hands? *What* is to be tested by what? (Who decides *what* stands fast?) And what does it mean to say that such and such stands fast?'[47] Again, we cannot say which comes first, something which is brilliantly captured in JLG/JLG by his continually turning back and forth pages of handwritten inscriptions. We see Godard reading from Wittgenstein's text, the cut to which is from a sheet of paper on which is written in hand 'Le fond du problème' ('The heart of the problem'), to Godard reading then covering the pages of *On Certainty* with his hands, then putting that book aside in favour of Diderot's *Letters of the Blind*. The first mention of these paragraphs in HISTOIRE(S) DU CINÉMA – but here their source goes unacknowledged – is at the end of Chapter 1A, TOUTES LES HISTOIRES. They are voiced by Godard over the flashing alternation of a still of Giulietta Masina in Fellini's LA STRADA, holding fingers to face, and the suicide of the young boy from the end of Rossellini's GERMANY YEAR ZERO, who closes his eyes with his fingers before jumping. The second mention is in Chapter 3A, LA MONNAIE DE

L'ABSOLU, in a section on error, where the book is seen being closed by Godard. Something similar to the effect of pages turning back and forth is achieved with the pulsing or flashing of images in PUISSANCE DE LA PAROLE. And the rhythm set up by the flashing of images and their alternation with intertitles, most notably in HISTOIRE(S) DU CINÉMA and the two television series, of a category or concept or idea flashed with, or even superimposed on or under images, is, I think, in the service of this claim that we cannot say which comes first, which over which. Throughout HISTOIRE(S) DU CINÉMA, and in a film almost contemporaneous with it, LES ENFANTS JOUENT À LA RUSSIE (the title of which is mentioned in JLG/JLG by his cleaning lady as she reads the journal kept by Godard during the making of the film), Godard's seriousness is his anguishing and hesitating over his words (stammering as both Dubois[48] and Deleuze[49], and indeed it seems Godard himself[50], put it). Insofar as Godard's style of irresolution and definite equivocation is a method (in another place Deleuze calls the 'before and after' Godard's 'generalised method'[51]), we might say that it is similar to Wittgenstein's manner of asking questions without insisting on an answer – it forms under the director's name a system of doubt. Paragraph 126 of *On Certainty* reads in part: 'My doubts form a system'.

As we have seen, Godard's subjective description, in which is born an objective uncertainty, seeks to give a 'feeling of the whole'. The viewer, and Godard himself, is required to decide or discover what that is. What the whole or totality cannot include is the decision as to what makes it the totality it is, the decision delimiting the frame. Godard's films try and make visible this necessary feature of representation. What the films can attempt to bring in is the limit of the before and after, the interval of decision, and make it the time inhabited by their characters; it is a limit which, as Deleuze puts it, the character himself has to step over 'in order to enter the film and leave it, to enter into the fiction as into a present which is inseparable from its before and after'.[52] This limit is also perhaps what Cavell is pointing to when he speaks of the way the camera can intervene in the character's part, interrupt his acting, rebuke or take vengeance on a character for his absence, indeed accompany the actor when that actor leaves the fiction, 'across the line of death'.[53] None of which, contra Deleuze, can be done without reference to the world. For how *can* an image be cut off from the external world? This would be possible only to the extent that the film-making process presupposes a point of view *external* to the diegesis, a presupposition which Godard suspends in the essentially interrogative way he composes his films. Necessary reference does not mean referential subordination. The task is to reintroduce an enduring interval in the moment between the before and after, to set this interval 'free', such that it stands on its own, becomes autonomous, and cuts the image off from the external world.[54] But by 'cut off' Deleuze must mean suspend or question (what else can we do?), perhaps transform. The autonomy of the image, its being for itself, is consequent of its awaiting a decision about its meaning, a decision about its relation to the external world. The camera records or reports the world; it presents my absence from the world in the form of its lacking my (Godard's) decision, the world is then becoming my decision about it, this is my responsibility. To say that the image is cut off or suspended is, of course, to have no less decided that relation in advance than were it to have been subordinated to a pre-established reference. But at least in its provisionalness that relation calls for a subsequent one on the part of the viewer. The viewer too is 'cut off' in that we have to decide. The 'and' between images is not simply an arbitrary one, the various and conflicting interpretations not merely those of multiple points of view;[55] the conjunction is Godard's, the various interpretations and options are those available to Godard. Godard insists on the facility afforded by the device of changing the rhythm of a scene, slowing a piece of footage down for instance, of perceiving possibilities inherent in the scene.[56] Does Godard want to say that the possibilities are unending (infinite), or are they the possibilities of – or in – one thing? If the task is to make sense of the connections between them and to discover the necessity linking them (what Godard calls their 'law'[57]), then surely the latter. And perhaps this is why Godard can make the matter of his being directed toward this or that object or person a question of conscience.[58]

Godard's later film and video works show how film can become itself by renouncing a claim over time, achieving their materiality not by presuming to objectify time, but by making time their proper object, requiring us to confront time, calling for an 'I' of history. Without the illusion of being in time we might see what time is capable of. There would not be a question here of whether we call this an indirect or a direct representation, for cinema's directness is its facility to present *that* as a problem of time. Hence, the seeming incompatibility – but only seeming – between Deleuze and Derrida: Deleuze: 'it is the direct presentation of time';[59] Derrida: 'there is not and never has been a direct, live presentation'.[60] When Godard states: 'The cinema, when it's well done, has a direct, total power... The cinema is live and direct...',[61] he is pointing to the way in which, materially, through its attending to the gap between two images, by making visible the temporal gap between the before and after, cinema can rend time rather than render it. What is made visible is not a present moment to which the before and after would belong, but a temporal limit belonging to neither, one that awaits its appropriation by the viewer as a matter of our responsibility.

5 Big Rhythm and the Power of Metamorphosis: Some Models and Precursors for HISTOIRE(S) DU CINÉMA

Michael Temple

In late 1950, Maurice Blanchot, literary critic and occasional philosopher, wrote the following pre-emptive description of Jean-Luc Godard's HISTOIRE(S) DU CINÉMA, a work that was only destined to come into being some fifty years later:

> There are some viewers who regret that Godard's video essays on THE HISTORIES OF CINEMA did not undergo more rigorous planning. The essays are found to be obscure, not in their language, which is clear – and even more than clear, brilliant – but in their development. Godard himself, at the end of the series, seems to have wished for better composition. Perhaps Godard is right, but his detractors are surely wrong. It is true that the ideas he develops have their whims: they are peremptory, sudden, they remain unresolved. They disappear and return. And since they often affirm themselves in formulas they find pleasing, they seem to think themselves thereby defined, and this achievement satisfies them. But the movement that abandons them, calls them back; the joy, the glory of a new formula once again draws them out of themselves.

This is already a strikingly accurate prediction. But it gets better:

> This movement – this apparent disorder – is most definitely one of the important aspects of these video-essays. The ideas do not thereby lose their coherence; it is rather from their contradictions that they escape, even though these contradictions continue to animate them and keep them alive. Godard's excuse lies not so much in the passion he devotes to the art he examines, nor even in the extraordinary admiration he lavishes upon it, but rather in this unique merit: the ideas, however they may tend, according to their own requirements, towards an important and general view of cinema, both in their attempted dialogue with film works and with the images they accompany, succeed at the same time – without losing their explanatory character – in illuminating themselves with a light that is not purely intellectual, in approaching an indefinable quality that is more open than their meaning, and in achieving for themselves (and for us who are destined to understand them) an experience that imitates art rather than describes it. Thus ideas become themes, motifs, and their somewhat

incoherent development, often criticised, expresses instead their truest order, which is to constitute and test themselves in their contact with History through a movement whose vivacity and seeming vagrancy make tangible for us both the progression in History of film works and their simultaneous presence in the virtual Museum where culture today assembles them.

Now how can Blanchot, with no discernible interest in the forms or fate of cinema, have made this astonishingly mature assessment of a future work whose creator, barely twenty years old at the time, had only just begun to frequent the legendary Cinémathèque of Henri Langlois in the avenue de Messine? There is a simple answer to this awkward question. Maurice Blanchot was not, of course, writing about Godard's HISTOIRE(S) DU CINÉMA at all.[1] He was, in fact, describing André Malraux's *Essais de psychologie de l'art*, a three-volume work of art history that was later to become *Les voix du silence* (1947-1965), arguably the most significant forerunner of HISTOIRE(S) DU CINÉMA along with (as we shall see) Élie Faure's *Histoire de l'art* (1909-1921) and *L'esprit des formes* (1927).[2] In the passage cited above, the name of 'Godard' replaces that of 'Malraux' and the title 'HISTOIRE(S) DU CINÉMA' supersedes '*La psychologie de l'art*'. A few additional adjustments complete the sleight-of-hand. Scholarship, we know, should not indulge in fakery, but the heuristic value of this 'truc à substitution', as Méliès would have called it, is too powerful to ignore. For this trick passage summarises most convincingly the first doubts and initial impressions of commentators who, in the late 1990s, finally saw the fully formed HISTOIRE(S) DU CINÉMA emerge from its manifold veil of mystery, from a decade of reports and rumours, official sneak previews and video contraband. But efficacious trickery also suggests, to this observer at least, that HISTOIRE(S) DU CINÉMA will demand some serious self-examination on the part of its critical spectators. Surely no film work has ever signalled more clearly to its viewers the redundancy of the hermeneutic word, precisely because its major innovation is to use sound and image, and the miracle of montage, as the basic tools of its historical investigations. How can one approach the material intensity and formal originality of such an enterprise, armed merely with pen and paper and hermeneutically good intentions? Should one perhaps follow Godard's example and mimetically respond in kind to the speed and complexity of what seems like a radically new object of critical enquiry? As if to 'the cinema alone' only the cinema (in its photographic, filmic, video, and digital manifestations) could reply on equal terms? While it is true that, further down the line, there will certainly be important practical questions for pedagogues and theorists alike, what I wish to do in the present essay is strategically to respond to that first impression of critical futility and redundancy by placing HISTOIRE(S) DU CINÉMA in some kind of French intellectual tradition of precursors and, more precisely, by introducing and examining some clearly identifiable models for the 'somewhat incoherent development' that rhythmically structures the 'seemingly vagrant yet vivacious movements' of Godard's late masterpiece. If fifty years ago Maurice Blanchot could magically foresee the shadow of Godard's histories in Malraux's *Les voix du silence* (and especially in its most famous volume, *Le musée imaginaire*), then surely one might now be able to identify similar prototypes and explore in detail the structural relationships between those models and their illustrious contemporary descendant. As was stated in the Introduction to this collection, whilst a considerable scholarly task of commentary and interpretation concerning the multiple meanings of HISTOIRE(S) DU CINÉMA clearly lies ahead, equally thoughtful attention must be paid to the structures, forms and rhythms sustaining those histories. Only in this way shall we reach a satisfactory understanding of the poetics of late Godard, thereby opening up the field to a proper reassessment of the Godardian corpus as a whole. With that broader perspective in mind, this essay seeks to contribute to the 'poetic' or 'modular' tendency.

In contrast to the fake exhibit with which we opened this discussion, let me now introduce some genuine material from HISTOIRE(S) DU CINÉMA. The passage in question, however, itself seeks to perpetrate a fairly scandalous act of deception. In Chapter 4A, LE CONTRÔLE DE L'UNIVERS, we see and hear the great French actor Alain Cuny declaiming in ghostly and moving tones a long text by Élie Faure.[3] At first glance, this appears to be describing and recounting the youth and senescence of cinema, but closer study of sources reveals that the term 'cinema' has in fact replaced what in Faure's original text was the ageing and youthful 'Rembrandt'. It is one of the longest textual passages in the whole of HISTOIRE(S) DU CINÉMA and, although we cannot reproduce Cuny's spine-chilling delivery, it merits a good hearing:

> In the early days, it merely felt but a few things, and it believed it knew everything. Later, inhabited only by doubt, pain, fear before the mystery of life, everything started to blur. And now that it felt everything, it believed it knew nothing. And yet, from insouciance to anxiety, from the loving recording of the early days to the hesitant but essential form at the end, it's the same central force that governed cinema. One can follow it from within, from form to form, with the shade and the ray of light prowling around, illuminating this, hiding that, making visible a shoulder, a face, a raised finger, an open window, a forehead, a little child in a crib. That which plunges into the light is the repercussion of that which the night submerges. That which the night submerges prolongs into the invisible that which plunges into the light [...] The cinema alone saw that if each person is at his task, the masses organise themselves alone, following an irreproachable equilibrium that the light falls where it should and ignores what it should, because it is useful that it illuminate one point of the scene

and that the shadows dominate elsewhere. It is alone in having been always present in everything that it looked at, the only one that could allow itself to mix mud with the light of someone's eyes, to introduce fire into ash, to make shine a rose in a shroud, or a pale blue as fresh as a rose. Its humanity is truly formidable. It is fatal like a devastating cry, like love, it is dramatic like the indifferent and continuous exchange between everything that is born and everything that dies. As it follows our march towards death, and the traces of blood that mark it, the cinema does not weep for us, it does not comfort us, because it is ourselves.[4]

Even at a purely literary level, this passage could stand as emblematic of Godard's late manner and historical method. Here are the main features:

1   At first glance the simple audacity of the substitution is immediately convincing. Of course cinema is Rembrandt, and Rembrandt cinema! But nonetheless, it leaves a strong impression that the mere act of rapprochement itself is at least as important as the precise senses it might generate. (One thinks again of Méliès, whose effects are always more special than any semblance of meaning or narrative they create.)
2   The illumination (to quote Blanchot) is not purely intellectual, it rather approaches an indefinable quality that is more open than its meanings, and achieves an experience that imitates art rather than describes it.
3   The theme or motif (Blanchot again) is neither an idea within an evolving argument nor the illustration of an historical thesis (of which, let us not forget, Godard has an abundant supply), but is rather a practical experiment in 'historical montage' (see Michael Witt's essay in the present collection), a process whose secret mechanism and purpose will always remain mysteriously deferred.
4   Beyond these instants of rapprochement, we sense the grander ambition to inscribe the story of cinema into the history of art. (Sharing such an ambition, neither Faure nor Malraux would have flinched at the prospect of comparing Rembrandt and cinema.)
5   That story's telling will require a complex, reflective, and fragile narrativity, in preference to the dull transparency of historical prose. (Faure's syntax, as evidenced here, provides both Godard and Cuny with a rhythmic model far richer and more resonant, for example, than the earnest plod of Sadoul or the turgid drone of Deleuze.)
6   At the heart of the historical narrative, a vital repetition maintains the story's impending end in ever closer proximity to its impossibly promising youth. (Both Faure and Malraux are part of that non-linear, Spenglerian tradition that draws its strength from the bloody cycle of crepuscular civilisations and terrible new worlds.)

7 Underlying all this is Godard's exemplary grasp of cinema's basic mission, its three fundamental traits: the duty to record, the image in process, the mystery of projection. (This is partly a familiar Godardian figure, of course, showing the cinematograph eternally bound to the contract of Lumière and Méliès, the compact of document and fiction, of image and montage; but one could equally remark the recent insistence on the public space of projection, the collective unknown of spectatorship, an aspect of Godard's thinking that has perhaps gone unrecognised.)

8 Finally, one must register the aspect of self-recognition, partly melancholic and partly resigned, within this picture of an artist in decline. (This brings us precisely to the cinema and Rembrandt, as well as to the broader question of self-portraiture in Godard's work as a whole...)

There may well be more, but the very quality of these correspondences (cinema/Rembrandt, Godard/Faure) demands a prior question. What order of relationship obtains in this exchange? The standard notion of influence, of great minds thinking alike, seems fairly impertinent here, although the spirit of Faure, one could say, informs Godard's vision. And Godard's switching process reforms in turn the dead historian's world. It's a Borgesian kind of reversal. As in the case of Blanchot's premonition, what strikes us even more than the uncanny fit between the disparate parts is the deeper notion of an underground network of relations, an ahistorical conference of spectral friends whose imbricated mutterings would somehow constitute the one true memory of cinema. Chronic but not logical. So what kind of company does Godard the film historian keep? Scarcely that of his fellow practitioners. Bardèche and Brasillach, Sadoul, Mitry, to name but the most obvious, none of these appears in the roll-call of great French critics ('from Diderot to Daney') that Godard intones and deploys across his later work.[5] Two reasons for this exclusion seem clear: a long-standing distrust of the very act of historicising, the dragooning of the diverse and the real into orderly lines and meaningful units; and an even stronger dislike of the subjugation of the visual realm to the rational empire of language, the subjection of cinema to 'my royal enemy, my number one enemy, the text'.[6] In contradistinction to the prosaic film historian, however, there stands the saintly and irreproachable figure of Henri Langlois, symbolic founder of the Cinémathèque and Godard's exemplary pedagogue.[7] Why is Langlois so precious an icon? Because he showed films. Not because he was an archivist (Godard famously told him to burn the collection), and certainly not because he was an administrator and cultural functionary. It was because he showed films, hundreds and hundreds of films, maybe without the soundtrack or in the wrong language, maybe with reels missing or in the wrong order, maybe without even knowing what might come out of the cans and on to the screen. But he showed films – in juxtaposition and contrast and series. And the act of film-history was therefore an art of projection. Such is, in résumé, the myth of Henri Langlois, his unique status placing him neither in the grand critical lineage nor in the pantheon of artists, but making him no less a saint of cinema than Jean Vigo or Serge Daney. Throughout his career Godard has remained faithful to the legend, but in particular we should signal the founding function of Langlois's death in the genesis of HISTOIRE(S) DU CINÉMA. The whole memorialising urge is born out of this absence, when Godard replaces Langlois at the Montreal film school in 1977, and consequently begins to work on 'an introduction to the true history of cinema and television'.[8] Twenty years later, in Chapter 3B, UNE VAGUE NOUVELLE, we see and hear Godard on screen still eulogising the man of the avenue de Messine:

> The identity of cinema. The identity of the New Wave. One evening we went to see Henri Langlois. And there was light. It's just (is it not?) that the true cinema did not even appear, to our provincial eyes, like the face of Madame Arnoux in the dreams of Frédéric Moreau. The cinema, we knew of it through Canudo and Delluc, but without ever having seen it. It had no connection with the Saturday night films, the Vox, the Palace, the Miramar, the Variétés, those films were for everyone. Not for us. Except for us. Because the true cinema was the one that cannot be seen. And it was only that one. It was, it was... it was Mary Duncan (isn't that right, Jean George Auriol?). But we would never get to see THE RIVER. And we had to love it blindly, and by heart. Same thing with the crowds of OCTOBER and those of QUE VIVA MEXICO (isn't that right, Jay Leyda?). Same thing with the tramways of SUNRISE (isn't that right, Lotte Eisner?). Because already forgotten. Still banned. Always invisible. Such was our cinema. And that's stayed with me. And Langlois confirmed to us that it was so. He confirmed – the term's exact – that the image is first and foremost a matter of redemption. Careful, though: the redemption of the real. We were, therefore, astonished. More so than El Greco in Italy. Than Goya, in Italy. Than Picasso, seeing Goya. We were without a past. And the man of the avenue de Messine gave us this gift of the past, transformed into the present. In the middle of the war in Indochina. In the middle of the war in Algeria. And when he projected L'ESPOIR, for the first time, it wasn't the war in Spain that made us jump. It was the fraternity of metaphors.[9]

The redemption of the real. Is that what cinema does? Is that what history does? Two names will help us to respond to these questions. The first is evoked at the end of the extract when Godard recalls L'ESPOIR, André Malraux's Spanish Civil War film drawn from his own war-time experiences and from his 1937 novel of the same name.[10] Across the whole span of HISTOIRE(S) DU CINÉMA, this film is probably cited more than any other single work, and fulfils diverse functions accordingly, but the mention of Malraux in relation to the 'redemption of the real' reminds us that one of the art historian's major theses in *Les voix du silence* is that throughout all cultures in history it is art that has helped man to triumph over death, momentarily but constantly redeeming that which has been surrendered to time, nature, the gods. That irrepressible power of metamorphosis enables man to achieve his 'anti-destiny', the victory of aesthetics over biology, of style over life. More immediately, in Godard's eyes L'ESPOIR represents an all-too rare instance of cinema performing its duty to record the real (the war was still in process whilst Malraux was shooting the film) by marrying document (one could almost speak of *actualités*) and fiction (the heightening of the action to the power of historical narrative, the necessary transcendence of the actual) into a unique form of contemporary testimony. Lastly, the work itself is an exemplary *film maudit* ('already forgotten, still banned, always invisible'), and so Langlois's retrieval of L'ESPOIR, projecting it into his own contemporary darkness, demonstratively 'confirms' the redemptive theory of the image, as does (in Godard's own dark times) the constant citation and remotivation of a few precious frames retrieved from Malraux's film. To speak the language of resurrection, however, within the general culture of French historiography inevitably evokes our second name, that of Jules Michelet, historian of France and (to revise Mallarmé's description of Hugo) the man who was personally history.[11] Inescapable model and precursor for the historian as artist, Michelet's self-portrait in the preface to the 1869 edition of *Histoire de France* provides the mission-statement for a certain way of doing history ('la résurrection de la vie intégrale') and a method or spirit that profoundly informs HISTOIRE(S) DU CINÉMA. Here are the essential features of that method (the reader may wish mentally to transpose certain key terms, such as 'cinema' for 'France'):

1   *Inspiration and perspiration.* 'This laborious work of almost forty years was conceived in a moment, in the lightning-flash of the July Revolution. During those memorable days, a great light came into being, and I saw France.'[12] It is an epiphany that reveals to the historian the massive responsibility and scale of the task ahead. Like a memorial stone for the future, the visionary moment is itself historicised, as is the life-long commitment and subjective *durée* that the project's completion will require. This fictionalisation of the sublimely impossible nature of the task (be it 'the History of France' or 'all the histories of cinema') thereby renders it paradoxically achievable. The rhetorical strategem of preterition (what I am about to tell you is unrelatable, but here goes anyway) is deployed throughout HISTOIRE(S) DU CINÉMA in a number of forms, some-

times by reference to others ('I examine carefully my plan; it is unrealisable', Bertold Brecht; 'to make a precise description of that which has never happened is the work of the historian', Oscar Wilde); sometimes by declaration of intent (the promise even to tell the stories of those films that were never made, the reconstruction of montage as cinema's lost art or missed opportunity, the necessary invisibility of true cinema, etc.), and sometimes by the figuration of Welles, or von Stroheim, or Vigo, whose very images (their work, their bodies) incorporate that trace of the sublime.

2   *Annals and history.* 'France had its annals, but in no way did she have a history [...] I was the first to see her as a soul and a person.'[13] The polarisation of genuine 'history' and plain old 'annals' (which we now often see reconfigured, somewhat ironically, as an opposition between 'memory' and 'history') is fundamental to post-Enlightenment historiography. Henceforth, France will be a star whose bloody and erotic legend can move us to love and murder. Lucidly, Michelet gives the lie to objectivity, however, by revealing that it is fiction that allows the *telos* into the recording process, it is fiction that shapes the raw materials and documents into the vast and moving image of 'France' (or the one true story of 'cinema'). For the artist-historian, France is a fictional character who inhabits Michelet as much as he inhabits it; or, as Godard would say, 'many people have loved the cinema, but few have been loved by it'.[14]

3   *Visible and invisible.* 'Until 1830 none of the remarkable historians of the period had yet felt the need to look for facts outside printed books, to look into primitive sources, mostly unpublished at the time, the manuscripts in our libraries, the documents in our archives.'[15] This aspect of the programme may at first surprise, since it counters the perhaps understandable impression that Michelet's (and Godard's) historiography is primarily or uniquely a matter of process, of phrase making and image making, to the grave detriment of hands-on archival digging. However lucid they are about the necessary fabrication of the past (which must endlessly be reinvented precisely to be redeemed), neither would deny the value of the document, the authenticity of the freshest trace. In Godard's case, it should never be forgotten that the first minister of montage is also a Bazinian fundamentalist. This has always been so, and for every constructivist slogan like 'it's not a just image, it's just an image' there is equally a credo such as 'photography is the truth and cinema is the truth twenty-four times per second'. Were more recent proof required, one need only reflect on the very idea of a sexagenarian filmmaker with fifty years of experience who still repeatedly compares cinema's efficacy to the Bazinian miracle of Veronica's 'true image', a cloth

that recorded Christ's face exactly and eternally, just as if it were simply an early type of film stock![16] Nor should one deride the mystical streak common to Michelet and Godard, since far from being exceptional or aberrant, the faith in 'primitive sources' is the very fundament of historical research, as is the sustaining belief that always there will come to light some undiscovered treasure and untold fortunes.

4   *Aesthetic and material.* 'So it's all or nothing. To rediscover historical life, one must patiently follow it in all its paths, all its forms, all its elements. But one must also, with an even greater passion, remake and re-establish the play [*jeu*] of all that, the reciprocal action of those diverse forces in a powerful movement that would once again become life itself.'[17] The link between Michelet and Godard is here furnished by Élie Faure, for whom 'the play of historical forces and movements' could stand as a working definition of his epistemological object. In Faure's *L'esprit des formes*, the figure of game or play is recast as the 'grand rhythm' of cultural time that Faure's historical prose will strive to capture and imitate. But the most important feature shared by Michelet, Faure, and Godard is the openness and unpredictability of the great historical play, whose 'unity is not that of a little five-act drama, but the powerful *work of self on self*, where France, by her progress, gradually transforms all its brute elements, and from pre-existing materials, creates for us absolutely new things.'[18] It is that receptiveness to the new and the unspoken that epitomises Michelet's legacy to twentieth-century historians, just as Godard's working example recommends to us the virtues of impurity, inclusiveness, and improvisation. As for cinema's five-act mystery play, it is two parts determinism (economic and technological), two parts human agency (individual and collective), and one part totally unknown and probably unknowable (art as factor 'X').

5   *Personal and impersonal.* 'My life was in this book, it has passed into it. It has been my only event [...] Because history, in the progress of time, makes the historian much more than it is made by him. My book has created me. It is I that was its work.'[19] Here is the moment, perfected in French culture by Proust and Montaigne, when the self-portrait at last emerges from 'the play of all that'. It's the point of self-recognition where the patient collector, collator, and creator finally 'passes into it', to the other side of the book, film or museum; and where even as he utters the phrase 'I was that man' it no longer has any currency, precisely because 'that man' has already become the reflection of his own self-portrait.[20]

These five methodical points could be added to the eight-point plan drawn up in relation to the 'Rembrandt/cinema' passage above. Even allowing for some repetition, we would still have a good ten or twelve general features from which to build a fairly solid model of how the late Godard might think and operate historically. That model, we have also seen, works in dialogue with certain voices from the past, but whereas in earlier years Godard's practise of reference and citation would seem to be most readily integrated into a system of disruption, correction and irony, now it appears quite clearly that those 'hard' or corrosive qualities, still tangible though they may be, function in counterpoint to a more responsive, reflective, and, one might say, communicative exchange. The temptation to interpret this 'soft and hard' modulation in personal or biographical terms may with equal legitimacy be developed or resisted. Certainly the piece of that name (sub-titled 'a soft talk between two friends on a hard subject') does display some of those communicative features, particularly in the closing sequences, which combine film-extracts (REAR WINDOW, BROKEN BLOSSOMS, LE MÉPRIS) and filmed dialogues between Miéville and Godard regarding their early encounters with cinema, thus announcing some of the dominant means and motifs elaborated in HISTOIRE(S) DU CINÉMA from 1988 onwards. In addition to our rather schematic thirteen-point model, we would need to recognise and attend to Godard's conference with other key precursors, a broad exchange that I have sought to illustrate with the snippets of overheard conversation between 'Blanchot', Malraux, Faure, Rembrandt, Langlois, Péguy, and Michelet... All of whom seem to be speaking the same mnemonic language, a common idiolect of cultural memory that itself would require a long and devoted study. But for now, I should like to focus more closely on two of these privileged precursors, Élie Faure and André Malraux, whose modular relationship with HISTOIRE(S) DU CINÉMA would appear especially close and communicative. Although the names of Faure and Malraux are frequently mentioned both in Godard's public discourse and in critical discussion of HISTOIRE(S) DU CINÉMA, it is noticeable that rarely is there any detailed analysis of their extremely voluminous works, and one could hazard a guess that few of the discussants have recently reread these materials first hand. In order to give a fresher sense of the cultural baggage that Malraux and Faure bring with them, let us now reconsider some basic information and examine some sample passages.

The writer Élie Faure (1873-1937) is best known for his *Histoire de l'art* (1909-1921), a multi-volume history of art guiding its broad public from ancient times to the modern world, and still available in paperback today, although it should be said that despite generations of readers, Faure is virtually non-existent as far as professional art historians are concerned. Is it in part this double aspect, popular and forgotten, that recommends Faure, like cinema, to the late Godard? An element of identification cannot be denied, but one should recall that Faure and Godard go back a long way, at least as far as the scene of Belmondo in PIERROT LE FOU lying in the bathtub reading Faure's sketch of Titian. Indeed, one wonders if research would not show that virtually all of Godard's taste in painting and his use of reproductions, from À BOUT DE SOUFFLE onwards, might not be traced back to Faure (and if not to Faure then to Malraux). This personal fidelity to certain writers and artists often goes unremarked (no doubt because it contradicts the myth of mercuriality), as does Godard's tendency to skip the more recent cultural generations in favour of intellectual figures such as Faure (and Charles Péguy, Denis de Rougemont, Jean Giraudoux, etc.) who are men of the nineteenth as much as the twentieth or even twenty-first centuries. Although *Histoire de l'art* is probably the one text that almost any Francophone art student or art lover will have read, it is important to remember that in 1927 Faure added to the basic narrative of *Histoire de l'art* a further double volume of a more philosophical or theoretical nature, known as *L'esprit des formes*. The relationship between these two works, their timing, scope, and intent, informs our discussion of HISTOIRE(S) DU CINÉMA, insofar as *L'esprit des formes* could best be described as a poetic and certainly non-linear re-edit of the flowing, chronological narrative that we witness unfold in *Histoire de l'art*. The latter, in other words, is a long, slow, wide-ranging panorama of the story of art, the development of cultures through historical time, whereas *L'esprit des formes* could be described as a kaleidoscopic complement to the panoramic view, absorbing all that linear real time as its raw materials (to put it crudely, its rushes) and profoundly reworking it, through comparison and compression, into the looser, spacier, more fluid, reversible and highly relativised timeframe that obtains in the editing suite (where past, present, and future are momentarily and materially in your hands).[21] It is the alternating rhythm emerging from these contrasting temporalities that will make itself felt so strongly in HISTOIRE(S) DU CINÉMA. A second significant point about Faure's intellectual legacy (which includes many other books on art, literature, philosophy, and politics) is that here was probably the first art historian to whole-heartedly embrace the coming of cinema. This recognition did not just mean that he deigned to take cinema seriously as an art form and allowed it a perfunctory role in his story of art. In Faure's grand scheme of things, cinema was born with a genuine mission, a cultural destiny to fulfil. In his many writings on the subject, posthumously collected as *Fonction du cinéma*, Faure consistently argued that cinema had arrived in Western culture in order to announce the new century and, beyond that, a new chapter in world history. In the short term, cinema would replace modern European painting and sculpture, which had reached, with Cézanne, a necessary conclusion or 'disintegration' as a form of individual and analytical expression. But it would then inaugurate, presumably on a global scale, an unknown and unpredictable era of popular art and mass communication that would massively express collective beliefs and ideals, echoing dance and theatre in ancient Greece or architecture in the Middle Ages. To express such a vision, one needs big eyes and big lungs. Certainly Faure had all the appropriate organs, as this passage from the opening of 'Introduction à la mystique du cinéma' (1934) should demonstrate:

> I can no longer believe henceforth that painting, the most individualist of all the arts, remains capable, at least in Europe, of presenting the image of a society that is evolving, with increasing certainty, towards anonymous and collective modes of production. And since expression has always been, and can only be, the daughter of production, we will sure enough have to decide which side we're on [...] We could easily console ourselves regarding the ruin of painting, if we managed to convince ourselves that the coming mystique has an expressive double, the cinema, whose beginnings precisely marked the appearance of the first common organs manifesting that mystique.[22]

As does this extract from the conclusion, this time, of 'De la cinéplastique' (1922):

> We are trying to escape, in all the countries of the world, from a form of civilisation that has become, by excess of individualism, impulsive and anarchic, in order to enter a form of material civilisation destined to replace analytical studies of states and crises of the soul with synthetic poems of the masses and groups in action. I imagine that architecture will be its principal expression [...] and *cinéplastique*, no doubt, will be its most commonly sought ornament, the social game [*jeu*] most useful to the development, amongst the crowds, of the need for confidence, harmony, cohesion.[23]

Alas, in order to convey a true sense of Faure's style, one would need to multiply such examples *ad infinitum* (indeed, one could just repeat the entire œuvre), since its essence lies in the very inexhaustibility of the lyrical lungs that carry the grandiose vision. At the other extreme, one could summarise Faure's philosophy in a few key phrases and big ideas, even in the titles of his major essays: 'The agony of painting', 'The universal language', 'The vocation of cinema', 'Defence and illustration of the machine', 'Introduction to the mystique of cinema'. We hear the same themes and motifs endlessly reprised and tirelessly reinforced, to the point that his fondness for the image of the public procession or *défilé* becomes emblematic of his thinking as a whole, as if one were attending the triumphal march of a horde of ideas and phrases who had just taken over the world. Seventy years later, rereading such slogans as 'the art of grand epochs is totalitarian', one may instinctively respond with democratic gratitude for minor times, but the passing

decades and changing contexts have not yet fatally diminished the intellectual force and syntactical power of Faure's cinematic world view, nor
should they obscure from our discussion the two key insights that feed most
directly into HISTOIRE(S) DU CINÉMA: the understanding of cinema's social
and aesthetic vocation and the sense of its essential continuity with the
grand flow of cultural history. This feeling of continuity is certainly shared
by Faure's direct successor, André Malraux (1901-1976). Of the two figures,
Malraux is by far the better known, and to some degree one could argue that
Malraux's great fame as a novelist and statesman (he was France's first ever
Minister of Culture and seems to have had a quasi-spiritual relationship
with General de Gaulle) has obscured the debt he owes to Élie Faure as an
art historian and cultural theorist. Indeed, if one reads Malraux's *Les voix du
silence* immediately after Faure's *Histoire de l'art* and *L'esprit des formes*, it is
like switching from one source to another of the same vast, overwhelming
energy. The four-volume *Voix du silence* is probably closer to *L'esprit des
formes* than to *Histoire de l'art* insofar as it subjugates linear historical narrative to a kaleidoscopic, perhaps even ahistorical view of cultural time and
human destiny. Where Faure's sense of basic cultural rhythm derives from
an alternation between the individual and the collective, between knowledge and faith, between periods of analysis and periods of synthesis,
Malraux's deep temporal structures are even more abstract (death and renaissance, destruction and redemption), with art always working as the primary agent of metamorphosis, the triumph of creative will over mortal
destiny. Art is born out of the ashes, *l'art est ce qui naît de ce qui a été brûlé*, a
formula that Malraux would even apply to the Nazi concentration camps,
which represented the very emblem of historical ineffability to his (and
Godard's) generation, and therefore the greatest contemporary challenge to
'the power of metamorphosis possessed by art':

> When men die, nothing remains of what was hideous in them, there only remains
> what greatness they had, as long as the transmission is made by art... And if, tomor-
> row, there were only to remain artistic testimonies of the gas-chambers, nothing
> would remain of the executioners, but the martyrs would remain.[24]

It is of course one of the central theses of HISTOIRE(S) DU CINÉMA that cinema
largely failed in its duty to represent these exemplary victims, to record their
terror and project their forms into the present. So here is an instance where
one could speak straightforwardly of influence, where Godard seems to
have taken the idea of art-as-redemption and adapted it to cinema's critical
moment of historic destiny in the middle of its century. Indeed, we could extend this argument by saying that Malraux's direct presence in HISTOIRE(S)
DU CINÉMA is materially much more substantial than Faure's. The latter is

materialised, as it were, through the voice of Cuny and the collage of cinema and Rembrandt, but otherwise his impact is felt at the deeper modular level. By contrast the very image of Malraux (cigaretted gaze into the camera) is repeatedly shown throughout HISTOIRE(S) DU CINÉMA, as are the afore-mentioned sequences from L'ESPOIR. In Chapter 4B, LES SIGNES PARMI NOUS, we even hear Malraux's voice, a recording of the famous *oraison funèbre* for Jean Moulin's entry into the Pantheon (and the Resistance's formal entrance into national mythology):

> Enter here, Jean Moulin, with your terrible procession, with those who died in the cellars without talking, like you, and even, which might be worse, having talked.[25]

Furthermore, there is evidence to suggest that at one stage Godard had planned to devote a whole sequence of HISTOIRE(S) DU CINÉMA to the filmed recitation of adapted extracts from *Esquisse d'une psychologie du cinéma*, the one text (albeit merely a series of notes) that Malraux directly addressed to the question of cinema. For example:

> From its infantile beginnings to the last silent films, the cinema seemed to have conquered immense domains. What has it gained since? It has perfected its lighting and its narrative, its technique, but artistically speaking? Here I call art the expression of unknown and immediately convincing connections between beings, or between beings and things.[26]

Perhaps it is precisely the direct address to cinema that discouraged Godard from using *Esquisse* so extensively. When he does quote verbatim from the text in Chapter 1A, TOUTES LES HISTOIRES, Malraux's words have already been transmuted into something much more enigmatic, indeed it may be the very question of the cinema-as-oracle that is posed:

> The masses love myth and cinema addresses the masses. But if myth begins with Fantômas it ends with Christ. What did the crowds hear when they listened to Saint Bernard preach? Something other than what he said? Perhaps, no doubt. But how can we ignore what we understand when that unknown voice plunges deep into our hearts?[27]

Even though he is at first glance textually and materially more visible than Faure, the real presence of Malraux in HISTOIRE(S) DU CINÉMA is, in fact, like Faure's, at the modular level. The only model that *Esquisse* might offer is the very notion of the 'sketch', the sense of Godard's histories as an open-ended series of essays rather than a definitive last will and testament. Otherwise, the actual details of Malraux's explicit theory of cinema are only relatively interesting and relatively banal: the purity of cinema before sound, the identification of montage and writing, the mythological aspects of stardom, the new dynamic of art and commerce... But what really counts, as with Faure, is the broad sweep and flux of the thinking, the philosophical dimension of cultural history, the preference for big ideas over linear exposition and material facts, and above all an uncompromisingly poetic approach to the actual fabrication of that history, its design, its composition, its rhythms. It is for these reasons that the clearest precursor for HISTOIRE(s) DU CINÉMA is not to be found in Malraux's sketches of cinema but in *Les voix du silence*, and most particularly in its founding volume, *Le musée imaginaire*. We need only sample the opening pages of this text in order to grasp the conceptual and material connections between Malraux's and Godard's projects. The first thing we notice, so obvious but so crucial, is that pictures are accorded equal status with words. Before the opening phrase, we are confronted by two images. One is a photograph of three paintings in a museum taken at such an angle that they appear to be exchanging glances, whilst the other is a portrait showing 'the archduke Léopold-Guillaume in his picture-gallery' by David Teniers. Together, they form a double 'image' of Malraux's task. The critical compiler and collector appears almost overwhelmed by this immensity of reflective and reflecting forms, this infinity of images and stories. And a phrase from Malraux's prose would provide the perfect caption for this diptych: 'there is a confrontation of metamorphoses' (*il est une confrontation de métamorphoses*). The reproduction of Teniers precisely recalls a famous photograph of Malraux himself standing in an empty artist's studio surrounded by hundreds of art reproductions that are scattered all over the floor. Today, this two-page collage of word and image by Malraux could stand on its own as another prescient critical essay on HISTOIRE(s) DU CINÉMA in general, and specifically on Godard's self-portraiture as the artist-historian overwhelmed by the excessive materiality of the task before and around him, but hanging on to his 'unrealisable plan' nonetheless. Such an effective and suggestive deployment of visual as well as prosaic materials is a key feature of Malraux's method. In fact, following on from Faure's example in *Histoire de l'art* and *L'esprit des formes*, Malraux made increasingly imaginative use of photographic reproductions, partly to illustrate his theory of the imaginary museum, but also to sketch out a potentially new form of art thinking, a visual as well as literary practice that would to some extent cede the initiative to forms, allowing the art works to perform their own self-criticism, to do their own critical work. Shown from as wide a range of angles and contexts as possible, in contrast and succession, in close-up and long-shot, in social function or on public display, the forms can thus do the thinking for themselves, and in so doing they instigate and sustain a vital counter-current to the prosaic flow of words and times and names and themes and images. Whatever the poetic qualities of the prose itself,

Malraux's example equally indicates a path of thinking, through and about the image, which his successors in art history have largely left undeveloped, despite the advent of television, video, and subsequent innovations in visual culture. Without the actual software or machinery, the concept of the imaginary museum, invented by Malraux at least as early as 1947, appears to pre-empt so much of our current discourse on virtualities and digitalities. His key insight is that, thanks first to the museum and now (in the 1940s) to contemporary forms of reproduction and distribution, we are able to inhabit an infinite cultural universe in which all arts of all epochs and all cultures are materially made available to us. Every cultural artefact becomes an *objet d'art*, an object of historical knowledge and aesthetic contemplation, whose function is a concept and whose meaning is a sign:

> Our relationship to art, for more than a century, has become increasingly intellectualised. The museum imposes a questioning of each of the expressions of the world that it brings together, an interrogation of what it is that brings them together. In addition to 'the pleasure of the eye', the succession and apparent contradiction of schools of art has made us conscious of a passionate quest, a recreation of the universe in the face of Creation. After all, the museum is one of the places that give us our loftiest idea of man. But our knowledge is now more extensive than our museums [...] Now that the art work has no function other than being an art work, now that the artistic exploration of the world continues apace, the collection of so many masterpieces, from which so many masterpieces are absent, convokes in the spirit *all* the masterpieces. How can this mutilated potential fail to invoke the entire potential?[28]

This is not, however, a discourse of decadence and loss. For someone seemingly so obsessed with death, Malraux has no melancholy, he focuses on death because it is the enemy to be defeated by art: 'The entire history of art, when it is that of genius, should be a story of deliverance: for history tries to transform destiny into consciousness, and art tries to transform destiny into freedom.'[29] Such a passage should serve to remind us that, despite his considerable foresight in some regards, Malraux's unwavering faith in his vision and his prose can also appear quite stunningly anachronistic. One hundred and seventy years ago, struck by lightning in July 1830, Jules Michelet might well have thought that the sheer power of his syntax could dictate the historical rhythms of the world. But in liberated Europe in 1945? With no more poetry at Auschwitz? With nothing seen at Hiroshima? In Malraux we must recognise that, as with Faure, these are basically still the prose-rhythms of the nineteenth century, as if all the world needed were a ceaselessly Hugolian harmony of light and shade, reason and romance, both all-embracing and all-conquering in its universal generosity.

Looking backward and seeing forward. It's a double-take that seems nicely to catch late Godard, as we suggested with our opening misquotation of Blanchot's text on *Le musée imaginaire*. It is clear that no-one has ever even tried to invent the historical art that Godard is undertaking in HISTOIRE(S) DU CINÉMA. But could such an innovation happen without this essentially anachronistic notion of the redemptive power of art and the efficacy of rememoration? Or without this paradoxical confidence in the grand rhythm, to use Faure's term, of historical play and recreation?

> The more I advance, the more I observe, the more I watch myself living, the less I conceive it possible to consider the history of peoples and the history of the spirit other than as a series of alternations, sometimes rapid and sometimes precipitate, between disintegrations through knowledge and integrations through love. It's the rhythm that Laplace, Lamarck, Spencer discovered in the evolution of the universal drama itself [...] it's the rhythm of the drama of chemistry in which synthesis and analysis alternately engender each other. It's the rhythm of the drama of physiology [...] It's the rhythm of the drama of biology [...] What we know of History is still and probably will always be very little. Perhaps, no doubt, History is only just beginning. But one must resign oneself to learning nothing of it unless one decides to seek in its unfolding an action, confused for sure, whose aspect one may only catch when one looks at it from afar and when, instead of considering it according to its so-called progresses, its so-called reverses, its so-called intentions or our so-called interests, one seeks resolutely that rhythm whereby the spirit, whether determined by its events or reacting to organise them, plays merely the role of regulator, but the unique regulator.[30]

At the risk of repeating ourselves, this sounds like a question of rhythm. Clearly, basically, fundamentally. And as in poetry, rhythm does not mean a metric template to which all sounds and senses must comply. It necessarily means an open and dynamic relation between different orders and perceptions of time. Some of those orders are relatively determined, such as fixed beats, set patterns and established forms, whilst others are relatively open, such as rhetorical strategies, syntactical shapes and semantic play; but the areas of indeterminacy are vast and mobile, expanding and contracting according to the attention of the listener, in direct proportion, perhaps, to the receptive commitment of its audience. What is true of poetry is certainly true of history. In Fernand Braudel's words, which are flashed on to the screen in Chapter 4A, LE CONTRÔLE DE L'UNIVERS: 'One history advances towards us with precipitate steps/another history accompanies us with slow ones.'[31] Or indeed as the poet Charles Péguy declares in *Clio, dialogue de l'histoire et de l'âme païenne*:

> It is undeniable that not all time passes at the same speed or according to the same rhythm. Not only individual time, not only personal time [...] But public time itself,

the time of an entire people, the time of the world. One is led to ask oneself if public time itself does not merely cover over, does not merely underlie, a specific duration, a duration of a people, a duration of a world.[32]

History's object would properly be this multiplicity of differential time-frames. Some slow and some fast, both long-wave and short-term. Experienced through an infinity of personal and collective *durées*, intersubjective perceptions of time that can slow the material down to a frozen image or speed it up to an imperceptible blur. Just as effectively as the editor holds the reel of images between his fingers and runs the frames of past-present-future back and forth. To develop an intelligence of that material complexity is the historian's true task. For the film historian, this means remaining receptive to all the diverse times of cinema and, more importantly, accepting the responsibility to recompose them. So Clio, the Muse of History, is not just 'the young girl who does the recording', as Péguy and Godard would disingenuously have her claim.[33] Certainly she plays the role of cinema's receptionist, secretary, treasurer, the faithful stenographer and videast of all its business, exploits, and affairs. But equally she aspires, desires to become a composer of big rhythms. This is why she reads Élie Faure on the sly, and carries *Le musée imaginaire* in her handbag. From Faure she derives anaphora, the figure of repetition and return. If ever there existed such a motif as the 'fauresque', it would be an historiographical gesture that endlessly retraces one serpentine, curvaceous line, always returning on itself but never exactly the same. The strength Clio draws from the fauresque can be seen in her clear grasp of temporal depth. Faure gives her the art historical version of all that patience and curiosity with which Bazin invested the techno-aesthetic concept of *profondeur de champ*. An historical plan or plane that is open to the unseen and the improvised. That can wait for the past duly to reveal its secrets, its surprises, if and when they come (talkies, colour, TV, digital...). That certainly has no fear of the future. You speak to her of the death of cinema? The disintegration, through analysis or exhaution, of her precious seventh art? Bring on the next phase of synthesis, the new wave of integration-through-love! Bring on the eighth, ninth, and tenth episodes of that famous serial 'The Mummy-Complex'! At the same time, looking to Malraux, Clio recognises and enjoys 'the power of metamorphosis possessed by art', the inexhaustible potential of change and human invention. For history also simply means the changing of forms, the metaphor or carrying over of the familiar into the strange, the regular and repeated twisting of the known sound or image into some new or monstrous shape, a soon-to-be beautiful trope. Change and return: it is this dual energy-source of *big rhythm and the power of metamorphosis* that enables Clio fully to deploy her historical forms and forces. Fidelity, patience, curiosity, such virtues come with the job. We

know she can believe her eyes when faced with the primitive source, the authenticity of the trace. Daily she rehearses the terms of her engagement: this
is a mark that resembles an event; this is an image that looks like someone's
world; this is a word that sounds like someone's life. Yet out of such recordings a history is fabricated and a story may unfold before the eyes of the
world. Identically, the cinema records, processes, and projects: the recording
of the real, the image in process, the projection into the dark. In the manner
of Jean-Luc Godard, lucid amid the mysteries of his art, Clio thus listens to
the counsel of Charles Péguy:

> You proceed by way of short-cut, allusion, reference, capture, grasp, play, nourish-
> ment, illumination, interference. Correspondence, resonance, analogy, parallelism.
> Re-excavation. Intelligence, understanding.[34]

So finally, what is a poet playing at, telling historians how to work? It's a
thankless task, but someone has to do it. Amongst their many gifts, poets
have a prescience. In that sense Godard can be a precursor, a model for future projects in the history of film and television. After all, if Péguy in 1913
can address an unborn artist and send him instructions for an art that is yet
to exist, then surely one can wait a while, re-excavate, and pray for an intelligence to rise from the dark unknown?

6 Mortal Beauty

Jacques Aumont

Something striking about HISTOIRE(S) DU CINÉMA – irritating or fascinating, depending on the moment and one's mood – is the playing with titles. Not the titles of the films, novels or paintings cited, but the fully systematic set of titles invented by Godard for his own use. At first, it must have been very simple: they were the necessary subtitles of the subdivisions of a work whose title was already complex. Like the chapter headings of a book, they ensured the work's frame, its plan, the sorting of its rich matter for reflection into fields or aspects, even, fantasmatically, into disciplines. As the project developed, from the second pair of episodes onwards, they began to circulate, to keep coming back, like some kind of litany, as if the film-maker sought to inscribe the list in the memory (his own, ours), or wanted to study this list in order to ask questions of it. Montage, that wonderful and terrible instrument, developed and perfected by Godard into an all-purpose instrument, comes into its own. When each title recurs, each time different and in a different site, each time it has a different significance, reconstructing the whole system. At the same time, like any of the elements of montage that constitute Godard's cinema, each has to begin by existing by itself and for itself. And the reprise of those elements, their constant return, poses each title each time as an enigma. One of the beauties of Godard's cinema has always been the capacity to say that what we look at, what it looks at with us and for us, is an enigma. Godard comes long after the classical film-makers who could look directly without having to tell us that they were looking and who could communicate directly the present of this opacity. Unlike them, Godard needs mediation, he has to say that the look exists, through Mireille Darc's ecstatic commentary on the worm in WEEKEND ('we are both "enigmas" you and I'), or through the ironic close-up on the coffee cup in DEUX OU TROIS CHOSES QUE JE SAIS D'ELLE. And yet, even to this second degree, it is still a cinema of contemplation which knows that by watching a sunset, a stream or, more simply still, a pebble, we can see the enigma of the world.

And this is how I see Godard looking at his subtitles (sometimes he really seems to be looking at them when he superimposes them on an absolutely inexpressive shot of his own face): 'What can these odd objects signify, this strange collection of verbal objects I have amassed?' Faced with these objects which were not discovered ready-made, the master of collage adopts the attitude of a painter in front of newspapers cut up for his canvas, and who suddenly realises that these words have a meaning – but what meaning? Sometimes, no doubt, we could project on to this Kuleshov-type face the expression of a memory: 'Ah yes, I remember having read that somewhere, in André Malraux's *La monnaie de l'absolu*, or perhaps in Sarah Kofman's *L'enfance de l'art*.' But always, whether as memory or surprise, these objects are placed there, like those worn-out litanies where the meaning must first disappear before acquiring, after a long labour of emptiness, another consistence. Chapters 2A and 2B foreground two of these titles (which at some point, no doubt, will have to be read together): SEUL LE CINÉMA and FATALE BEAUTÉ. I don't know if these are part of the original plan of the series, or whether they express an inflection of it, nor do I know what state of the author's mind is thus revealed; all I see is the enigma of this pairing: the solitude of cinema, the fatality of beauty. Cinema is alone, 'all alone', a solitary and melancholic figure, out of which Godard makes a character in a film; cinema is a fictional character, one that says, with Paul Verlaine and the hero of BANDE À PART: 'here it is lonely and frozen'. And beauty is fatal. Fatal? This is not so clear. Does it mean a particular beauty, or Beauty itself, and what destiny can we imagine of which beauty would be the operator?

Cinema is melancholic because it is nearing its end, or is perhaps already dead (we have heard this one before). In Godard there is the hope that to tell the history of cinema is to find in the pious memory of great figures some consolation for their loss – and beyond that, consolation for the loss of the past, of Time, of the self. None of this is new, and we can all no doubt imagine seeing something – if it is only what Jacques Lacan calls 'one's own stupid and ineffable existence' – from the perspective of the end, or as finished. What is striking in Godard's proposition is the association with a fatality, a destiny. A fatality, moreover that implicates or concerns the Beautiful, beauty. What is the knot that binds together these elements: beauty, the end or endings, and destiny? This is precisely the object of Chapter 2B of HISTOIRE(S) DU CINÉMA, unequivocally titled FATALE BEAUTÉ. In the beginning, beauty, at the end, happiness – a profound value, of which glory is only the 'brilliant mourning', the flashy surface. Beauty is the faces of women or, as in the poet Malherbe (distant source of the 'my beautiful care' formula): 'what we find on the faces of beautiful women, what we see there and cannot define'.[1] As for happiness, that is a painting by Pierre Bonnard (*Table servie et jardin*, 1934) brilliant with the very colour which photography and cinema had suppressed and which deathly Technicolor had failed to retrieve. The faces of women and the colour of paintings are both apparitions, enchanting and pleasing surfaces that please. Beauty, happiness (or pleasure) are made materially visible through these pleasing images and, in the process, eroticised, hyper-eroticised. As Jean-Marie Pontévia says: 'Eros is Nature's most beautiful feature. What does "the most beautiful" mean? The Orphic name of Eros may tells us: Eros is Phanes, the brilliant one.'[2] It all connects. As Robert Graves put it: 'in the Orphic myth the love god Phanes is a loudly buzzing celestial bee, son of the Great Goddess. As Phaëthon Protogenus, Phanes is the Sun, which the Orphics made a symbol of illumination.'[3] The poet Godard, great-grandson of Orpheus, builds his fable of beauty on an equivalence with light, but he knows that beauty illuminates only on condition that it is brought back to its sole true source, i.e. lyric intuition.

In this Chapter's neo-Platonic meditations, with Hermann Broch's *The Death of Virgil* as its epicentre, the beautiful is thus 'explained' by light. But in what sense is this an explanation? What is light, and in what way could it be not just the symbol but the actual presence of the good and the beautiful? Several times in HISTOIRE(S) DU CINÉMA the following (rearranged) passage from *The Death of Virgil* is recited by the voice of François Périer (taken from the soundtrack of SOIGNE TA DROITE): 'As if everything were once again simply a waiting for the morning star, as if nothing else were legitimate... And at first, very softly, as if trying not to frighten him, the whispering that Man had already discerned long ago – so long ago, long before Man existed! – the whispering begins again.' Whispering: the loudly-buzzing Orphic bee, possibly, but also, and more immediately, the impersonal being, the impersonal existent of French phenomenology: Merleau-Ponty's *one*, Levinas's *there is*, Blanchot's neuter or outside or *interminable murmur*. In the meditation of Virgil dying, light can be identified with this *there is*, this murmur of being; the whispering he hears, worrying and reassuring at the same time, comes with the promise of light as salvation. Simple *Dasein*, a simple human being like any other, the poet is thrown into existence, *geworfen* (as Husserl and Heidegger would say), and his sole salvation is the light of the sun.[4]

The metaphor becomes limpidly clear, and it is not surprising that Godard has warmed to these vibrant pages. What are the thoughts, during his last meditation on earth, of the most famous artist of his time, cherished by patrons and emperors, misread by the public, and so deeply discontented with himself and his work? He thinks of existence as anonymity and as murmur; he thinks of the vanity of fame and of the survival of his work (which he means to destroy); he thinks of the good warm light that despite everything will come as a salvation, a salvation of body and soul; he resolves to believe – to believe in his art, in Art. We can understand why this text has haunted the work of the most famous and most misunderstood film-maker of his time. All the more so because Godard, a film-maker and not a literary artist, can grasp the idea of light in all its dimensions, in its fullness and physical reality. Like Virgil who sang the great historic myths, the poet-historian of cinema trusts in the grain of light, in the interminable whispering of light rising from the shadows; but it is not only the light of dawn that he awaits, the divine and impersonal light that symbolises salvation: he also knows concretely that cinema is a light that ceaselessly traverses shade. Cinema is a salvation-machine, and thereby a salvatory machination: the first and last metaphor of this virtue is what Josef von Sternberg called 'an adventure of light', invoking Goethe's 'mehr Licht'.

Beauty is fatal: this is what Godard sees when he lifts his gaze towards the title of Chapter 2B of HISTOIRE(S) DU CINÉMA. Fatal – *fatum*, destiny – because beauty cannot help invoking light or the idea of light, but it lacks the power of light to reach the supreme sphere, that of the Good and the True. This is pure Plato: corporeal beauty refers us to the essences, to the suprasensible, but is unable to go further than its minor, secondary, delegated and very dangerous power, the power to represent them. The idea is a painful one: if Beauty is only corporeal beauty, then it is only surface and is therefore perishable. This is, in the first place, the common experience that every young man learns for himself, and that cinema has rendered more directly than literature. To desire a girl is to use oneself up looking at her, in the constantly disappointed hope that this gaze will assuage a little of the suffering essential to desire: never to know the desired one from the inside and as one knows oneself; never to be able to enter into it. All these male gazes – the staple of amorous experience and also the beginning of its symbolic or even mythic formalisation – have just one meaning: they designate the beautiful corporeal form as the brilliant but invariably disappointing and painful substitute for that which desire really addresses, i.e. the quite other brilliance of being.

This is already violent, even if we have had to learn to domesticate in desire this brilliance of beauty. But beauty is all the more fatal because (as Godard says) 'we always show it in its youthful forms, while wishing it to be eternal, though it cannot be so'.[5] It is, in the end, a feminine version of the Faust myth, or at least it has a feminine accent. 'Fatal' beauty is the beauty that makes us forget the necessity of death, and that is why the apparently casual gesture of montage that Godard allows himself, seeming once more to give in to his passion for puns, is on the contrary directly thetic and theoretical. 'Always the fatal instant will arrive to distract us': citing this line by Raymond Queneau, the episode suggests a broad range of significations: to distract us from the thought of death no doubt, but also to dis-tract us (Queneau was a good Latinist), to tear us, to detach us (from life), to pull us (into nothingness). The fatal instant is as much the instant that language un-

derstands by these terms (the definitive passage to death) as it is other instants, such as the instant of birth, of *jouissance*, of the 'little death', or the
instant of the birth of love. We are still in the slightly banal nexus of love and
death that the montage of this whole sequence has constructed.

This is first said with pathos, with emotion. The whole sequence is accompanied by Paco Ibañez's song, *Palabras para Julia*, a song of farewell from
a dying man to a woman he has loved: stay alive, remember that when I
lived I thought of you. Meanwhile we see images of women dying or suffering (DUEL IN THE SUN, ROME, OPEN CITY, SOME CAME RUNNING, Gretchen in
the snow in FAUST); we see Beauty going towards the Beast and King Kong
gazing upon Fay Wray, coming up against another kind of suffering, that of
not being able to love the other who is too other; we see women riding men
(RANCHO NOTORIOUS), transforming them into beasts; we see deaths that are
negative miracles (John Cassavetes in THE FURY). Death and love, women
and suffering. Fatal beauty as fatal instant, because beauty distracts us from
our sense of time, including the obligations of memory. Fatality of the instant, the temporal destiny of man (of the being, the *Dasein*). Fatal beauty, always the fatal instant. The slippage from one fatality to the other is one of
these sudden shifts fabricated by montage. But, as often with Godard, it is
montage that, despite the arbitrary appearance, contains or invents the idea.

The text read by Godard while these images of death and love follow on
from each other, departing from the *eros-thanatos* cliché, speaks of the
trauma of birth. The mortal instant is placed in brutal relation with the instant of parturition, fixing a common term that is no longer fatality but the
instant; and in both cases, it is the instant as the supreme violence that time
inflicts on the living being by making it disappear or appear. Suddenly an
entire subtext comes to the fore: surely Godard, no stranger to existential-
ism, precisely by insisting on the fatality of the instant – of any instant, and
not only of traumatic instants – is echoing the fundamental intuition of
Heidegger, i.e. that the present is born not of the past, but of the future, as
the permanent irruption of 'ex-static' time? The destiny of man, says the
philosopher, the fate of this *Dasein* cast into the world and into time, is to be
subject to the fatal law of the instant, as pressure and violence, as imminence
and as threat (the precise range of meanings of the Latin *instans*). This is one
of the major themes of *Being and Time*, separating datable and significant
time, time measured by the clock, by 'once' and 'then', from time as permanent irruption. Time is 'tempered' by the future, as in the following image:
time is not a river we go down in a boat, it is a wind, a violent wind against
which we walk, like Jean Cocteau's Orphée in the Zone. The fatality of the
instant, its quality of destiny, is that it never ceases to arrive, to blow upon us
or to enter us – without knocking. Destiny knocks on the door only in works

of art (which is why they protect us). Time is what we would be protected from, but against which the *Dasein* has no armour (except art); the instant is the sharpened point with which Time pierces our defences, wounds us and makes us naked. The false depth of the present is simply a tiny shield, fragile and from the outset bound to give way, held up against the violence of time that arrives – that arrives, always, and never passes.

Cinema, as art, plays for and promises potential control of this destiny – the destiny of the being-for-death – insofar as cinema can be seen as that which has allowed this coming of the instant to acquire symbolic form. Cinema is the art of the fatal instant, not so much because of the false self-evidence that cinema is an art of duration, but because of its place in the system of the arts and of the ideologies of art, and because of the concepts to which it has given birth. The numerous categories of 'movement-image' and 'time-image' constructed by Deleuze have this meaning: cinema is the instrument that allows us to retrieve the conceptualisation of time – to reread Henri Bergson, i.e. to rewrite him, to envisage differently what *Being and Time* fixed for the immediately preceding generations. The history of art – 'our' history of art – starts from this premiss that God became incarnate, giving concrete foundation to the possibility of a legitimate *mimesis* ('we have no other culture', as Jean Louis Schefer puts it). Cinema-art as it is realised by Godard presupposes the completion of another *mimesis*, of another prospect of salvation, or perhaps eternal despair. It incarnates the essential pressure, the insistence or the instance of the future in the present. Recounting cinema (for Godard and Deleuze) or thinking cinema (for Deleuze and Godard) means addressing a form that in its stories and its very texture has manifested the passage and the coming of time.

I return to Godard's demonstration or meditation; or rather, I have never left it, even if, in following it, we quickly seem to have deviated. The instant is what comes, and at the same time what distracts; in a basic contradiction, it is both what makes time pass over us by manifesting our being-for-death, and that which distances us from the thought of death, from care. (There may be a hint of moral condemnation in the 'coming to distract us'; I am not concerned with this.) This is the fatality: being in time and being distracted. If the historian and the critic are defined by their struggle with fatality, Godard must be doubly determined to re-establish the rights of History over destiny, and the rights of meaning over the erosion of time and the frivolity of distraction. This is the sense of many of the episode's collages, beginning with the coincidence of the monologue on birth ('the voice of Jean Cocteau saying "the light's red: I entered illegally" – but when I was born, did I not enter illegally into the blood of my mother?') and this resonantly Hegelian or Bataillian inscription: 'Only the hand that effaces, that effaces, that effaces, can write.' To write history is to efface the past, throwing light on a future that is always to come; history gives birth to history, but in violence and murder; the future kills the past. 'Murnau and Freund invented the lighting of Nuremberg when Hitler didn't even have beer money in the Munich bars': cinema pre-empts this birth of history in history, it gives the sign or premature symptom thereof, presenting itself, perhaps derisorily, as a mastered form precisely where the event cannot be mastered. As for the historian, let him not forget the lesson of Charles Péguy's *Clio*: we can only make history on the basis of absence, after the lack of the lack of documents has come to an end (a technical formulation of the self-evidence that forgetting is the pre-condition of the coming of memory). Thus to efface is the gesture of the historian, his ethical gesture, the symbol of his responsibility. 'To have or have not' (hands, that are dirty).

'Fatal instant', because it manifests the pressure of being on the living being, the violence of time that is to-come, and also because it distracts us from the thought of death or from the possibility of memory (in a way it is the same thing).

'Fatal beauty', restating in a brilliant, eroticised form our pain at being separated from the world of Ideas (the ravishing of women, at the beginning of the episode, is the painful and despairing attempt, doomed to failure, to ravish Beauty herself).

Cinema is the form that in the twentieth century these two destinies, these two Fates, have found to express themselves. The painful destiny of Beauty: inaccessible, unthinkable, or thinkable only as transcendence – and that is cinema in its aspiration to the condition of art, always a frustrated aspiration. The terrible destiny of Time, the passage of time over me, this pressure of time coming towards me and destroying me little by little – that is cinema as the terrible machine of 'death at work' (Cocteau) or 'death making us its promises via the cinematograph' (Jean Epstein). The history of cinema starts from this thought of an impossible transcendence, a destructive time. But at the same time, cinema is the operator and the symbolisation – i.e. the possibility of perpetuation – of the struggle between these two fatalities: a struggle for the preservation of memory through the constant signification and citation of death at work; a struggle to restore beauty's true, deep and essential signification, to allow us to attain the light of thought. The great films are those that give us 'that saturation of magnificent signs bathed in the light of the absence of explanation' (Manoel de Oliveira). But the magnificence of this light, its greatness, is precisely that it is able to give its own explanation: 'things are the only occult meaning of things' (Fernando Pessoa).

Fatality of beauty. And to begin with, in the art of film, the fatality of the division between two opposing values of brilliance. Here is the Godardian lesson:

– the bad brilliance, the vulgar brilliance of spotlights, of the Oscars, of Technicolor, of starlets and blockbusters. A deathly brilliance, the mask of mourning; the brilliance of putrefaction, like the iridescent sheen of decaying meat. Mortification: from the moment of its birth, and because it was immediately industrialised and Hollywoodised, cinema has stolen life from life, not so as to live itself, but only to deprive the real of life. More malign than the demon who steals the shadow of poor Schlemiel, since at least the Devil has no qualms about appearing as what he is. In its efforts to appropriate the world (and to nullify it), cinema has adorned itself with violent trappings that placed it from the outset among the products or by-products of the century's major incarcerating enterprise: advertising. (Beneath the fluidity imparted to bodies in the advertising campaigns for Dim Tights, Giorgio Agamben sees the exact equivalent of Busby Berkeley dance sequences: a fascist cinema *in pectore*, intended, it goes without saying, to conceal a sinister reality beneath its brilliance, the concentration camps, and later the reduction of Man to the condition of consumer. In his only politically interventionist film intended for a mass audience, TOUT VA BIEN, Godard had said the same thing: making adverts for Dim Tights provided a living for the director, a Sartrian 'hypocrite' racked by remorse, who was played by the ex-communist Yves Montand. The future author of adverts for Marithé and François Girbaud, for Darty, and for Nike, had noted in passing that, whatever you do, the gesture of advertising also affects art cinema.)
– the major, sublime brilliance of solar illumination: that of beauty and *eros*, or that of being itself (or, in the Orphic myth, that of knowledge). This brilliance cannot be seen with the eye, it does not burst through the screen and it advertises nothing. Certain conditions or certain adventures of the light of cinema might perhaps give an idea or a glimpse of it, but it is aimed at the soul, or at a certain state of consciousness. This brilliance is here called 'happiness', but we could also think of 'joy' as in Bernanos, '*élan vital*' as in Bergson, or 'dance' as in Nietzsche.

This is the first stage of the thesis – one easy enough to accept, after all. Brilliance can decay, beauty can decay; beneath the mask of the most beautiful Queen in the world there is the wicked Witch, whom the laboratory of Hollywood is always ready to reveal; publicity is the kidnapping of beauty, its imprisonment, its rape, its terrible murder. It is all very simple, then, a question of ethics; the artist need simply cultivate true, ideal beauty: already we see that this naïve reversal, this 'angelicism' will not suffice. But the second stage of the thesis is more painful still; it concerns not perverted or insulted beauty, but intact Beauty, in its most positive powers. Left to herself, Godard reveals, Beauty passes from the martyred Justine to the Sadeian Juliette. 'Beauty is the beginning of the terror that we are able to bear': the filmmaker has often used this line from Rilke (Isabelle Huppert tells how she received it on a postcard, alone and enigmatic, as preparation for her role in SAUVE QUI PEUT (LA VIE)). Beauty and terror; beauty is terror; but bearable, delicious; the opposite of joy, but still joy, as we have learnt from Bataille; and delicious terror is nothing less than the pre-Romantic delight whereby Edmund Burke had defined the sublime. But in Rilke's poem, the next line is: 'and as such we admire it, because it disdainfully neglects to destroy us'. Fatal beauty, this time as a haughty goddess who could reduce us to nothing. The close connection between this divinity and splendour terrifies (to 'sublimate' also means to heat a solid such that it evaporates immediately, without passing through the liquid stage). The double destiny of beauty: to be a false beauty, disguising the real and stealing its life; to be Beauty, confronting us with what we are unable to bear.

Rilke makes of beauty a disdainful but benign goddess who could destroy us in a wink or with a click of the fingers (let us suppose she has fingers and eyes) but refrains from doing so. He is completely caught in the historical moment of the West when Beauty was the last vestige of the celestial Ideas; when after the end of Romanticism there remained this belief in the beautiful as definitive substitute, definitively appropriated by art, for the values of truth and goodness. Broch goes further, destroying even this Romantic assimilation: Beauty's crime is to have mimicked the divine intercession between our feeble human endeavours and the Ideas – giving us only the appearance of these Ideas, whether through impotence or sadism (if we must have an explanation). 'That's why Beauty is also a fall back into pre-divinity, and why for Man it is a reminiscence of something. Oh, return to the native land! The return of the one who doesn't need to be invited!' These words from *The Death of Virgil* appear both in SOIGNE TA DROITE and HISTOIRE(S) DU CINÉMA but Godard might also have cited the following: 'All that is done for Beauty alone must remain the share of nothingness and the void, and deserves to be condemned; for even in the coldness of the harmonic balance proposed by Beauty, this enterprise is governed by intoxication, is mere regression, no more than pure representation, and does not aspire to knowledge, which is the exclusive abode of the gods.'

In his lyrical meditation, the dying poet (Virgil but also Dante, and also Hölderlin, and also Broch and Godard) wishes to destroy his work because he has only been able to attain beauty, and not the real. Beauty is not a quality often accorded cinema, long considered as a mere subsection – no more noble than popular song or fiction – of the culture industry. Cinema's claim to legitimacy, in the diverse forms this has taken from the start, spontaneously avoided seeking to establish the beautiful as a value of the 'seventh' art; it is even the basis of the claim to distance cinema from beauty as value, whether by virtue of a modernist ideology of art (that of the Simultaneists and Cubists, from Guillaume Apollinaire to Fernand Léger), where the beautiful is 'outdated'; or by virtue of an existentialist conception whereby cinema, attaining the real directly, has no need of classical beauty (or else produces a beauty *sui generis*, whose beauty is nothing more than that of the world); or because, confused with a concern for form, the beautiful is seen as obstructive and derivative by a political enterprise of denunciation or exposure; or because a 'living art' (Gilbert Seldes) must cultivate values other than those of the traditional arts; or finally, because the very word has no sense for a conception of cinema as an art of event. Furthermore, cinema was born more or at less at the moment when, within aesthetics, Benedetto Croce was postulating that beauty is in no sense a problem or notion within aesthetics or in art, but 'a simple psychological and empirical concept'; I can find a work of art to be beautiful, I can even, through this opinion, experience something more general that for me would be beauty: this would not say something about the work of art but only, at most, about my state of mind.

It is significant that Godard has leapt over the entire *aesthetic* history of the seventh art, in order to address directly a classical *ethos* that is harder and more despairing. For the dying Virgil of Broch, beauty is the (fatal) error of art, its 'desperate effort to create the imperishable out of perishable things'; it is a value, but a negative one. The quotation from *The Death of Virgil* in Chapter 2B is long and heavily reworked (cutting together ten or so dispersed fragments). Its composition (its framing and duration) is strict, the mirror image of the cosmetic face of Death ('Lady Max Factor') of Sabine Azéma, the actress who recites Broch's text. It is hard to overemphasise the importance of these Platonic notions of a beauty that troubles us, body and soul, in order only to turn us from the way of knowledge. Obviously, to return to this classical rejection of beauty as the temptation of a 'game in itself' is also to avoid the question of the beautiful, in the cinema and today. With what beauty, that would be neither the erotic surface of bodies nor the eroticised surface of the image's pictorial values, should cinema be concerned?

Alongside the terrorist, terrorising version of a divine beauty with the power to annihilate, Godard sustains throughout HISTOIRE(S) DU CINÉMA another version – not to be confused with the bitter affirmation that beautiful bodies have been stolen from beauty by advertising and industrial cosmetics. This other version is banal: cinema shares the fate of any art of representation, linking beauty to the figuration of women. Cinema is a vast symbolic form of the gaze of young men upon the body of women: therein lies its fiction. FATALE BEAUTÉ is dedicated to two women, Michèle Firk and Nicole Ladmiral; it opens with three female faces and the photograph of a woman writer (Simone de Beauvoir) before the brief montage of shots on the theme of rapture; meanwhile, on the soundtrack, a song by Paco Ibañez. Firk was a critic on the journal *Positif* who committed suicide in 1967 during the guerilla war in Guatemala; Ladmiral was the young actress who played Chantal in Bresson's JOURNAL D'UN CURÉ DE CAMPAGNE and committed suicide a little later. The dedication conceals, then, the nonetheless forceful presence of female figures of resistance. Together with the allusion to feminism via Beauvoir, they are in sharp contradiction with the figure of rapture – of masculine power, embodied by a man carrying off a woman, fainting and at his mercy – while in the song a sentimental, paternalistic man comforts a woman. At the other end of the film, the reflection upon mystery comes to a close, just after the 'explosive mourning of happiness', in a brusque pirouette: Godard as burlesque actor at the beginning of SOIGNE TA DROITE alternating quickly with Lartigue's photograph of Suzanne Lenglen jumping, while Léo Ferré sings that he's just an entertainer.

This is the theme's resonance, a Godardian resonance, but not exclusively so. Beauty is beautiful women; young girls in bloom or in tears, Lolita, Lili, Monika, Zoia, Baby Doll (1B); women once loved or who have inspired a kind of tenderness (I am not concerned with biographical truth), Karina, Ladmiral, Wiazemsky, Bardot (4B); women who create and who resist, Anne-Marie Miéville, Camille Claudel, Sarah Bernhardt, Colette, Hannah Arendt, Virginia Woolf (4A). This is an entirely benign procession of beautiful women, so different from each other and at the same time so similar and so eternally feminine, i.e. natural, i.e. eternally mysterious. This is no longer the misogynist Godard of LE MÉPRIS, where the woman is abominable because we understand nothing of her, not even her smile ('is it a mocking or a tender smile?'); but woman, *la femme*, remains there, with that generic singularity of the definite article, as in the text by Élie Faure read by Alain Cuny, where woman opens her legs to 'us' no less maternally than when she breastfeeds (4A). From the 'creature' to the Mother, has there really been a change in the philosophy of feminine mystique? We may wonder.

'Might there not be a situation where alterity is borne by a being positively, as essence? I think that the contrary that is absolutely contrary, the contrariness that allows a term to remain absolutely other, is the feminine.' These astonishing words from *Time and the Other* are contemporary with *The*

Second Sex. Emmanuel Levinas defines the feminine as 'a mode of being that consists in avoiding the light', essentially unknowable, instituting thereby an absolute of alterity (far from the conception of the other as liberty that reaches exhaustion in the Hegelian dialectic of master and slave). 'By positing the alterity of others as a mystery, I do not posit it as a liberty identical with my own liberty, and in contest with it, I do not posit another existent facing me, I posit alterity. As with death, it is not an existent that we have to deal with, it is the event of alterity. We have sought this alterity in the absolutely original relation of *eros.' Eros* once more meets *thanatos*, but what emerges from this encounter is another given of my existence: others exist – and above all, that necessarily other other that is Woman – and in the same movement whereby they exist, they escape me.

One can see the place accorded by the film-maker to woman, to the feminine, in his thinking and images. At the most superficial level there is, no doubt, what we see in all films, whether Hollywood or New Wave: the necessity that Albertine constantly disappear so that time may be recovered. There must be stories if History is to come, and they are always stories of distance and flight, stories of the disappearance, the evanescence of women, the story of their entirely-other otherness, the story of the gaze's powerlessness to fix the beauty of their bodies. And there is the depth of these stories where the theme of beauty is the key: the role of glorious *hors-d'œuvre* accorded women – the place of Beauty, the place of absolute alterity – is simply the signifier, elegantly disguised, of the certainty that the essential mystique of the feminine seals a fatal relation between beauty and the knowledge of death. It is on the sacrifice of the happy dimension of the beautiful – 'mourning of happiness', renunciation of the Platonic identification of the Beautiful with the Good or of the Romantic identification of Beauty with Truth – that is built the possibility of memory. What remains of beauty is what woman brings to stories: seduction, sex appeal; the mystery of absolute otherness, necessarily dangerous. In all this, what suffers and disappears is art, i.e. poetry, i.e. thought. (We understand the melancholy of the artist historian, the sense of mourning and loss. In passing, however, we should note that woman remains the being most readily sacrificed. In the very first chapter of HISTOIRE(S) DU CINÉMA (1A) Gilda sings 'Put the blame on Mame', and these images of beautiful Rita Hayworth are followed – sinister presage – by images of the burning witch from Dreyer's DIES IRAE. It is not entirely certain that Godard, at this moment, is on the side of the witches. And here it is still a matter of women to whom humanity is accorded; there are more worrying figures in Godard's cinema, not adequately accounted for by the Marxian-Weberian analysis of prostitution as vast metaphor. Endless hesitations of a man who had, so astonishingly, been able, at least in one film – SAUVE QUI

PEUT (LA VIE) – to give a female point of view. The indecision regarding women of a man 'no better than any other'.)

I have perhaps over-insisted on the theoretical value, and didactic tone, of an episode of HISTOIRE(S) DU CINÉMA that does not differ essentially from the others. It may be more provocative, through the split between the erotic seductiveness of 'pretty girls' and Platonic beauty, resituating philosophically the question of the Beautiful on its original terrain. But rather than clarify, it makes more complex the role of beauty in the art of film. Erotic seduction is one thing, often acknowledged in cinema (in the cosmetic industry of cinema); quite other is the Beautiful, from the faces of beautiful women where we see the Beautiful without knowing what it is, to the Rilkean goddess who strikes us dumb and might turn us to stone. Art theory and art history in the twentieth century have more or less abandoned beauty as a value and even as a concept, whether out of revolt against beauty as classical value, as a value of order, hence bourgeois, or out of revolt against beauty as the submission of the work to an external ideal. As for cinema, it has not concerned itself with beauty but only with those other values in the Platonic paradise that are interchangeable with beauty: the true and the useful. To denounce the superficial forms of brilliance, of spotlights adorned by the sun's rays, is a little facile. At first sight it concerns only the cultural industry of cinema, its non-artistic side. But that presupposes that we can effect this separation, something that Godard's films throw into doubt (hasn't Godard himself shown women with the false and vulgar appearance of beauty?). Godard's Olympian sadness on this matter is surely sincere. He seems seriously to regret not being able simply to discover this 'happiness' of the beauty of girls or women one might love, admire and at the same time consider beautiful, a happiness sadly lost, with, as sole compensation, the fame of stars and starlets – degraded, vicious forms of femininity playing on vulgar seduction.

The emotional or sentimental aspect, always to the fore in HISTOIRE(S) DU CINÉMA, gives flesh to something else, something more profound. In the first instance: beautiful bodies (beautiful women, let's say; a man's body for Godard, and generally in the cinematographic system, is something else) are the manifestation of the beautiful, its evidence according to that primary, unsurpassable affirmation – as in the opening arguments of the *Symposium* – that the Beautiful is firstly given us by beautiful things and beautiful bodies. What has cinema done with these beautiful bodies? Godard's answer is bitter: instead of exalting them, which it could have done (it had the capacity do to so), cinema has made of them the flesh of desire and pornographised them (and that includes art cinema: Hitchcock filming Tippi Hedren, Godard filming Myriem Roussel). Cinematography, the art of vision and light, could have consciously directed its efforts towards giving form to the gaze as desire, as the lifting of the secret of beautiful bodies. But when cinema has spoken of desire, it has separated desire from this attempt to symbolise beauty. Despite or because of its brilliance, the star is a pornographised state of the beautiful body – the equivalent, within the cosmetic industry of cinema, of the academic nude in painting, the Venus or Phryne of the extravagant potboilers in the Musée d'Orsay. As for art cinema, it sought to be the Manet or the Courbet of these academic painters; but in offering up as *Olympia*s or *Births of the world* these naked bodies in their 'real' misery, cinema has at the same time distanced itself from the happy relation to the (beautiful) feminine body. Unlike photography, cinema has no academic nude, that hypocritical state of the beautiful body's degradation. From the first, cinema has given this degradation for what it is, an unhealthy, ephemeral sheen. No Venus in cinema – neither academicised nor, as Godard bemoans, offered up in her sublime beauty (symptomatically, Venus is the name of one of the two poor girls in LES CARABINIERS).

And if we go on, if we move from these fictional beings to the form these fictions take, if we consider the concern for beauty in general, outside or beyond this presentation of bodies, what do we find? Is there something like a sentiment, a desire or a temptation of the beautiful form in cinema? There are two ways of answering, depending on the philosophical reference we have in mind. In Platonic terms, a beautiful form is what escapes time, what leads to eternity. In cinema, there is a certain contradiction, an ontological one if you like, in this idea of a passage to eternity. It is almost a malediction: how can one imagine a form which of itself gives to the art of capturing the present a touch of the eternal? In fact, all avant-gardes that have sought to define a pure form have had to do so in the name of other concerns, sometimes aesthetic, more often ethical. Ultramodernist presuppositions were necessary for the purified movement and light of the films of Henri Chomette or Eugène Deslaw; a fascist credo was needed to authorise the pure manifestations of steel in Walter Ruttmann's ACCIAIO, and the optical tricks of the Whitney brothers presupposed the mantra.

In Hegelian terms, beauty can better, or differently, accommodate the contradiction between the eternal and the perishable. The parable of the young girl who follows on from the Muses, and offers us the fruit she has picked, is crystal clear: this fruit, detached from the tree and hence severed from the rising sap, is removed from excessive ripening and corruption and so will maintain an unalterable sensuality. This young girl is the museum, and it is art that gives flavour, taste and sensuality to beautiful form. French cinephilia, however ignorant of Hegel it may have been, has sensed this, even if it is as the aberrant pseudo-Nietzschianism of the Macmahon extremists of the late 1950s and early 1960s. The aesthetic problem of cinema at this point is thus the difficulty of finding or defining beautiful form. What pure beauty might the cinema possess that would be its own? Just as the cinema as social apparatus, as site of personal expression and as mimetic technique, has used a considerable number of solutions and means derived from other apparatuses and other techniques, so no formal beauty conceivable for the cinema could belong to the cinema alone. This is the deep meaning, fifty years on – i.e. finally rid of the 'aesthetic correspondences' straitjacket, in the flat, too quantitative sense given it by Étienne Souriau – of Bazin's major intuition that cinema is an impure art. It is an impure art because neither its objectives nor its origins can be its own (see the famous texts on the place of theatre and literature in the art of film), but also, I would add, an impure art because its beautiful form is not its own. A film's beauty is not its own (it is in the end the world's beauty, according to the credo of Eric Rohmer the critic), nor is its beautiful form, because there is still no sensorial or aesthetic terrain on which could be qualified as 'beautiful' pure arrangements of durations and tonalities (as has been done for music and, retrospectively, for painting).

Cinema has, then, inevitably had to go via beautiful bodies in order to encounter beauty, and that is why cinema has found beauty only in narrative. Perhaps the most pregnant sentiment in all of Godard's HISTOIRE(S) DU CINÉMA, the one that stays with us on leaving a screening and thereafter, is that it is impossible to separate the intensities of movement, the brilliance of gesture, the emotion of faces, all these deeply moving traits which Godard has extracted from the films he has watched for us, and which he has made, in short, into traits of beauty – it is impossible to separate them, to remove them from their narrative charge, or rather from the fact that they carry a narrative charge (which itself need not be known). When they used to say that every film is a fiction film, that all films are narrative, it was for the bad reasons of an abstract theoretical enterprise. The way this is said by HISTOIRE(S) DU CINÉMA is infinitely concrete: the work ceaselessly reaffirms that it is through fiction, through narrative, that beautiful bodies, i.e. beauty, i.e. beautiful form, are possible in cinema. The equation of woman, death and time, no doubt a revival of the *eros-thanatos* cliché, is thus a part of the Godardian thesis (or, it matters little, of the thesis I derive from Godard), a thesis regarding the poetics of film: the filmic is born from this interlacing because it embodies the passage of time. Narrative serves to 'make reality arrive' (André S. Labarthe) and, in this sense, it resists the transformation of cinema into an 'art of the image' – whatever we include in this formulation. The fatality of cinema – not in its apparatus but clearly in its history – is thus to tell stories, fated to tell stories of desire, that are fated to be knotted

around women and their alterity and the gaze that will not satisfy 'us', fatally knotted around the pain of the desire to possess beauty. Cinema's aesthetic fatality is to have been able to produce no other formal beauty than
this. Its ethical fatality is to have to this degree coincided with a definition of
desire that ties it to a painful conception of the exercise of the gaze. But that
is another story, perceived by Godard but not told.

Godard's invention – in these essays that, on this point as on many, can be
seen as the culmination of all his work and all his inventions – is to have said
this in a film that, precisely, brings to bear the essence of its work on this
knotting of desire, death's fatality and time, and to have said it through a
formal invention. The cinematograph as 'death at work' (Cocteau), as
'death making us its promises via the cinematograph' (Epstein), i.e. the cinema of desire, of fiction, of the mortal beauty of bodies, is commented upon
here, and in the process somehow replaced or substituted by another cinematography that seeks to extract from time something quite different: energy. This is, in the end, the value, meaning and bearing of a form that
Godard, who has been experimenting with it a long time, puts forward decisively and definitively in HISTOIRE(S) DU CINÉMA: the alternation of images.
The rapid alternation of two images, whether they cover each other completely or sometimes penetrate and tear through each other; a mixture of ul-
tra-short montage, superimposition and sectioning, achieved with the help
of video techniques invented for television. It is an eminently emotional
form (through its own dynamic and through the overwhelming impact of
an image inserted into another), and is also an explicatory, demonstrative
form; the most striking example of this in HISTOIRE(S) DU CINÉMA, the water
from the fire-hose in Eisenstein's STRIKE becoming the flame of the tor-
turer's blowtorch in Rossellini's ROME, OPEN CITY, plays perfectly with these
two dimensions: terror, horror, at the same time didacticism (repression is
always the same, always terrible). With this form, Godard has in some sense
found the new *Pathosformel*, the new formula of pathos, which, unlike that
formula noted by Aby Warburg in painting, does not entirely disguise emotion beneath fictions and characters, but brings forth a pure energy. Pure
emotion because pure rhythm; pure form because pure movement (not
beautiful but pure and energetic) – this is the beautiful form Godard invents
for cinema.

Cinema has been a gigantic machine for systematically organising the
disappearance of the body, allowing just a perceptual trace to survive. It
needed a film-maker who has, in his time, made more than one casting error
(casting the wrong body) to invent a beautiful cinematographic form that
leaves the body's beauty intact.

7 European Culture and Artistic Resistance in HISTOIRE(S) DU CINÉMA Chapter 3A, LA MONNAIE DE L'ABSOLU

James S. Williams

A topos of Godard's recent work, the opposition between art and culture, is best formulated in JLG/JLG: AUTOPORTRAIT DE DÉCEMBRE: 'there is culture which is the rule/which is part of the rule/there is the exception/which is art/which is part of art/everyone speaks the rule/cigarettes/computers/t-shirts/television'.[1] This general opposition, which can be likened to many such statements made earlier in the twentieth century by Theodor Adorno about the state of the culture industry and the market, could be taken in a variety of ways. For example, as a contrast between the absolute autonomy of art and the contingencies of democratised culture, or as part of a gendered distinction Godard often draws between culture as education and production (an essentially feminine, maternal principle), and art as the adult domain of creativity (the masculine principle).[2] A little later in JLG/JLG, however, Godard is far more specific about the exceptional status of art, bringing together artistic heavyweights such as Flaubert, Pushkin, Dostoevsky, Gershwin, Mozart, Cézanne, Vermeer, Antonioni and Vigo to develop the notion of art as an essentially European phenomenon and experience. He states: 'it is the nature of the rule/to wish the death/of the exception/no/it is/no/it is therefore the rule/of Europe/of culture/the rule of Europe/of culture/to organise the death/of the art of living/which was blossoming/still at our feet'.[3] Let us unpack this set of ideas carefully. For Godard, art is necessarily 'high' due to its origins in the Church and has served throughout history as an index of western morality, cinema being in his view its last representative. It can be defined (following André Malraux) only as something that ultimately surpasses the bounds of human comprehension. Yet in Godard's opinion the exception of art is now threatened from within Europe itself by the promotion and proliferation of European culture for all. JLG/JLG was released the year after the GATT (General Agreement on Tariffs and Trade) talks of 1993 when France successfully pursued a policy of *exception culturelle*, that is, the exception of 'cultural products' such as cinema from world trade agreements. The extracts from JLG/JLG just cited could thus be viewed as an acerbic comment by Godard on French cultural policy advocated in the name of an integrated Europe ('a Europe of Cultures'), and its misplaced wish to legislate in matters of art wrongly conceived as culture. Certainly, if the hegemony of commodified American culture and its reactionary forces of merchandising and distribution devoid of a sense of history have always constituted a natural enemy in Godard's work (one thinks in particular of films of the mid-to-late 1960s like DEUX OU TROIS CHOSES QUE JE SAIS D'ELLE), it is now the 'new Europe' that has become his most immediate foe. As Godard declared in brutally simple terms during a conference in London in 1991 on the theme of European identity in cinema: 'We have in Europe more or less lost our identity, mainly through an acceptance of American culture. For me, painting and movie-making is not culture. A novel is not culture – it's art. Mozart is not culture, but distributing Mozart on RCA compact disc is culture. This is very different. But I don't think the cure for this lost identity is to try to construct a bigger identity and call it "European".'[4]

How do Godard's recent public pronouncements on art and Europe actually relate to his films? PASSION, set in a TV studio in Switzerland (the neutral and, for Godard, often empty centre of the old continent) against the distant backdrop of martial law in Poland, marked, of course, Godard's first direct attempt to consider the status and legacy of European art, in particular its engagement with European history in the form of historical narrative. Paintings by (among others) Rembrandt, Goya and Delacroix are presented in the film in the form of *tableaux vivants*. Ien Ang has written convincingly that PASSION displays a specifically European nostalgic melancholy, part of a general longing for the impossible in European idealist thought which has resulted historically in failed Utopias, from the Enlightenment to German unification. Moreover, it radically stages this melancholic passion for the impossible as 'the impossibility of cinema itself, the impossiblity of narrative, the impossiblity of love, the impossibility of arriving at anything'.[5] In the same doomed European vein as PASSION are more recent films by Godard such as NOUVELLE VAGUE, in which Europe is presented as a murky, bureaucratic world of corporate capital where international industrialists and financiers circulate oblivious to the beauty and mystery of nature, and HÉLAS POUR MOI, where Europe is treated more as a background extra, a passing object of irony (a Swiss boat named 'Italy' passing in and out of the frame, a travelling salesman hauling his suitcase of goods 'Made in Europe' everywhere and nowhere, a soldier always on the point of leaving for Bosnia, etc.). That said, Godard's work of the late 1980s and 1990s has dealt in increasingly serious fashion with contemporary events in Europe. ALLEMAGNE ANNÉE 90 NEUF ZÉRO, for example, where the issue of language and culture is directly thematised (German, French, English and occasionally Russian all overlap each other), is one of the most dense and intensive of Godard's recent films and offers an aesthetic and philosophical meditation on the solitary 'state' of post-communist East Germany. FOR EVER MOZART charts the doomed progress of a young drama troupe bound for Sarajevo and exposes along the way the hypocrisy of western countries during the Bosnian war (euphemisms such as peacekeepers). As for HISTOIRE(S) DU CINÉMA, it is literally flooded by the images of twentieth-century war in Europe, from the Spanish Civil War to the Second World War, the Holocaust and Bosnia.

What is striking, however, is that those current events in Europe with which Godard now chooses to engage have almost no link at all with the rich heritage of European art that he draws on and cites so profusely. Godard's is an essentially classical sense of European art and culture that advances no further into the story of modern art than Picasso, Francis Bacon and Nicolas de Staël, that last gasp of the Paris School before the centre of modern art moved to New York and Abstract Expressionism became the order of the day. As for European cinema, it means essentially for Godard a cinema of the past, that is to say, as Jacques Aumont has emphasised, 'une Europe à trois' – Germany, Italy and France.[6] It is significant that apart from the odd fleeting reference to film-makers such as Coppola, Angelopoulos, Garrel and Kiarostami, Godard makes virtually no reference to contemporary cinema in HISTOIRE(S) DU CINÉMA. Similarly, many of those quintessentially European thinkers and writers to whom he refers consistently in his recent work, such as Charles Péguy, Oswald Spengler and Denis de Rougemont, were writing much earlier in the century and all agonised in different ways over the sad predicament of contemporary Europe and European culture. Péguy's posthumously published *Clio* (1917) (subtitled 'Dialogue of history and the pagan soul'), parts of which are read aloud in the last chapter 4B, LES SIGNES PARMI NOUS, is a visionary work of faith that upholds the French tradition, in particular the 'genius'of Victor Hugo in whom history and poetry, matter and spirit are fully interwoven. Written under extreme personal stress and shadowed by a calm intimation of approaching war, Péguy's dialogue between Clio, the Muse of history, and the reader is a meditation on remembrance and the creative intelligence of memory.[7] Spengler's mammoth *Decline of the West* (1923), invoked in ALLEMAGNE ANNÉE 90 NEUF ZÉRO in terms of the final battle between blood and money, predicts the end of western civilisation by finding analogies with the declining civilisations of the past. It is a Cassandra-like work poised between optimism and faith on the one hand, and pessimism and spleen on the other. According to Spengler, cultures rise and fall in defiance of linear progress and leave nothing behind.[8] Denis de Rougemont's *Penser*

avec les mains (1936) is quoted at length in Chapter 4A of HISTOIRE(S) DU
CINÉMA, LE CONTRÔLE DE L'UNIVERS, with Godard reading out key phrases
and extracts covering the entirety of the text in chronological order. De
Rougemont wrote this now little-read essay about the threatening decadence of western culture during the rise of National Socialism, and with it
he sought to reinstate the powers of active, individual thought and a western principle of community and friendship based on a new order of moral
ethics (what he called the 'seven virtues' such as creative imagination). This
he contrasted with culture which is always 'a ready-made thing and not a
thing to be made or being made. It's the idea of the cultivated man rather
than the creator that is associated quite naturally in our minds with culture;
the idea of luxury rather than work, spiritual struggle and power in process'.[9]

Underlying these very different works by Péguy, Spengler and de
Rougemont is, of course, a profound sense of what Europe and European
culture should stand for. For Godard, such certainties can be viewed now
only as a matter of the past, as what Europe and European art and culture
once embodied or symbolised. In cinematic terms, a reconstructed notion of
Europe might entail the regular programming of European-made films in
every country: 'The day when every televison station in Europe regularly
shows a Greek, Portuguese or Slovak film, whether dull or not, Europe will
be created. Otherwise it will remain American.'[10] A genuinely new Europe
could mean nothing more than this, yet equally nothing less than this,
which is to say an impossible ideal. Thus, when Godard turns to a writer
like de Rougemont, the author of other works such as *L'amour et l'Occident*
(1956), it is above all to help himself diagnose the disunited, moribund state
of contemporary European culture rather than to establish a clear social or
political prognosis. He will never engage, for instance, with de
Rougemont's numerous later essays and reports on the future of European
union such as *Les chances de l'Europe* (1962), published under the auspices of
the Centre Européen de la Culture which he founded in Geneva in 1950, or
L'un et le divers, ou la Cité européenne. Deux discours (1970), both of which argue strongly for a European federation. Yet if 'Europe' and European art is
fast becoming only the stuff of memory for Godard, by the same token it
constitutes a privileged site of the imaginary, part of an open and often
fantasmatic process of association, tension, transition and translation (in the
literal sense, too, of moving a (dead) body). A film like ALLEMAGNE ANNÉE
90 NEUF ZÉRO revels in a polyglot, pan-European artistic and historical past
and imaginary, complete with frontiers, homelands, and dragons. Indeed,
what Godard calls his 'cinematographic unconscious', the product of his
childhood reading of German literature, and specifically German Romanti-

cism, his imaginary 'motherland', is what can make possible an image of Don Quixote riding through the industrial wastelands of the former East Germany.[11]

It is by virtue of their floating status in the relentless flux of Godard's videographic montage in HISTOIRE(S) DU CINÉMA that European art and culture past become, in fact, essentially open questions, or questions of form. I would like to explore these questions, and in so doing try to establish the specific nature of artistic 'exception' and opposition to the rule in Godard's current film practice, by examining one particular episode of HISTOIRE(S) DU CINÉMA, Chapter 3A, entitled LA MONNAIE DE L'ABSOLU, literally, 'The change [as in exchange, or barter] of the absolute', although the title is clearly intended as a reference to the fourth and last part of Malraux's *Les voix du silence* (1951), translated into English as *The Twilight of the Absolute*. I have chosen this chapter because it is perhaps the most self-consciously European episode of HISTOIRE(S) DU CINÉMA, offering an explicit and extensive enquiry into the relations between European art and history, specifically war, during the nineteenth and twentieth centuries. It also constitutes a virtual case study *à la* Malraux in the transformation of forms, from writing (Victor Hugo) to painting (Edouard Manet) to cinema (Roberto Rossellini and post-war Italian cinema) across the course of historical time. The European aspect is highlighted in the book of HISTOIRE(S) DU CINÉMA by the very first image of the third volume (p. 4), a superimposition featuring William Blake's *Europe* (an image not available in the video and even preceding the general subtitle of the book's four volumes, *Introduction à une véritable histoire du cinéma*). This illustration, where the Creator bends down with his compass, served as the frontispiece to Blake's book *Europe: A Prophecy* (1794), and it constitutes in turn a kind of foreword to Godard's own work in Chapter 3A by sounding a note of destiny and fatalism. While many of the key themes of HISTOIRE(S) DU CINÉMA are showcased here (notably the power – and weakness – of cinema and television, the Holocaust as a zero point in western history and civilisation, human suffering and death, the moral necessity of memory), LA MONNAIE DE L'ABSOLU falls into four distinct thematic parts: Europe, art, the Second World War, and cinema as a national event. I intend to examine each of these four parts in turn in order to show how together they present interrelated sites of crisis, struggle and resistance. I do not propose an exhaustive close reading since the intricacy and depth of Godard's videographic montage here would require an entire book in itself. However, a detailed analysis of Godard's use of European painting and art in Chapter 3A and of the effects of his poetic and historical formulation of montage will reveal that what he is elaborating in HISTOIRE(S) DU CINÉMA is really a 'trans-national' and 'trans-aesthetic' project sustained in part by resistance to the very idea of Europe as a unity and whole. I will then use this discussion to explore the general process of figuration within the rhetorical movements of Godard's videographic montage. I will argue that figuration functions essentially as a means of resistance in HISTOIRE(S) DU CINÉMA, and that this internal resistance constitutes the very fabric of the work at the most immediate level of videographic form.

Europe

LA MONNAIE DE L'ABSOLU begins with Godard reciting in a choked whisper a political speech by Hugo entitled 'Pour la Serbie' originally delivered on 29 August 1876 (Godard types the author and date at the end of the three-minute sequence). The speech was written by Hugo out of a sense of outrage at the actions of rival warring fictions in the build up to the Russo-Turkish war of 1877-8 (the second major Balkan War). In it, he lambasts the reluctance of western European nations to respond to the war in Serbia and exposes the hypocrisy of the diplomatic position adopted by western governments when they say that to assassinate a man is a crime, while to assassinate a nation is a 'question' requiring careful consideration. 'What humankind knows, governments are unaware of', Hugo states, before asking: 'When will the martyrdom of this small heroic nation end?'[12] The irony of Godard's choice of this speech is underscored by television footage of carnage during the recent Bosnian war, the shot of a magazine cover with the title *Bosnie: les années high-tech*, and a photograph of François Mitterrand hidden behind sunglasses. It is extended by Godard's repetition of Hugo's mocking words 'et cetera, et cetera' and the periodic tolling of a bell. At the same time, Godard presents us with a bewildering concatenation of painted images of violence, war, barbarism and the grotesque. Goya's *Saturn*, one of his tragic *Black Paintings*, is first flashed in and out of Artemisia Gentileschi's brutal portrayal of Judith beheading Holofernes with the help of her maid. With this second image, which is suspended and repeated (and over which, in the standard restating of all the chapter titles at the beginning of each episode, the title of Chapter 2B FATALE BEAUTÉ appropriately falls), Godard reminds us that the Judith and Holofernes story is linked expressly to warfare and military strategy (a Jewish widow's successful attempt to drive out the Assyrian invader and save her people). However, through sustained rapid spot editing which accentuates the violence represented in both images (the phrase 'MONTAGE' is flashed up in triplicate), Godard is clearly provoking us into imagining the possible links between the represented scenes, a question that we take to the next series of images. These are mainly details of further works by Goya (including *Great exploits with dead bodies* from the *Disasters of War* series, *The Fire*, *Miracle of St. Anthony of Padua* (in the cupola of the Church of San Antonio de la Florida, Madrid), *Group on a balcony*, and the chalk drawing *Saturn devouring his children*), Fuseli (*Lady Macbeth sleepwalking*), Delacroix (*Pietà*), Grünewald ('The Temptation of Saint Anthony' scene from the *Isenheim Altarpiece*), El Greco (*Christ driving the traders from the temple* (the third, so-called 'Toledo' version)), and Uccello (*Deluge* and *The Battle of San Romano* (the Louvre panel)). This controlled visual conflagration is also punctuated by moments of black leader, a glimpse of Velázquez's *Portrait of a court dwarf*, newsreel images of a Nazi death camp, and the sequence (slowed-down) from Rossellini's 1948 film GERMANY YEAR ZERO where the little boy Edmund walks through the rubble as he heads towards his voluntary death. The sequence comes to a rest with Monet's extraordinary portrait of his dead wife Camille on her deathbed (painted in 1879 three years after Hugo made his speech).

Godard leaves us breathlessly trying to assimilate this eclectic assemblage of French, Spanish, Italian and Swiss historical and biblical imagery. Are we meant to consider the images primarily as a demonstration of western culture and history in crisis or as signs of a particular national culture? The penultimate image, Goya's *General Antonio Ricardos*, emphasises the state of confusion: over the portrait of this Spanish general (killed, as it happens, during the Franco-Spanish Wars shortly after the portrait was painted in 1794), Godard types the words 'Monsieur le vicomte le laquais d'Orsay', a loaded reference to the home of the French Foreign Office. He is perhaps hereby suggesting that France succeeded in blocking stronger United Nations and European Community actions against Serbia during the recent Bosnian War, a perception shared by many at the time. The exhilaration, yet also difficulty and frustration, induced by the fragmentation and defamiliarisation of images is exacerbated by other methods employed by Godard, including the filtering of images (for example, black-and-white images discoloured a bloody red), the splintering of text (words cut in two, or into and sometimes over each other), and Godard's desire to use artists with and against each other (for instance, the mysterious main figure of *Deluge* is superimposed over a Renaissance image of the Ponte Vecchio). Yet in addition to the images' link with the culture that produced them and their possible new connection with each other lies the formal question of their original context. This question is articulated explicitly a few seconds later when Godard offers perhaps the most commonly recognised detail from Grünewald's *Isenheim Altarpiece* – the bent right arm and pointing finger of St. John the Baptist in the Crucifixion scene which shapes into a triangle the words: 'Illum oportet crescere me autem minui' ('He must increase, but I must decrease'). In presenting just the detail of St. John, a key aspect of this supremely Catholic monument and its project of affirming a harmonious Catholic world view on the brink of spiritual crisis with the Reformation, Godard is quite deliberately gesturing towards a narrative unity and whole located forever off-screen and thus forever deferred. This fact is paralleled on the soundtrack, for Godard reproduces about two thirds of Hugo's devastating speech almost word for word before cutting it dramatically after the statement that humanity ('*nous*') has its own 'question' – the little child in the mother's stomach. He thus denies Hugo's conclusion that the only possible solution to war in the Balkans is a 'United States of Europe', or 'Republic of Europe' (the 'last port'), i.e. a continental Federation, with Paris, the city of light and capital of liberty, at its head. By stopping it where he does, an act as decisive as Judith's decapitation of Holofernes, Godard ends on a note of unresolved crisis and horror.

Godard's refusal even to entertain the notion of a European solution premissed on the universality of French culture and civilisation (a political card played by France over a century later during the GATT talks[13]) clearly reflects a belief that human war and suffering are a universal concern more important than any warped utopian notion of State or Republican unity. This approach can be linked perhaps to Jacques Derrida's recent treatment of Paul Valéry, another quintessentially European writer quoted at length by Godard at the beginning of Chapter 4A. In *L'autre cap: mémoires, réponses et responsabilités* (1991), Derrida revises Valéry's 'Notes sur la grandeur et décadence de l'Europe' by arguing that it is no longer possible for Europe to think of itself as the universal 'brain' of a vast body, or indeed as anything more than simply a geographical 'head' ('cap') to the Asiatic continent. Instead of heading towards some new form of European 'capital' (in all senses of the word), it is crucial, Derrida insists, to respect 'the other heading' ('l'autre cap'), or better still, 'the *otherness* of the heading' ('l'Autre du cap').[14] Certainly, the (inter)textual commitment in HISTOIRE(S) DU CINÉMA and all Godard's recent work to movement and circulation must be read as an aesthetic move against any attempt at an imposed and fixed 'European' unity, especially a vision of Europe that includes no proper account of the painful and complex experience of the Second World War. Sometimes, however, the threat of stasis is so great that it finally prevails. ALLEMAGNE ANNÉE 90 NEUF ZÉRO, for example, a 'border' film like so much of Godard's recent work in that it feeds into and out of HISTOIRE(S) DU CINÉMA, draws abruptly to a halt when Lemmy Caution finally reaches the capitalist neon of the new Germany, part of the new American World Order, where the 'phantoms' that greeted him when he crossed the border can no longer find their 'verdigris' home.

Art

If, then, division and fragmentation are privileged over unity both formally and thematically, should one talk primarily in terms of a 'national' – as opposed to European – art and culture, and if so, how? How, that is, can one create and maintain a 'free' work of art which, unlike the work of an artist like Velázquez in the pay of the court, resists the rules of the State that underwrite wars. Goya, who consciously asserted the freedom of invention (or 'caprice') of the artist, provides the obvious point of contrast to Velázquez and a possible model for Godard who, even more than in PASSION where three Goya paintings were reconstituted (*The nude maja*, *The parasol* and *Madrid, 3 May, 1808: Executions at the mountains of Prince Pius*), gives us here a glimpse of Goya's enormous range. However, any attempt at a proper answer to the question remains lacking. After evoking the mad and capricious lust for power of Golden Age Hollywood with its empty 'UNIVERSAL' wish to make the world weep in its seat – a wish, Godard argues, that has now been rendered banal by American television and its 'groupies' – LA MONNAIE DE L'ABSOLU then passes via a short bridging episode featuring a detail of Goya's own representation of *Judith* (from the *Black Paintings* series) to a more calm and reflective sequence on Manet. The link between Manet and Goya is enforced by Godard's repetition of the image of Saturn (this time a close-up detail) which is followed immediately by a detail of Manet's *Le balcon*, an innocent group portrait featuring Berthe Morisot that reworks Goya's *Group on a balcony*, a Hogarthian view of two women shadowed menacingly by two demonic gallants. The story of Goya's great influence on Manet is well-known in art history, and in *Les voix du silence* Malraux provides concrete evidence of Manet's use of Goya as a model (*The nude maja* for *Olympia*, *Madrid, 3 May, 1808* for *Exécution de Maximilien*).[15] What is important here, however, is that the terms of their connection are precise for Godard. It is not really a question of an artist outstripping his precursor and model due to an anxiety of influence, in the manner, say, of Saturn desperately ingesting his offspring for fear they might become unstoppable rivals. Nor is it a question of the two artists' similar yet different representation of human violence, or of their status as representatives of a national school of painting. It is rather their link in an ongoing, universal chain and metamorphosis of artistic form. In this regard, Godard is utterly faithful to the spirit of Malraux in *Les voix du silence*, and it is this which will ultimately enable him at the end of LA MONNAIE DE L'ABSOLU to formulate the uniqueness of cinematic form. To paraphrase Godard's voice-over: all Manet's women appear to be saying: 'I know what you're thinking of' ('Je sais à quoi tu penses'), no doubt because Manet was the first painter to link the internal world to the cosmos. Even the famous pale smiles of Leonardo da Vinci, Vermeer and Corot (examples of which Godard provides for the reader's scrutiny) proclaim 'me first, the world after'. It is for this reason, according to Godard, that Manet initiated modern painting, that is to say, the cinematograph, or form becoming speech, or more precisely, 'a form that thinks' ('une forme qui pense'). In Godard's version of the beginnings of modern art, which names Georges Bataille's study *Manet* as its point of departure, Manet is promoted as a 'man of cinema' not simply because his career coincided exactly with the beginnings of photography and he looked for truth without falling into naturalism, but because his work facilitates creative thought. This is an intrinsically human moment, one of sudden mutual recognition between the viewer and subject, self and other, self and the world. Godard repeats here a central thesis of HISTOIRE(S) DU CINÉMA: that cinema was initially designed for the purposes of thought but that this was forgotten immediately, the flame being definitively extinguished at Auschwitz.

But there is more at stake in Godard's appreciation of Manet, and it will become clearer if I quote a key passage from Bataille's study: 'what counts in Manet's canvases is not the subject, but the vibration of light [...] To break up the subject and re-establish it on a different basis is not to neglect the subject; so it is in a sacrifice, which takes liberties with the victim and even kills it, but cannot be said to *neglect* it. After all, the subject in Manet's pictures is not so much "killed" as simply overshot, outdistanced; not so much obliterated in the interests of pure painting as transfigured by the stark purity of that painting [...] No painter more heavily invested the subject, not with meaning, but with that which goes beyond and is more significant than meaning.'[16] In Godard's scheme, cinematography essentially follows through the operation of modernity initiated by Manet since it sacrifices the real literally by putting it to death and then mourning it. Although 'killed off', however, the real does not totally disappear; instead, the sacrifice returns the real to us and allows us to regain access to it because the projected image is effectively resurrected in light. One of Godard's primary aims in HISTOIRE(S) DU CINÉMA is clearly to privilege and celebrate this resurrecting power of film and to reveal it – ironically through the medium of video – as the opposite of what Philippe Sollers has dismissively called in his discussion of the work 'the barter of cinema', that is, a negative illustration of what must be undergone – a 'flood' of phantoms from the past – before a true work of painting with transcendent qualities of completeness and 'thereness' can be successfully realised.[17] Indeed, one of the determining formal tensions of HISTOIRE(S) DU CINÉMA derives precisely from the struggle played out between the destabilising flux of cinema and cinematic history and the static pictorial image that manages effortlessly to impose itself however much Godard subjects it to the vibrations of the video machine, as at the start of LA MONNAIE DE L'ABSOLU. Godard's purpose is surely to reverse cinema's negative status (what Sollers terms its 'enormous fantasmagoria') *vis-à-vis* other more 'refined' arts and instead reconfigure painting as the change or barter of cinema. The key here is montage which for Godard constitutes style, cinema's – and video's – unique ethical and moral code. This leads us to the next and third sequence concerning the Second World War which exemplifies Godard's method of historical montage.

World War II

The bridge between the two sequences takes us from the world of Manet's *Nana*, via his *Fifrelin* accompanied by a fifing tune, to that of Zola pictured with his photographic camera and the last words of his novel *Nana*, 'à Berlin! à Berlin! à Berlin!', pictured in close-up (this is the influence of technology on the evolution of literary form, here naturalism). This in turn leads to Jean Renoir's silent 1926 film NANA starring Catherine Hessling (claimed by Godard incorrectly as the first co-production with UFA[18]), to Goebbels and the shot of Jean Gabin being gunned down in Marcel Carné's QUAI DES BRUMES of 1938, a film originally meant to be filmed in Berlin as the last UFA co-production but which was banned by Goebbels. This quick-fire chain of connections is merely a preparation, however, for the core element of the six and a half-minute sequence: the crossing in time of two trains and the elaborate train of associations it produces. To summarise in brief: in 1942, Danièle Darrieux, along with other French stars such as Suzy Delair and Junie Astor, travelled from Paris to Berlin as guests of UFA. In the same year, Irène Némirovsky, a young French Jewish writer, returned to Paris from the South in order to retrieve a bracelet and was promptly arrested before being deported from the same station to Auschwitz. Godard refers to Némirovsky as 'that fool Irène' (a reference also perhaps to Louis Aragon's *Le con d'Irène*, published clandestinely in 1928). These two facts become a site for further criss-crossings of associations. Némirovsky had scored a blockbuster hit in 1930 with her book *Le bal* which was immediately adapted for the screen by William Thiele in the 1931 film of the same name starring Darrieux in her first major role (pictured in close-up is a page of her *Journal* describing the success of *Le bal*). Notable by their absence on the train, however, were Alain Cuny and Marie Déa who starred together in Marcel Carné's LES VISITEURS DU SOIR of 1942, a still from which is shown featuring Cuny as Gilles (one of the two envoys of the Devil with Arletty) and Déa as Lady Anne, both chained up and turned to stone. Godard intones 'their hearts were beating, beating, beating' ('leur cœur battait, battait, battait') in honour of a love that cannot be suppressed but which serves to express the momentous urgency of the decision taken by Cuny and Déa not to take the train and effectively collaborate. The sequence continues with the caption 'Le train suivant' matched by a detail of a painting by Kandinsky entitled *Murnau, view with railway and castle* (1909), and concludes with contemporary footage of Cuny repeating the question he posed to Déa in 1942 concerning the train, this time to Juliette Binoche as she reads aloud a poem by Emily Brontë on impending death.[19] The last image, superimposed over the contours of Binoche's body, is of a reclining nude by Nicolas de Staël.[20] This dizzying procession of wartime references is already dense enough but the resonances proliferate even further if we consider that Catherine Hessling was first noticed by Renoir's father, Auguste Renoir; that the typed word 'la romance' produces an image of Viviane Romance from LA VÉNUS AVEUGLE (a 1943 film by Abel Gance), an actress who also took the train with Darrieux and her group; that the phrase 'Gilles, no, not that of Drieu' refers also to the title of an autobiographically inspired novel by the writer and collaborator Drieu la Rochelle;[21] and that finally, inscribed in segments across the middle of the sequence, is the phrase attributed by Godard to William Faulkner, 'The past is never dead, it has not even passed' ('Le passé n'est jamais mort, il n'est même pas passé') (Faulkner's first novel, we recall, was *Soldier's Pay* (1926) about the uneasy return of a war hero, translated into French as *Monnaie de Singe*).

Taken as a whole, the sequence is structured as a site of intersection between various journeys positive and negative, all of which feeds into a double movement of repetition and reversal. The term *battement* itself functions as a double movement since it indicates not only the beating and palpitation of the heart but also an interval of time (as in the phrase 'un battement de vingt minutes', a wait of twenty minutes between trains). All the elements are, as it were, crossed through and in some cases crossed out, for Godard also pursues a process of self-correction initiated earlier in Chapter 3A when the caption 'erreur' flashed up shortly after his erroneous statement that Eric Pommer was the founder of Universal (it should have been Carl Laemmle). The process continued with the correction seconds later of Dolores del Rio ('Erreur Virginia Mayo'), and, in the Manet episode, with the almost spontaneous correction of the pianist he evokes, 'my Miss Clara Haskil' (a Jewish performer hounded by the Nazis), by the caption 'erreur Martha Argerich' stamped over the image of one of the latter's CD recordings. In this third sequence Godard recognises his confusion over the dates in the war, 1942 and 1944, and signals this with the caption 'Error two years before'. I would like to argue that this series of double movements corresponds to the rhetorical figure of the chiasmus, or the placing crosswise of elements, which can take the form of practically any strategy of reversal or specular reflection that crosses the attributes of inside and outside.[22] As such, it does no more than formalise the many key features of Godard's videographic style evident from the beginning of LA MONNAIE DE L'ABSOLU, including the inter-flashing of images, their fading in and out, superimposition and absorption, whereby each image opens up to another in a continuous process of traversal. The very first images of Goya and Gentileschi, specifically their representations of human arms engaged in unbearable violence – from man as perpetrator of violence (Saturn holding up his child – son or daughter? – to eat[23]) to man as the victim of violence (Judith beheading Holofernes) – indicate that the central drive and direction of this chapter is inversion and reversal. Images bridge anonymously over each other, as in the first bridging episode of Chapter 3A itself where the phrase 'Don't tell stories, my child' ('Ne raconte pas d'histoires, mon petit'), typewritten over a shot of Godard, is immediately reversed as: 'Tell stories, my man' ('Raconte des histoires, mon grand').

Hence, if each image – defamiliarised, decontextualised and deallegorised – is effectively transformed metaphysically into a kind of epiphany, a manifestation of the mystery of cinematographic creation (one thinks ahead to Godard's appreciation in Chapter 4A of Hitchcock as the greatest creator of forms this century on account of the fact that what one remembers of his films are not the narratives but the visual details – objects at their most concrete because suddenly thrown into light), nevertheless it is the case that each image has the potential to be motivated rhetorically in recurring patterns and structures.[24] Moreover, it is precisely because Godard's poetics of montage embraces all forms of image and can subject them to similar processes of reversibility that it manages to reverse the overwhelming autonomy and self-sufficiency of painting – all images become equally 'present'. In short, Godard's videographic montage displaces and disperses the potential power of painting and prevents it – if only temporarily – from overwhelming and blocking the video flow. What counts above all is the performability and transformability of the image within a larger signifying system rather than any innate expressivity it may possess. Furthermore, this process, which, as the episode of the trains highlights, traces the relations between life and art, possesses a specifically historical dimension. Robert Bresson's 1945 film LES DAMES DU BOIS DE BOULOGNE, for example, produced during the last months of the Occupation and the beginning of the Liberation, is presented by Godard as a film of French resistance for lack of any other. Its penultimate scene of Élina Labourdette whispering 'I will fight' ('Je lutte') is linked poetically to the moment when the 'maquis of the Glières plateau' (a photograph is offered of Jean Moulin) was about to fall (in 1944). It is also juxtaposed on the soundtrack with a speech by General de Gaulle from London during the last stages of the war proclaiming the need for collective struggle. Such editorial manoeuvres allow Godard elsewhere even to suggest that montage – or the act of creating relations between people, objects and ideas – is, of itself, a form of history, indeed, that montage and history are the same process.[25]

Cinema as national event

What value, though, ought we to ascribe to Godard's rhetorical crossings? Do they carry Christian connotations of the cross as symbol of the crucified Christ, the Saviour and Word, an idea potentially at odds with the Jewish significance of the episode (Némirovsky, Haskil, the Holocaust, etc.)? This question is elaborated in the fourth and last sequence of 3A, where Godard develops the notion of cinema as a means of national renewal at a precise historical juncture. We move from a highly symbolic instance of aesthetic resistance – the lovers of LES VISITEURS DU SOIR – to the notion of cinematic form itself as resistance. There is once again a short bridging episode where Godard considers institutionalised remembrance – the celebrations for the fiftieth anniversary of the Liberation of Paris – and laments the present state of cinema and television. Such a media spectacle, he claims rather wildly, ostracises the likes of Guy Debord because French cinema never liberated itself from the Germans and Americans. Similarly, Japanese cameras will allow the dead to remain unburied and thus abandon once and for all the role once performed by poets. Godard then generalises the idea of resistance, moving from poetry as essentially a form of resistance (the example given is Osip Mandelstam) to a case of resistance in cinema, i.e. the only film to resist the occupation of cinema by America and Hollywood uniformity, Rossellini's ROME, OPEN CITY of 1945. It was natural that this event occurred in Italy because the country had twice betrayed according to Godard, and thus needed to reverse its total lack of identity. With ROME, OPEN CITY, the only time a (commercial) film was not made by people in uniform, Italy refound itself as a nation ('Italy simply regained the right of a nation to look at itself in the face'). Godard's further controversial claim here is that no other European country produced resistance films as such, not even Poland. Indeed, he summarily dismisses Munk's uncompleted THE PASSENGER (1963) (briefly glimpsed) and Jakubowska's THE LAST STAGE (1948) as films of expiation. After all, Poland, he states, ended up welcoming Spielberg, where 'never again' ('plus jamais ça') became 'it's better than nothing' ('mais c'est toujours ça', literally: 'but it's still that'). France during this period, meanwhile, was producing films like Claude Autant-Lara's SYLVIE ET LES FANTÔMES, a romantic comedy.

What is so remarkable about the nostalgic roll-call of Italian post-war films that follows, which seems more like an extended advert for an already well-covered period of Italian cinema (brief sequences juxtaposed from SENSO, THE LEOPARD, BICYCLE THIEVES, THE SWINDLERS, PAISÀ, GERMANY YEAR ZERO, STROMBOLI, BITTER RICE, LA STRADA, UMBERTO D., LA TERRA TREMA, AMARCORD, and THEOREM), is that Godard presents it in the form of silent cinema. A song by the popular Italian singer Ricardo Cocciante celebrating the glories of Italian as an all-embracing, inclusive and universal language is simply dubbed over the parade of images and allowed to play unhindered to its natural end. Godard also superimposes snatches of extracts (in their original) from Dante's *The Divine Comedy* and Ovid's *Art of Love*, assorted phrases of Latin interwoven with Italian around the themes of vision, imagery, light, change and divine power, ending with a statement on the immanence of love: 'Qui nimium multis non amo dicit, amat' (literally: 'He who says much and to many that he does not love, loves'). By allowing the images essentially to speak for themselves (some sequences, like that of de Sica's UMBERTO D., even retain their original editing, rare in HISTOIRE(S) DU CINÉMA), Godard is actually respecting the common production method of Italian cinema during that period. His argument is that what made ROME, OPEN CITY so unique and served to create a tide of Italian Neorealist films by Fellini, Visconti, Pasolini, de Santis, and so forth, was that the Italian and Latin poets of the past effectively 'passed over' the images since sound was never recorded on location at the same time as the images. Godard would seem thereby to be utterly faithful to Rossellini's adage (famously endorsed by the primary theorist of cinematic presence, André Bazin) which he types in at the end over an image of the director: 'Reality is there, why manipulate it?' ('Les choses sont là, pourquoi les manipuler?'). If important aspects about the production and technique of ROME, OPEN CITY are omitted here (the fact, for example, that despite its frequent newsreel appearance the film comprised simulations and reconstructions of recent events shot in the same location), it is because Godard proposes the film pri-

marily as an act of resistance against American cinema (a scene from a western in colour is briefly viewed). ROME, OPEN CITY was a totally unexpected
and spontaneous free artistic act, shot in adverse conditions beyond the limits of the studio system, and it realised cinema's full potential, unique
among the visual arts, to operate at a popular and national scale, literally
projecting an entire people's new, future self-identity. The sudden moment
when Italy beheld its own image was a rare, cinematic gesture of historical
incarnation, one that, as Marie-José Mondzain has shown, also originally
occurred in America where cinema provided the new country with an account of its history, the story of its birth.[26] For this reason, ROME, OPEN CITY
allowed cinema in some way to redeem itself after its abject failure to record
the Holocaust. Yet Godard actually goes further when he argues elsewhere
that only a Christian country like Italy could retrieve its identity so successfully in the image, since only the Christian religion is directly concerned
with images.[27] It is as though the history of a new cinematic movement must
necessarily enact a major transformation according to the narrative of the
Passion, the miraculous process whereby God incarnates himself through
Christ who, through His Passion (the Crucifixion and then Resurrection),
restores the visible and the fallen image of Man. This idea may help to explain the attention given here and throughout HISTOIRE(S) DU CINÉMA to the
agony of the Communist Manfredi's torture by the Nazis in Rossellini's
film. The idea is pursued in the following Chapter 3B, UNE VAGUE NOU-
VELLE, where Godard claims that the image is of the order of redemption
('careful, that of the real'), thus giving further significance to the quote attributed by Godard to St. Paul and which he cites constantly throughout
HISTOIRE(S) DU CINÉMA: 'The image will come only at the time of the resurrection' ('L'image ne viendra qu'au temps de la résurrection').

   ROME, OPEN CITY exemplifies Godard's idea of art as freedom and as exception (the sudden advent of Rossellini), and of identity through difference
(the Italian nation within Europe). Yet it is not on this social and historical
high note that Chapter 3A actually ends, since Godard also needs himself to
perform the specificity of film and video as a medium over and beyond its
capacity to record visual reality. What is at issue is precisely cinema as a process and art of manipulation. There is thus a sudden return to French in the
last series of captions, 'une pensée qui forme/une forme qui pense', a chiastic formation that harks back to the Manet episode (where we note *en passant*
that the idea of silent cinema was already evoked in Godard's phrase 'it was
silent cinema in the company of my Miss Haskil'). This chiasmus effectively
repeats the chiastic play of repetitions, double movements and corrections
that we have traced throughout Chapter 3A as one single moment of reversal. Indeed, one might say that the previous compulsive play of error and

association, encapsulated by the phrase flashed earlier on the screen 'the mechanical sentence starts up again', and where, for example, a reference to a wartime tune about a girl Marguerite was enough to justify an image of the young Marguerite Duras counterpointed by a phrase about torture from her late work *La douleur* (1985), has now been reversed into a single message. The perpetual movement of displacement, of error and *errance* has been finally controlled by a folding together of the Italian Renaissance and Italian modernism at the turning point of a chiastic inversion. The first part of the sentence is written over a black-and-white photograph of Pasolini head down and hidden by shades – this is intellectual thought in the agonising process of being formed – and then reversed over the small detail (almost impossible to recognise out of context) of a figure from Piero della Francesca's cycle of frescoes, *The Legend of the True Cross*. The detail – a head, elegant and serene, staring out of frame into the distance – is taken from the scene entitled 'The Exaltation or Restitution of the Cross' in reference to Heraclius's return of the cross to Jersualem according to the Golden Legend. Once again, therefore, we are dealing with a Christian image in terms of resurrection, and it is worth noting historically that this fresco was commissioned as part of an attempt to renew the Catholic Church by bringing together its different parts and engineering a *rapprochement* with the Eastern Church.

The linking of Pasolini with Renaissance art is, of course, a pure act of montage on Godard's part, a simple yet wilfully ironic manipulation which directly contradicts the spirit of Rossellini and his idea – typed by Godard on to the screen – that 'The camera is the screen'. Moreover, in conversation with Alain Bergala, Godard connects directly the idea of 'a thought that forms' not only with bad cinema (Pasolini is not specifically mentioned) but also with the State, i.e. with the controlling of thought rather than its spontaneous revelation through montage. Godard states: '"The State is the thought that forms." I believe more in a form that thinks [...] In cinema it's the form that thinks. In bad cinema, it's the thought that forms.'[28] The unexpected linking between Pasolini and della Francesca that Godard makes at the end of LA MONNAIE DE L'ABSOLU, one that ties together the two principal art forms explored during the episode, is exemplary of the type of transfer and poetic – as opposed to intellectual – thought proposed earlier in the Manet sequence. As such, it may to said to herald a new relationship between self and other and self and world defined in general historical terms, since Godard insists here on historical incarnation as part of a larger process of continuity and evolution, including that of Latin into Italian. Montage, not available to the other 'finer' arts, is what enables cinema to become something more than cinema and so qualify as art as defined by Malraux. It therefore has the value of an absolute with an extra-aesthetic, or rather trans-aesthetic, dimension. (To recall Adorno: where art is experienced purely aesthetically, it fails to be fully experienced even aesthetically.)

Of course, this is only a temporary point of resolution. HISTOIRE(S) DU CINÉMA comprises a serial structure and the proceeding *à suivre* already reverts back self-reflexively to Pasolini: a shot of the intellectual talking bird from his 1966 film, HAWKS AND SPARROWS. Yet what the sequence brilliantly reveals is that the figure of the chiasmus not only constitutes one of the defining features of Godardian montage, but also possesses in his work a specifically Christian dimension as the visual epitome of the Saviour's Passion and Redemption. It can be linked in this respect to another formal process in HISTOIRE(S) DU CINÉMA: Godard's identification by means of a small cross of the saints and martyrs of French cinema such as Jean Vigo, Jean Cocteau and Jean Renoir. Moreover, if we consider LA MONNAIE DE L'ABSOLU in its entirety, it could justifiably be argued that the four sequences constitute in themselves a (loosely defined) chiastic structure, the turning point of reversal being the crossing of trains: war/art/war/art (i.e. cinema as an art reborn after Auschwitz). Finally, Godard's joint emphasis on the physical aspect of montage and the spiritual act of incarnation accounts perhaps for his resurrection of de Rougemont's essay *Penser avec les mains* which, at a key historical juncture, preached the decisive and liberating violence of creative thought as an integral part of a universal 'dialectics of incarnation' to which even divine thought yielded with the agony of God's son on the cross.[29] For this reason, in addition to the phrases extracted by Godard in LE CONTRÔLE DE L'UNIVERS which conclude with the statement that an act is the judge of time and justifies Man's hopes for salvation, we might just as appropriately select others from *Penser avec les mains* such as the following: '*incarnation* is an act reducible neither to conformity nor an escape, and what is more – and this is crucial – will arise out of a surge of thought towards an end it invents or has seen. It's the thought that acts, which knows where it's going' (pp. 223-224; original emphasis); 'the act reincarnates us. The primacy of the spiritual is the primacy of the person creating, of the "thought that thinks" over "the thought that is thought"' (p. 247); and 'man in his capacity as man is truly a creator, but a creator created [...] and his limits are those of personal incarnation. That is his order and reality, and the place of his redemption' (p. 248). The transformative power of individual creative thought is what, both for Godard and de Rougemont, allows for and demands a personal moral judgment. In his own account during an interview of the complex train episode in Chapter 3A, Godard remarks: 'That is where the connection is. You can show the past and the present. A thought is there. A wish also to judge. There is a story.'[30] (Compare de Rougemont in a passage cited almost word for word in Chapter 4A: 'I believe in the appeal of facts. Let us consider the times and the places in which we live, our given particular situation, and the concrete appeal that thus emerges; and after that LET US JUDGE' (*Penser avec les mains*, p. 125).)

LA MONNAIE DE L'ABSOLU, then, offers a continually evolving analysis of the national and universal status of art. At the beginning, European art is presented as a reflection of European history and the constant struggle for power and conflict between city- and nation-states. This is to be contrasted with the direct encounter with the cosmos in Manet. By the end, however, a kind of clearing and resolution is reached: art must be seen above all in national terms since this is what ensures continuity, in the case of Italy, from the painting of the Renaissance to the renaissance of Italian cinema and Italy as a country with Rossellini. Indeed, the historical need for state and national identity is what gives art and cinema its primary motivation and meaning. Exceptionally, Italian Neorealism, being a genuine movement of the people – and this is Godard at his most residually Marxist – had nothing directly to do with the State which seeks above all to reproduce an image of itself. In fact, as a 'free act' ROME, OPEN CITY contradicted the many kinds of State-sponsored and sanctioned art that Godard is fond of listing in HISTOIRE(S) DU CINÉMA and elsewhere. In ALLEMAGNE ANNÉE 90 NEUF ZÉRO, for example, in addition to Velázquez and Giotto, he offers the example of Dürer who 'destroyed nature in his canvases' and is even proposed as the precursor and predecessor of Nazism. In FOR EVER MOZART, the message could not be more clear: nation opposes state. The rather conservative implication of this form of national aesthetics is that there can never be a total break with the past: even the most radical avant-garde expression or statement (e.g. Manet, Picasso), when placed and viewed in its national context, represents only a temporary and minor discontinuity within a larger, more fundamental continuity, that of artistic tradition. Yet in Chapter 3A Godard suggests, paradoxically, that it is as a direct result of being formed in regional and national terms that cinema as an art can accede to something transnational and therefore universal, eternal and transcendent. A film by Rossellini is of the order and sublimity of a fresco by Piero della Francesca.

The problem today, of course, is that in a unifying, post-Cold War Europe based on the free flow of capital, where the traditional model of the nation-state has become outmoded and with it the notion of national boundaries, a narrative of nation is no longer available to bridge the necessary recontextualising of meaning. It thus makes an event on the national scale of Italian Neorealism impossible to duplicate. Indeed, with the narrative of nationhood so deformed (Serbia being an obvious case in point),[31] and with all distinctions between East and West, past and present, at risk of being lost, art is increasingly irrelevant to the construction of a national identity. As Jeffrey Skoller has argued in his Deleuzian reading of ALLEMAGNE ANNÉE 90 NEUF ZÉRO, rather than ideas becoming universalised knowledge they are simply ill-remembered signifiers of a vague memory. Germany has become a deterritorialised world of signifiers of past events, he suggests, and the film in turn constitutes a flea market of allusions and references to a past of German culture and ideologies (Freud's Dora turns into Goethe's Charlotte Kestner, which leads to Thomas Mann's *Lotte in Weimar,* then Schiller, and so on).[32] Yet it could be argued, perhaps, that Godard's stubborn belief in some profound and always complex notion of national culture and identity within his massive elaboration of a pan-European imaginary is of salutary value at the present political juncture, since it serves to avoid what Jürgen Habermas has called in his discussion of the formal and functional transformations of the nation-state in post-Wall Europe 'the arrogance of post-nationalism'.[33] It is perhaps in this light, too, that we can best appreciate Godard's affinity with the French writer and media theoretician Régis Debray, with whom he has been the most forthright in his views on art as a specifically western (read: Christian) phenomenon now at its end.[34] Part of Debray's general project is a defence of the image and a reawakening of our obligations and duties to it. He is the author of *Vie et mort de l'image: une histoire du regard en Occident* (1992) which bemoans the current tyranny of the visual (the realm of the videosphere) and emphasises the need for otherness, incompleteness and the transcendental (as opposed to mere transparency). What is interesting, however, is how this approach goes hand in hand in Debray with a kind of national Republicanism expressed most recently in *Le code et le glaive: Après l'Europe, la nation?* (1999), an essay that proposes to examine 'a Republican conscience' and delivers a hatchet job on 'Euroland'. For Debray, the supra-national or federal model will lead to the worst possible outcome: nations without a State (i.e. inorganic bodies), and, at the top, a State without people (i.e. an organ without body), leading in the case of France back to the feudalism of the Ancien Régime.[35] While I do not wish to claim Godard as a political theorist in the same mould as Debray (Godard is, after all, an artist not a politician, and Debray needs to be viewed within a particular French political context that stretches from de Gaulle to the resurgence of the far right), nevertheless it is striking to note the similarities in tone and emphasis between Godard's strong sense of nationhood in cinema and Debray's desire to restore the discourse of passion and war (if not *la patrie*) as part of a tradition of nation-states that recognises the 'values' of a nation accreted over time, i.e. the barter (*monnaie*) of history which, Debray asserts, is currently being buried under the vocabulary of international banking and legalese. Debray argues vigorously that the concept of a new European mega-State based in Brussels denies the essential role of *lieux de mémoire* and of what he calls 'le tragique de l'histoire', which includes myth, the people, a shared heritage and a common will, factors equally foregrounded and valorised in HISTOIRE(S) DU CINÉMA.

I would like now to return to LA MONNAIE DE L'ABSOLU since the new Europe may, in fact, be only the most obvious figure of impossible unity and of the ongoing crisis of fragmentation and decontextualisation in Godard's endlessly self-reflexive work which is sustained by other forms of missed totality. I am thinking, for example, of the extracts and cited ideas linked poetically and chiastically across different forms and media in each main episode of Chapter 3A, in particular the details of paintings that refer to an outside whole and which alone justify Godard's repeated use in HISTOIRE(S) DU CINÉMA of the phrase: 'The perfect union of several voices prevents all in all the progress of one towards another' ('L'union parfaite de plusieurs voix empêche somme toute le progrès de l'une vers l'autre'), as well as of the statement (one of many by Robert Bresson cited in the work): 'If an image looked at separately expresses something clearly, and if it presents an interpretation, it will not transform itself on contact with other images. Other images will have no power over it, and it will have no power over images. Neither action nor reaction.'[36] I would argue, in fact, that Europe is really only a privileged metaphor for the more immediate problem of the process of cinematic and videographic form, specifically montage, because it operates for Godard as an eminently reversible concept. After all, his definition cited above of an ideal Europe in cinematic terms is similar to his dream scenario for the State funding of films in France, which imagines that if the State were really serious about funding cinema, it would out of obligation pay repertory cinemas to show a certain number of films a guaranteed number of times, even those lacking an audience.[37] Such reversibility of ideas raises the question of whether, in fact, there are any aesthetic limits to Godardian montage, for so omnipresent is the theme of Europe and European art and history, a veritable memory bank of images, that at times it seems merely to act as the spur for yet further chiastic formations, i.e. as a bankable quotient of recorded reality available for videographic creativity and its endless self-reflection. The more forms to be crossed through, the greater the possibility for reversibility, transfiguration and resurrection. From the painting of history to the history of painting, the trace of history becames essentially just another 'sublime' element, in the Kantian sense, too, of history being beyond our immediate comprehension.[38]

Yet again, therefore, what value ought we to attach precisely to the many chiastic moments crafted by Godardian montage? Do they represent simply

a compromise solution, a temporary stopgap of sense in lieu of a total meaning, whether of Europe or art or nation or history? I would like to suggest
that Godard's rhetorical play of montage itself forms part of the only theme
that can be said to unify Chapter 3A, that is, war and its resistance, a theme
which, as we have seen, is kept on the move in different forms as a political,
military, and artistic concept. To say that montage is itself the subject of interrogation and displacement for Godard is not simply to say that it constitutes a form of resistance to encroaching uniformity, that of the unified,
global super-present supplied by today's televisual and digital communica-
tions, where the different processes of history and memory, as well as of art
and culture, all risk being flattened if not cancelled out. Certainly, Godard's
practice of desynchronisation, translation, ambivalence, tension, mystery in
the complex folds and texture of videographic form, which results in a continued openness to the Other (whether defined as image, form, or idea),
amounts to a form of aesthetic and ethical resistance. In the concluding
chapter of HISTOIRE(S) DU CINÉMA, LES SIGNES PARMI NOUS, where he positions himself almost over-rhetorically as a film-maker/artist engaged in
combat with France as a morally bankrupt nation, Godard berates (in terms
not too far removed, ironically, from Gaullist fears of globalisation) 'the sys-
tematic/organisation/of unified time/the instant/that global tyranny'
(*Histoire(s) du cinéma*, vol. 4, pp. 279-286). Yet the question of montage in
HISTOIRE(S) DU CINÉMA is at once more involved and original than that. Let
us revisit Godard's inter-crossings of form.

These are, as we have seen, intense and dynamic moments of combination and crossing through artistic form, history, idea, even gender. Whether
Godard is moving into or away from details, filtering images (black and
white discoloured a bloody red at the start of 3A), splintering and reversing
texts (words cut in two, or into and sometimes over each other, the same
with music and the sounds of war), counterpointing art and cinematic image, or playing off an artist with and against himself or another (e.g. the different shades of Goya at the start of 3A, the pictorial image of a bridge
superimposed over the detail of another), the emphasis is always on movement and process, or *trans*, rather than on 'the between' (Deleuze)[39] or the
'*entre-images*' (Bellour).[40] Indeed, HISTOIRE(S) DU CINÉMA pushes to new limits what Kaja Silverman and Harun Farocki have correctly identified in PAS-
SION, namely a process (or trope) of transferral, transition, transposition and
transformation. In PASSION, they argue, where crosscutting is a privileged
vehicle for establishing the derivations of a term from its ostensible opposite, 'the transfer between the senses of sight and hearing represents a critical component of the Godardian sublime [...] a potentiality specific to
cinema'.[41] A full measure of the Godardian sublime operating specifically in

HISTOIRE(S) DU CINÉMA can be gained by referring to one of the most stunning aesthetic moves in HISTOIRE(S) DU CINÉMA, one that has already become a sticking point for the philosopher Jacques Rancière.[42] Towards the end of Chapter 1A, TOUTES LES HISTOIRES, where Godard evokes the power of wartime newsreels to redeem cinema's primary documentary status by presenting brief clips of George Stevens's colour footage of the Ravensbrück concentration camp ('39-44 martyrdom and resurrection of the documentary'), we are suddenly confronted with an extraordinary composite image: the moment from Stevens's own 1951 film, A PLACE IN THE SUN, when the rich heiress Liz Taylor rises from the embrace of Montgomery Clift, her right arm outstretched, and declares that she intends to marry him. The original soundtrack is replaced by a short extract from a viola sonata by Paul Hindemith, a key composer for Godard since the late 1980s,[43] and the action is stop-started. The image is then enframed by the operative detail from Giotto's *Noli me tangere* (the 'Easter Morning' scene in the Arena cycle of frescoes at Padua) which is turned around 90° so that it appears as if Mary Magdalene is descending from the clouds like an angel (the hands of the risen Christ are just visible bottom right of frame). This is a *détournement*, so to speak, of the sacred kind. In addition, Mary's outstretched hands seem to encircle Taylor, drawing her up into the heavens as if in the form of an iris shot. Christ's prohibition against touching ('Don't touch!') has been stunningly reversed in a new and unheralded form of touching across form, encompassing art, cinema and video – a kind of hyper-tripping and troping by Godard such that all the various elements banal and divine are stretched to their limit and reversed. It is accentuated by Godard's voice-over which states: 'O what wonder to look at what one cannot see/O sweet wonder of our blind eyes', words which rework those of the priest in Georges Bernanos's novel, *Journal d'un curé de campagne* ('O what wonder to be able thus to give what one does not own oneself, O sweet miracle of our empty hands').[44] As such, it forms a metapoetic comment on Godard's own process: on the subtlety of vision and recognition as opposed to mere sight, and, more specifically, on the videographic process itself, whereby a wake for the dead (the recorded trace of history as a graveyard of the dead) is transformed at moments like these into rapture ('martyrdom and resurrection').

Sublime crossings and transfigurations of this kind are the result of Godard's manipulation of montage as a form of thought, that is to say, 'thinking with one's hands' (de Rougemont). They constitute what Youssef Ishaghpour has aptly called *'images-pensées'*,[45] and display Godard's conceptualising power and consummate skill in inventing 'forms that think'. For this reason, they may be said to exemplify the authority of Renaissance painting that he is so fond of citing, that is to say, its force as an instrument of scientific knowledge and innovation. But these 'maximal' instances of metaphorical mastery, proof of Godard's enormous creative and poetic will, also risk becoming in themselves totalising interpretations. Sollers talks of Godard's incessant cogitation and meditation,[46] and Godard himself virtually admits that the process is compulsive, irresistible and potentially unstoppable when he types on the screen at one moment in LA MONNAIE DE L'ABSOLU that 'the mechanical sentence starts up again'. Chiastic formations even extend between chapters (1B, UNE HISTOIRE SEULE/2A, SEUL LE CINÉMA). In fact, Godard is always so far ahead of the viewer in making the intellectual connections and processing links across form and time that the result can feel like the opposite of a free, creative act. Moreover, it is hard not to question or even simply reject Godard's leanings towards the transcendent with his clutching of the details and shards of religious ideas and iconography as a nostalgia for the plenitude of meaning in cinema and art, another manifestation, perhaps, of that European nostalgic melancholy for the impossible. As Rancière has rightly stated, in the case of Giotto's *Noli me tangere*, Godard has effectively divorced the figures from their plastic and dramatic context (whose meaning, after all, was absence, separation and the empty tomb) in order to impose an absolute image, that of cinema's redemption.[47]

This is not the whole story, however. There is another way of looking at mystery in HISTOIRE(S) DU CINÉMA, one that is not necessarily religious, for there exists in Godard's videographic montage a secondary, counter-movement, what we might call a 'minimal' moment of metonymy. For despite their many obvious and different formats, physiques and dimensions, frames, some images are linked and moulded together by shape, contour, line, gesture, profile and outline. For example, at the start of LA MONNAIE DE L'ABSOLU, the image of one of the children's bodies being devoured by Saturn appears to marry the form of a *Disasters of War* image over which it is superimposed. Similarly, the shape and contours of some of the deathly forms from Goya's *Disasters of War* are taken up in the spread-out arms of Fuseli's *Lady Macbeth*, while superimposed approximatively over the figure of Binoche is de Staël's *Nu Couché*. To take the sublime episode of TOUTES LES HISTOIRE(S) that we have just encountered, a few seconds before, and as if in preparation for it, a Rembrandt etching *Self-Portrait: Wide-Eyed*, an eternally youthful expression of western subjectivity peering as if in disbelief at the horror down the line at Auschwitz, arises out of an image from Munk's film THE PASSENGER of prisoners performing Bach, such that the black lines of Rembrandt trace and link up with the black-and-white lines of the prisoners' uniforms (on the soundtrack Godard cites Malraux: 'art, that is to say, what is reborn in what has been burnt' ('l'art, c'est à dire, ce qui renaît dans ce qui a été brûlé'). Shortly afterwards, and following further instances of metaphorical crossing through Impressionism and different periods of religious painting (the black-and-white images of Rembrandt and Munk merging into Monet's (blue) *Impression: Sunrise*, which leads to the central sacred detail of Mary with the infant Christ from the Isenheim Altarpiece (in red), reversed immediately into the main detail of a St. John the Baptist's beheading), we see a still from Murnau's NOSFERATU of Count Dracula, his outstretched, cloaked arms interlocked with a detail multiply flashed of Picasso's *Guernica* (a major point of reference in HISTOIRE(S) DU CINÉMA because inspired by real and traumatic historical events and possessing eternal, resurrecting power). Finally, pictorial images of human faces looking up in agony and terror (again from Goya's *Disasters of War* series) complement Stevens's colour images of the gaping, open-mouthed, disembodied victims of the camps.

What we are witnessing here are really 'horizontal' moments of confluence, contiguity, conjunction and coincidence within the 'vertical' pull of Godard's rhetorical and imaginary manœuvres. They trace the inter-relations of human form at the level of silhouette, shape and figure. The roll-call of Italian Neorealism in LA MONNAIE DE L'ABSOLU, a series of emotional movements and gestures running from pain to sensual joy, is only the most overt example of this type of basic and spontaneous association and connection which is always material, proximate, local and specific. Moreover, such play of detail operates in complete silence since it is never directly commented on or integrated and rationalised as part of an argument or thesis. It is a pure, affective moment of seeing and feeling rather than of interpretation, and might even appear sentimental and naive in comparison with some of the dense, aggressive intellectual processes and formations that we have unpacked and described. A continuity in Godard's later work might be established if, like Aumont, we acknowledge that since FRANCE/TOUR/DÉTOUR/DEUX/ENFANTS, which explores the human body as the very paradigm of representation and expression, Godard has shared the former desire of western art to paint and show human feelings directly beyond language.[48] To put it another way, the non-linguistic resists any totalising conceptualisation or theorisation in HISTOIRE(S) DU CINÉMA and preserves its mystery. In the terms proposed by Jean-François Lyotard in *Discours, figure*, the sensible or figural is privileged over discourse. Lyotard's book was, of course, an attack on the structuralist project which, in his opinion, was too quick to translate things (historical material reality) into signs, thereby erasing the force or desire intrinsic to seeing. For Lyotard, on the contrary, the work of art offers desire not images in which it will be fulfilled and lost, but forms whereby it will be reflected as play and as unbound energy. Although he did not refer specifically to film, the views Lyotard presents are perhaps just as pertinent, if not more so, in the cinematic context. 'The transcendence of the symbol', he writes, 'is the figure, that is, a spatial manifestation which linguistic space cannot incorporate without getting disturbed, an externality which it cannot internalise into signification. Art is posited in alterity in its quality of plasticity and desire, curved extension, opposite to invariability and reason, diacritical space. Art wishes for figure; "beauty" is figural, unbound, rhythmic [...] All discourse has its *vis-à-vis*, that to which it is opposite [...] The cognitive function carries within itself that death which sets up the *vis-à-vis*, that death which makes the density of reference [...].'[49] In HISTOIRE(S) DU CINÉMA, the figural is above all the human figure at its most concrete and literal, and the work's meaning ultimately lies somewhere between the figural and the awesome reach of Godard's Sublime. That is why, finally, the concluding chiastic sequence of LA MONNAIE DE L'ABSOLU which marries the tortured face of Pasolini with the calm, enigmatic Piero della Francesca detail is so important, since it also marks a temporary break and resolution in the work's inherent struggle between sense and the sensible.[50]

The problem of resistance has thus become even more fundamental than our analysis of Chapter 3A had prepared us for, since the very form of HISTOIRE(S) DU CINÉMA seems consistently to be resisting the logic of Godard's rhetorical manoeuvres. The greater, more radical question of artistic 'exception to the rule' is therefore actually the work's resistance to its own constructions and primary processes through, paradoxically, a direct and immediate 'collaboration' of forms. The work essentially cuts itself loose at regular moments from Godard's guiding drive towards aesthetic sense and knowledge. Whether one sees this as a necessary masochistic move on Godard's part – and by that I mean as a healthy expression of creative impotence that preempts the pitfalls of total mastery and potential inaccessibility – is a matter for debate. What can certainly be said is that HISTOIRE(S) DU CINÉMA's own internal self-resistance through the tracing of boundaries between figures and objects is what, in fact, makes possible the general (metacritical) thematisation of resistance in LA MONNAIE DE L'ABSOLU. One might say further that Godard's singular oppositional stance in HISTOIRE(S) DU CINÉMA, by which he self-consciously resists totalisation (his own), is arguably the only artistic position possible when, in the face of the continuing massive horror of European history that he relays so powerfully to the viewer, he would surely prefer to court impotence, deadlock and failure indefinitely rather than risk the dogmatics of affirmation. The highly paradoxical nature of this last-ditch act of aesthetic affirmation, forced *in extremis* like the highly charged statement made in FOR EVER MOZART that: 'To resist means not to be had (from behind) by History' ('Résister, c'est ne pas se faire avoir par (derrière) l'Histoire'), might usefully be compared with that of the philosopher whom we mentioned at the very beginning of our discussion, Theodor Adorno. Like Godard, Adorno viewed the Holocaust as an end point of human civilisation and as a result had a sense of permanent catastrophe. Out of a defeatist politics of political pessimism, however, Adorno generated a compensatorily rich negative dialectics that constantly undermined and defeated any idealising synthesis, even though he never fully abandoned the concept of totality, or totalising idealism.[51] HISTOIRE(S) DU CINÉMA seems at times to move in the particular direction indicated by Adorno of contemplating 'all things as they would present themselves from the standpoint of redemption'. Perspectives, Adorno explained, 'must be fashioned that displace and estrange the world and reveal it to be, with its rifts and crevices, as indigent and distorted as it will one day appear in the messianic light'.[52] Godard's similar aesthetic strategy in HISTOIRE(S) DU CINÉMA perhaps explains his hesitant and oneiric final resort, but resort nonetheless, to one of the ultimate totalising and idealist concepts, that of creator, in the closing moments of the work.

In the end, HISTOIRE(S) DU CINÉMA defines itself above all by the notion of struggle and resistance, but not simply against culture, Europe, the State (to some degree all synonymous now for Godard), nor even, as was the case with Adorno, against easy readability (for Adorno, we recall, only difficult art and philosophy such as his own escaped reappropriation by the market system). More crucially still, the work is engaged in a process of internal self-resistance and struggle whereby it forms a connection, however uncertain, contingent and minimal, with the immediately human and social. If, in the last analysis, this unique creative resource is also to be described as a 'European art film' – and I think it should – it is precisely because it interrogates and reverses relentlessly the meaning of each of those terms and demands that we, in turn, reconsider and redefine received notions such as national and European art and cinema as part of our duty of discovering what Godard calls – in the form of an open, eternal mystery – 'the signs amongst us'.

8 The Evidence and Uncertainty of Silent Film in HISTOIRE(S) DU CINÉMA

Vicki Callahan

The radicality of Jean-Luc Godard's HISTOIRE(S) DU CINÉMA lies not so much in the dizzying bombardment of images drawn from the collected archives of cinema history, but rather in the parallel dislocation, equally vertiginous, presented by the problematic of the project itself. This project, a meditation on the relationship between the historical, cinematic, and moral planes of the twentieth century, is perhaps more concretely a reworking of the Bazinian question: 'What is cinema?' While this fundamentally ontological project is hardly new for film theory, or even for Godard (and is, in fact, the question posed by *every* Godard film), what is striking about this work is his invocation and utilisation of the silent era, and particularly the films of Louis Feuillade, as a pathway to answering this question. In this essay, I will argue that Godard's use of silent cinema, and particularly the cinematic mode of 'uncertainty' that Feuillade's cinema represents, serves as the foundation in HISTOIRE(S) DU CINÉMA for a poetic rewriting of the century's cinema and social history, a rewriting which, I shall suggest, has consequences not just for historiography but also for philosophy and, in particular, ethical issues of gender and identity.

A reference to Louis Feuillade's 1913-1914 silent serial FANTÔMAS appears near the end of Chapter 1A, TOUTES LES HISTOIRES, via an abbreviated quotation from André Malraux's *Esquisse d'une psychologie du cinéma*, and sets in place the ethical and epistemological frame for the rest of HISTOIRE(S) DU CINÉMA. The quotation in the video is as follows:

> The masses love myth and cinema addresses the masses. But if myth begins with Fantômas it ends with Christ. What did the crowds hear when they listened to Saint Bernard preach? Something other than what he said? Perhaps, no doubt. But how can we ignore what we understand when that unknown voice plunges deep into our hearts?[1]

Of particular importance in this quotation is the gap or hesitation between the word and thing (as evidenced by the gap by what is spoken and what is understood) – the inability of language to convey *directly* its intended meaning. And this gap between word and thing goes to the heart of Godard's at-

traction to silent era film-making, for silent film gives us the thing prior to
the oppressive conditions put in place by the name:

> The image doesn't name. Silent cinema was a great cultural and popular revolution.
> It didn't name, but we recognised everything and knew everything. With the sound
> film industry, we started naming again.[2]

As we can see from the full text of the original quotation by Malraux,[3]
Fantômas represents for Malraux a highly dualistic and moralistic universe
where good and evil are clearly demarcated. But Malraux's judgment of
Fantômas appears less interesting to Godard than the commentary's ability
both to foreground our gaps in speech-driven knowledge and to highlight
an alternative, but rarely pursued or recognised, mode of thought ('what we
understand when that *unknown* voice plunges deep into our hearts').
Godard's use of Fantômas in this instance is neither casual nor accidental,
and despite the fact that the references to Feuillade's films throughout
HISTOIRE(S) DU CINÉMA are often oblique and fleeting (beyond the Malraux
quotation, our only references to the crime serials are a FANTÔMAS poster
and the title: JUDEX), the debt to Feuillade is clear.

Feuillade's films, especially the crime serials, represent an alternative
path or counter history that defies the usual categories of cinema history –
the 'cinema of attractions' and 'classical cinema'. Neither exclusively driven
to 'show' a spectacular event nor to 'tell' a story, Feuillade's films present,
rather, a preoccupation with the limits of knowledge. In the FANTÔMAS series, for example, the overarching Manichean structure of good and evil
(implemented by the detective's pursuit of the criminal, Fantômas) is itself
put into question by the inability to discern what good and evil might be exactly. Indeed, the most salient trait aligned to the master criminal Fantômas
is that he is elusive or *insaisissable*, a 'quality' that is founded not so much on
strength or skill but on the fact that he is *unrecognisable* to the police or public
– or even his lovers and accomplices. Ultimately, this problem of
misrecognition in FANTÔMAS speaks to the larger issue of a crisis in *visible
evidence* – a crisis that is replayed in numerous Feuillade films.

A second, and important, reference to Feuillade occurs in HISTOIRE(S) DU
CINÉMA Chapter 1B, UNE HISTOIRE SEULE. The presentation of a photograph
of the silent era film-maker overlaid with the text, ERREUR TRAGIQUE, the title of a two-reel drama made by Feuillade in 1913, points to an ongoing fas-
cination that Godard has with the film. The title recurs in Chapter 3B, UNE
VAGUE NOUVELLE, and is mentioned both directly and indirectly in interviews with Godard.[4] The film's primary concern, like FANTÔMAS,[5] is with the
status of visual evidence. In ERREUR TRAGIQUE, a husband discovers his
wife's 'infidelity' via a close examination of a film strip (his wife has been

photographed accidentally in the background of a short comic film). While the raw data during the husband's examination of the film's individual frames irrefutably reveals the wife to be in the company of another man, the infidelity is merely the husband's projection. However, it is the apodictic quality of the image that serves as the legitimation of the husband's narrative. As Godard notes, the cinema's (and the photograph's) scientific side produces compelling testimony:

> Because even these days, if someone says your wife's cheating on you, you don't necessarily believe them. But if you see a photo there's something about vision which is considered irrefutable.[6]

However, Feuillade's film ruptures the closure of the banal story of adultery by *continuing* the story line (and better still, the obvious 'reality'). There is another narrative: the wife was in the company of her brother, thereby falsifying the husband's story line. What happens, Feuillade's film asks, between the individual frames, beyond the seemingly irrefutable given?

What is fascinating about HISTOIRE(S) DU CINÉMA is that Godard's method throughout the series *mimics* the husband's investigation of the search for evidence, but with a very important difference. At the very opening of Chapter 1A, we see a progressive and associative link of images from the still camera (the shifting, searching eyes of Jeffries (James Stewart) in REAR WINDOW as he looks through a telephoto lens) to an iris shot of a character with a magnifying glass, and then to a close-up of the eye itself *through* a magnifying glass. The still camera, the magnifying glass and the eye's isolation of data, or the single frame of information in the case of *Erreur Tragique*, all point to the *mistaken* vision found in the image in singularity – what Bergson calls the deception of ordinary or cinematographic knowledge. This is the idea that reality is but an assemblage of fixed moments or 'snapshots' which can be abstracted from time without any loss of veracity.[7] Thus, Godard moves to show us the way out of error with a shot of an editing machine presented in close-up, from an investigation of vision and the image to the complications put in place by *cinematic* vision, an image in *movement*. Here we can see not only a larger field of information to survey under the microscope, but the added dimension that a slice of time can be run forward, backward, or stopped, which the opening demonstrates to us via the actions of the Steenbeck as it appears to search a strip of film repeatedly. This process is then doubled by a fade-in of Ida Lupino (as Mildred Donner in Lang's WHILE THE CITY SLEEPS) dropping a slide into a hand viewer for inspection, and then the overlap of the two images together (Lupino and the Steenbeck). The soundtrack, slowed to an indistinguishable groan, now matches Lupino's every move (the first soundtrack 'matched' with the Lupino image, was from a separate film). As the image is slowed and then stopped, we see not only the subtleties of gesture as the woman drops the slide into the viewer, but also the space between the frames, since Godard places black frames into the sequence to highlight the illusion of movement and the simultaneously scientific (the detail of movement) and false information provided by the cinema. The scientific dimension emerges from the cinema's ability to give us any possible alteration from frame to frame, thus mimicking our own *ethical* options (we can choose one option over others at every instant), and highlighting the need for precisely such a tool of measurement. But the illusion is our daily belief that no other alteration or choice is available to us, in cinema or in everyday life. By foregrounding the black frames in the sequence, Godard points to other cinemas, other edits, other actions, other choices.

The crisis of singular vision is underlined for us by another important reference that occurs in the voice-over at the end of Chapter 1A (and is also seen in a soundless video clip from JLG/JLG: AUTOPORTRAIT DE DÉCEMBRE in Chapter 3A, LA MONNAIE DE L'ABSOLU). The voice-over, an abbreviated quotation from Ludwig Wittgenstein's *On Certainty*, is as follows:

> 'You have two hands?', asks the blind man. But it isn't in looking at my hands that I assure myself of this. Yes, why should I have confidence in my eyes if I am in doubt. Yes, why isn't it my eyes that I'm going to verify when I look if I see my two hands.[8]

The use of Wittgenstein here suggests more than a general skepticism about the limits of vision. What I believe is at stake, and what accounts for Godard's use of Wittgenstein in the opening of HISTOIRE(S) DU CINÉMA, is rather a larger consistency of philosophical method across these two theorists' works.

Wittgenstein's text is in large measure a response to the philosopher G.E. Moore's essay 'Proof of an External World'. To summarise Moore, there is a certain ontological *obviousness* to what we see and, in turn, a whole range of things that we can *know* based on sight. This is provided that the thing in question is not merely 'presented' but can be 'met with in space',[9] and is '*logically independent* of my perception of it at the time'.[10] Now this last caveat is particularly interesting in that this *eliminates* things like dreams, shadows, hallucinations, mirror images or reflections of any sort, that is to say, the very entities that are used ordinarily to call into question the truth status of vision. Thus, to prove existence of an external world, Moore says simply: 'Here's one hand and here's another'.[11] According to Moore, this is an event which we could all test, that is, physically investigate to see if it is true. No doubt such a test would not satisfy the skeptic, who could propose an *infinite* number of possible scenarios to invalidate the claim, but in that case, *nothing* would be useful as evidence.[12] To put this another way, Moore claims he *knows* the existence of an external world because to dispel the skeptical alternative (that I may be dreaming, for example) would be a *logical impossibility* (i.e. there would never be enough tests which could be performed as proof).

Wittgenstein's response to Moore is not simply to say, 'yes, but what if you were dreaming, etc.'. Rather, he takes issue with Moore's comment that to *know* his hands are in front of him is the same thing as *knowing* that an external world exists. Moreover, we would like to believe, Wittgenstein states, that what we know 'guarantees it is a fact'. However, 'one always forgets the expression, "I thought I knew"'.[13] The use of the term 'I know' does not at all provide the obvious certainty implied by Moore as the phrase is not dependent on any sort of fixed standard or tests. Wittgenstein writes:

> 'I know' often means: I have the proper grounds for my statement. So if the other person is acquainted with the language game, he would admit that I know. The other, if he is acquainted with the language game, must be able to imagine *how* one may know something of the kind.[14]

Thus, certainty has, paradoxically, a particular quality of contingency. It is not that the word 'certainty', or any other word, is meaningless or illegitimate, but rather that it is dependent upon our ability to use the term correctly in a given context, or, as Wittgenstein puts it, in a 'language game'.[15] That is, there is no essential quality to the meaning of any word but rather *similarities*, or *family resemblances*,[16] that enable the consistent use of a term, like certainty, in a particular setting. Our participation in a language game is thus the correct *performance*[17] of a given word's usage. To put this another way, words have no essential meaning in *isolation*.

It is this slippery and *performative* status of the term 'knowledge' or 'certainty' that Godard appears to appropriate. Furthermore, this is the lesson of the silent era's cinema before the naming, that is, the cinema before the fixity of language, narrative, and sound. This is also the lesson from Feuillade's ERREUR TRAGIQUE since, despite the most careful scrutiny of the image, the husband still did not account for the gap in the narrative. Before condemning the wife, we need to know the context of the image, the field of frames that surround it, no matter how much we believe the truth to be definitely before us. It is this factual illusion of the image in isolation – or in the seeming isolation of the cinematic image endlessly flowing onward without a break between the frames – which provides for a form of tyranny in the image, and even tyranny in our everyday lives. Thus, the *'usine de rêves'* is easily transformed into a factory of horrors as Godard demonstrates for us with an extremely slow overlap dissolve between Chaplin and Hitler in

Chapter 4B, LES SIGNES PARMI NOUS (Chaplin seems to mutate gradually into Hitler).

What is of interest here is not only the proximity of good and evil and our inability to discriminate between the two, but the fluidity and potential alteration of matter in the frame. This is what the cinema shows and alternatively attempts to conceal through language and narrative: that even matter can be transformed by time. The cinematic frames register this process of transformation. A predictable and sequential organisation of the frames lends us the notion of certainty as obvious, natural and immutable. But any disruption of linearity, or the sequential, points us toward an 'escape' from matter as a fixed or certain entity. Hence, Godard defines the cinema as 'doing' metaphysics, that is, *performing* the possibilities of being:[18]

> Cinema is there to do metaphysics. Moreover, that's what it actually does although no one sees it, or rather those who do it don't say so. Cinema is something extremely physical on account of the fact that it is a mechanical invention. It is there for escape, and to escape is of the order of metaphysics.[19]

There is no break or contradiction between the metaphysical inclinations of the cinema and its scientific or mechanical qualities. Rather, what you have is an ongoing exchange of possibilities and experimentation. It is not a teleological explanation of being that such a metaphysics implies, but a radical notion of movement and choice in any direction as possible. In this light, it is easier to read the second iteration of ERREUR TRAGIQUE in Chapter 3B. Now the film title is overlaid on a blank cinema screen – the empty screen drawing attention to the multiple possibilities contained therein rather than a fixed image.

The empty screen suggests not only the myriad possibilities of the next frame, but can also be seen as referring to the space between the frames itself. One might read ERREUR TRAGIQUE's projection on the white screen as the reversal – both metaphorical and literal – of the black space between the images. The attention to gaps or the interstitial space between the frames is a key element of HISTOIRE(S) DU CINÉMA.[20] Beyond the often long stretches of black frames noted above in the Lupino example, Godard also uses short and sometimes single-frame edits, inserting (or more accurately cross-cutting) black-and-white frames within a film clip to induce a type of flicker effect. This technique is in place in the opening moments of Chapter 1A as Godard edits extra black frames into a sequence from KING KONG (when Fay Wray is filmed by an on-screen cameraman) as a way of demonstrating the spaces between the unfolding frames of the cinema image. Hence, the *potential* arbitrariness of the linking of images is clear, and, like ERREUR TRAGIQUE, another narrative can emerge. Godard also points to another history coextensive to our fictional film past by juxtaposing and relentlessly cross-cutting not only Hollywood and Nazism throughout the series, but also Lenin and Soviet montage film-making (indeed, sometimes all these groupings interspersed). The title for Chapter 1A is TOUTES LES HISTOIRES, that is, 'all the histories,' and as Godard notes at one point in the chapter, this entails a plural sense of history (the commentary states at first, 'avec des s', and then a reminder of the Nazi heritage, 'des SS';[21] the Chapter 4B slow dissolve noted earlier between Chaplin and Hitler demonstrates the proximity and intersection of these histories). He follows this comment with remarks that point to the breadth of the possibilities therein: 'all the histories that could have been, that will be, that were'.[22] Between these shifts in verb tense are the possibilities of other histories to be witnessed. The gap has not been closed for us, and there are multiple histories to be written.

This understanding of history is consistent with Godard's use of Wittgenstein. For while Godard's reference to Wittgenstein's language game foregrounds the context of an image, it is also important to remember that the notion of context is itself somewhat specialised. The larger epistemological lesson of Wittgenstein's 'language game' is that there are no *fixed meanings*, although they are somewhat fixed with the context of the game (this distinguishes Wittgenstein's position from radical skepticism or relativism). Godard clues us into his historical method in Chapter 1A which starts with the Bresson quotation, 'Don't go showing all aspects of things. Leave for yourself a margin of indeterminacy'.[23] To be precise, the quotation, like many if not all quotations by Godard, is altered from the original Bresson text which states: 'Don't show all aspects of things. Leave a margin of indeterminacy.' Godard's alteration of the Bresson statement shows us a philosophy as action, process, movement.

Moreover, what might be inserted in this undefined margin, in the historical/narrative gaps, is also of interest in terms of methodology. In one extraordinary sequence from Chapter 1A, immediately after announcing the range of his historical project, 'all the histories that could have been', Godard induces a type of false flicker effect through the overlap of three separate images: (i) Godard in his library, (ii) a Norma Shearer publicity photograph, (iii) the crop duster sequence from Hitchcock's NORTH BY NORTHWEST. He then intercuts the three images with the Hitchcock sequence slightly dominant (i.e. in terms of time on screen). The 'flicker' effect is produced by overlapping at least two of the images and bringing the individual images into view by quick iris-ins and iris-outs with the white background of Shearer's publicity photograph enhancing the effect. Godard thereby inserts himself into the history of Hollywood cinema and foregrounds his position as a *commentator* on that history. That is to say, Godard is not at all implying that this history is *objective* or *the only true history*. In addition, Godard's opening of 1A includes the vertically positioned and disjunctive spelling out of the word *histoire(s)*, so that *toi* (you) appears alone in the gap of the word and is repeated. The technique suggests both an interpellation of us as viewers to this history and a place for us within this history (as agents, spectators, historians).

The crucial dimension behind these multiple histories is that they are neither autonomous nor relative. Rather, we are forced by the juxtaposition of images and the gaps in between to make a relational inference or correspondence amongst the materials. It is, in effect, a *poetic* history, as Godard makes clear to us with the ending of Chapter 1B, UNE HISTOIRE SEULE. Here, Godard quotes a passage (again, an edited or altered passage) from Martin Heidegger's essay, 'What are Poets for?':

> Poets are those mortals who sing solemnly sensing the trace of the gods that have fled, who stay on the gods' tracks and so trace for mortals, their brethren, the road for turning back. But who, among the mortals, is capable of detecting such a trace? Traces are often not apparent and are always the legacy of a summons that is barely foretold. To be a poet in a destitute time means to attend, singing, to the trace of the gods that have fled. That is why at the time of the world's night the poet utters the sacred.[24]

The tone of Heidegger's essay, the 'time of destitution', is matched by Godard's relentless display of images from the most horrific moments of this century. But for Heidegger (and Heidegger is using a reading of Rilke's poetry to make his point), the period is 'destitute' not only as a result of the events themselves – it is also a product of our perspective and memory:

> The time remains destitute not only because God is dead, but because mortals are hardly aware and capable even of their own mortality. Mortals have not yet come into ownership of their own nature. Death withdraws into the enigmatic. The mystery of pain remains veiled. Love has not been learned. But mortals are. They are, in that there is language. Song still lingers over their destitute land. The singer's word still keeps to the trace of the holy.[25]

Thus, the 'turning back' from the destitution requires a new mode of thought performed for us in HISTOIRE(S) DU CINÉMA by the Steenbeck's replaying and forwarding of the film and the restoration of a certain amount of memory ('the trace of the holy'). Before we can turn away, we must first face the horror: 'In the age of the world's night, the abyss of the world must be experienced and endured. But for this it is necessary that there must be those who reach into the abyss.'[26] The poet leads us to a different awareness and into a type of being 'in the world', which Heidegger demarcates as the

'Open', a 'space' that cannot be accessed by representation and exists independently of human consciousness.[27]

How does the poet help us reach the 'Open'? The method of organisation in Godard is not strictly speaking an association but rather, as Gilles Deleuze notes, a process of 'differentiation'.[28] We can see this mode of operation at work in other Godard films, for example COMMENT ÇA VA, a film that is also an extended exploration on how we see and what we know. It opens with the statement: 'a film between the active and the passive'. The key term as Deleuze points out in another context (ICI ET AILLEURS and SIX FOIS DEUX) is the conjunction 'and':

> It is the method of BETWEEN, 'between two images', which does away with all cinema of the One. It is the method of AND, 'this and then that', which does away with all the cinema of Being = is. Between two actions, between two affections, between two perceptions, between two visual images, between two sound images, between the sound and the visual: make the indiscernible, that is the frontier, visible (SIX FOIS DEUX). The whole undergoes a mutation, because it has ceased to be the one-Being, in order to become the constitutive 'and' of things, the constitutive between-two of images.[29]

But how precisely does this method of 'and' operate in Godard? Most crucially, we need to look at the workings of montage which, as we know, is one of Godard favourite topics (and Chapter 4A, LE CONTRÔLE DE L'UNIVERS, features a special homage to the master of montage, Alfred Hitchcock). Godard depends, like early cinema and Feuillade, on the 'shock' cut. The clearest proponent of this editing strategy from the silent era is, of course, Georges Méliès. In Méliès the use of stop motion photography is used to create a 'trick effect': a person disappears, limbs and heads are excised from the body (and sometimes reassembled), vehicles are subjected to precipitous falls (which crumble but leave the occupants to emerge none the worse for wear). This is usually done, however, within the context of a science fiction or performance venue (the conjurer) and produces laughter and surprise, rarely disorientation or disturbance. In the case of Feuillade, the 'trick' effects and 'shock' cuts occur within a seemingly everyday setting. In the crime serials, Feuillade mixes realist *mise-en-scène*, the long take (and usually deep space) tableau, and an urban detective narrative in *conjunction* with the 'shock' cut. Here the cuts are not playful or performative, but rather traumatic and unexpected. *Suddenly,* the character falls from an upper story window or over a cliff with often an equally *sudden* appearance of someone below to rescue or capture the person imperilled.[30]

It is this ongoing juxtaposition of the 'realistic' and the 'illusory', of the 'documentary' and the 'fictional', that propels forward so much of

HISTOIRE(S) DU CINÉMA. Of course, the slippage between real and unreal states is not new for Godard (nor the interrogation of the modes therein), but what is new, or at least qualitatively different, is the speed with which we must deal with the shock. We move from beautiful, and indeed sublime, images from art and nature to explicit and gruesome scenes of animal slaughter, war, executions and imprisonment. Functioning much like the lingering static shots of resplendent nature (in terms of Deleuze's 'differentiation') in JLG/JLG and NOUVELLE VAGUE, there is a certain relentless focus on the images of the grotesque in HISTOIRE(S) DU CINÉMA. This is yet another parallel with Feuillade as a number of unusually gruesome crimes are carefully detailed for us, especially in FANTÔMAS. HISTOIRE(S) DU CINÉMA challenges the viewer to watch the brutality, and, anticipating our glance away, repeats the images for us again and again. Thus, there is a doubled effect of the repeated shock within the frame (the grotesque) and across frames (from the sublime to the grotesque). And, of course, the strategy is consistent with our journey to Heidegger's 'abyss'.

Deleuze calls this radical disjunction between edits an 'irrational cut', a technique that produces a particularly interesting effect. Deleuze is referring to UNE FEMME MARIÉE but his remarks are equally descriptive of the structure of HISTOIRE(S) DU CINÉMA:

> From this perspective, the internal monologue gives way to sequences of images, each sequence being independent, and each image in the sequence standing for itself in relation to the preceding and following ones: a different descriptive material. There are no longer any perfect and 'resolved' harmonies, but only dissonant tunings or irrational cuts, because there are no more harmonics of the image, but only 'unlinked' tones forming the series. What disappears is all metaphor or figure.[31]

This disappearance of metaphor and figure does not signal the death of all meaning in Godard and thereby an exclusive focus on *aesthetics* rather than language or politics. Rather, what Godard is gesturing towards are new forms of meaning, expression, and thought, and the politics that emerge as a result. However, if perception is suspect and metaphor vanishes (direct and indirect access to a thing), then can we still communicate, can we still 'write' an *histoire(s)*? Perhaps the most explicit answer to this question comes in Chapter 2A, SEUL LE CINÉMA. The episode opens with Godard in discussion about the 'work of the historian' and he underlines there the need for a 'precise definition' or 'scientific' quality in his method. Shortly after we are presented with a segment entitled 'Envoi 1' which features a lengthy video sequence (almost to the end of the episode) of a young woman reading excerpts from Baudelaire's 'Le Voyage'. In the context of Godard's comments about science and history, we can see the poem directing us away from linear or rational methodology. As the text from Baudelaire as cited in HISTOIRE(S) DU CINÉMA reads: 'Man's fortune is absurd; the goal can change its place,/ And, being nowhere, can perhaps be anywhere!'[32] The slippage and ambiguity of meaning noted in Baudelaire's poem is visualised for us by a clip from THE NIGHT OF THE HUNTER cross-cut with an earlier part of the reading. Here, the children escape the threat of the preacher (Robert Mitchum) by taking a boat down the river, this voyage passing quite quickly from immediate danger to an idyllic and dreamlike universe where an inversion of nature to man, in terms of foreground and background, seems to take place. As Deleuze points out in his discussion of the sequence, 'the whole of nature takes on the responsibility of the children's movement of flight, and the boat where they take refuge seems itself a motionless shelter on a floating island or conveyor belt'.[33] To put this another way, the human subject is no longer defining or controlling the universe exclusively. Nor is a shift of background meant to foreground an absence of meaning or to imply man's fundamental passivity. It is as if the film has flipped sides of a mirror or performed a type of rapid inverted rack focus to give us a reversal of perspective. The effect is to open up vision or thought and promote what Heidegger might call a 'releasement' towards the world (and into the 'Open') – a type of knowledge or thought 'beyond the distinction between activity and passivity'.[34] The interesting aspect of 'releasement' or 'meditative' thought (as opposed to calculative or rational thought) is that it is always in *movement*, a process of 'going toward' an object or 'moving-into-nearness'.[35] But this meditative thinking can never be an end point, for 'we presage the nature of thinking as releasement. Only to forget releasement again as quickly'.[36]

It is this movement of thought and history that Godard's cinema projects for us, a movement between beauty, sexuality, eroticism, pornography, and back again, or between nature, children, machines, war, death, and back (or any other number of variations and linkages). The pattern of progression is not linear, but rather *recursive*. As Douglas Hofstadter comments:

> Sometimes recursion seems to brush paradox very closely. For example, there are recursive definitions. Such a definition may give the casual viewer the impression that something is being defined in terms of itself. That would be circular and lead to infinite regress or paradox. This is because a recursive definition never defines something in terms of itself, but always in terms of *simpler versions of itself.*[37]

The visual style of recursion is seen most clearly according to Hofstadter in M.C. Escher's works. Here, the reversal is in place from foreground to background and back again, but simultaneously, in the space of one image.[38] Godard's HISTOIRE(S) DU CINÉMA functions similarly, perhaps most strik-

ingly in a sequence from Chapter 3A, LA MONNAIE DE L'ABSOLU. Godard
uses multiple fade-ins and outs with two overlapping sequences: one from
Hitchcock's THE BIRDS (the moment when the birds attack the school house),
and a documentary clip from wartime footage of a bomber on the attack
(this second clip was actually used in Chapter 1A over the Malraux commentary on FANTÔMAS). The sequence is initiated by the words 'What is cinema?' ('QU'EST-CE QUE LE CINÉMA?') written over a close-up of the
tortured and bloodied resistance fighter Manfredi (Marcello Pagliero) in
Rossellini's ROME, OPEN CITY, then cuts to documentary scenes of massacres
(two shots in sequence, one repeated from the first episode). The audio track
is taken from Jean Cocteau's LE TESTAMENT D'ORPHÉE: 'what horror' ('quelle
horreur'). The first answer we receive in text form to the question 'what is
cinema?' is 'nothing' ('RIEN') placed on an all black screen. Now the recursion becomes most explicit. The bird sequence and the bombing sequence are overlapped so that both appear equally visible in the image: the
birds are flying up and off the playground bars to begin their attack on the
children as the bomber drops down in the sky, the counter motion up and
down within the frame by the two images mapping a type of recursion in itself. Again, alternating back to the black screen, the text asks us: 'what does
it [cinema] want?' ('QUE VEUT-IL?'). Another angle of the visual recursion
within the frame is displayed: the children run down the hill towards the
camera at a diagonal as the other image has the plane cutting across the
frame left to right in a lateral movement. The text answers (still on black
background): 'everything' ('TOUT'). Now a new level of reversal takes over,
and one image fades up or down in relation to the other with first the Hitchcock sequence dominating, then the bombing. It produces a type of flicker
effect similar to Chapter 1A's NORTH BY NORTHWEST/Shearer/Godard sequence. The text poses another question: 'what is it [cinema] capable of?'
('QUE PEUT-IL?' over a black background), which is followed by another title card: 'something' ('QUELQUE CHOSE'). The absolutes put in place by
the text ('RIEN'/'TOUT') are displaced by the end of the sequence by an
ambiguous 'quelque chose' – not the thing in itself, but the possible, which
is demonstrated by the visual recursion. It is also interesting to note that this
particular sequence is followed rather quickly (within a few frames) by another visual reference to the JLG/JLG sequence that quotes Wittgenstein's *On
Certainty*.

Of course, most cinema tries to shut down these gaps, the possible rever-
sals, and this is usually done through the workings of narrative. Like the
husband in ERREUR TRAGIQUE, classical cinema will fill in any gaps in evidence by supplying the most 'obvious' or 'self-evident' story line. Here, the
woman's trip to the park, to the space outside the home, cannot be innocent

but is being overdetermined by a sexualised scenario (cinema being, as Godard frequently notes, obsessed with only two stories, the girl and the gun). When the narrative inevitability of this trajectory is altered a type of dislocation may occur. The husband runs to his wife's rescue but is too late to save her from his act of sabotage (her carriage has an accident). Neither relieved that the husband has arrived on time (although fortunately the wife survives), nor filled with grief that he is late (since she does live), we are rather left only with a vague sense of disturbance... with something. This is the general pattern and effect of Feuillade's crime serials. In the early serials, FANTÔMAS and LES VAMPIRES, the detectives and journalists chase the criminals endlessly. The criminals constantly metamorphose (through costume or, in LES VAMPIRES, through multiple leaders of gangs) beyond recognition. The structure is not only non-linear (circular and repetitive, but without any real end point or achievement), but also, like the visual pattern described above, recursive (gangs pursue the virtuous and vice versa). Or often in Feuillade's crime films the narrative lines are multiplied – there is more than one gang, sometimes working against, sometimes working for the main gang. And some criminals turn to 'the other side' (the law), but often only to turn back again. We are then made aware that there is not one narrative but *numerous* narrative lines that we must follow... numerous *histories*.

HISTOIRE(S) DU CINÉMA also makes an explicit link with the narrative suspension of silent serials. The ending (or lack thereof) of the serial film is mimed at the close of each episode of HISTOIRE(S) DU CINÉMA with its use of the title card 'à suivre' ('to be continued'). But these open endings might also be read as a reference to the multiple histories in circulation. Anne-Marie Miéville's LE LIVRE DE MARIE is connected physically to Godard's JE VOUS SALUE, MARIE via the title card 'en ce temps-là' ('at that time'), a type of structure found repeatedly in the silent serial. For example, the scripts for FANTÔMAS are filled with expressions like 'au moment où' ('at the moment when', or 'just as'). The imminent reversibility of all events signified by the phrase is then visualised by those abrupt or irrational cuts seen in both Feuillade and Godard. In the case of LE LIVRE DE MARIE and JE VOUS SALUE, MARIE, by linking their two films in this manner (Godard repeats the phrase throughout JE VOUS SALUE, MARIE), Godard and Miéville appear to be suggesting not so much that the two Marys are one and the same, a child then a woman,[39] but rather that there is a multiple pathing of history(ies) and narratives.

It is important to remember that the strategy of recursion in Feuillade's films, as in Godard's, operates not only at the level of narrative but also at the visual. The bodies and costumes of the master criminals Fantômas (René Navarre), in the series of the same name, and his *femme fatale* counterpart

Irma Vep (Musidora) in LES VAMPIRES, function as moving screens (or frames within frames). These mobile screens, signified by the black *maillot de soie* (a tight form-fitting bodysuit), have the eerie effect of both drawing attention to, and denying, the physical properties of difference. They are a type of moving reversal image; the stark black figure on the often brightly lit and spare surroundings are the ultimate recursion. And if one recognises that the recursion happens across films, from FANTÔMAS to LES VAMPIRES, as well as across sex/gender boundaries, then the potential of the recursive moment to visualise the political implications of the poetic comes to the foreground. The centered, cohesive self drops out in poetic language, where, as the theorist/film-maker Trinh T. Minh-ha notes:

> There is no 'I' that just stands for *myself*. The 'I' is there; it has to be there, but it is there as the site where all other 'I's can enter and cut across one another. This is an example of the very strength and vitality of poetical language and of how it can radically contribute to the questioning of the relationship of subjects to power, language and meaning in theory. Theory as practised by many is often caught in a positioning where the theorist continues to stand in a 'safe place' to theorise about others.[40]

The poetic is not then in this instance an example of solely formal preoccupation, but a radical rethinking of fundamental categories, beginning with the subject, the 'I'.

At times, Godard's HISTOIRE(S) DU CINÉMA seems to be an elegy written particularly for the silent era – a series in mourning for the lost promise of another kind of cinema, a cinema of uncertainty and possibility. There is another important silent film reference that must be addressed in this context. Léonce Perret's LE MYSTÈRE DES ROCHES DE KADOR of 1912 occurs prominently in Chapters 1A and 2A of HISTOIRE(S) DU CINÉMA, and glimpses of the key image from the scene flash repeatedly throughout the entire work. While the particulars of the narrative are too convoluted to do it justice in a brief exposition, it is perhaps instructive to note the following. A young woman (Suzanne de Formel) has been led to believe (in error) that she has shot and wounded her beloved (Captain Jean D'Erquy). This piece of misinformation induces in turn amnesia. In an effort to cure his fiancée, D'Erquy enlists the aid of a professor whose area of research includes 'the application of cinematography to psychotherapy'.The professor *restages* the original trauma of the shooting, and thereby demonstrates that Suzanne was, in fact, drugged throughout the shooting. The amnesiac suddenly emerges from her catatonic state, stands before the now blank screen, gestures wildly and faints. The woman's *true* history is restored, and, as the title card states: 'she cries... she is saved!'.

It is this last sequence of the woman rising before the all white screen that is repeated in Godard's series. Here, Godard points not only to the curative powers of the cinema, but more particularly to a desire to restage and restore a *history* (and *histories*) of the cinema and the traumatic events of this century on this empty screen. That this cure is acted out on the woman's body is not without interest. Women scholars, especially feminists, have discussed at length the role of women in Godard's films, but it is a matter of some debate within this group whether or not Godard is critiquing or reinforcing patriarchal representations of gender.[41] While it is beyond the scope of the present article to address the many difficulties raised by women scholars with respect to Godard's presentation of gender and sexuality, I would like to propose that we use the silent film LE MYSTÈRE DES ROCHES DE KADOR as a starting point to rethink some of the issues of gender raised by Godard's films, or at least in the work dating from his first collaboration with Miéville, ICI ET AILLEURS, to the present.

The woman in LE MYSTÈRE DES ROCHES DE KADOR is an hysteric, her body excessively acting out both loss of memory (the catatonia) and the cure (the melodramatic gesture on memory's return, the flailing arms, the loss of consciousness). But where precisely are the curative powers of the cinema in LE MYSTÈRE DES ROCHES DE KADOR? Suzanne's encounter with the screen is much like our encounter with HISTOIRE(S) DU CINÉMA, that is, we see a history that runs back (the restaging) and forward (the alternative narrative possibility). So it is the movement backwards as much as forwards that is crucial here, indeed the very aspect of movement itself. Suzanne's immobility mirrors her rigid reading of the Captain's wound – that it must have come from her hand. Her illness is the product of her inability to perceive an alternative possibility or an image in movement. But this is not the only part of the cure. Suzanne's renewed health, signalled by the movement of her hands to her face in recognition, is interestingly enough not a *self*-recognition (the reenactment has been staged without her help, with another woman). That is to say, Suzanne's cure is the result of the image on the screen projecting a 'truth' back to her about the possibilities of the event, and in turn herself. Her cure is not simply being able to see the 'truth' of the shooting, but also her identification as a *possibility other than herself*. Or rather, she identifies beyond her presumed self, to another aspect of her self – a type of simplification or recursive experience yet again.

The emphasis, then, is on the performative quality of the states. It is not only that the body is signalling the change, but that the change itself can be sudden and dramatic – a quantum shift. We have a type of 'irrational edit', but now at the level of the body rather than the film material, and the radical gesture draws our attention to our recursion between figure and ground,

between two seemingly opposing entities (mad/sane). Critical attention
should thus be focused not so much on *if* Godard uses oppositional pairs of
women (the virgin/whore dichotomy is particularly troublesome), but on
how he uses the oppositions to foreground manifestations of gender as *per-*
formances of gender. The slow and stop motion of HISTOIRE(S) DU CINÉMA returns to a scientific investigation of the gesture (e.g. Lupino and Ray in the
opening moments of Chapter 1A), which runs parallel to a similar scrutiny
of the voice (think of the screams and groans from the Steenbeck and
Godard's manipulation of his own voice throughout). There is also the reference in both JLG/JLG and HISTOIRE(S) DU CINÉMA to Ray's JOHNNY GUITAR,
'lie to me, tell me all these years you've waited'. In all of these instances, the
dissonance created between sound and image, or between words and inflection, functions like the 'irrational cut' focusing our attention to the gaps
in our performance of gender. More radically, if we remember that Godard's
larger understanding of cinema is read through his filter of 'metaphysics'
(the openness or emptiness of *matter*), then an attention to the woman's *body*
would be consistent with Judith Butler's reading of the category of sex as itself a type of performative utterance – a category that is constituted
through, and naturalised by, the reiteration of particular norms. This process is not a unilateral or always efficient one since an ongoing series of constructions and destabilisations of the 'subject' is enacted. Perhaps most
importantly for our context here, these repetitions or performances of sex
occur in *time*.[42]

And this, I think, is the key to Godard's 'métaphysique': the break in the
sequencing of the frames is a break in time, in that process of repetition and
naturalisation. Godard's project thus remains 'faithful' to the altered opening quotation from Bresson, 'Leave for yourself a margin of indeterminacy'.
It is the ongoing process of alteration at every level of the text that prevents
the closure of the 'one' margin. To put this another way, the recursive strategy embedded at the heart of HISTOIRE(S) DU CINÉMA (the quoted text/im-
age only slightly different) opens up the text into a matrix organisational
structure, where the 'I' and the 'not I' and the 'you' all intersect. To put this
back in the poetic language of Trinh T. Minh-ha: 'I am not I can be you and
me'.[43]

It may seem peculiar to some feminists to utter Minh-ha and Butler's
names in the same breath as Godard's. However, if we look at the larger theoretical framework and politics behind these different projects, I would argue there is more than a little intersection of methods and goals. Some have
chosen to read this methodology spiritually (in the sense of transcendence)
or formally (ambiguity read solely as aesthetic experimentation). Yet I
would like to suggest that Godard's HISTOIRE(S) DU CINÉMA has potentially

profound ethical implications (and his comments about the cinema of resistance throughout HISTOIRE(S) DU CINÉMA – especially Chapters 3A and 4B –
and in interviews would reinforce that perspective). As Deleuze notes,
'Godard's aim is "to see the boundaries", in other words, to make the imperceptible visible'.[44] The cinema of the impossible is more radically a cinema of
the possible. It cannot be emphasised enough just how boldly Godard's
later work demonstrates by example rather than precept the infinite possibilities for change that lie within our reach – starting with the thing Godard
knows most intimately, his past experience of the cinema and his current
hands-on practice of the transformation of the moving image. At several
points throughout HISTOIRE(S) DU CINÉMA, Godard asks us, with Denis de
Rougemont in mind, to 'think with our hands' ('penser avec les mains'), a
radical merger of body and mind where matter is not *determined* by rational
ideas, social constructs, and essentialist politics, but reaches outside this oppressive modality to embrace alterity as a way of being.

9 The Crisis of Cinema in the Age of New World Memory: the Baroque Performance of KING LEAR

Timothy Murray

> Monads 'have no windows, by which anything could come in or go out'. They have neither 'openings nor doorways'. We run the risk of understanding the problem [of Leibniz] vaguely if we fail to determine the situation. A painting always has a model on its outside: it always is a window. If a modern reader thinks of a film projected in darkness, the film has nonetheless been projected. Then what about invoking numerical images issuing from a calculus without a model? [...] The painting-window is replaced by tabulation, the grid on which lines, numbers, and changing characters are inscribed (the objectile) [...] Folds replace holes. The dyad of the city-information table is opposed to the system of the window-countryside.
> (G. Deleuze, 'What is Baroque?')

In *The Fold: Leibniz and the Baroque*, Gilles Deleuze borrows from the late twentieth century to visualise the curvilinear patterns of thought that distinguish Leibniz's 'folds' from Descartes's 'lines'. For a rather simple comparison, Deleuze turns to the cinematic apparatus to contrast the illumination of its projections with those 'lines of variable inflection' which are characteristic of numerical images. The code of the latter highlights a radical structural change that Deleuze attributes initially to the thought of Leibniz. The shift occurs when 'the surface stops being a window on the world and now becomes an opaque grid of information on which the ciphered line is written'.[1] Although Deleuze here cites the grids of Rauschenberg and the lines of Pollock, he concludes *The Fold* by dwelling on the 'new Baroque' quality of the numerical music of Boulez and Stockhausen. At the heart of the Baroque 'fold' for Deleuze lies the transformational force of its cultural impact: 'To have or to possess is to fold, in other words, to convey what one contains "with a certain power". If the Baroque has often been associated with capitalism, it is because the Baroque is linked to a crisis of property, a crisis that appears at once with the growth of new machines in the social field and the discovery of new living beings in the organism.'[2] Rather than illuminate a pregiven process of conceptualisation and its concomitant social order, the growth of new social machines, from the line painting to the digital sound, provides the mechanism for 'deterritorialisation' and new sets of previously incompatible social groupings and fabulations.

If the promise of the Baroque can be thought as a crisis of property, its contemporary spectre is nowhere more haunting and baffling in Deleuze than in the field of cinema. While *The Fold* contrasts the projection of cinema with the Baroque lines of numerical painting and synthetic sound, *Cinema 2: The Time-Image* turns to Leibniz and the crisis of perspectival 'property' to understand the radicality of the shadow and the depth of field which Welles introduced to cinema. This same book concludes similarly to *The Fold* by reflecting on the 'change of force' wrought by the procedures of 'serialisation' shared this time by Boulez and... Godard. In cinema, insists Deleuze, this serialisation results in a transformation through which characters are less windows of the world than serial elements 'of the will of force' through which the world view becomes open to new and unpredictable procedures of 'fabulation'. The 'property' of cinema is understood by Deleuze in relation to the radicality of its unfolding tales and representations. Yet few social fields have been placed into so much crisis by the growth of 'new Baroque' machines as has cinema. The new machines are those of electronic replication, of course, with their digital duplicating systems that sometimes make redundant the need for actors, props, and craft itself, from design to lighting to cutting. Digital editing systems, to cite one example, both shorten the process of production and transform the messiness of crude, manual procedures of visualisation into slick, technical translations of virtualisation. Many of the most difficult techniques of montage can now be enacted by the unpractised initiate through the simple procedure of clicking a mouse. Segments of film, moreover, can be downloaded on the web or burned on to DVD in a way that challenges the integrity of the print and its distribution. Even the culture of cinema has been transformed by the growth of digital cinematic machines. Not only are cinematic segments readily downloadable on the internet but the amateur discourse of cinema has proliferated with list-serves, celebrity sites, amateur cinema reviews, electronic journals, CD-ROMs, and DVDs. Just such a crisis of cinematic property, from the specialised magic of computer generated imagery (CGI) to the generalised terms of amateur net chat, must be understood as constituting essential threads of the growth of cinema and the terms of its theorisation.

It may seem ironic to readers now mournful of the cutting-edge dominance of Godard and his French peers, those readers convinced also of the death of (French) cinema (which Roger Leenhardt once lauded as 'Baroque'), that I understand the crisis of cinematic property wrought by the digital revolution and its new film culture to be somewhat of a natural extension of the legacy of Godard and the uncanny prescience of his tenets and practices. Discussion of this suggestion, however, necessitates a shift of focus away from many of the New Wave's critical innovations, such as its break from the traditional of literary adaptation promoted by the French Cinema of Quality and its celebration of the singular role of the cinematic 'auteur', not to mention its distancing in the early sixties from the Left Bank movement and its emphasis on the political value of cinema. What Godardian cinema shares with the new media, notably with its independent strains, is its particularly baroque sensitivity to a crisis of property that links the new and the old. By this, I am thinking not simply of the representation of property in crisis, such as is figured differently from the sides of East and West, in ALLEMAGNE ANNÉE 90 NEUF ZÉRO, or represented in FOR EVER MOZART as a horrifying struggle over the property of ethnic identity 'in this Europe not purified but corrupted by its sufferings'.[3] In Chapter 4A of HISTOIRE(S) DU CINÉMA, LE CONTRÔLE DE L'UNIVERS, Godard appropriates passages from Denis de Rougemont's *Penser avec les mains* (1936) to suggest that the crisis pertains to the soul of Europe and its self-representations: 'in this Europe of today, there are two sorts of nations, those one calls old and those one calls rejuvenated, those that have maintained a certain number of possibilities but don't know much what to do with that freedom which they brag about, and those that have waged or suffered since the wars a revolution of the masses and have maintained freedom of opinion, that is to say, the freedom to protest, but without deep passion'.[4]

This double crisis of action and passion is linked further by Godard to the crisis of representation itself. Again citing de Rougemont: 'I wouldn't want to speak ill of our tools but I would like them to be employable/if it's generally true that the danger lies not in our instruments but in the weakness of our hands/it is no less urgent to specify that a thought which abandons itself to the rhythm of its mechanisation renders itself literally proletarian.'[5] For Godard, the popular mechanisation of the apparatus reflects not merely the numbing split of the European condition but also the concomitant decline of the thoughtful promise of cinema itself. Godard consistently voices concern about the ability of late twentieth-century cinema to match the ontological fabric of the twentieth century whose traces he laments as fading on the miniaturised monitors of television and its digital offspring: 'Cinema is higher than us, it is that to which we must lift our eyes. When it passes into a smaller object on which we lower our eyes, cinema loses its essence. One can be moved by the trace it leaves, this keepsake portrait that we look at like the photo of a loved one carried with us; we can see the shadow of a film on the television, the longing for a film, the nostalgia, the echo of a film, but never a film.'[6]

Embalmed in such an enigmatic discourse is something like a chiaro-scuro-effect. The shadow, the longing, and the echo – the composite picture of Godard's scattered thoughts on cinema and culture requires his readers' frequent adjustment to his prose's quick and jarring movements between the apparatus, property, thought, and cinema. Consistently evident, however, throughout HISTOIRE(S) DU CINÉMA and his later interviews is Godard's linkage of the property of the transformation of cinema to how his cinema thinks the crisis of property, particularly in relation to past terms of troubled growth in the social field. This conflation of cinema with a crisis of property is, I hope to suggest in the following pages, what uncannily aligns Godardian cinema (and its thought) with the coda of a 'new Baroque' aesthetic caught between clashing systems of visual projection and digital information.

The mess of avoidance

A vibrant picture of the clash of new film culture with the memory of the privileged visual systems of the past appears in Microsoft's CD-ROM, 'Cinemania', in which the likes of Roger Ebert or Leonard Maltin share their casual responses to cinema with the user of the personal computer who now has the 'full' repertoire of history, shorts, publicity stills, and star data at her finger tips. One two-star review by Maltin speaks so presciently to the crisis faced by the legacy of Godardian cinema that I've decided to shape the framework of this essay around an excerpt: 'Bizarre, garish, contemporary punk-apocalyptic updating of the Shakespeare classic. There's little to be said about this pretentious mess except... avoid it'. The 'pretentious mess' is none other than a film by Godard, his 1987 adaptation of KING LEAR. To some degree, this film certainly represents the slippage of cinema in the face of a resurgent American film culture and the resistance of Godard himself to the demands of this culture. The idea for the film is said to have arisen spontaneously at the 1986 Cannes Film Festival when Godard met the infamous Menahem Golan and Yoram Globus of Cannon Films. Their first and only exchange while crossing the street led immediately, according to Godard, to 'a fast deal' penned on a cocktail napkin for a $1,000,000 adaptation of KING LEAR, to be directed by Godard and to feature the writer of its script, Norman Mailer, as King Lear.[7] Godard's film opens by replaying the director's taped phone conversation with Golan who called to pressure the director to make good on the promise to deliver the film by the 1988 Cannes Festival. The film then screens footage of the two initial takes of the first scene in which Mailer protests Godard's shaping of his script, followed by Mailer's sudden and permanent departure from the set (along with his $100,000 scriptwriter's fee and his $250,000 actor's salary). Add to this folly the fact, recounted by Godard, that he, the director, had never read Shakespeare's play prior to signing the deal ('Of course I'll read it before I shoot. People tell me it's a great story, but it's just one I've heard of, like the story of Carmen or the story of Mary'[8]). The prehistory of Godard's film thus bears all of the traces of the mess it is reported to be by more than one critic: 'By turns slapstick and funereal, self-mocking and pretentious, Godard's LEAR could almost pass for a student film were it not for some talented presences [Norman Mailer and his daughter, Kate, Burgess Meredith, Molly Ringwald, Peter Sellars, and Woody Allen].'[9] Clearly not a film by a student of Shakespeare, Godard's KING LEAR stands out at the end of the twentieth century as much more than a platform for marquee actors. I will argue that it conveys a stunning portrayal of the challenges of the cultural loss of property and the recovery of 'a certain power' in the new social field of cinema. What is recovered, however, is less a classical adaptation of Shakespeare than a thoughtful reflection on the promising structures of cinema in the post-traumatic condition of its cultural decline.

Twice early in the film, a voice-off evokes the post-nuclear trauma that sets the stage for Godard's take on the great story: 'And then suddenly, it was the time of Chernobyl and everything disappeared, everything, and then after a while everything came back, electricity, houses, cars, everything except culture and me.' While perhaps a reference to the waning value of the auteur directing the action, the 'me' here actually refers to the film's central protagonist, William Shakespeare, Jr. the Fifth (played by Sellars), whose voice provides the grainy texture of many of the film's voice-overs. The task of young William is to fulfil the charge set jointly by the Royal Library of the Queen and the Cultural Division of Cannon Films: 'to capture what had been lost, beginning with my famous ancestor'. Throughout the film, Will, Jr. walks around with a notebook jotting down overheard phrases that seem hazily familiar to him. Is it merely coincidental that William shares the task faced by Jean-Luc, his director, to capture the loss of the cultural capital of the (more and more frequently) unread Shakespeare, if not to recoup the losses of cinema itself? Could lack of acknowledgment of this linkage between cinema and the mnemonic losses of Shakespeare account for the extreme dislike of the French KING LEAR as expressed by both critical slants cited above, which reflect the amateur tastes of American movie culture and the cultural expectations of 'classic Shakespeare' on film?

There is certainly no reason why Shakespeareans would need to appreciate Mailer's Mafioso rendition of the plot in which Dom Learo attempts to divide his entertainment laden crime kingdom between his daughters. Similar modernisations of *King Lear* have been accomplished more successfully in innumerably different ways. Yet what should not be undervalued here is Godard's repositioning of the text, post-Mailer, in the discourse of the modernist genre *par excellence*, cinema. In addition to respecting the play's insistence on a father's confused struggle with his three daughters, Godard introduces the terms of his film as he speaks from voice-off following Mailer's sudden departure from the set. In addition to Lear with the three daughters, Godard picks up the script with a sensitivity for the theme of 'Kate with three fathers': 'Mailer as star, father, me as director: too much indeed for the young lady from Provincetown'. What appears initially to be yet another adaptation of Shakespeare *on* film, evolves from the opening moments into an articulation of Shakespearean themes *in* cinema, in the history of cinema. This becomes particularly apparent when Godard's KING LEAR is considered in the context of the film-maker's retrospective sense of its place in HISTOIRE(S) DU CINÉMA. Given the relative obscurity of his messy KING LEAR in film history and criticism, it is fascinating that HISTOIRE(S) DU CINÉMA includes multiple references to the film's conceptual dialogue and the Shakespearean text, as well as multiple stills from the film and conceptual commentaries on many of its visual strands whose status is rather obscure in the Shakespearean adaptation. This relative prominence of KING LEAR is particularly evident in the telescopic version of the printed text, *Histoire(s) du cinéma*, notably the fourth volume, where textual and imagistic references to the film stand out. As suggested by its conceptual prominence in HISTOIRE(S) DU CINÉMA, what remained to be captured by Godard in creating his KING LEAR might be said to be twofold: cinematic representation and the thought of cinema *as* representation.

Cinematic representations

Cinematic representation is harnessed throughout the film via frames and traces of the artistic images of civilisation that remain with us in the hazy decline of post-nuclear/post-Cold War culture. Although William's voice-offs in KING LEAR are focused primarily on textual retrieval, they reveal that post-nuclear/Cold War cultural recovery – the kind called for in ALLEMAGNE ANNÉE 90 NEUF ZÉRO and FOR EVER MOZART – will go astray if it sticks too close to the misleading academic insistence on the convenient separation of histories of image and text, of theatre and cinema, of Shakespeare and Godard. Exemplary of Godard's classic montage of text and image, the characters of KING LEAR reveal that the post-nuclear age has fused moving images with static words in a way that lends little solace to previously comforting cultural points of view and orientations which now lie 'twisted without reason, as if perspective has been abolished... [as if] the vanishing point has been erased'.

Echoing Cordelia's match of attractive body and frozen tongue, silent images from the history of art that are screened prominently throughout the film, from the delicate female drawings of da Vinci and Vermeer to the female subjects of Manet, Morisot and Renoir which Cordelia (played by Molly Ringwald) peruses during her many quiet moments. It is almost as if painting's silencing objectification of female beauty figures the condition triggered by Cordelia's forceful silence in Shakespeare's play, and, conversely, as if the contemplative female subjects of classical painting best represent the silent cinematic introspections of Cordelia. The legacy of painting is evoked at the commencement of the film (directly after Mailer's departure) as William, Jr. flips through a photo album that includes a shot of Renoir with three actresses, about which William says that '[Renoir] was keen on young girls like his father Auguste, father, father'. The three girls, the three fathers, the history of the leer, might not these branches of the family tree of cinematic painting be signified by the film's enigmatic intertitle, '3 Journeys In To King Lear'? The same images by da Vinci, Vermeer, and Manet that fill the space of Cordelia's solitude are reprinted in *Histoire(s) du Cinéma*, vol. 3 (pp. 49-57). Succeeding the double framed phrase 'des ténèbres de l'absolu' on pages 46-47 (an interesting conflation of Chapter 3A's title and subtitle, LA MONNAIE DE L'ABSOLU and LA RÉPONSE DES TÉNÈBRES), these silent female images evoke, haunt, or supplement the loss of cinematic plenitude: 'les célèbres et pâles sourires/de Vinci et de Vermeer/disent d'abord moi/moi/et le monde ensuite'.[10] Regarding the painterly quality of HISTOIRE(S) DU CINÉMA, Godard stresses that the video

> belongs to painting history and it's pure painting, but cinematic painting – it's a part of cinema that been given away by most people... But I like those people [in the painting] to say words, and then there is a drama – but drama painted like that. Not like in a novel. Very often I look at paintings and I say to myself: What is he saying? Those people – what are they thinking of? I remember my very first article was a comparison between a Preminger picture and Impressionist painting. Maybe it's not possible, but to me it seems possible – it is my cinema.[11]

Might not just this performative aspect of the painterly subject be precisely what Godard stages in KING LEAR when the spectator watches Cordelia looking at paintings in a way that opens the space of thought: those people, what are they thinking? Might not Cordelia herself stand in for the figure of

Berthe Morisot in Manet's *Le Balcon* whose image reprinted in *Histoire(s) du Cinéma* (vol. 3, p. 49) bears a montaged interpellation preempting the spectator's question in a way that reclaims thought for the silenced subject: 'Je sais à quoi tu penses'? As made evident by the interweaving in HISTOIRE(S) DU CINÉMA of pictures featured in KING LEAR, the historical stuff of artistic visualisation is as much the property of cinematic adaptation as is the composite memory of Shakespeare on the screen (with the significant difference being how the Cinema of Quality's faithfulness to fictional narratives gives way here to the imagery of art history and the weird jump cuts and dissolves of their screened memory and mediated thought).

In a similar fashion, the figures and sounds of cinema itself, from the European cinema of Grigori Kozintsev, Robert Bresson, Jean Renoir, to the American movie culture of Woody Allen, Burgess Meredith, and Molly Ringwald, intrude frequently in KING LEAR as the shadow of something about Shakespeare and cinema which remains to be noticed. How KING LEAR bears the marks of the history of cinema itself is made evident from the beginning of the second opening of the film, after the departure of Mailer and his Kate. Here William Shakespeare, Jr. wonders 'why did they pick me? Why not some gentleman from Moscow or Beverly Hills? Why don't they just order some goblin to shoot this twisted fairy tale?' As young William flips through his album of famous directors, stills of famous directors appear on the screen as William enumerates the ghostly presence of cinema's past by imagining which gentleman might be appropriate for the task: 'Marcel [Pagnol], yes. "Kenji [Mizoguchi] yes, of course... François [Truffaut], I'm not sure, Georges [Méliès], yes, definitely, Robert [Bresson], yes, Pier Paulo [Pasolini], yes, Fritz [Lang], yes, of course, of course'.

In the wake of this ghosting of cinema's many fathers, this viewer is struck by the curious surfacing of stills and citations from Godard's KING LEAR at key moments in Godard's HISTOIRE(S) DU CINÉMA, as if somewhat of a retrospective homage to the enigmatic traces of the history of cinema itself. Consider how the overhead shot of waves crashing against the shoreline which opens and closes KING LEAR follows in the wake of the graphic, 'SEUL LE CINEMA/LA BEAUTÉ', in HISTOIRE(S) DU CINÉMA 4A. Crucial to an understanding of the role of representation in Godard's KING LEAR, this shot and intertext are accompanied in HISTOIRE(S) DU CINÉMA 4A by a cautionary voice-over concerning the need for the urgent return of artistic thought and its vicissitudes. Of course, the inclusion of KING LEAR's waves in HISTOIRE(S) DU CINÉMA also alludes coyly to the prominent legacy of the textual classics and their thoughtful provocations in Godard's KING LEAR. Godard's film depicts how the Shakespearean text is recognised and transcribed in bits and pieces by the interloping descendent who seems to recognise Shakespearean verse as if aided by something of a trans-generational phantom: 'As you wish, which, watch... wITchcraft... As You Like It, that's it', exclaims young William after eavesdropping on the conversation between an old man ('Learo') and his young daughter at an adjoining table. While Virginia Woolf's modernist experiment *The Waves* is discovered in its entirety amidst the refuse of the shoreline (references to this text open and close the film), the classical text of Shakespeare is recovered only by the arbitrary reassemblage of its language, line by line, phrase by phrase, as uttered by the cultural unconscious of the post-nuclear public. Readers of the book *Histoire(s) du Cinéma* will surely notice how the Shakespearean text once unknown to Godard surfaces to provide the lines voiced over the montaged images of the New Wave's 'intensity'. In volume 3, following the phrase typed over a photograph of Woolf: 'Dieu, que je peux souffrir! C'est terrible d'avoir le don de tout ressentir avec une telle intensité' ('God, how I suffer! It is awful to have the gift of feeling everything with such intensity'), we read the words: 'she's gone for ever/I know/when one is dead/and when/one lives / lend me a looking glass'.[12] This extract is juxtaposed visually with an image from the climax of Godard's 1968 film ONE PLUS ONE, the moment when Anne Wiazemsky is borne aloft on the platform of a crane which is also carrying a camera. At issue throughout both KING LEAR and HISTOIRE(S) DU CINÉMA, then, is a challenging reflection on the possible recovery of visual representation in the wake of the loss of its most cherished figures, from image to thought.

Abolished perspective

Perhaps something like the missing mist of the stone, the failed mimetic return of the looking glass, constitutes the representation of the perspectival shift that links the challenge of the new (media) age to the crisis of representation so prominent in Shakespeare. One of the most enigmatic moments in *King Lear* occurs in the final moments of the play, when Lear makes his final plea to the unyielding stone:

> And thou no breath at all? Thou'lt come no more,
> Never, never, never, never, never!
> Pray you, undo this button. Thank you, sir,
> Do you see this? Look on her! Look, her lips,
> Look there, look there!
>   (Act V, Scene iii, pp. 306-311)[13]

In Shakespeare, Lear's enigmatic command appeals to his audience to act as a sort of go-between, to join him in seeing and acknowledging the captivating enigma of the figure of nothing: the death of the daughter and the disempowerment of sovereign perspective. Re-enacting his imagined representation of Cordelia's living trace on the stone, Lear dies while redirecting the viewer's vision to a side-view of whatever it is that we imagine remains 'there' and the fragmented conditions of interpersonal relations promised by it.[14] In Godard's KING LEAR, young William's mournful line 'as if perspective has been abolished' transfers into the cinema the enigmatic deictic gesture with which Lear leads us to his death: 'Look there, look there!' Reenacting Lear's imagined representation of an abolished perspective in need of reparation, Godard's KING LEAR positions the enigma of the empty look as the deictic gesture most characteristic of the challenge of this film (just as HISTOIRE(S) DU CINÉMA similarly cites these lines to imagine the living trace of the New Wave's expired 'intensity').

The film's intertitles describe KING LEAR three different times as a film 'Shot in the Back'. Clearly related to the film's destruction of perspective (which is traditionally established from a frontal view), this provocative intertitle might also refer to Godard's betrayal of the realistic codes of cinematic and dramatic adaptation. More than once, for example, Godard positions his two primary protagonists, William, Jr. and Cordelia, so that they face away from the camera at important moments in the film. The viewers' first introduction to William comes from the back, as he faces away from the camera and gazes out across a body of water while asking in voice over, 'Am I in France?'. During their first cinematic interaction in the elegant restaurant of the Hôtel Beau Rivière in Nyon, Cordelia sits with her back to William as he addresses her from his adjacent table (in response to which Don Learo, as Mailer terms his Mafioso protagonist, punningly accuses Shakespeare of 'making a play for my girl'). In the following scene, when three silent muses follow William down a country road, one of them mimes Shakespeare's writing gestures from behind his back. And two scenes later, when Cordelia reads aloud to her father her sisters' rhetorical telegrams attesting to their unbridled love for Learo, she does so while looking out on a hotel balcony so that her back is turned to the camera, her father, and her viewers. 'Shot in the Back', Shakespeare and Cordelia are portrayed less as the tragic presences of this tale with whom the viewers will identify, and more as the mediating screens through which – and between which – the performance of language, affect, and cinema must pass via the abolition of conventional cinematic perspective and Shakespearean pity and fear.

This reversal of convention also animates the form of Godard's productions. In contrast to the architectonics of the film palace through which, we learn late in the film, 'light must come from the back', Godard prefers to in-vert the conventions of lighting in production to achieve a consistently enig-matic chiaroscuro effect. Rather than positioning artificial lights behind the camera, Godard reverses the process so that the camera shoots light coming from the back of the set:

> I see contrast. It's a way of having two images, far away from each other, one dark and one sunny. I like to face the light, and if you face the light, then contrast appears and then you are able to see the contours [...] I like to not have the light in the back, be-cause the light in the back belongs to the projector, the camera must have the light in front like we have ourselves in life. We receive and then we project.[15]

Godard situates light 'There', 'in the Back', as if to thrust the viewer on to the horizon of deictic space whose iterative referent 'there, there' is cut free by Lear from the clarity of perspective's anchor. What follows, 'there, there', is the uncertain trace of projection.[16]

No thing

Just such a framework of the uncertainty of perspective's loss is foregrounded by one of the voice-overs opening the film as 'a good way to begin'. It is the sound of Norman Mailer who, in his short-lived role as Lear, introduces the viewer to the central epistemological dilemma bequeathed to Godard from William Shakespeare the Senior: 'words are one thing, reality another thing: between them, NO THING'. Between them, in other words, lies the enigmatic thought of cinema as epitomised by Godard's 'way of having two images, far away from each other, one dark and one sunny'. Be-tween them is also the voice-over description of William, Jr.'s arrival in Nyon, 'between Italy and Germany, between the woods and the water'. Also between them lies the graphic intertitle that reappears at infrequent in-tervals throughout the film as a marker of cinematic thought itself: NO THING. 'So that [Don Learo] can silence this silence of silence', says Shake-speare Junior in a voice-over midway through the film, 'he listens as if he's watching television. But Cordelia, what she shows in speaking is not NOTHING but her very presence... her exactitude'. Between them, between Learo and Cordelia, then, lies not the amnesiac sounds of televisual viewing through which Learo, in listening to his daughters, 'hopes to see their entire bodies stretched out across their voices', as Junior so electronically states it. Between them lies something much more exact: Cordelia's presence, or what lies between reality and words. NO THING.

Conversely, this phrase split between itself of what lies there, between frames, between images, between words, and between Lear and Cordelia, doubles as the graphic embodiment of the interval itself, NO THING. It seems plausible that the thought of culture missing from the casino and entertainment world of Don Learo resonates on the horizon of the interval whose temporal resistance to the different folds of the present, past, and future was annihilated by the NOW of Chernobyl and its expansive nuclear fusion.[17] 'Holding/in both hands/the present/the future/and the past', so Godard writes in HISTOIRE(S) DU CINÉMA 4B, 'un roi peut/achever un règne/mais on n'achèvera/jamais l'histoire/de ce règne' ('a king may complete a reign but the history of that reign will never be completed').[18] It seems likely that the recovery of the thought of history will entail a rethinking of the horizon itself, marked as it is by the postnuclear, postcommunist reality of Chernobyl and by the dispersion of the frontiers of national and ethnic identity, from Kozintsev's Russia and Kurosawa's Japan to Godard's France and Woody Allen's America.[19] If we think back to William, Jr.'s first appearance in KING LEAR, moreover, we will realise that the rethinking of the horizon of history must also entail the rethinking of cinema itself: 'I remembered what Pluggy told me years later about editing, "handling, physically, in both hands the future, the present, and the past".'

The challenge of positioning the horizon in relation to the productive suspension of the analogue movement of temporality is brought home by the film's seeming refusal to mark its end with the traditional credits that fix the boundaries of its national locations and financial sponsors. After a graphic intercut declares 'The End' of KING LEAR, the film begins anew, however briefly, by introducing viewers to the man in charge of editing Cannon Pictures now that 'Chernobyl is long past'. After Chernobyl, the conventions of closing the film seem to have been altered as much as those that opened Godard's KING LEAR. Played by Woody Allen, the editor sports the appropriate name of Mr. Alien. Introduced literally as the cinematic 'Other', Mr. Alien's role is singled out quizzically by William, Jr. (who himself is covered by yards of celluloid), 'Why not some other gentleman from Moscow or Beverly Hills?'. In a way that positions the film in the loop of '*déjà vu*', as if doubling Shakespeare's return of Cordelia to Britain to redeem, with the aid of France, the lost perspective of her father's reign, Mr. Alien (punning perhaps on Sigourney Weaver's return from the dead in ALIENS) comes to life here in the wake of cinema's apparent passing to handle film with the temporal sensibility prescribed by Godard in HISTOIRE(S) DU CINÉMA. As he literally sews film at the editing table (accompanied by the graphic intertitle, 'So Young, Sew Tender'), Mr. Alien addresses his cinematic viewers with the same lines presented by Godard in HISTOIRE(S) DU CINÉMA in relation to the boundlessness of history, as well as those remembered by William, Jr. at the outset of the film in relation to the openness of memory. Fingering his celluloid footage, Alien speaks aloud his self-consciousness about how he is 'holding in both hands the future, the present, and the past'. The place of cinematic thought here again lies anew on the frontier, on the border, on the margin, on the horizon of history and its cinematic passing: Look there, look there.

Outside resemblance

As for the holder of thought, the server of epistemological wisdom, this task lies in Godard's KING LEAR neither with the managing director of Learo Jet, his dutiful daughter, nor the obedient scribe, Shakespeare Junior. 'They seemed to be looking for something', says Junior of Lear and Cordelia midway through the film, 'no one knows, only the Professor knows'. Alongside Shakespeare Jr., Learo, Cordelia, and much later Mr. Alien, enters the persona of cinematic thought itself, the inimitable Professor Pluggy. 'I don't know if I made this clear before', Junior reminds the viewers in two subsequent voice-over intervals, 'but this was after Chernobyl. We're in a time now when films and more generally art have been lost, do not exist, and they have to somehow be reinvented. Thanks to the old man and his daughter I had some of the lines but I was told this old man Pluggy had to go together with the lines.' Pluggy, who says he 'hates light', bears the name of his twenty years in the chiaroscuro dark, hidden in the editing room lit obscurely from the back, just as his face is partially obscured by the parodic headdress of his electronic brotherhood with flowing cords and dangling jacks.

Hidden beneath the plugs and wires that denote the electronic transformation of life in the editing cave, Godard himself stands-in jokingly for the Professor of Cinematic Thought. He plays Pluggy, the genius of cinema whose epistemological quest is fuelled by the fact that, as he tells Junior, he knows that what he is looking for 'doesn't exist: since nobody does it'. After he utters these lines, the Professor responds to William's question, 'what are you aiming at?', by shifting the underside of his seated body to surround the cinematic space with the baffled resonance of a loud fart. Epistemological aim, in this context, is tantamount to an aggressive bilabial fricative, a pure sound-event, one that may have no corollary or analogy other than the invisible waste of nuclear fallout or the perlocutionary effect of NO THING.[20] 'The result of what is obtained immediately', says Pluggy to Junior, 'controls the truth of association...What is great is not the image but the EMOTION which it provokes...The emotion thus provoked is true because it is born outside all imitation, all evocation, and all resemblance.'

Just such a distancing from an art of 'resemblance' for the sake of a cinema of 'affect' lies at the heart of later Godardian cinema, as well as at the core of its prescient representation of what I termed earlier a new Baroque era caught between clashing systems of analogue and digital representation. Godard can be said to lay bare the virtual scaffolding of his cinema when he distances his artistic practice from systems of analogue representation, i.e. from those practices based on formal codes of progression and analogy through which a picture demonstrates its mimetic resemblance to its realistic source (and through which a cinematic adaptation of the Cinema of Quality marked resemblance to the source text). In agreeing with Gavin Smith in a 1996 interview that cinema has 'imprisoned the image', Godard indirectly positions himself on the digital frontier when he differentiates moving 'pictures' from cinematic 'images': 'An image doesn't exist. This is not an image, it's a picture. The image is the relation with me looking at it dreaming up a relation at someone else. An image is an association.'[21] By shifting cinematic practice from the terrain of 'resemblance' with what exists to that of 'association' with – or simulation of – something as nebulous as the haptic affect of a fart, Godard can be said to inscribe his work retroactively in the virtual interactivity now so characteristic of digital aesthetics.

Rather than celebrate film's imitation of nature, its adherence to well-established artistic genres such as adaptation, documentary, or realistic narrative that set the parameters of 'resemblance', or even its perspectival solicitation of spectatorial attention and wonder, digital aesthetics can be said to position the viewer on the threshold of the virtual. As put succinctly by Pierre Lévy, the image thereby 'abandons the exteriority of spectacle to open itself to immersion'.[22] The promise of digital aesthetics is its enhanced zone of 'interactivity' through which the users' entry into the circuit of artistic presentation simulates or projects their own associations, fantasies, and memories in consort with the artwork. It is just such a simulation that Godard terms the virtual, unrealised promise of 'true montage':

> *La vraie mission*, the true goal of cinema, was to arrive at a way of elaborating and putting into practice what montage is. But we never got there; many directors believed they had reached it, but they had done other things. Particularly Eisenstein. He was on the way to montage but he didn't reach it. He wasn't an editor, he was a taker of angles. And because he was so good at taking angles, there was an idea of montage. The three lions of OCTOBER, the same lion but taken from three different angles, so the lion looks like he's moving – in fact it was the association of angles that brought montage. Montage is something else, never discovered.[23]

'Born outside all imitation, all evocation, and all resemblance', the image of true montage or true emotion in Godard's KING LEAR can be only a simulacrum of the production and the affect of representation, whether the simulacrum is understood in terms of its founding, philosophical articulation in Plato's cave or its later electronic actualisation in Godard's studio. A most eerie sequence in KING LEAR cuts between both of these scenes of the cave and the studio during William's second interrogation of Pluggy about the status of cinema. It happens inside a chiaroscuro-lit editing studio, a space viewers have come to associate with Godard's self-representation in films dating back to NUMÉRO DEUX, where he works in front of two video monitors from which he reshot video footage on 35 mm.[24] Peeking around the doorway into a darkened space where flashes of light are doubled by the whirring sounds of electronic equipment, Junior notes that 'there's a lot of noise around here, huh? What's it for? What's it all for, Professor?'. Signifying the cinematic crisis that appears with each growth of new machines in the social field, from silent cinema to video and digital editing, this conflation of cinema with a cacophony of sound positions the contemporary editing studio in continuous variation with the earlier trauma of the talkies' break from the pure image of silent cinema. It is the allusion to this break and its confusing discovery of new beings in the cinematic mechanism (thinking back to Deleuze's notion of the baroque) that prefaces Pluggy's discourse on the image as 'a pure creation of the soul; it cannot be born of a comparison but of a reconciliation of two realities that come from more or less far apart'.

One of the realities shown at intervals during this sequence is that of a crude light box illuminating tiny plastic models of prehistoric creatures that hearken back to cinema's primal scene of the cave. At precisely the moment of Pluggy's assertion that 'the image is a pure creation of the soul', footage of the prehistoric lightbox is intercut with an image resembling the silhouetted spectacle displayed to the imprisoned spectators of Plato's cave. To grasp the cinematic relation between these two distinct prehistoric realities of lightbox and cave, one need merely recall the theoretical legacy of Jean-Louis Baudry's emphasis on the importance of the allegory of Plato's cave to the ideology of the cinematic apparatus: 'we can thus propose that the allegory of the cave is the text of a signifier of desire which haunts the invention of cinema and the history of its invention'.[25] At issue for Baudry, but perhaps lost after Chernobyl, is how the cinematic apparatus provokes the simulation not of the reality of cinema and its representations but of its dream, its desire, to such an extent that 'it is indeed a simulation of a condition of the subject, a position of the subject, a subject and not reality'.[26] Baudry's apparatus, from cave to film palace, is thus no more than a subject's machinery of desire and its signifying practices.

While this model fits the cave, it might well constitute a cinematic reality more or less far apart from that of KING LEAR where we learn from young William that everything reappeared after Chernobyl, 'everything except culture and me'. Culture and me, the apparatus and the subject. Where do they lie in the post-apocalyptic wasteland of Godard's KING LEAR? Is the machinery of desire here represented as grounded in the subject or might the culture of the subject itself have disappeared in the machineries of cinema and their signifying practices: 'cinema is higher than us, it is that to which we must life our eyes'?

Add, then, to the primal image of the cave in this same intriguing sequence the simulacrum of the studio itself, whose dual video monitors and electronic mixing board attest to Godard's own enigmatic position between the duelling realities of cinema and video which have ushered in the digital age. The uncanny return of this scene, which leaves the director in the dark as he lurks in the shadows of new age machineries, clearly harks back to Godard's stance in NUMÉRO DEUX, where he spoke prophetically about the link of his cinema to the crisis of its property: 'Mac machine. No Mac, only machine'.[27] While Godard had no way in 1975 of foreseeing the digital developments that have unfolded in Silicon Valley, his repetitive staging of the doubling of the video monitor presciently situates the future promise of the Mac in relation to the logic of his doubled image.

Harun Farocki could easily have been referring to KING LEAR, rather than NUMÉRO DEUX, when he wrote that:

> the idea of doubling the image must have come to Godard from working in video. Video editing is usually done while sitting in front of two monitors. One monitor shows the already edited material, and the other monitor the raw material, which the video-maker may or may not add to the work-in-progress. He or she becomes accustomed to thinking of two images at the same time, rather than sequentially.[28]

It is this break from the mastery of analogue sequence that repositions the subject in the disjunctive gap of the cinematic machine, in the space of the between, in the thought of the dislocation of two realities more or less far apart, whether those of the cave and the editing room or those of cinema and video. In KING LEAR's editing room sequence, the jocular alternation on two monitors of the figure of Liberty and the caricature of Pluto (an animated embodiment of the fricative) attests to the irrational dissonance of the quest that brings Pluggy and Junior together in an attempt to redefine post-apocalyptic culture. Here the quest differs from the confident recreation of authorial vision, artistic harmony and narrative development – the humanistic project shared by literary history and classical cinema and the pedagogical project now lamented for its supposed death by the National Association of Scholars and the National Alumni Forum, whose recalcitrant members cannot acknowledge the radicality of the Shakespeare they lament nor the Shakespearean dissonance of Godard's emphasis on what lies between KING LEAR's NO THING.[29] In effect, this fascinating sequence, with its cave-like studio setting, reproductive lights, electronic feedback, video monitors, and enigmatic sounds, attests to the disparate forms and realities through which contemporary cinema now responds to the new frontiers, horizons, and representational possibilities opened up by the politics and machineries of the post-Chernobyl age. This is a representational challenge not at all contrary to that posed by Shakespeare's *King Lear*, providing we apply pressure to the uncertainty of Lear's dying deictic, 'Look there, look there!', an uncertainty embraced as representationally empowering by Edgar who subsequently speaks the play's closing lines: 'Speak what we feel, not what we ought to say'.

Deleuze in the shadows

Sandwiched between the electronic editing board and the editing room's two monitors so different in their exact similarity lurks a figure darkened in silhouette who appears to stand-in for the off-camera voice of Pluggy. Although it turns out at the scene's end to be the same Edgar who utters Shakespeare's lines about speaking feelingly, I've frequently found myself fantasising this silhouette to be the spectre of the other Professor of Cinema and its Thought, the one who in wrote the chapter on 'Thought and Cinema' in his 1985 book, *Cinema 2: The Time-Image*, in which Godard figures so prominently. I was first enraptured by this fantasy that Deleuze appears as if in hologram in Godard's 1987 film upon hearing Pluggy's assertion about the reconciliation of two realities that are more or less far apart. 'The more the connections between these two are dissimilar', Pluggy informs us evoking Pierre Reverdy, 'the stronger the image will be, the more it will have emotive power... Two contrary realities will not draw together their opposing selves; one rarely attains power and forces from these oppositions'.

The emotive reconciliation of such dissimilarities can be understood to be fuelled by the force of Deleuze's notion of 'incompossibility'. Incompossibility is Deleuze's baroque term borrowed from Leibniz for two coexisting incommensurables. In a footnote to *Logique du sens*, Deleuze provides a summary of the three serial elements of the world that inscribe the

Leibnizian monad on the margins of incompossibility: one that determines the world by convergence, another that determines perfect individuals in this world, and finally another that determines incomplete or rather ambiguous elements common to many worlds and to many corresponding individuals.[30] Deleuze is interested in how these elements fail to converge while still not negating or rendering each other impossible. Rather than either converging or remaining impossible for each other, they stand in paradoxical relation to one another as divergent and coexistent: as 'incompossible'. Deleuze dwells most explicitly on the serial nature of post-Leibnizian incompossibility in *Difference and Repetition* and *Cinema 2*. He contrasts Leibniz's example of different points of view on one town, 'not necessarily true pasts', with the bifurcating fabulations of seriality, 'incompossible presents' through which each series tells completely different stories which unfold simultaneously.[31] The forced coexistence or 'chaoerrancy' of seriality, Deleuze adds in *Cinema 2*, results in a crisis of truth that knows no solution but only a pause or a delay, say, within 24 frames a second.

What one does attain, suggests Deleuze in his writing on Godard, is the trademark of (post)modern cinema through which 'the whole undergoes a mutation, because it has ceased to be the One-Being, in order to become the constitutive "and" of things, the constitutive between-two of images'. 'The whole thus merges', adds Deleuze, 'with what Blanchot calls the force of "dispersal of the Outside", or "the vertigo of spacing": that void which is no longer a motor-part of the image, and which the image would cross in order to continue, but is the radical calling into question of the image (just as there is a silence [this is still Deleuze writing before Godard's KING LEAR] which is no longer the motor-part or the breathing-space of discourse but its radical calling into question)'. 'False continuity', Deleuze concludes, 'takes on a new meaning, at the same time as it becomes the law.'[32] The brilliance of Godard's KING LEAR is how it situates the new electronic meaning of cinema in relation to the contemplation of the radicality of silence and its impact on the law in Shakespeare: 'Bear them from hence [instructs Albany at the end of Shakespeare's *King Lear*]. Our present business is general woe. Friends of my soul, you twain Rule in this realm, and the gor'd state sustain.' Just as false continuity, the breathing-space of NO THING, become the law of Lear's Britain (since saved by France) whose twained rule sustains the gor'd state, so the doubled image, the silence of the break, and the gap of sequentiality sustain the rule of what Deleuze calls Godard's cinema of incommensurability.

It is almost uncanny how much Godard's KING LEAR exemplifies Deleuze's argument about the cinema of Godard. One can almost imagine

Godard falling upon *Cinema 2* after the sudden departure of Norman Mailer to come upon the idea for a saving protagonist of the film, the Professor of the Thought of Cinema. A brief summary of Deleuze's reading of Godard provides almost a pony for the reading of this film Shot in the Back. The hallmark of this cinema is what Deleuze calls its irrationality:

> The cut has become the interstice, *it is irrational and does not form part of either set, one of which has no more an end than the other has a beginning*: false continuity is such an irrational cut. Thus, in Godard, the interaction of two images engenders or traces a frontier which belongs to neither one nor the other.[33]

This visual irrationality brought home by Godard in his morphing play with Goofy Liberty pertains as well to the many different parts of KING LEAR, which begins and ends twice, as well as its disparate protagonists, intertitles, and voice-overs. Three features of such false continuity provide a particularly apt means for summarising Godard's performance of the cinematic frontiers of the film: 'free indirect vision', the interstice between sound and vision, and finally the fabulation of modern political cinema.

What Deleuze calls 'free indirect vision' is the excessive seriality of Godardian cinema which flows in continuous variation from one sequence to another. Through this offshoot of 'free indirect discourse', Deleuze writes,

> either the author [think here of Shakespeare as well as Godard] expresses himself through the intercession of an autonomous, independent character other than the author or any role fixed by the author, or the character acts and speaks himself as if his own gestures and his own words were already reported by a third party.[34]

If this seems all too abstract, just think back to the intercession of Professor Pluggy on the one hand, or how Shakespeare Junior speaks words already reported by a third party on the other. The practical result is the effacement of a controlling interior monologue, the inversion of a totalisation of images or whole in favour of an outside inserted between them, and the erasure of the unity of man and the world in favour of a break, leaving Godard's viewers with, at best, only a frail belief in the promise of the post-nuclear world.[35] These results could be summarised in the series of intertitles repeated at intervals throughout Godard's film in a way that disrupts the narrative flow of KING LEAR: A Picture Shot in the Back, A Study, An Approach, A Clearing, A Thing, Fear and Loathing, Three Journeys into King Lear.

Such a repetition of intertitles in continuous variation constitutes the seriality of KING LEAR through which two images or the fold of sound and vision are said by Deleuze to engender or trace a frontier belonging neither to one nor the other. Just such a stress on the showing (*faire voir*) of the indiscernable, of the in-between, of 'Look there, look there!', motivates the project of Godard with its mixed media, intertitles and intersecting narratives, as well as the discourse of Professor Pluggy who responds to Young Shakespeare's timid request, 'Tell me, Professor', with the abrupt corrective, 'SHOW, SHOW, DON'T TELL'. Perhaps it is something like the violence or the bloodiness of Godard's show that prompted the viscerality of Leonard Maltin's negative reaction to the mess of KING LEAR. Or perhaps it has as much to do with the stress on fabulation deriving from Godard's seriality, a fabulation described by Deleuze as characteristic of political, feminist, postcolonial cinema (not as strange a category for Shakespeare's *King Lear* as one might think, and one worth entertaining in its postnuclear cinematic apparition). Fabulation – the reciting, retelling, reconceiving of the ancestral story – is the truly cinematic image-event in Deleuze through which the colonising myths of culture, whether those of Shakespeare, Hollywood or the National Association of Scholars, achieve something akin to a contrary world-memory of an infinity of peoples who remain to be united, or even who should not be united. The new world-memory of Shakespeare *in* cinema, as suggested by the post-apocalyptic project of Godard and his stress on the recovery of the passion of cinematic history throughout HISTOIRE(S) DU CINÉMA, is marked not so much by the coherence of authorial perspective and cultural patrimony as by the intensity, disparity, dissemblance and *différend* of cinematic nomadism and its chao-errancy. Through radical transformations of the conditions of Shakespearean production, Godard can be said to join Cordelia in her pact with Virginia Woolf to constitute, as Professor Deleuze would say, 'an assemblage which brings real parties together, in order to make them produce collective utterances as the prefiguration of a people who are missing'.[36] Such fabulation on the eve of the new digital era of cinema needs to be understood, moreover, as just as dissimilar as it is drawn together. At one moment, it might constitute no more than an abrasive cinematic fricative; at others, it might amount to an assertive, feminist counter-charge such as that spoken by Cordelia to Shakespeare, Jr.: 'You write what is against me, you do not write for me.' But at all times, the new world-memory of post-Chernobyl cinema – let us call it: HISTOIRE(S) DU CINÉMA – testifies to the prescience of Godard's cinematic practice which champions the idealism of pure montage and the generative passions of the clash of its incompossible systems of analogue and digital representation.

10 The Power of Language: Notes on PUISSANCE DE LA PAROLE, LE DERNIER MOT and ON S'EST TOUS DÉFILÉ

Jean-Louis Leutrat[1]

> 'I often have the feeling of an image that speaks,
> that there is a word behind the image.'
> (J.-D. Pollet)

All of Godard's films accord an important place to the written and spoken word, to language in all its forms: luminous signs, letters, postcards, handwritten pages, stylised credit sequences, spoken and recomposed texts, etc.. Perhaps it is a question of impressing (*imprimer)* or expressing (*exprimer*) language, of *imprinting* words into the cinematic image, since from quite early in his career, Godard, following Cocteau's star, literally prints his writing on the screen. In his later films, the 'late' Jean-Luc Godard goes a lot further in this direction of 'ceding the initiative to words', as the poet Stéphane Mallarmé would have said. In this perspective the year 1988 produced three short video works, PUISSANCE DE LA PAROLE, LE DERNIER MOT and ON S'EST TOUS DÉFILÉ, which together pose an intriguing series of questions about the power and potential of language, particularly in relation to its sibling rival, the filmic or videographic sound-and-image. The three titles are themselves revelatory, the first two explicitly (literally 'the power of the word' and 'the last word') while the third takes its lead or inspiration from the type of poetic wordplay that one finds in the works of Mallarmé, a poet for whom the possibilities of language were infinite and whose writings, it so happens, provide the textual base or 'pre-text' for ON S'EST TOUS DÉFILÉ. Here we shall focus mainly on this 'Mallarméan' videowork, partly because it encapsulates the kind of themes and effects that we find in the other two pieces, and partly because it can be seen as a precursor or messenger of Godard's exuberant late style, which was, of course, to flourish and evolve from 1988 to 1998 under the aegis of HISTOIRE(S) DU CINÉMA.

Before dealing with this work from 1988, however, it is worth drawing attention to how Godard uses language in the films of the 1960s, especially since his experimentations in the field of wordplay and language function through an incessant resumption and enrichment across different works. A remark by Godard about Gilles Deleuze is intriguing in this regard: he reproaches him for writing very badly.[2] This predilection for 'classical' writing (from what point of view is it possible to say that Deleuze writes badly?), accompanied by a less significant preference for traditional diction, draws our attention to an aspect of Godard's personality that we might have been led to neglect: his taste for 'correct' language. His explicit reference in LE DERNIER MOT to the seventeenth-century grammarian Vaugelas is revealing as well as amusing: 'I am going away, or I go away, since both one and the other is or are gramatically correct, and is said, or are said.'[3] Émile Récamier adapts this sentence in UNE FEMME EST UNE FEMME, responding to the question 'Why is it women who suffer?' with the following: 'Because it is they, or it is them, who make others suffer, since both one and the other are gramatically correct, and is said, or are said.'[4] Before these questions of proper grammar, however, there is the alphabet itself which precedes words even before they can be correctly combined. In cinema, the opening title sequence is the perfect place and opportunity for this pre-eminence of the letters of the alphabet, manifestly conspiring to compose themselves into the names of the actors and the words of the film title (see PIERROT LE FOU for an eloquent example of this). The alphabet provides another form of motivation in the opening scenes of À BOUT DE SOUFFLE, where the letter A of the title seems playfully to predetermine the bodily gestures, the alternating movement of faces, the spread legs of the young girl in the newspaper, the crocodile clips, the opening of the car bonnet, the chevrons on Michel Poiccard's jacket, etc.. Everything at the beginning of the film develops the shape specific to the letter A. In a similar vein, the initials of the hero of the film are M.P, like Monogram Pictures, and the petrol sign B.P can read Belmondo-Poiccard. Of course, playing with letters and their graphic form is part of a wider realm of word play, and certainly the younger Godard playfully exploits schoolboy humour, repetition, and visual-verbal puns. This characteristic of his early work is well known. Again at the beginning of À BOUT DE SOUFFLE, Michel Poiccard leans back against a wire fence (*grille*); he is chain-smoking (*griller des sèches*); burning with the desire to join Patricia, but also scorched or burnt out in advance (*grillé, flambé*), i.e. dead, without a future, his destiny branded into his being. As the police-motorcyclist says to him shortly after: 'Move and I'll burn you' (*bouge pas ou je te brûle*). Language, to an extent, programmes the *mise-en-scène* but in an underhand way.

The names of characters can also be transparent. Pierrot le fou ('Pierrot the fool') is the famous gangster ('Mad Pierre') but he also becomes in turn Raymond Queneau's character 'Pierrot mon ami' ('Pierrot my friend'), 'mon ami Pierrot' ('my friend Pierrot') from the popular song, Picasso's *Paul as Pierrot*, and Piero della Francesca (an echo of LE MÉPRIS). Likewise, 'the fool' becomes the mad Van Gogh, the love-crazy Raymond Devos character (*dites que je suis fou*), and Pierrot/Ferdinand's catchphrase 'I don't care' (*Je m'en fous*). Language is always present and homophony makes the films jump from one thing to another. Thus, an entire scene of PIERROT LE FOU is constructed from a chain of associations starting with Paul Valéry's famously paradigmatic sentence 'The Marquise went out at five o'clock' (a phrase that Valéry uses ironically to generate an infinite number of novelistic intrigues). Thus Marianne hums 'Everything's gone bad, Madame la Marquise' (a variation of a famous French song, 'Everything's fine, Madame la Marquise'); the dancing joint is called La Marquise; the figure five appears in the words ('I'm coming back in five minutes', 'ah, what an awful five o'clock in the afternoon'), and a suspicious character makes a hand-gesture signalling the figure five... And so on. One could multiply these examples ad infinitum. The point is that Godard's early films thus have a mimological aspect, not in the sense understood by Gérard Genette (i.e. of language imitating reality) but in the sense of profilmic reality imitating language. Not only does language suggest or 'create' both objects and gestures, but also it programmes the wider *mise-en-scène*, a montage of visual and sound effects.

It would be tempting to argue that during this period of Godard's work, discontinuity seems to be valued for itself as the standard of a cinema of modernity anxious to put distance between itself and the idea of totality (the word 'total' reoccurs often, either through the signs of the well-known petrol company Total, which advertises itself with the three colours red, white and blue, or adverbally, as in this phrase from LE MÉPRIS: 'I totally love you...'). One could say of the work of Godard what Roland Barthes has said of the art of Schumann: 'In the end, there are only *intermezzi*, whatever interrupts is itself interrupted, and so on...'. This describes excellently a certain cinema of Jean-Luc Godard. From filled-in gaps to immediately dissolved plenitudes, the splits and divisions seem only to expand or multiply as each film draws its form and force from the fractures and digressions that might just as easily engulf it. Continuity of meaning is subverted, spatial and temporal coordinates are altered, and logical links are disjointed. But there is clearly another side to this eminently poetic mode of composition. One could equally argue that thanks to these puns and word-associations of every kind, a double movement is created, a paradox that separates what seems closely related and, just as importantly, brings together what seems far apart. The renewal of perception, allied to a remotivation of language, is an ethical task familiar to poets since time immemorial. Mallarmé speaks of 'secret identities': 'the entire mystery is there: to establish secret identities through an oscillation that gnaws and wears through objects, in the name of a central purity'.[5] Could one perhaps suggest that if separation and detachment were the chief strategic aims of the 1960s, then rapprochement should now be seen as the stronger tendency in more recent times? From LETTRE À FREDDY BUACHE to HISTOIRE(S) DU CINÉMA, Godard has certainly foregrounded the idea of poetic rapprochement by citing and reciting the poet Pierre Reverdy's famous definition of the 'image': 'The image is a pure creation of the mind, it cannot be born from a comparison, but comes from the bringing together of two distant realities [...] An image is not powerful because it is brutal and fantastic, but because the association of ideas is distant and true.'[6] Reverdy's statement has a value that exceeds the domain of words, but it is significant that Godard relies on the words of a poet for whom the term 'image' has a necessarily different meaning from that understood by the film-maker. This rapprochement of Godard and Reverdy already suggests that the verbal and the visual will be increasingly and intimately interrelated and that the 'image' may bring together cinema and poetry in new ways.

Certainly, the more recent films have not ceased to rely on linguistic permutations, quite the contrary. An example of creative sound association occurs at the beginning of NOUVELLE VAGUE where the inscription on the lorry 'Harsh' prepares us in turn for the title of the magazine 'Cash', the moment when Richard Lennox plays 'squash' and the sound of falling into water, 'splash'. The title of PUISSANCE DE LA PAROLE is adapted from 'The Power of Words', a text by Edgar Allan Poe featuring a long dialogue between two angels on the nature of the cosmos and the creative potential of language. Godard quotes Poe's text extensively, mixing it with a violent, confrontational dialogue between two separated lovers that is borrowed from James M. Cain's novel *The Postman Always Rings Twice*. (Incidentally, *La puissance de la parole* is also the title of a book by Jean Breck, first published in 1986, about orthodox hermeneutics. Hence, Godard as usual is taking his inspiration from whatever sources he finds and telescoping ideas and information according to his needs.) In Poe's text we read: 'And while I [Agathos] thus spoke, did there not cross your mind some thought of the *physical power of words*? Is not every word an impulse on the air?' (original emphasis).[7] In the video work we see, on one side, tremendous natural, even cosmic forces unleashed, displaced, entering into dramatic movements and explosive confrontations with one another. But at the same time these powerful *forces* also become *forms* that are taking aesthetic shape before our very eyes and ears, and are combining and composing themselves rhythmically to establish a relative stability and harmony. PUISSANCE DE LA PAROLE thus reveals a

Lucretian vein in Godard's thinking: we witness the telescoping and bombardment of visual and sonorous atoms, the acceleration of particles, phenomena of reverberation and superimposition. But this atomic discontinuity is counterbalanced by a continuity of flux and flow. It is as if Godard were attempting at the same time to render or convey both the constancy of the 'infinite springs' (mentioned in Poe's texts) and the infinite differenciation implied by the multiplicity of atoms, sparks, flashes and crashing waves. The materiality of the voices we hear and the corporeality of the lights we see become fused into the torrential flows of water or volcanic lava which PUISSANCE DE LA PAROLE presents to us in the form of powerful documentary images. On another level, the collision of the texts by Poe and Cain finds its equivalent in the clashing of the separated lovers. The couple has split or broken up, and in the fall-out we witness the impotence of speech from one side (silence, refusal) and the power of speech from the other (anger, abuse). The lovers are caught up in furious movements, violent transports and dislocations that reflect the dramatic shifts of a love story, the history of two bodies confronting each other and even collapsing with exhaustion. In the terms of Reverdy's definition, we might say that PUISSANCE DE LA PAROLE produces images that are indeed 'brutal and fantastic'.

By contrast, what 'distant realities' does ON S'EST TOUS DÉFILÉ attempt to bring together? A fashion parade by the Swiss fashion designers Marithé and François Girbaud, and texts by Mallarmé from *Divagations* ('Le nénuphar blanc', 'Solennité', 'La cour', 'Sauve-garde'). The punning formula shown as an epigraph to the piece reads: 'A throw of the dice / a bit of a fashion-parade will always abolish chance' (*un coup de dé(filé) abolira toujours le hasard*). The association of ideas is immediately foregrounded, combining an inversion of Mallarmé's most famous line of verse ('a throw of the dice will never abolish chance') with an explicit allusion to the well-known fact that the poet also wrote idiosyncratic fashion articles in *La Dernière Mode*. This is the 'distant but true association of ideas' that gives strength to the image and sparks the remotivation of the all-too familiar poetic cliché. Following on from this epigraph, Godard shows us that, again like Mallarmé, he can find inspiration even in the everyday words of the dictionary. In the opening sequence, Godard reminds us of the etymology of *angoisse* (anxiety) – the Latin *angustia*, meaning a narrow passage, a 'defile' in the sense of a passage so narrow and tight that one can only go through it in single 'file'. He does this with two captions, a word underlined in each: 'anxiety, from the Latin *angustia*', and: '*défilé*, from the Latin *angustia*'. Then the word 'anguish' appears on its own associated with two images, one of which comes from an advertisement for a brand of shoes (Charles Jourdan) reproducing a figure from Michelangelo (the nude above the Persian Sibyl in the Sistine chapel). Due to an effect of montage, the image seems to be held by a woman of whom we see only her legs (with high-heeled shoes) and her hands and varnished nails. The idea of abduction is strongly suggested. The word 'an/ guish' (*an/goisse*) then reappears, split in the middle by the neck of a female silhouette seen from the front. This echoes the link between the procession and the throat (*la gorge*) through the meaning of *défilé* as a 'narrow pass' or 'gorge', as well as signalling the homophony between *coup* (throw, strike, etc.) and *cou* (neck). This sense of anxiety and violence is linked, of course, to the literal but enigmatic meaning of the title: 'we all ran away'. What were 'we' so scared of? Why did we hide, escape, dodge, run away? Who is this 'we'? And what duty has been dodged or avoided? Perhaps one of the first reproductions shown in the film, that of the tortured souls in Giotto's *Last Judgment*, might suggest an answer to this question.

One of the other short pieces from 1988, LE DERNIER MOT ('The last word'), concerns a young French philosopher, Valentin Feldman, who was tortured and shot by the Nazis during the Occupation. The 'we' might therefore designate the Swiss population that remained apart, distanced from the sound and the fury around its frontiers during the Second World War. In the sounds of *défi-lé* one can also hear an echo of the word *défi* – a challenge, perhaps of the kind that Feldman issued to his executioners: 'Fools, do you not see that it's for you that I'm dying?' This may well in turn provide an incidental echo of Godard's general historical claim that cinema 'ran away' from its responsibilities during this crucial period of History, a period that was both a critical moment in his own personal history (he grew up in a right-wing Swiss banking family) and a critical challenge which cinema clearly failed to meet. Such an echo might be heard in the piece's use of a passage from a symphony by Arthur Honegger, a composer whose family background was also Swiss. Honegger's *Liturgy* is entitled 'Dona nobis pacem' or 'Give us peace', a plea that reinforces the essential paradox implicit in the title: on the one hand, the graceful parade, the orderly procession of beautiful bodies; on the other, the sense of panic, disorder and abdicated responsibilities. This paradox of the parade or procession is a recurrent figure in Godard's later works: the procession of unemployed extras in GRANDEUR ET DÉCADENCE D'UN PETIT COMMERCE DE CINÉMA (reprised in FOR EVER MOZART); the procession of robotic bodybuilders in ARMIDE. These deadly parades seem like a vision of cinema robotically going through the motions, merely turning up to make a pointless appearance or empty succession (*défilement*) of images. The march of robots leads us further to the idea of a military procession, also *défilé* in French. The distance between this form of parade ('the theme of human stupidity', according to Honegger) and the fashion parade is apparently incommensurable. Is it possible for Godard to bridge the gap merely by 'throwing a parade' (*un coup de défilé*)? The kind of associative leaps that he performs in ON S'EST TOUS DÉFILÉ are impressive, vertiginous... and hazardous. One is reminded of the *métaphore filée* or elaborate conceits that were practised by Gongorists, Marinists, and other 'metaphysical' poets of the sixteenth century. They, too, combined a sense of humour and danger, and likewise prided themselves precisely on the extreme heterogeneity of the 'distant' elements that the image could truly bring together. The most celebrated contemporary descendant of that metaphysical tradition is none other than... Stéphane Mallarmé. In Godard's case, it is as if montage were conceived and executed as a highly risky form of acrobatic thinking, a high-wire video artistry that not only jumps from art to art (painting, music, poetry, film) but also, within each art, attempts the most prodigious and precarious leaps. Gravity may well insist that at any and every moment the acrobatic *monteur* will fall spectacularly on his face. But as we hear Godard say in Chapter 4A of HISTOIRE(S) DU CINÉMA quoting Denis de Rougemont: 'It is high time that thinking became again what it is in reality: dangerous for the thinker and transformative of the real.'[8]

If we consider another short section found near the beginning of the film, we see that the visual montage brings together shots of ordinary Parisians walking through the streets (similar to the people of Lausanne that one sees in LETTRE À FREDDY BUACHE) and a series of portraits by Longhi (*The Rhinoceros*), Gainsborough (*Heneage Lloyd and her sister*) and Boucher (*La Marquise de Pompadour*). These contrasting images of society are intercut with close-ups of the face of the designer François Girbaud and the lower body of one of the fashion-models who is seen raising her legs one after the other in order to undo her sandals. In a manner reminiscent of Eadweard Muybridge, Godard applies to the whole sequence an analytical video eye, decomposing the human movements with extreme slow motion and reverse motion, thereby creating an impression that the film-image itself is an object of video scrutiny and that we are watching the hesitations and interrogations of the editor viewing and reworking the raw photographic materials. As for the sound montage, it alternates between Mozart (*Concerto No. 5*) and Sonny Rollins, another kind of distant and true association. We can also detect a fragment of Mallarmé, the beginning of 'Le nénuphar blanc':

> I had rowed a great deal, stupefied by the broad, clear stroke, my inner gaze fixed on the total forgetting of movement, whilst around me flowed the hour's laughter. So much immobility was idling away that, touched by a dull sound wherein the skiff near disappeared, I recognised our halt only by the steady sparkling of initials on the

naked oars, which recalled me to my wordly identity. What was happening, where was I?[9]

The first distant and true association (of Mallarmé's dice and the fashion-parade) now leads us to interpret the poet's text – which already flees from us in each of its words or phrases – as a meditation or dramatic monologue by the creator Girbaud-Godard. Having worked so intensely hard ('*ramer*' in French slang), the *couturier-monteur* asks himself some serious existential questions when it comes to the actual moment of the parade ('while around me flowed the hour's laughter'). What happens, where am I when suddenly awoken from this inner reverie of designing, confecting, cutting and piecing together rags, 'making up' my art from these mundane basic materials? What happens when I return to my worldly name? It is tempting to see in this montage a portrait of the film-maker as poet (Mallarmé) and designer (Girbaud), in other words, of the artist caught up in the chaos and confrontation of production and exhibition but secretly longing for those still moments of illusory calm and creative self-presence which only montage can provide, albeit fleetingly. As with the elaborate play on *défilé* the self-portrait is a paradoxical figure of cinema as orderly display and violent dispersal, artistic control and worldly chaos, the catastrophic failure of the film-making process on set or location and the miraculous redemption of all that 'rush' in the rhythm and grace of montage.

So what is this 'Mallarméan' Godard that ON S´EST TOUS DÉFILÉ apparently brings to light? First of all, one can understand the comparison in the banal sense of being obscure or unintelligible. The film-maker also has a reputation for cultivating opacity. What is said of the beauty of Mallarmé's poetry ('firmly closed up in what separates it from clear elocution'[10]) could be said of Godard's own works of the 1980s and 1990s, particularly ON S´EST TOUS DÉFILÉ which is quite characteristic of the procedures invented by Godard during this period. There is in these works no transparent meaning which can be unproblematically penetrated, just as in Mallarmé's poetry the reader must work both to construct and unpack signification. No more than in the latter, Godard is not looking for an obscurity based only on arbitrary associations; a decoding is needed that must strike a harmony with emotion. Reversing the proposition 'a throw of the dice will never abolish chance', the film-maker is simply reformulating the poet's famous – if futile – ambition to deny the role of chance in creation by seeking effectively to abolish it. But like Mallarmé in 'Le nénuphar blanc', he maintains the balance between improvisation and the calculation of a project ('the broad, clear stroke'), between the passage of time ('around me flowed the hour's laughter') and immobility, i.e. the balance in cinema between music and sculpture. A similar aesthetic-economic preoccupation has been traced by

Bertrand Marchal right across the poet's writings, most notably in *Divagations* where it often takes the form of speculation on the cult of gold and the cult of the Book: 'Mallarmé in a certain sense turns money over. Behind the brutal number of gold-metal, behind economic theocracy, the "sacred jongleur" attempts to reveal the hidden figure of an imaginary gold, for which he finds the unique and inexhaustible mine in the dark depths of the human mind.'[11] In the Parisian street scenes of ON S'EST TOUS DÉFILÉ, we repeatedly see the word 'gold' (*or*) written on a sandwichboard in the middle of the crowd. It is a moment of pure chance reinvented within the material design of the piece and reinvested by a more global symbolic economy. For Mallarmé, this sense of a vast but virtual symbolic system found its expression in the grand project of the Book, the poetic idea of a self-sufficient universal Work that would symbolically represent, or perhaps literally replace, the whole world of being and becoming. In ON S'EST TOUS DÉFILÉ, we again hear the voice of Godard intoning this passage from 'Solennité': 'What a representation! The world is there. A book, in our hand, if it expresses some august idea, replaces all theatres, not through their obliteration, which it causes, but on the contrary, by bringing them all together, imperiously.' Like most commentators, Godard interprets Mallarmé's Book as a *fin de siècle* version of the alchemical 'Great Work' (an analogy which the poet himself often encouraged). But Godard is in all probability thinking also of his own great late project, HISTOIRE(S) DU CINÉMA, that unique body of work of which ON S'EST TOUS DÉFILÉ is but a brilliant fragment or sample. Is it perhaps 'the marvel of a lofty poem such as here' (as Godard the commentator declaims, clearly taking such pleasure from the rhythms of Mallarmé's peerless prose). But the referent of 'here', the here and now of performance and spectatorship, is at least threefold. We cannot say for sure whether it refers to the fashion-parade itself as a cinematographic object and display, to the video work of which the parade has become a precious, shimmering, corporeal fabric, or indeed, to the greater marvel of Godard's late 'divagating' and, as we have suggested, 'Mallarméan' manner.

If Deleuze can define modern cinema as an oscillation between the word and the image, we could perhaps add a third term: language. Not necessarily the language of the spoken word or written text but an invisible language that, although it may develop from these, implicitly and silently structures the *mise-en-scène*. This is the power of language, its unseen potential for cinema. In a quasi-materialist manner, Godard's later work makes perceptible this potential, its influence in the interstice or disjunction between hearing and vision. Through the imbrication of images and words, but more importantly through the permanent subterranean working of language's 'notes from underground', a piece such as ON S'EST TOUS DÉFILÉ shows itself to be receptive to this potential of language, in the same way that PUISSANCE DE LA PAROLE receives (literally so, with a satellite receiver) the cosmic dialogue of Edgar Allan Poe's angels, and LE DERNIER MOT receives (in an almost religious sense) the final paradoxical words of a dying philosopher to his uncaring and unhearing executioners. One might even claim that it is only in LE DERNIER MOT that Valentin Feldman's words have finally been received. How close does this idea of reception take us to what Michel Chion calls 'the audio-image'? We think of receiving a film as primarily a visual experience, but according to Chion, this is an illusion. The audio-image is in effect mental, and no more exclusively to do with vision than it is to do with sound. Chion argues that in this complex process which is partially 'natural' (psychological and physiological) and partially 'cultural' (conditioned by practices, codes, cultural conditionings), sounds and images are not the only important factors. The Word as such should be included, very often present orally or visually.[12] We have certainly seen in our discussion of these three pieces from 1988 (the year that the first chapters of HISTOIRE(S) DU CINÉMA appeared) that language is present at the centre, determining and privileged, yet also ex-centric. But Chion only envisages the tangible appearances of language in the form of a written or oral text, whereas we have also witnessed in ON S'EST TOUS DÉFILÉ the presence of an invisible, spectral language whose efficacy is underground (*souterrain*) and sovereign (*souverain*). It is impossible to escape it, impossible to fix it. 'Flee from language, it pursues you. Pursue language, it flees from you.'[13] It might even be said, finally, that ON S'EST TOUS DÉFILÉ opens up in Godard's work a 'spectral' period dominated by NOUVELLE VAGUE and HISTOIRE(S) DU CINÉMA, and that perhaps the phantoms that haunt the latter in the form of a crypt will awaken to the invisible life of a spectre. In such a context it is no surprise that Godard should turn to Mallarmé, the poet who made a virtue out of virtuality.

11 Investigation of a Mystery: Cinema and the Sacred in HÉLAS POUR MOI

Lætitia Fieschi-Vivet[1]

'Neither an art nor a technique, but a mystery.'

(HISTOIRE(S) DU CINÉMA)

'Are you familiar with the ten historical propositions on the Old Testament?
According to Scholem the truth is preserved in a certain tradition,
which means that the truth can be communicated.
Well, I find that funny since the truth we're after has all sorts of properties,
but certainly not that of being communicable.'

(HÉLAS POUR MOI)

Like Giraudoux, Molière and Plautus, Godard in turn has set out in search of the legend of Alcmena and Amphitryon. [2] In HÉLAS POUR MOI, he focuses the story on a mysterious, strange and unlikely event. In the ancient myth Jupiter adopts the guise of Amphitryon (who has gone off to fight in a war) in order to possess Amphitryon's wife, Alcmena. In HÉLAS POUR MOI it is possible that God descended to earth to impersonate Simon (who has left on a business trip) in order to sleep with Simon's wife, Rachel, whose virtue and faithfulness are beyond question. This may be what happened, but it is equally possible that no such thing happened at all. Perhaps it was Simon who returned that evening, or perhaps it was 'the god whom we'll call Simon #2 from now on since he looks exactly like Simon'. [3] A man arrives on the scene of the hypothetical event in order to conduct an enquiry. His name is Abraham Klimt. His investigation begins at the same time as the film. What exactly happened? From the point of view of the characters, no-one knows; the protagonists themselves have doubts or deny what is supposed to have happened and the evidence provided by flashbacks is contradictory. The method of montage using enigmatic cutting and pasting increases the sense of uncertainty. The sequences are fragmented and broken down into a succession of random shots whose origin remains uncertain and whose arrangement is always mysterious. The investigator picks up a series of clues whose significance is anything but obvious. Visually, aurally and diegetically, the clues mask and obstruct the reconstruction of the event. Since the film takes the form of Klimt's enquiry, with all its unusual configurations, the film problematises any connection with the event. What traces remain of what probably happened? Klimt's 'historiographical' approach is not equipped to penetrate the mystery. It is caught out by its own futility in the face of the improbability of what he is trying to uncover. To succeed, he needs the help of another character, the visionary poet Aude Amiel. The combination of these two figures, the investigator and the poet, with their complementary approaches, brings images of the event back to the surface. The relationship between fiction and documentary is being invoked here since these two forms are implicated in any historical reconstruction. It is worth remembering that this dichotomy has always been at the heart of Godard's preoccupations with the medium of film and the practice of film-making.[4]

This chapter proposes that the question of the sacred, which is central to Godard's work during the 1990s, emerges at the intersection of the two axes of the poetic and the historical and culminates in HÉLAS POUR MOI. I will demonstrate how this process develops by looking in particular at the internal composition of certain shots, or in other words at their formal experimentation. On the one hand, the reason why there is something hindering the power of sight in the film is because it is impossible for the historical approach to provide a complete vision of the past. On the other, when something does appear amidst the blurred superimposed images of Aude's poetic vision, it escapes detection by either sight or hearing. The invisible 'something' can be said to acquire a virtual body but only thanks to elements that remain obscure and unknown, and stay hidden and blurred. The principle of indeterminacy therefore plays a crucial role not only because it directs Klimt's investigation and Godard's film, since both are attempting to find what cannot be seen, but also because it acts as the dynamic force governing its own emergence at a formal level. What is more, the degree to which this principle determines Klimt's method of investigation and the form of the film decides how great the distance is between the spectator and the essential elements of the film. Small wonder, then, that at the time of the film's release in September 1993 it received a fairly bad press from critics who were not familiar with Godard's work. Leaving aside the many misinterpretations of the film, the critics' reactions revealed that they were perplexed by the difficulty of HÉLAS POUR MOI.[5] The fundamental importance of this film, which plays a defining role in Godard's later œuvre, is precisely due to the fact that the written word has no control over the film's hiatuses, its resistance to interpretative closure, its multiple resonances, its echoes and infinite correspondences, all of which lay the foundations for a truly musical creation. While Godard himself has decided to admit publicly that the film is not what it should have been due to lack of time[6] and overambition,[7] and even that 'it's a failure', he has also said that 'in the very incompleteness there is something which works'.[8] When in JLG/JLG the assistant editor, a blind woman, says of HÉLAS POUR MOI that 'it's a film that still has to be made', Godard replies, 'ah, what you say is true: it's a film nobody has seen'. Repeated in HISTOIRE(S) DU CINÉMA, a work which, by contrast, has been acclaimed by the critics, this conversation ends on a note of tonal harmony, suggesting a direct and hitherto unexplored link between HÉLAS POUR MOI and HISTOIRE(S) DU CINÉMA (indeed, HISTOIRE(S) DU CINÉMA contains several extracts, visual and aural, from HÉLAS POUR MOI). How then should we respond to the film's negative reception? Godard: 'We've seen that the film was somewhat abandoned. But, after all, the Son of Man was also abandoned.'[9] And: 'Almost all the good films in the history of cinema have been abandoned children. People are afraid of expressing their emotions.'[10] The present essay does not in any way claim to offer an exhaustive analysis of the film. Since the film would not respond to such an approach, an attempt is made to address the very elements in the film which cannot be completely grasped. This study is concerned with the numerous ways in which the film establishes a margin of undefined space, in other words, the notion of the impossibility of seeing or hearing. I have opted to analyse how the film's sense of mystery is deepened by the relationship between the montage and the *mise-en-scène*,[11] while also looking at the impact on this process of the material [*plastique*] composition of the shots. My aim therefore is to preserve the mystery of HÉLAS POUR MOI, bringing to the surface the underlying forces that constitute what I call its 'poetic historiography', and showing thereby how the film is 'a cinematic proposition' ('une proposition de cinéma'), as Godard chose to subtitle it.

Mise-en-scène considered as a way into the film: the figure of the investigator

'My name is Abraham Klimt. I'm a publisher. I'm trying to find out what happened in the late afternoon of 23 July 1989 [...] Three months ago my firm received a book telling the story, if you can call it that, of what in any case happened here. You were all involved [...] There are some pages missing, so I've come to find them. That's my job' (Screenplay, pp. 65-66). So, notebook in hand, Klimt is looking for a story which he will tell while looking for it, since the film and the investigation begin at the same time (cf. Orson Welles in MR. ARKADIN). While Klimt goes around asking questions of himself and others, we see the characters recollecting, and, since the film respects the genre's conventions, we are shown their stories. Although the figure of the investigator harks back to the heyday of the private investigator in Hollywood film noir and detective films with strong literary and British influences (notably Sherlock Holmes), this figure is not limited to the 'private' variety of investigator. One can include several other investigating characters who share the aim of casting light on a secret or lie: the psychoanalyst trying to uncover a patient's traumatic or fantasised secret (e.g. SPELLBOUND); the amnesiac in search of his own story (e.g. Mankiewicz's SOMEWHERE IN THE NIGHT); and the confessor who, unlike the others, can of course give nothing away (e.g. I CONFESS, which is in fact referred to on several occasions in HÉLAS POUR MOI). It is also worth recalling that the investigator is a recurring figure in Godard's own films (most obviously DÉTECTIVE) and that he appears in different guises, of which the most famous is the secret agent Lemmy Caution (in ALPHAVILLE and ALLEMAGNE ANNÉE 90 NEUF ZÉRO). This is not to forget that most of Godard's films contain a male character who is trying to reconstruct something (KING LEAR, PASSION) without ever fully managing to do so ('it's not quite right', as Klimt says). Lastly, the minister, the doctor, Simon #2 (the god), and Klimt all wear raincoats, the conventional attire of the inspector from Philip Marlowe to Colombo... A film investigation is usually expected to answer the questions implied by the presence of the investigator, such as 'What happened?' and above all 'What is he looking for?'. Moreover, the exposition of such a film will normally be taken up by the events leading up to the drama in question. The investigator, dear to the American detective story, slowly pieces together the connections between the definite clues and those based on belief, intuition and suspicion. All the intricate details of the 'crime' are gradually revealed during the investigation, right up until the *dénouement* when the motive and the guilty party (or parties) will be unmasked, the film generally ending with a solution to the mystery. Thus, we have a genre of film that, like the investigator himself, is searching for something. It records what has happened. In the pursuit of signs, the film observes, stays alert, takes note, records the existence of hidden phenomena, reveals secrets and unmasks pretence. In contributing to the revelation of a truth, the detective gives dramatic form to the experimental or documentary aspect that is present in every film. Investigation is a metaphor for cinema itself, as Godard has long maintained: 'At times, you see, I'm trying in my own way to conduct an investigation.'[12] The particularity of Klimt's investigation compared with the conventional enquiry film is not just that in terms of *mise-en-scène* its object remains hidden and mysterious, but also that the nature of the film's montage increases and emphasises the impossibility of arriving at an irrefutable version of events. Instead of resolving the issue, the sort of investigation carried out in HÉLAS POUR MOI seems at first to offer only partial and unconnected clues. In view of the stress laid on the hermetic quality of what happened, the form the investigation takes itself becomes problematic. As Pascal Bonitzer has said: 'Mystery means what happens, not just in normal time, but rather in eternal time, outside time. However, something did happen, someone [...] comes back to the scene of the crime [...] There is therefore a before and an after, except that, as is often the case with Godard, the tenses get mixed up. There is no ending possible because everything is already over and at the same time has never begun.'[13] Klimt's entrance into the film is recorded by two shots in the prologue.[14] They announce his arrival on the scenes of the mystery and indicate the role he is going to play. The first shot of the film shows a country road with a village in the distance. Klimt is standing to the left with his back to the camera. He does not move at the beginning, but then sets off on foot towards the village, carrying a briefcase, umbrella and raincoat. The opening credits are intercut with various establishing shots until we see the same shot of Klimt on the country road. This time we see him face on. Now he's moving in the opposite direction, walking up the road towards the camera from where he set off in the opening shot. He moves forward, stops in front of the camera, looks at it for a moment and then lowers his eyes... According to Marc Vernet, the look into the camera, together with the use of a voice-off, are two stylistic features conventionally associated with the figure of the inspector in a detective film.[15] The distinctive feature of HÉLAS POUR MOI is the non-linear or 'anachronic' approach adopted by Klimt's investigation. The motif of the return journey associated with Klimt is now established: Klimt goes and comes from elsewhere. The elsewhere in question is the place where an apparently strange event perhaps occurred and/or is going to occur. In an apparent paradox, it is also the place where Klimt goes and from where he also returns. The film is a journey through water, sky and earth, but these are also the sites or locations of a mystery. Thus, Klimt walks by the lake in search of signs and reflections. We also see him approach the pontoon by which he will later leave. The formal question addressed by the film is how to represent the return of images of a mysterious event.

Uncertainty on the screen: 'the investigation'

The atypical features of Klimt's investigation pose obvious difficulties for the *mise-en-scène*. The numerous obstacles facing Klimt at first prevent a reconstruction of what took place. But rather than devaluing the event, the *mise-en-scène*, precisely because it conceals the event, raises it to the level of an enigma. Initially, none of the characters Klimt meets and questions can provide him with a single firm clue. Nonetheless, while his interview with the old servant Clémence, for example, does not reveal anything about the event, other clues about the nature of his investigation do slip into the conversation: 'I had the impression that there was something that could neither be said nor written and that the minister knew this' (Screenplay, p. 46). Next, the denials of the characters themselves literally hinder any exact reconstruction on the basis of their testimonies:

> Simon: Nothing happened.
> A. Klimt: That's not true. What happened was not normal.
> Simon: It was me. I turned round and came back. (Screenplay, pp. 133-134)

Klimt's investigation is limitless and inherently flawed since what he has set out to discover cannot be communicated, the characters being unable to reveal anything. The uncertainty principle underlies all discussion of the event so that the very impossibility of saying anything certain about it itself 'says' something, even if it is only to indicate the event's fundamentally hermetic and untransmissible nature... At the same time, by making it necessary to ask over and over again 'What happened?', and by introducing a multitude of details that obstruct the recovery of the truth, the film proposes some theories that are invitations to further speculation, even for the filmmaker himself: 'You wonder whether it's Simon who returns. He comes back and says "I've come back". Perhaps the other one let him come back, I cannot say.'[16] Thus many probable facts are based on something doubtful. An unspecified premiss sets off a series of questions and the general uncertainty leads to the irruption of insinuations and the ebb and flow of secrets and revelations. Klimt again: 'So, in your view, nothing special happened that afternoon? [...] Neither in terms of content nor form?' (Screenplay, p. 69).

As well as the ambiguity of the *mise-en-scène*, we need to consider the way that the editing heightens the mystery and increases the confusion. The indeterminacy principle can be seen to emanate from an enigmatic process of cutting and pasting that one could just as easily call 'collage'. Let us look at a specific example of how doubts raised in the *mise-en-scène* about the possibility of the accurate reconstruction of the event are exacerbated by the montage. When Klimt questions Rachel's friend Nelly about that afternoon, he receives three different versions of the same moment, each of which reappears on the screen:

> Nelly: I remember that afternoon, we were early, so was Mrs. Monod. Rachel was sitting on the pontoon...
> Voice of Benjamin: Definitely not. She arrived swimming!
> Tennis player: That's not true. She was walking in the water.
> We see the three versions of Rachel's arrival:
> – Rachel sitting on the pontoon.
> – Rachel arriving swimming.
> – Rachel walking in the water. (Screenplay, p. 66)

Here, what matters is not whether Rachel was sitting, swimming, or walking, nor that we learn exactly what happened, but rather that we realise that we are seeing eyewitness accounts where the act of forgetting, memory's counterpart, interferes in the reconstruction. The witnesses' subjective and contradictory accounts constitute a proliferation of ambiguous traces and the investigation succeeds only in collecting a mass of relative truths. The testimonies of the witnesses cannot easily be appropriated by the investigator, thus contributing to the narrative only indirectly. Denying the possibility of a truthful reconstruction of events, they lose their status as authenticated elements in the narrative and therefore as clues. The visual evidence is completely relativised by the *mise-en-scène*. We no longer know how much 'reality' we should ascribe to the visible, either in the sense of what we believe or what is likely to have happened. The only thing we can be sure of is the uncertainty principle underlying the visible. The only certainty is that nothing is certain! However, the film's form takes one stage further these questions raised about the reliability of what is shown. When Klimt asks Nelly what happened that afternoon, she replies: 'I remember. Rachel was sitting on the pontoon...'. And in the previous shot we indeed saw Rachel sitting on the pontoon. 'Definitely not. She arrived swimming.' 'That's not true. (Shot of Rachel getting out of the water.) She was walking in the water.' Several shots follow.[17] But then the third 'book' or section of the film begins with Rachel swimming up to the pontoon. Although the *mise-en-scène* already multiplies the number of points of view, these contradictory testimonies are edited together in a chaotic manner. The emphasis on dispersal, which was decided during the editing process, increases the proliferation effect, underlining the extinction of the film's internal coherence and its complete diegetic confusion. For example, the connection between the image of a character thinking and remembering and the image of the thing remembered is totally unclear. When seen for the first time, the film's apparent lack of visual cohesion adds to its obscurity. We begin to realise that the blurred images, black screen, and close-ups do mark transition, but these are only detectable as such after the film has been viewed carefully several times. Points of view are fragmented, testimonies and time scales become entangled, contaminated and muddled. Although the soundtrack, especially the voice of a character recounting what he or she has seen, often links images of the past with images of the 'present', Godard himself admits that there are too many things happening at once and that it is difficult to follow the different strands of the story.[18] The normal criteria of filmic organisation – time, space and meaning (the way the sequences are arranged) – cannot help the spectator to get his or her bearings. The montage creates disparate viewpoints and a polyphonic structure whose parts are only identifiable as a mass of uncertain fragments. It also brings about the disappearance of any chronologically based causality linking the shots. The disjointed character of the film contributes to its enigmatic serial organisation and creates a bizarre polyphony, defying all narrative logic. The soundtrack provides the only anchorage, acting as a 'binding agent' principally in the form of the narrator's voice. Godard has said that he, too, has been struck by the apparent discontinuity between the images in HÉLAS POUR MOI: 'It's a failure, but in its non-completion there is something that works: a sequence or shot is seen, but then it's completely forgotten. You don't remember anything anymore, you see only the pure present which is the present shot only and which does not have much presence since it depends on what is about to come. But since you haven't seen it yet that doesn't help much. I myself was struck by that. I like it, it's a new element in my work. The image we see now depends on the one about to come. The one which comes before is, so to speak, the ex-present and so has disappeared.'[19] If every image functions as an indicator of its predecessor, the normal sequence is reversed. This situation not only works against a film's conventional organisation but also against its very 'unravelling'. The juxtaposition of shots therefore involves a paradox. At the same time as freeing images from the slavery of narrative, the film's organisation proposes a new connection between images in a form that reverses the usual movement in cinema. This heightened irrationality (in terms of montage) may offer an opening on to the mystery of cinematographic creation and perception.

'A form that thinks' and appromixates speech: argument for a cinematographic historiography

The argument of this essay is that the configuration of Klimt's investigation gives it a form that points to something else, so that the film, in itself an enigmatic object, can articulate a series of questions. The original premiss underlying the form of the film suggests that a thorough and chronological reconstruction of the event is unlikely. In this way the relationship between historiography and cinematic form is questioned. As Godard says: 'Cinema is the legend you can see with your eyes and partly hear, or at least you can make out some fragments of it [...] The rise and fall of the cinema, superseded by other means of communication, took place in order to remind men that there is such a thing as memory, that they indeed have memories and that the word itself means "history" in Greek.'[20] The film, in the form of an investigation, attempts to explore the maze of memory. The device of formal fragmentation challenges the ability of film to incorporate mental and sense impressions, as well as the shadows and traces of subjectivity. The past's images intervene like memories and return like ghosts, appearing on the screen as if in the mind of someone remembering. If cinema has the ability to give visual and aural expression to the labyrinths of subjective memory, then the fact that a linear and complete reconstruction of an event is impossible means that the whole question of a 'cinematographic historiography' is being addressed here. Besides, according to its Greek etymology, 'historia' means investigation. At the centre of the investigation carried out in HÉLAS POUR MOI, neither absolute certainty nor clear-cut meaning is relevant any more, since all we are left with are different points of view. To return to the film, the garage is the first place where Klimt stops to make enquiries: 'Abraham Klimt looks around him and spots something in the corner of the workshop. It's a small picture in a glass frame consisting of two photographs, of a man and a woman: Simon and Rachel. ("I'm looking for someone called Simon and someone called Rachel.") Klimt approaches the picture and we see his reflection in the glass. He is standing just in front of the window looking on to the lake' (Screenplay, p. 2). Seeing Klimt's reflection superimposed on the framed photographs leads us to consider that we will be seeing Rachel and Simon through his eyes. Such an interpretation is born out by the following title that recurs throughout the film: 'History is created only through its telling.' This supports the view that Klimt's actions constitute a sort of historiographical enquiry. Indeed, were Klimt to attempt it, he would only be able to write the story by respecting the uncertainty principle, in other words by recognising the failure of the positivist approach to the writing of history. Alain Bergala has written of HÉLAS POUR MOI in the following terms:

> The suspicion created by all the shots of this film of a false present is doubtless the reason why we find in Godard's later films the search for a new sort of image, one that will bring both resurrection and redemption: as if the images of today might even compensate gradually for the past sins of cinema, even those committed by others. However, one condition would apply: time is not linear and the present always connects with a past of which it is at once the rather dream-like repetition and a slightly corrected version. This is exactly the case in HÉLAS POUR MOI, the moment when Simon leaves Rachel, for example [...] Godard will never pretend that he can achieve an exact reconstruction of what that scene was like at the time. Any resurrection of that moment will involve a slight alteration and a very small shift in perspective. Godard is seriously suggesting that what took place was also what didn't take place, or rather that what occurred was also something else: Simon both did and didn't leave. He both did and didn't come back. To Rachel, he was her husband and not her husband; her husband and also her lover, her man and also the god.[21]

By recognising the improbability of what happened that night and the impossibility of achieving an authentic reconstruction, something of the truth of the event can emerge and be born, or reborn. Doubt, or in other words the wisdom of uncertainty, enables Klimt precisely to look for what he is duty-bound to recall to the present in the name of exactitude. The film is testimony to what he achieved within the limits of his abilities. As Youssef Ishaghpour has remarked during his discussion of HISTOIRE(S) DU CINÉMA with Godard: 'The relationship between the urgency of the present and the salvaging of the past rules out the possibility of a story that simply recounts how events unfolded or claims to illuminate the past through the present and vice versa. On the contrary, what is required is a story that rejects linear narrative and stresses instead breaks and jumps, seeking to release the unrealised potential contained within the past. As you put it in one of the paradoxical quotations placed at the beginning of each section of the HISTOIRE(S) DU CINÉMA: "Providing a detailed description of what never happened is the real task of the historian" (O. Wilde).'[22] We are led to wonder whether the disrupted chronology and the scattering of sequences into uncertain fragments constitute the quest for the invisible part of the event. If so, the confusion would act as a dynamic catalyst and promise of discovery. Indeterminacy is the *sine qua non* for making images of the event reappear and becomes the very site (even if unknown) from which those images might spring. As Aude declares in the film: 'In "impossible" there is "possible".' Just as doubt both separates us from knowledge of the event and is the necessary condition of its possible re-emergence, however fragmentary, so the constant use of visual and aural *caches* [masks] has a similar effect (the case of the hand that rests on the camera and the continual reappearance of black screen). Preventing a clear view of certain shots, the *caches* force us to concentrate on them and make the scenes in question very enigmatic. On numerous occasions the soundtrack occludes the dialogue in a similar way by using aural *caches*, such as the superimposition of sounds by the noise of passing trains (especially, for example, in one of the final scenes, where the minister and the doctor shout out the 'theorem'; a scene to which we shall return). At the level of individual shots, these obstructions can be seen as indications of the method of enquiry adopted by Klimt who gets stuck and stumbles over the forbidden character of what he is trying to see. But it is this 'ostracism' that gives the image its potential. Because each fragment possesses visual incompleteness it is as though it demands completion, even provoking the feeling that the sense of mystery opens on to something, namely the imminent emergence of the invisible, able to restore a fragment to its former wholeness. As Aude puts it: 'What prevents us from seeing is also what allows us to look directly at the sacred or the beautiful.' The basic definition of the sacred refers to a secret, forbidden and inviolable domain. With the necessary reverence prior to any possible emergence of the sacred, a series of visual, auditory and conceptual detachments thus establish a necessary 'gap'. These function as both obstacles and springboards. By inscribing the absence which they signify, they point to the dimension of the secret and prepare the ground for its emergence. The visual and auditory obstacles potentially open up access to the film's dominantly poetic character, itself a passageway towards what it is impossible to see. They require the mediation of another form of backward glance, a look that declines the reconstruction of the visible in favour of a furtive glimpse of its veil...

> Klimt: You sell images, so you should know, one should surely be able to say whether there are things that it is impossible to see.
> Nelly: Invisible things?
> Klimt: Things that it is impossible to see. (Screenplay, p. 68)

Aude, visionary poetess

Since Klimt's is the only voice-over we hear in the prologue, we naturally think that he will play the role of storyteller in the film and that the affair which he is unravelling will be revealed through his investigation. But his investigation is quickly seen to constitute a kind of failure and requires the help of another method of enquiry, using intuition, imagination and vision.

When it comes to the epilogue, Aude has joined Klimt in the voice-over, and indeed hers is the main voice. This suggests that the meeting of these two figures brings about the combination of their respective approaches of historiographical enquiry and poetic vision. As Klimt says to Aude: 'I've received your letter. You mention that you saw something' (Screenplay, p. 8). Aude is in effect the one who will allow Klimt to find out what might have happened, what could have happened, and what never happened: 'That afternoon she noticed what others did not see: neither the minister nor Ludovic seemed to see or hear the god and his companion Max Mercury, although they were nearby at the time. Aude, on the other hand, perceives something of the scene taking place before her: "Be quiet, I'm listening to something"' (Screenplay, p. 80). Visual perception is no longer relevant for Aude's 'vision', which works by hearing and touch, and also operates beyond the visible using intuition. In the section of JLG/JLG devoted to HÉLAS POUR MOI, Godard teaches the blind assistant editor where, and above all, how to cut the reel of film. She memorises the places where the film has to be cut with her hands, unrolls the reel, repeats the dialogues and pretends to cut the film. The film is 'in-corporated', i.e. memorised by the body. Next, Godard asks her to imagine a geometrical figure. When she is asked: 'How do you manage to see all that?', she replies: 'In my head, just like you'.[23] The blind assistant editor suggests that there are two forms of vision: sight (which perceives what is visible) and vision ('clairvoyance' giving access to the invisible):

> Klimt: So what are you talking about? I don't see what you're saying.
> Aude: You put it very well: 'I don't see'. (Pause) And yet I saw it. Or rather, I heard it. Yes, that's how I'd put it. (Screenplay, p. 51)

Aude closes her eyes to see again what she heard that afternoon, and images of it return to the screen. She puts her hand and her head on Klimt's shoulder and says, 'Seeing the invisible is exhausting'. Her vision performs the office of mediation. Following the argument that the figure of Abraham Klimt stands for the function of investigation in cinema, the figure of Aude Amiel can be seen to represent cinema's poetic function. This interaction between the investigator and the poet makes possible the notion of HÉLAS POUR MOI as itself a 'visionary investigator'. It is certainly true that cinema is always an enquiry and a vision, which are also promises made by any writing of history. It bears witness to what happened and what could (have) happen(ed) by recording the visible and showing the invisible in their possible moments of coincidence. This essay proposes that these two properties of cinema are represented in HÉLAS POUR MOI by Klimt and Aude respectively. Both 'go and look elsewhere in order to bring back images' using two complementary methods that can be connected with the documentary-fiction dichotomy that recurs in Godard's discourse. In terms of montage, with Aude and Klimt's encounter the past and the 'present' do indeed coincide. During this sequence, space and point of view fuse in a here-and-now where the figures respond to each other. The shots representing their meeting are edited in parallel with those of the event involving Simon #2 and Rachel. Like the shot in JE VOUS SALUE, MARIE where Marie at last bares herself naked to Joseph, towards which the entire film is directed, this shot acts as a visual and auditory climax in HÉLAS POUR MOI, *il momento culminante*, the place where the spirit meets the body. We see Klimt standing at a window with one hand pressed against the glass, looking outside, astonished. It is raining. The rain is trickling down the window. We hear the Minister in a voice-off: 'Do not enter gently...'. There follows a shot of the lake's surface superimposed over a shot of a hand stroking someone's sex. Then we hear Simon #2, voice-off: 'This will be your daily prayer.' An extremely quick succession of shots follows (twelve in two seconds): sunrise (dawn), female genitals, the sun, darkness, male and female genitals uniting, darkness, genitals, darkness, genitals, darkness, genitals, darkness. The unrepresentable here emerges through the use of techniques that no longer work to exclude the eye, the ear, or the intellect, but rather allow something to be unveiled that will nonetheless elude our grasp. Like the shimmering reflections of the sky and the light upon the smooth, opaque surface of the lake of which we see only intermittent flashes and scattered, refracted rays, something luminous allows itself to be perceived but escapes capture by sight or thought: 'Ah, Simon, not into space [*le vague*], but into the waves [*les vagues*]' (Screenplay, p. 91).

At the end of the 1930s, Bataille noted in *Cahiers d'Art* that the sacred is 'that which flees as soon as it appears and cannot be captured'.[24] There are certain shots in HÉLAS POUR MOI where we see the daylight through the branches of the trees, and this photographic effect, particularly in the frequent shots taken directly into the sun, illustrates materially both the veil and its transparency. A whole series of shots, such as the veiled body of Rachel (which can be made out through her thin, transparent nightshirt), also contribute to this sense of unveiling and revealing, the latter term recalling once more the link with investigation. Here the *cache* is literally a veil, letting through rays of light without allowing us to determine distinctly the object hidden from view. In the central scene of the vision, for example, it is difficult to tell whether the shot of the hand on the genitals, seen beneath a shot of the lake, is showing the sex of a man. In similar fashion, the use of the off-screen (*hors-champ*) makes it difficult to identify the characters since we cannot see their faces. For example, the shots of Rachel in the water show a man

facing the lake with his back to the camera, so his face is off-camera, although we can guess that it is Max Mercury. Similarly the shot of Rachel in
pitch dark, half-naked from her neck to her knees is lit by a single sparkler. A
multitude of framing devices creates a tension that is not just between the
seen and unseen, but also in this case between the specific and the non-specific, between the clear and the vague, light and dark, all of which contribute
to the interference caused by the sound track during most of the sequences.
The continuous hubbub, doors constantly slamming, the polyphonic array
of random quotations in the bookshop and the cacophony of incongruous
sounds out of synch with the images all contribute to the masking effect of
the sound. The phrase 'Be quiet, I'm listening to something' is barely audi-
ble simply because the statement is itself part of Aude's 'vision', i.e. she sees
and hears things which the others, the minister and Benjamin, do not notice.
A conjunction of sound and visual effects occurs in the shot of Rachel reciting the Lord's Prayer with her back to the light, inaudible and barely visible.
Finally, the enigmatic editing used in the film also adopts this strategy with
its superimpositions, ultra-rapid intercutting of shots (as in the central scene
of the 'vision') and repetition of hiatuses (Simon's departure). Once again,
we see that the factor of indeterminacy functions as a catalyst for the emergence of the intangible. Instead of being a sign of fracture, the sense of
visual, sonorous and conceptual distance within the film, and the concomitant play of gaps between these elements, result in subtle revelation. To return to the form of the film's inner composition, there is one beautiful and
original shot that characterises this way of getting the indeterminate to
emerge. On this occasion we are not dealing with a *cache* but something
vague, something only mumbled... The shot in question is one of Rachel
standing in profile, glowing in the golden light surrounding her body. Indeed, the camera does not focus on her and only her silhouette can be made
out since the edges remain vague. A visible aura envelops Rachel so that
visually her body fuses with – and becomes indistinguishable from – its surroundings. The luminous halo encircling her abundant red hair evokes the
golden halo used by artists to depict the heads of saints, especially in religious icons. The disruption of reality in the film enables us to see what we
would not normally perceive. This shot of Rachel's hair conveys a degree of
intensity that surpasses the ordinary, its diaphanous quality having the
blurred form associated with the sacred. The passage from the blurred to the
clear is not achieved by the camera for it is when the character moves forward into focus that the blur progressively gives way to a clear image. In the
sense that the blurred space is where the clarity emerges, it can be seen to
mediate between the visible and the invisible. Godard: 'I tried to sustain the
feeling of doubt: we don't know and neither does Rachel. Perhaps this film

is like the ones they used to make, where the haziness of the image led the viewer to the awakening of the characters.'[25] Just as Joseph learns to revere the distance between his hand and Marie's belly in JE VOUS SALUE, MARIE, so we see that once the reality effects of cinematographic naturalism have been eschewed in HÉLAS POUR MOI, a gap or separation enables the latter to reach the realm of the sacred. Since the attempted reconstruction of the event cannot be observed according to the conventions of realism, the play with the possible effects of a blurred image extends indefinitely the questions raised by the film.

The sacred in Godard's œuvre of the 1990s

Although Godard's recent work has involved a constant engagement both with the world and cinema, it has never neglected the sacred, understood as that which cannot be represented but rather only evoked according to the Bressonian aesthetic.[26] On the contrary, it has been Godard's aim to subvert this entire tradition of the stylised evocation of the sacred, whereby reality is filtered down in an ascetic operation enabling the sacred finally to emerge.[27] The horror film[28] may be seen as its disreputable opposite, since in that genre the supernatural irrupts on to the screen when a disparate element disturbs the apparently harmonious world of 'normality'.[29] For Godard, however, giving some sort of material form to the impossibility of seeing lies at the centre of the cinematic project. It is no longer a matter of what lies hiding beyond the facade of an austere, everyday world; the sacred is what cinema has a mission to discover and show materially in this world. 'Not beyond, but this side of [en-deçà] the images and sounds', as one character says to Klimt. In JE VOUS SALUE, MARIE Godard is looking for the 'right' shot, with the requisite distance and appropriate framing, in order to film the body, in this case the belly of Marie. In HÉLAS POUR MOI, the multiple areas of tension resulting from the interaction between the seen and unseen, the precise and the blurred, day and night, constitute the 'body' of what cannot be seen. Being forbidden was the condition of the emergence of this body in JE VOUS SALUE, MARIE, while in Klimt's investigation the hidden becomes the very substance where seeing ('vision') can take shape. In my view, HÉLAS POUR MOI is the conclusion of this search in material terms. What escapes understanding can be attained through 'vision'; feeling replaces guesswork. The promise contained within an interdiction can be made to appear.[30] The cinema is a mystery, the dramatisation of which is proposed by Godard in HÉLAS POUR MOI. Film is where the spirit seeks to incarnate itself; the god may indeed have returned to earth in order to possess Rachel... The religious vocabulary used by Godard during the 1990s seems to point to such a quest: 'And anyway you don't argue about a vision. Perhaps the image will come to us, sir, at the time of the redemption. (Pause) As St. Paul said' (Screenplay, p. 97).[31] The recurrence of religious terms in Godard's work should not be read in terms of supposed religious convictions,[32] but rather insofar as those terms share a semantic field with the history of art: 'The cinema is of the order of a revelation as the Church describes it. Something that happens within. I prefer to say "a mystery", that's all... I've adapted a quotation from Wittgenstein. Referring to Christianity, he said: "Whatever happens, believe". I've simply added that the same is true in cinema.'[33]

Clearly, the words 'redemption', 'resurrection' and 'atonement' that feature so regularly in Godard's recent discourse have to be understood in a cinematic context, especially in terms of cinema's relationship with the history of art, and in terms of the social function that cinema might have performed (cf. Élie Faure). One may wonder if this choice of terminology refers to the condition of the image (suggesting a 'third' image created by the editing of two others), its position of importance for each of us and the power it possesses:

> Aude and A.K. are sitting on the low wall in front of the church, both looking at the lake. The light catches Aude while A.K. is in shadow.
> A. Klimt: I can't see much.
> Aude: Seeing is something different. Don't try to see all aspects of things. Leave room for a degree of indeterminacy. (Screenplay, p. 97)

Unlike in a riddle where to finish the game you try to resolve the secret of an enigma, in HÉLAS POUR MOI the participant must let go. The secret can neither be seen nor heard but rather perceived in a brief flash, 'in-corporated' like a momentary emotion. This is where the quality of 'resistance' in Godard's films is really seen, and where the indeterminate has a crucial role to play. In addressing what is this side of [*en-deçà*] the visible, all the diegetic, visual, and sound obstacles can in fact help to overcome the institutionalised blindness of cinema which denies the possibility of astonishment and bewilderment. As Martine Joly remarks of the image: 'Our indignation is caused by the breaking of the contract of trust: even if we expect more than with any other medium to be able to believe in images, this credibility has been shown to be uncertain and illusory. It's the uncertainty that is unbearable because our particular expectations of accuracy and truth are disturbed. The overwhelming desire that an image should be accurate and the visible synonymous with truth originates precisely in an awareness that our personal histories are deeply ingrained in us and never forgotten.'[34] This uncertainty, synonymous with the loss of an all-knowing point of view, is the central feature of HÉLAS POUR MOI where knowledge has to be based on doubt just as vision starts with the non-specific. The film's achievement is to depict this indeterminacy; the 'incredible' is expressed in and through the very substance of the film.

Conclusion

The collaboration of Aude and Klimt illustrates and questions the articulation of documentary and fiction. These two opposites, which represent two modes of historical reconstruction, cohabit to such an extent that they are indistinguishable. HÉLAS POUR MOI takes the form of a 'visual investigation' into a legendary past treated as an event. The enquiry depicted addresses the coexistence of, on the one hand, the invention and clairvoyance of all filmic reconstruction, where 'what could happen' is imagined; and, on the other, a film's historiographical competence, i.e. recording what did happen. The question the film addresses is how proofs and miracles, documents and fiction, can inhabit the same technical elements and meet the necessary conditions that will permit the 'historical' somehow to convey the inexpressible. The historical fabrication seen at work in HÉLAS POUR MOI echoes the project undertaken in HISTOIRE(S) DU CINÉMA which has informed indirectly the whole of my study, for there Godard interrogates the possibility of resurrecting cinema to its full potential following its early, and untimely, 'death'. Godard argues forcefully in HISTOIRE(S) DU CINÉMA for cinema's poetico-visual potential as well as its documentary function, and, as we have seen, the very substance of HÉLAS POUR MOI attends to both these aspects. Ishaghpour has stated the following:

In HISTOIRE(S) DU CINÉMA, Godard sets out to retrieve certain shots from the entire history of cinema. Each shot bears the imprint of a moment from the past, whether more or less distant, which the succession of filmic images is intended to revive for the viewer in the form of a present that has been miraculously preserved. These shots of the past have become unrecognisable, as if aware that they were once the present and are now only traces of it, proof thus of a lost present of which only the outline survives. They have become evidence in the investigation undertaken by Godard (Abraham Klimt's alter ego) to trace the moment when the major crime in cinema took place – the crime of failing to fulfil its role of capturing the present at the time of the Nazi terror. If cinema missed the only present it was important to show, as Serge Daney said, Godard has committed himself to searching relentlessly, shot after shot,

for the exact moment when the system faltered, the moment when cinema allowed itself to be disconnected from the present and desynchronised.[37]

In the same way, the two epistemological breaks in the history of cinema de-
tected by Godard, namely, the loss of the aura of silent film with the arrival
of the talkies, and the misunderstanding of the historical function of cinema
during the period of the concentration camps, could be compared with the
two approaches discussed above in relation to the uncertainty principle. On
the side of documentary, indeterminacy relativises the veracity of eyewitness accounts with the denials, doubts, omissions within the *mise-en-scène*,
and the proliferation and subsequent dispersal of points of view in the montage. Our ability to recognise things is thwarted, omniscience is deflated
and the investigation becomes bogged down. However, some part of the ineffable truth of the event does manage to emerge from the impasse of
historiographical reconstruction. At a material level, the *caches* may block
our view, putting in place and enacting the invisible, but they require us to
find another way of looking back, offering a path towards what it is impossible to see. On the side of fiction, meaning the fabrication inherent in any
historical account, the indeterminacy principle manufactures a partial access to the buried past, returning film to the sphere (or poetics) of vision
close to the experience provided by the cinematograph at the time of early
cinema. Freed from the requirement to distinguish and define, which can
become an impasse within historical thought, film can be positioned within
a multiplicity of networks with infinite possibilities. Invoking the powerful
resonance of the cinematograph's early ambitions, Godard's underlying
principle attempts to restore its magical potential. Ishaghpour again: 'Art
and God have reappeared in Godard's work from the perspective of the redemptive relationship between the poetic and the historical.'[38] The secret of
HÉLAS POUR MOI concerns the enigmatic presence of cinema at the heart of
the twentieth century.

Filmography of Jean-Luc Godard*

OPÉRATION BÉTON (1954) (35 mm). 20 mins.

UNE FEMME COQUETTE (1955) (16 mm). 10 mins.

TOUS LES GARÇONS S'APPELLENT PATRICK (CHARLOTTE ET VÉRONIQUE) (ALL BOYS ARE CALLED PATRICK) (1957) (35 mm). 21 mins.

UNE HISTOIRE D'EAU (1958) (35 mm). 18 mins.

CHARLOTTE ET SON JULES (1959) (35 mm). 20 mins.

À BOUT DE SOUFFLE (BREATHLESS) (1960) (35 mm). 90 mins.

LE PETIT SOLDAT (1960) (35 mm). 88 mins.

UNE FEMME EST UNE FEMME (A WOMAN IS A WOMAN) (1961) (35 mm). 84 mins.

'LA PARESSE' (episode in LES SEPT PÉCHÉS CAPITAUX) (1961) (35 mm). 15 mins.

VIVRE SA VIE (FILM EN DOUZE TABLEAUX) (MY LIFE TO LIVE) (1962) (35 mm). 85 mins.

'LE NOUVEAU MONDE' (episode in ROGOPAG) (1962) (35 mm). 20 mins.

LES CARABINIERS (1963) (35 mm). 80 mins.

'LE GRAND ESCROC' (episode in LES PLUS BELLES ESCROQUERIES DU MONDE) (1963) (35 mm). 25 mins.

LE MÉPRIS (CONTEMPT) (1963) (35 mm). 105 mins.

BANDE À PART (BAND OF OUTSIDERS) (1964) (35 mm). 95 mins.

UNE FEMME MARIÉE (A MARRIED WOMAN) (originally LA FEMME MARIÉE) (1964) (35 mm). 98 mins.

ALPHAVILLE. UNE ÉTRANGE AVENTURE DE LEMMY CAUTION (1965) (35 mm). 98 mins.

'MONTPARNASSE-LEVALLOIS' (episode in PARIS VU PAR... (SIX IN PARIS)) (1965) (16 mm blown up to 35 mm). 18 mins.

PIERROT LE FOU (1965) (35 mm). 112 mins.

MASCULIN FÉMININ (MASCULINE FEMININE) (1966) (35 mm). 110 mins.

MADE IN USA (1966) (35 mm). 90 mins.

DEUX OU TROIS CHOSES QUE JE SAIS D'ELLE (TWO OR THREE THINGS I KNOW ABOUT HER) (1966) (35 mm). 90 mins.

---

*   This largely follows the authoritative filmography compiled by Alain Bergala for *Godard par Godard* II

'ANTICIPATION OU L'AMOUR EN L'AN 2000' (episode in LE PLUS VIEUX MÉTIER DU MONDE (THE OLDEST PROFESSION)) (1966) (35 mm). 20 mins.

'CAMÉRA-ŒIL' (episode in LOIN DU VIETNAM) (1967) (16 mm).15 mins.

LA CHINOISE (1967) (35 mm). 96 mins.

'L'ALLER ET RETOUR ANDATE ET RITORNO DES ENFANTS PRODIGUES DEI FIGLI PRODIGHI' (episode in VANGELO 70) (1967) (35 mm). 26 mins.

WEEK-END (1967) (35 mm). 95 mins.

LE GAI SAVOIR (1968) (35 mm). 95 mins.

CINÉ-TRACTS (1968) (16 mm). 11 x 2-4 mins.

UN FILM COMME LES AUTRES (A MOVIE LIKE ANY OTHER) (1968) (16 mm). 100 mins.

ONE PLUS ONE, AKA SYMPATHY FOR THE DEVIL (1968) (35 mm). 99 mins.

ONE AMERICAN MOVIE (ONE A.M.) (1968) (16 mm). 90 mins.

BRITISH SOUNDS (SEE YOU AT MAO) (1969) (16 mm). 52 mins.

PRAVDA (Dziga Vertov Group) (1969) (16 mm). 58 mins.

VENT D'EST (WIND FROM THE EAST) (Dziga Vertov Group) (1969) (16 mm). 100 mins.

LUTTES EN ITALIE (LOTTE IN ITALIA) (Dziga Vertov Group) (1969) (16 mm). 76 mins.

JUSQU'À LA VICTOIRE (Dziga Vertov Group) (1970) (16 mm) (unfinished)

VLADIMIR ET ROSA (VLADIMIR AND ROSA) (Dziga Vertov Group) (1971) (16 mm). 103 mins.

TOUT VA BIEN (with J.-P. Gorin) (1972) (35 mm). 95 mins.

LETTER TO JANE (with J.-P. Gorin) (1972) (16 mm). 52 mins.

ICI ET AILLEURS (with A.-M. Miéville) (1974) (16 mm). 60 mins.

NUMÉRO DEUX (with A.-M. Miéville) (1975) (35 mm). 88 mins.

COMMENT ÇA VA (with A.-M. Miéville) (1975) (16 mm). 78 mins.

SIX FOIS DEUX (SUR ET SOUS LA COMMUNICATION) (with A.-M. Miéville) (1976) (video in 6 parts). 600 mins.

FRANCE/TOUR/DÉTOUR/DEUX/ENFANTS (with A.-M. Miéville) (1977-8) (video in 12 parts). 318 mins.

SAUVE QUI PEUT (LA VIE) (EVERY MAN FOR HIMSELF, aka SLOW MOTION) (with A.-M. Miéville) (1979) (35 mm). 87 mins.

'SCÉNARIO VIDÉO DE SAUVE QUI PEUT (LA VIE)' (1979) (video). 20 mins.

LETTRE À FREDDY BUACHE (1981) (video). 11 mins.

'PASSION, LE TRAVAIL ET L'AMOUR: INTRODUCTION À UN SCÉNARIO'/ 'TROISIÈME ÉTAT D'UN SCÉNARIO' (1981) (video). 30 mins.

PASSION (with A.-M. Miéville) (1981) (35 mm). 87 mins.

SCÉNARIO DU FILM PASSION (1982) (video). 54 mins.

'CHANGER D'IMAGE' (episode in series LE CHANGEMENT À PLUS D'UN TITRE) (1982) (video). 10 mins.

PRÉNOM CARMEN (with A.-M. Miéville) (FIRST NAME: CARMEN) (1982) (35 mm). 85 mins.

JE VOUS SALUE, MARIE (HAIL MARY) (1983) (35 mm). 72 mins.

'PETITES NOTES À PROPOS DU FILM JE VOUS SALUE, MARIE' (1983) (video). 25 mins.

DÉTECTIVE (with A.-M. Miéville) (1984) (35mm). 95 mins.

SOFT AND HARD: A SOFT CONVERSATION BETWEEN TWO FRIENDS ON A HARD SUBJECT (with A.-M. Miéville) (1985) (video). 52 mins.

GRANDEUR ET DÉCADENCE D'UN PETIT COMMERCE DE CINÉMA (1986) (video). 52 mins.

JLG MEETS W.A./MEETIN' W.A. (1986) (video). 26 mins.

'ENFIN, IL EST EN MA PUISSANCE', aka 'ARMIDE' (episode in ARIA) (1986-7) (35 mm). 12 mins.

KING LEAR (1987) (35 mm). 90 mins.

SOIGNE TA DROITE OU UNE PLACE SUR LA TERRE COMME AU CIEL (KEEP UP YOUR RIGHT) (1987) (35 mm). 82 mins.

'CLOSED' (10 small adverts for Marithé et François Girbaud) (1988) (video). 10X15-20 secs.

ON S'EST TOUS DÉFILÉ (1988) (video). 13 mins.

PUISSANCE DE LA PAROLE (1988) (video). 25 mins.

'LE DERNIER MOT'/'LES FRANÇAIS ENTENDUS PAR' (episode of LES FRANÇAIS VUS PAR) (1988) (video). 13 mins.

LE RAPPORT DARTY (with A.-M. Miéville) (1988-9) (video). 50 mins.

NOUVELLE VAGUE (1990) (35 mm). 89 mins.

'L'ENFANCE DE L'ART' (episode in COMMENT VONT LES ENFANTS?/HOW ARE THE KIDS?) (with A.-M. Miéville) (1990) (35 mm). 8 mins.

ALLEMAGNE ANNÉE 90 NEUF ZÉRO (GERMANY YEAR 90 NINE ZERO) (1991) (35 mm). 62 mins.

CONTRE L'OUBLI (with A.-M. Miéville) (1991) (video). 3 mins.

LES ENFANTS JOUENT À LA RUSSIE (1993) (video). 60 mins.

HÉLAS POUR MOI (1993) (35 mm). 84 mins.

JE VOUS SALUE SARAJEVO (1994) (video)

JLG/JLG: AUTOPORTRAIT DE DÉCEMBRE (JLG/JLG: DECEMBER SELF-PORTRAIT) (1994) (35 mm). 62 mins.

2X50 ANS DE CINÉMA FRANÇAIS (with A.-M. Miéville) (1995) (video). 50 mins.

FOR EVER MOZART (1996) (35 mm). 84 mins.

ADIEU AU TNS (1996) (video).

PLUS OH! (1996) (video clip originally shot in 35mm). 4 mins 15 seconds.

HISTOIRE(S) DU CINÉMA (1988-1998) (video). 265 mins.

1A: TOUTES LES HISTOIRES (51 mins): UNE HISTOIRE SEULE (42 mins)
2A: SEUL LE CINÉMA (26 mins); 2B: FATALE BEAUTÉ (28 mins)

3A: LA MONNAIE DE L'ABSOLU (26 mins); 3B: UNE VAGUE NOUVELLE (27 mins)

4A: LE CONTRÔLE DE L'UNIVERS (27 mins); 4B: LES SIGNES PARMI NOUS (38 mins)

THE OLD PLACE (with A.-M. Miéville) (2000) (video).

ÉLOGE DE L'AMOUR (2000) (35 mm/DV).

L'ORIGINE DU VINGT ET UNIÈME SIÈCLE (2000) (video). 15 mins.

Discography of Jean-Luc Godard

Nouvelle Vague (Munich: ECM 'New Series', 1997). Complete soundtrack of NOUVELLE VAGUE in a boxed set of 2 CDs accompanied by a booklet of illustrations and an essay by Claire Bartoli.

Histoire(s) du Cinéma (Munich: ECM 'New Series', 1999). Complete soundtrack of HISTOIRE(S) DU CINÉMA in a boxed set of 5 CDs accompanied by a four-volume transcription (incomplete) with English and German translation.

Selective Bibliography

I Works by Jean-Luc Godard (including short texts since 1985 not included in *Godard par Godard II*)

Introduction à une véritable histoire du cinéma, Paris: Éditions Albatros, 1980.

Jean-Luc Godard par Jean-Luc Godard, vol. 1 1950-1984, ed. Alain Bergala, Paris: Cahiers du Cinéma, 1985 (includes and supplements material published earlier in three parts by Flammarion under the general title *Godard par Godard: Les années Cahiers, Les années Karina, Des années Mao aux années 80*). Reprinted in 1998 with an additional text, 'Le cercle rouge'.

Godard on Godard [1972], ed. and trans. Tom Milne and Jean Narboni, New York: Da Capo, 1986 (texts from 1950 to 1968).

'C'est la nuit qui parle', in: Philippe Garrel and Thomas Lescure, *Une caméra à la place du cœur*, Aix-en-Provence: Éditions Admiranda/Institut de l'Image, 1992, pp. 9-13.

JLG/JLG: phrases, Paris: Éditions P.O.L., 1996.

For ever Mozart: phrases, Paris: Éditions P.O.L., 1996.

'Lettre aux *Cahiers*', *Cahiers du Cinéma*, no. 508 (1996), pp. 14-27.

'Sans-papiers: avant qu'il ne soit trop tard' (with Patrice Chéreau, Anne-Marie Miéville and Stanislas Nordey), *Le Monde*, 13 May 1998, p. 1.

2x50 ans de cinéma français: phrases, Paris: Éditions P.O.L., 1998.

Allemagne neuf zéro: phrases, Paris: Éditions P.O.L., 1998.

Les enfants jouent à la Russie: phrases, Paris: Éditions P.O.L., 1998.

Jean-Luc Godard par Jean-Luc Godard, vol. 2 1984-1998, ed. Alain Bergala, Paris: Cahiers du Cinéma, 1998.

Histoire(s) du cinéma, 4 vols, Paris: Gallimard-Gaumont, 1998.

2 Major interviews with Godard since 1985 not included in *Godard par Godard II*

'La curiosité du sujet': interview with Dominique Païni and Guy Scarpetta, *Art Press*, Special Issue 4 – 'Godard', December 1984-February 1985, pp. 4-18.

'Jean-Luc Godard-Philippe Sollers: L'entretien', *Art Press*, no. 88, January
   1985, pp. 4-9 (a transcription of the video *L'Entretien* produced by Jean-
   Paul Fargier in 1984).
Katherine Dieckmann, 'Godard in His Fifth Period', *Film Quarterly*, vol. 39,
   no. 2 (1985), pp. 2-6 (reprinted in: David Sterritt (ed.), *Jean-Luc Godard: In-
   terviews*, Jackson, Miss.: Mississippi University Press, 1998, pp. 167-174).
'Beaucoup d'intelligence': Interview with Léon Mercadet and Christian
   Perrot, *Actuel*, no. 103, January 1986, pp. 73-79, 115-117.
'ABCD...JLG': interview with Olivier Péretié, *Le Nouvel Observateur*, 18 De-
   cember 1987, pp. 50-52.
'Le cinéma meurt, vive le cinéma!': interview with Danièle Heymann, *Le
   Monde*, 30 December 1987, pp. 1 and 10.
'Godard arrêt sur images: Le cinéaste commente quelques photos de SOIGNE
   TA DROITE': interview with M. Halberstadt, *Première*, no. 130 (1988), pp.
   56-59.
'Une place sur la terre': interview with Raphaël Bassan and Hélène Merrick,
   Revue du Cinéma: Image et Son, no. 434, January 1988, pp. 51-55.
'Cultivons notre jardin': interview with François Albéra, *Cinémaction*, no. 52
   (1989), pp. 14-17.
'Wenders interviewt Godard', *Suddeutsche Zeitung* (Munich), 16 November
   1990, pp. 59-62.
'Jean-Luc Godard in Conversation with Colin MacCabe' (London, 1991), in:
   Duncan Petrie (ed.), *Screening Europe: Image and Identity in Contemporary
   European Cinema*, London: British Film Institute, 1992.
'Le Briquet de Capitaine Cook': interview with François Albéra and Mikhaïl
   Iampolski, *Les Lettres Françaises*, 19 April 1992, pp. 17-21.
'L'homme qui en savait trop': interview with Samuel Blumenfeld, Christian
   Fevret and Serge Kaganski, *Les Inrockuptibles*, no. 49, September 1993, pp.
   75-82.
'Jean-Luc Godard: "Je viens d'ailleurs"': interview with M. N. Tranchant, *Le
   Figaro*, 30 August 1993.
Interview with Bernard Pivot, 'Bouillon de Culture', France 2, 10 September
   1993.
'Jean-Luc Godard Now': interview with Andrew Sarris, *Interview*, no. 24,
   July 1994, pp. 5-6.
Interview with Gavin Smith, *Film Comment*, vol. 32, no. 2, March-April 1996,
   pp. 31-40 (reprinted in: Sterritt, *Jean-Luc Godard: Interviews*, pp. 179-193).
'Le Petit Soldat': interview with Frédéric Bonnaud and Serge Kaganski, *Les
   Inrockuptibles*, 17 November 1996, pp. 22-29.
Interview with Noël Simsolo, 'À voix nue', Radio France Culture, April
   1998.

Jonathan Rosenbaum, 'Godard in the 90s: an interview, argument, and scrapbook', *Film Comment*, vol. 34, no. 5, September-October 1998, pp. 52-61.

'La légende du siècle': interview with Frédéric Bonnaud and Arnaud Viviant, *Les Inrockuptibles*, no. 170, October 1998, pp. 20-28.

'Godard refait le cinéma', *Libération*, 7 October 1998, pp. 1-5

'Jean-Luc Godard, maître d'ouvrage d'art', *Le Monde*, 8 October 1998, p. 33.

'J'ai fait une échographie': interview with P. Murat and J.C. Loiseau, *Télérama*, 11 November 1998, p. 38

'Godard fait son cinéma': interview with Pascal Mérigeau, *Le Nouvel Observateur*, no. 1773, 29 October-4 November 1998, PP. 76-78.

'Jean-Luc Godard: Des traces au cinéma': interview with Michel Ciment and Stéphane Goudet, *Positif*, no. 456 (February 1999), pp. 50-57.

Jean-Luc Godard and Youssef Ishaghpour, 'Archéologie du cinéma et mémoire du siècle', Dialogue I, *Trafic*, no. 29 (Spring 1999), pp. 16-35.

Jean-Luc Godard and Youssef Ishaghpour, 'Archéologie du cinéma et mémoire du siècle', Dialogue II, *Trafic*, no. 30 (Summer 1999), pp. 34-53.

'Avenir(s) du cinéma': interview with Charles Tesson, *Cahiers du Cinéma* (hors série – 'Aux frontières du cinéma'), May 2000, pp. 8-19.

3   Periodicals: Special Issues or Dossiers on Godard since 1985

'Godard', *Art Press*, Special Issue 4, December 1984-February 1985.

'Jean-Luc Godard: les films', *Revue Belge du Cinéma*, no. 16, 1986.

'Jean-Luc Godard: Le Cinéma', *Revue Belge du Cinéma*, nos. 22-23, 1988.

'Le Cinéma selon Jean-Luc Godard', *CinémAction*, no. 52, 1989.

'PASSION', *L'Avant-Scène Cinéma*, no. 380, April 1989.

'Spécial Godard – Trente ans depuis', *Cahiers du Cinéma* (hors série), November 1990.

'NOUVELLE VAGUE', *L'Avant-Scène Cinéma*, nos. 396-397, November-December 1990.

'LE MÉPRIS', *L'Avant-Scène Cinéma*, nos. 412-413, May-June 1992.

'Godard' (dossier), *Blimp*, no. 21, Autumn 1992.

'Jean-Luc Godard: Au-delà de l'image', *Études cinématographiques*, nos. 194-202, 1993.

'Face au cinéma et à l'Histoire à propos de Jean-Luc Godard' (dossier), *Le Monde*, 6 October 1995 ('Supplément livres', pp. x-xi)

'Jean-Luc Godard' (dossier), *METEOR (TEXTE ZUM LAUFBILD)*, no. 6, December 1996.
'HISTOIRE(S) DU CINÉMA de Jean-Luc Godard' (dossier), *Cahiers du Cinéma*, no. 513, May 1997.
'JLG' (dossier), *Vertigo* (British), no. 7, Autumn 1997.
'Godard, toutes les histoire(s) qu'il y aurait' (dossier), Cahiers du Cinéma, no. 529, November 1998.
'Le Siècle de Jean-Luc Godard: Guide pour HISTOIRE(S) DU CINÉMA', *Art Press*, hors série, November 1998.
'Spécial HISTOIRE(S) DU CINÉMA', *Cahiers du Cinéma*, no. 537, July-August 1999.
'The Godard dossier', *Screen*, vol. 40, no. 3, Autumn 1999.

4   Critical Works on Godard

Aumont, Jacques, *Amnésies: fictions du cinéma d'après Jean-Luc Godard*, Paris: P.O.L., 1999.
– 'Beauté, fatal souci: Note sur un épisode des HISTOIRE(S) DU CINÉMA', *Cinémathèque*, no. 12 (1998), pp. 17-25.
– 'La mort de Dante', *Cinémas* (Canadian), vol. 8, nos. 1-2, Special Issue – 'Cinéma et Mélancolie' (1997), pp. 125-145.
– 'Godard peintre', in: *L'œil interminable: Cinéma et peinture* , Paris: Librairie Séguier, 1989, pp. 223-247.
Bellour, Raymond, *L'entre-images: photo, cinéma, vidéo*, Paris: La Différence, 1990, pp. 330-7
– and Mary Lea Bandy (eds.), *Jean-Luc Godard: Son+Image, 1974-1991*, New York: Museum of Modern Art, 1992.
Bergala, Alain, 'HÉLAS POUR MOI, ou du présent comme passé légèrement corrigé,' *Cinémathèque*, no. 5, (1994), pp. 19-27.
– 'La maison de cristal', *Cahiers du Cinéma*, no. 508 (1996), pp. 28-31.
– *Nul mieux que Godard*, Paris: Cahiers du Cinéma, 1999.
Biette, Jean-Claude, 'Les enfants de Godard et de Pasiphaé', *Trafic*, no. 15 (1995), pp. 118-130.
Bonitzer, Pascal, 'Dieu, Godard, le zapping', *Trafic*, no. 8 (1993), pp. 5-12.
Bouquet, Stéphane, 'Des livres, Le livre', *Cahiers du Cinéma*, no. 529 (1998), pp. 58-59.
Buache, Freddy, 'La rumeur des distances traversées,' *Cinémathèque*, no. 8 (1995), pp. 43-49.

Censi, Rinaldo, 'HISTOIRE(S) DU CINÉMA: Lo splendore delle rovine', *Cineforum*, no. 366, July-August 1997, pp. 12-17.
– 'Jean-Luc Godard: Panegirico in dieci movimenti', *Cineforum*, no. 383, April 1999, pp. 45-47.
Cerisuelo, Marc, *Jean-Luc Godard*, Paris: Lherminier/Quatre-Vents, 1989.
Ciment, Michel, 'Je vous salue Godard', *Positif*, no. 324, February 1988, pp. 31-33.
Cohen, Alain J.-J., 'Godard et la passion du féminin: cas extrêmes de Marie ou d'Armide', *Vertigo*, no. 14 (1995), pp. 111-117.
De Baecque, Antoine, 'À la recherche d'une forme cinématographique de l'histoire', *Critique*, nos. 632-633 (2000), pp. 154-165.
Deleuze, Gilles, *Cinema 2: The Time-Image* [1985], trans. Hugh Tomlinson and Robert Galeta, London: Athlone Press, 1989.
Delvaux, Claudine, 'Tirer son plan et puis le voir: cinq fragments sur SOIGNE TA DROITE de Jean-Luc Godard', *Revue Belge du Cinéma*, nos. 22-23 (1988), pp. 190-205.
Desbarats, Carole and Jean-Paul Gorce (eds.), *L'effet-Godard*, Toulouse: Milan, 1989.
Dior, Julie, 'À la poursuite du je: JLG/JLG', *Cinémathèque*, no. 12 (1998), pp. 24-33.
Dixon, Wheeler Winston, *The Films of Jean-Luc Godard*, Albany: SUNY Press, 1997,
Douin, Jean-Luc, *Godard*, Paris: Rivages, 1989.
Eisenschitz, Bernard, '"Une machine à montrer l'invisible": Conversation à propos des HISTOIRE(S) DU CINÉMA', *Cahiers du Cinéma*, no. 529 (1998), pp. 52-56.
Farassino, Alberto, *Jean-Luc Godard*, Milan: Il Castoro,1996.
Frodon, Jean-Michel, *L'âge moderne du cinéma français: De la nouvelle vague à nos jours*, Paris: Flammarion, 1995, pp. 774-778.
– 'Jean-Luc Godard, autoportrait de mélancolie', *Le Monde*, 9 March, 1995, p. 26.
Giavarini, Laurence, 'À l'ouest, le crépuscule', *Cahiers du Cinéma*, no. 449, November 1991, pp. 82-86.
Goudet, Stéphane, 'Splendeurs et apories de la dernière écume', *Positif*, no. 456, February 1999, pp. 58-59.
Grafe, Frieda, 'Whose History. Jean-Luc Godard between the Media', *documenta documents*, no. 2 (Kassel: documenta GmbH,1996). Trans. Stephen Locke.
Harcourt, Peter, 'Calculated Approximations of Possibilities: Rhetorical strategies in the late films of Jean-Luc Godard', *Cineaction*, no. 48 (1998), pp. 8-17.

Ipacki, David, 'Le Verbe ressuscité et l'image crucifiée: JLG/JLG de Jean-Luc Godard', *Cinémathèque*, no. 8 (1995), pp. 33-42.

Jameson, Fredric, 'High-tech collectives in Late Godard', in: *The Geopolitical Aesthetic: cinema and space in the world system*, London and Bloomington: Indiana University Press, 1992, pp. 158-185.

Jousse, Thierry, 'Lettre à Jean-Luc Godard' (on HÉLAS POUR MOI), *Cahiers du Cinéma*, no. 471 (1993), pp. 30-32.

–, 'Melancholia: JLG/JLG', *Cahiers du Cinéma*, no. 489 (1994), p. 36.

Kramer, Robert, 'Sur et autour de HÉLAS POUR MOI', *Positif*, November 1994, pp. 66-68.

Leutrat, Jean-Louis, 'HISTOIRE(S) DU CINÉMA, ou comment devenir maître d'un souvenir', *Cinémathèque*, no. 5 (1994), pp. 28-39.

– 'Ah! les salauds!' (on ALLEMAGNE ANNÉE 90 NEUF ZÉRO), *Cinémas* (Canadian), vol. 4, no. 3 (1994), pp. 73-84.

– 'Un besoin de distance' (on ON S'EST TOUS DÉFILÉ), *Vertigo*, no. 18 (1999), pp. 124-128.

– *Jean-Luc Godard, un cinéaste mallarméen*, Paris: Schena-Didier Érudition, 1998.

– *Des traces qui nous ressemblent: PASSION de Jean-Luc Godard*, Seyssel: Éditions Comp'Act, 1990.

Locke, Maryel and Charles Warren (eds.), HAIL MARY: *Women and the Sacred in Film*, Carbondale: Southern Illinois Press, 1994.

Loshitzky, Josefa, *The Radical Faces of Godard and Bertolucci*, Detroit: Wayne State University Press, 1995.

MacCabe, Colin, *Godard: Images, Sounds, Politics*, London: BFI/MacMillan, 1980.

Mazabrard, Colette, 'Godard revigorant', *Cahiers du Cinéma*, no. 92, May 1989, pp. vi-vii.

– 'Ruptures: *Je ne vois pas, mademoiselle*' (on HÉLAS POUR MOI), *Vertigo*, nos. 11-12 (1994), pp. 42-47.

Mesnil, Michel, 'Blier, Godard: la vérité en cinéma', *Esprit*, no. 197, December 1993, pp. 121-130.

Nesbitt, Molly, 'History Without Object', in: Kerry Brougher (ed.), *Art and Film Since 1945: Hall of Mirrors*, New York: Monacelli Press/Los Angeles: Museum of Contemporary Art, 1996, pp. 280-97.

Paech, Joachim, PASSION *oder Die Einbildungen des Jean-Luc Godard*, Frankfurt: Deutsches Filmmuseum, 1989.

Rafferty, Terrence, 'Double Godard: The director revisits ALPHAVILLE and presents a self-portrait', *The New Yorker*, 6 February 1995, pp. 92-96.

Rancière, Jacques, 'La sainte et l'héritière: À propos des HISTOIRE(S) DU CINÉMA', *Cahiers du Cinéma*, no. 536 (1999), pp. 58-61.

Richard, Frances, 'Jean-Luc Godard: Swiss Institute', *Artforum*, vol. 38. no. 3, November 1999, pp. 146-147.

Robinson, Marc, 'Resurrected Images: Godard's KING LEAR', *Performing Arts Journal*, vol. 11, no. 1, 1988, pp. 20-26.

Roloff, Volkor and Scarlett Winter (eds.), *Godard Intermedial*, Tübingen: Stauffenburg, 1997.

Rosenbaum, Jonathan, 'Godard in the 90s: an interview, argument, and scrapbook', *Film Comment*, vol. 34, no. 5, September-October 1998, pp. 52-61.

– 'Trailer for Godard's HISTOIRE(S) DU CINÉMA', *Vertigo* (British), no. 7 (1997), pp 12-20.

– '*Le vrai coupable*: two kinds of criticism in Godard's work', *Screen*, vol. 40, no. 3, Autumn 1999, pp. 316-322.

– *Placing Movies: The Practice of Film Criticism*, Berkeley: University of California Press, 1995, pp. 18-24, pp. 184-189.

Rubenstein, Meyer Raphael, *Postcards from Alphaville: Jean-Luc Godard in Contemporary Art, 1963-1992*, Long Island City, NY: Institute for Contemporary Art, P.S.1 Museum, 1992.

Seguin, Louis, 'Le brouillard et son reflet', *La Quinzaine littéraire*, no. 587, 16-31 October 1991, pp. 27-28.

Shafto, Sally, 'Saut dans le vide: Godard et le peintre', *Cinémathèque*, no. 16 (1999), pp. 92-107.

Silverman, Kaja and Harun Farocki, *Speaking about Godard*, New York: NYU Press, 1998.

Skoller, Jeffrey, 'Reinventing Time, Or The continuing Adventures of Lemmy Caution in Godard's GERMANY YEAR 90 NINE ZERO', *Film Quarterly*, vol. 3, no. 3 (1999), pp. 35-42.

Sollers, Philippe, 'Il y a des fantômes plein l'écran...': interview with Antoine de Baecque and Serge Toubiana, *Cahiers du Cinéma*, no. 153 (1997), pp. 39-48

– 'JLG/JLG: un cinéma de l'être-là', *Cahiers du Cinéma*, no. 489 (1994), pp. 37-39.

Stam, Robert, 'The Lake, The Trees' (on NOUVELLE VAGUE), *Film Comment*, vol. 27, no. 1, January-February 1991, pp. 63-66.

Sterritt, David, *The Films of Jean-Luc Godard: Seeing the Invisible*, New York: Cambridge University Press, 1999.

Temple, Michael, 'It will be worth it', *Sight & Sound*, vol. 8, no. 1, January 1998, pp. 20-23.

– 'The Nutty Professor: teaching film with Jean-Luc Godard', *Screen*, vol. 40, no. 3, Autumn 1999, pp. 323-330.

- 'Godard, écrivain', in: Vérène Grieshaber (ed.), *Contemporary Swiss Writing*, London: Institute of Romance Studies/Interstice, forthcoming.
Temple, Michael and James S. Williams, 'Jean-Luc Godard: Images, Words, Histories', *Dalhousie French Studies*, no. 45, Winter 1998, pp. 99-110.
Theweleit, Klaus, *One+One*, Berlin: Brinkmann & Bose, 1995.
Toffetti, Sergio (ed.), *Jean-Luc Godard: un hommage du Centre culturel français de Turin et du Museo nationale del cinema de Turin*, Turin, 1990.
Wajcman, Gérard, '"Saint Paul" Godard contre "Moïse" Lanzmann, le match', *l'Infini*, no. 65, Spring 1999, pp. 121-127.
White, Armond, 'Double Helix: Jean-Luc Godard', *Film Comment*, vol. 32, no. 2, March-April 1996, pp. 26-30.
Williams, James S., 'The Signs Amongst Us: Jean-Luc Godard's histoire(s) du cinéma', *Screen*, vol. 40, no. 3, Autumn 1999, pp. 306-315.
- 'Identité et situation de Krzysztof Kieślowski dans le contexte des dernières œuvres de Jean-Luc Godard', in: Jean Macary (ed.), *Francographies: Création et Réalité d'Expression Française, Actes II*, New York: Société des Professeurs Français et Francophones d'Amérique, 1995, pp. 125-133.
- 'Beyond the Cinematic Body: human emotion vs. digital technology in Jean-Luc Godard's HISTOIRE(S) DU CINÉMA', in: Scott Brewster, John J. Joughin, David Owen and Richard J. Walker (eds.), *Inhuman Reflections: Thinking the limits of the human*, Manchester: Manchester University Press, 2000, pp. 188-202.
- and Michael Temple, 'Jean-Luc Godard: Images, Words, Histories', *Dalhousie French Studies*, vol. 45, Winter 1998, pp. 99-110.
Wilson, Emma, 'Conclusion: Histories of Cinema', in: *French Cinema Since 1950: Personal Histories*, London: Duckworth, 1999, pp. 137-144.
Witt, Michael, 'L'image selon Godard: théorie et pratique de l'image dans l'œuvre de Godard des années 70 à 90', in: Jean-Pierre Esquenazi, Gilles Delavaud and Marie-Françoise Grange (eds.), *Godard et le métier d'artiste*, Paris: L'Harmattan (Actes du colloque de Cerisy), forthcoming 2000.
- 'On Gilles Deleuze on Jean-Luc Godard: an Interrogation of "la méthode du ENTRE"', *Australian Journal of French Studies*, vol. 36, no. 1 (1999), pp. 110-124.
- 'The death(s) of cinema according to Godard', *Screen*, vol. 40, no. 3, Autumn 1999, pp. 331-346.
- 'Qu'était-ce que le cinéma, Jean-Luc Godard? An analysis of the cinema(s) at work in and around Godard's HISTOIRE(S) DU CINÉMA', in: Elizabeth Ezra and Susan Harris (eds.), *France in Focus: Film and National Identity*, Oxford: Berg, forthcoming 2000.
Wollen, Peter, 'When the beam of light has gone', *London Review of Books*, 17 September, 1998, pp. 19-20.

Notes

Notes to 1: Introduction to the Mysteries of Cinema, 1985-2000

1   'C'était ça, la Nouvelle Vague/la politique des auteurs/pas les auteurs/les œuvres', spoken by Godard as the guard to the Museum of the Real in HISTOIRE(S) DU CINÉMA 3B, UNE VAGUE NOUVELLE. His character agrees with the sentiments expressed here: 'Your friend is right, Miss: first the works, then the people' ('Votre ami a raison, Mademoiselle/d'abord les œuvres/les hommes ensuite'). Variations on the formula have been deployed by Godard in many interviews, including his reply to Serge Daney's suggestion, coincidentally, that he might be the 'guardian' of cinema: 'I believe in man to the extent that he creates things. Men are to be respected for creating things, whether it be an ashtray, a remote control, a car, a film, or a painting. From that point of view I'm not a humanist at all. François [Truffaut] talked about the *politique des auteurs*. Today, only the word 'auteur' remains, but what was interesting was the term *'politique'*. Auteurs are not what's important. These days we supposedly respect man so much that the result is we don't respect his work' ('Godard fait des histoires': interview with Serge Daney, in: *Libération*, 26th December 1988, included in Alain Bergala (ed.), *Jean-Luc Godard par Jean-Luc Godard*, vol. 2 1984-1988, Paris: Cahiers du Cinéma, 1998, pp. 161-173 (p. 162)). This interview has been translated as 'Godard Makes [Hi]stories': Interview with Serge Daney' in: Raymond Bellour and Mary Lea Bandy (eds.), *Jean-Luc Godard: Son+Image 1974-1991*, New York: Museum of Modern Art, 1992, pp. 159-67.

2   See 'Beaucoup d'intelligence': interview with Léon Mercadet and Christian Perrot, *Actuel*, no. 103, January 1986, pp. 73-79, 115-117 (p. 117).

3   *Ibid.*.

4   Carole Desbarats and Jean-Paul Gorce (eds.), *L'effet-Godard*, Toulouse: Milan, 1989.

5   Examples of Godard's recent personal visibility include a long radio interview on France Culture in May 1995 entitled 'Le bon plaisir de Jean-Luc Godard', and in September of the same year his public acceptance of the Adorno Prize in Frankfurt. In 1996 he starred in Anne-Marie Miéville's film NOUS SOMMES TOUS ENCORE ICI, and in 1998 he received a César in honour of the Nouvelle Vague while interviews with Bergala were relayed in retail outlets like FNAC to promote the commercial release of the four-volume book *Histoire(s) du cinéma* (it sold out almost immediately in France). In May 1998, Godard was also co-signatory to a declaration published in *Le Monde* against the French government's actions towards the *sans-papiers* (those people not in possession of valid legal documents and threatened with deportation).

6   See Josefa Loshitzky, *The Radical Faces of Godard and Bertolucci*, Detroit: Wayne State
    University Press, 1995; Wheeler Winston Dixon, *The Films of Jean-Luc Godard*, Albany:
    SUNY Press, 1997; David Sterritt, *The Films of Jean-Luc Godard: Seeing the Invisible*,
    New York: Cambridge University Press, 1999; and Kaja Silverman and Harun
    Farocki, *Speaking About Godard*, New York: New York University Press, 1998.

7   Exceptions include the following: Bellour and Bandy, *Jean-Luc Godard: Son+Image
    1974-1991*, op. cit. (featuring chapters by Bellour, Jean-Louis Leutrat, Peter Wollen,
    Jacques Aumont, Philippe Dubois, Alain Bergala and Laura Mulvey), Michael Tem-
    ple and James S. Williams, 'Jean-Luc Godard: Images, Words, Histories', *Dalhousie
    French Studies*, vol. 45, Winter 1998, pp. 99-110, and Michael Witt, 'L'image selon
    Godard: théorie et pratique de l'image dans l'oeuvre de Godard des années 70 à 90',
    in: Jean-Pierre Esquenazi, Gilles Delavaud and Marie-Françoise Grange (eds.),
    Godard et le métier d'artiste, Paris: L'Harmattan (Actes du colloque de Cerisy), forth-
    coming. See also Molly Nesbitt, 'History Without Object' in: Kerry Brougher (ed.), *Art
    and Film Since 1945: Hall of Mirrors*, New York: Monacelli Press/Los Angeles: Mu-
    seum of Contemporary Art, 1996, pp. 280-97 (ALLEMAGNE ANNÉE 90 NEUF ZÉRO),
    Jeffrey Skoller, 'Reinventing Time, Or The continuing Adventures of Lemmy Caution
    in Godard's ALLEMAGNE ANNÉE 90 NEUF ZÉRO', *Film Quarterly*, vol. 3, no. 3 (1999), pp.
    35-42, and Klaus Theweleit, *One+One*, Berlin: Brinkmann & Bose, 1995. For work
    based more around HISTOIRE(S) DU CINÉMA, see Jean-Louis Leutrat, 'HISTOIRE(S) DU
    CINÉMA, ou comment devenir maître d'un souvenir', *Cinémathèque*, vol. 5 (1994), pp
    19-24 (on the first part of Chapter 1A); Jacques Aumont, 'Beauté, fatal souci: Note sur
    un épisode des HISTOIRE(S) DU CINÉMA, *Cinémathèque*, vol. 12 (1998), pp. 17-25 (on
    Chapter 2B) (translated for the present volume); Michael Witt, 'On Gilles Deleuze on
    Jean-Luc Godard: an Interrogation of "la méthode du ENTRE"', *Australian Journal of
    French Studies*, vol. 36, no. 1 (1999), pp. 110-124; Armond White, 'Double Helix: Jean-
    Luc Godard', *Film Comment*, vol. 32, no. 2, March-April 1996, pp. 26-30 (followed by
    an interview with Godard by Gavin Smith (pp. 31-40)); and James S. Williams, 'Be-
    yond the Cinematic Body: human emotion vs. digital technology in Jean-Luc
    Godard's HISTOIRE(S) DU CINÉMA' (on Chapter 1B), in: Scott Brewster, John J.
    Joughin, David Owen and Richard J. Walker (eds.), *Inhuman Reflections: Thinking the
    limits of the human*, Manchester: Manchester University Press, 2000, pp. 188-202.
    Aumont has since published *Amnésies: Fictions du cinéma d'après Jean-Luc Godard*,
    Paris: Éditions P.O.L., 1999.

8   For the best general perspective in English on HISTOIRE(S) DU CINÉMA, see the 'Godard
    Dossier' in *Screen*, vol. 40, no. 3, Autumn 1999, pp. 304-347, edited by Michael Witt,
    which includes articles by Witt, James S. Williams, Michael Temple and Jonathan
    Rosenbaum. See also Michael Temple, 'It will be worth it', *Sight & Sound*, vol. 8, no. 1,
    January 1998, pp. 20-23 (although the work as described is not the definitive version),
    and Jonathan Rosenbaum, 'Godard in the 90s: an interview, argument, and scrapbook',
    Film Comment, vol. 34, no. 5, September/October 1998, pp. 52-61 (a slightly modified
    version of 'Trailer for Godard's HISTOIRE(S) DU CINÉMA', *Vertigo* (British), no. 7, 1997,
    pp. 12-20). Introductions in French include the Godard special issue of *Cahiers du
    Cinéma*, no. 537, July-August 1999 (which includes short individual descriptions of
    each episode) and the November 1998 issue of *Art Press* (hors série) intended as a
    'guide' to HISTOIRE(S) DU CINÉMA featuring articles by Dominique Païni, André S.
    Labarthe, Philippe Forest, Jean Douchet, Kent Jones, Pascal Convert, Eric Rondepierre,

Cyril Beghin, Gary Hill, Hans Belting and Anne-Marie Bonnet, Bernard Tschumi, Melvin Charney, Gilles Tiberghien, Marc Augé, Alain Badiou and Marie-José Mondzain. See also 'Face au cinéma et à l'Histoire à propos de Jean-Luc Godard', *Le Monde*, 6 October 1995, 'Supplément livres', pp. x-xi, a published transcription of a round-table discussion on HISTOIRE(S) DU CINÉMA held between writers, historians and philosophers during the 1995 Lugano Film Festival, at which Godard was present.

9 Jean-Luc Godard, HISTOIRE(S) DU CINÉMA (Gaumont, 1998). During the autumn of 1999, the entire series was broadcast on Canal Plus so one could claim that *de facto* there is a free, legally reproducible copy of the work, whereas numerous semi-pirated copies of the work in progress had previously been in circulation for some years.

10 See Filmography for English versions of film and video titles.

11 Jean-Luc Godard, *Histoire(s) du cinéma*, Paris: Gallimard-Gaumont, 1998, 4 vols.. The boxed set of CDs produced by ECM (New Series) a year later also includes a five-volume transcription (incomplete) of the soundtrack of HISTOIRE(S) DU CINÉMA translated into English and German.

12 All of the following are published in Paris by Éditions P.O.L.: *JLG/JLG* (1996), *For ever Mozart* (1996), *2x50 ans de cinéma français* (1998), *Allemagne neuf zéro* (1998), *Les enfants jouent à la Russie* (1998).

13 See 'Hitchcock est mort', in: Alain Bergala (ed.), *Jean-Luc Godard par Jean-Luc Godard*, vol. 1 1950-1984, Paris: Cahiers du Cinéma, 1985, pp. 412-416 (p. 416).

14 See 'La curiosité du sujet', *Art Press*, Special Issue 4 – 'Godard', December 1984-February 1985, pp. 4-18 (p. 5).

15 Godard claims that the writer Marguerite Duras always referred to him as a 'poète maudit'. We have discussed the symbolic importance of their relationship as an encounter between Word and Image in Temple and Williams, 'Jean-Luc Godard: Images, Words, Histories', op. cit., and Michael Temple, 'Godard, écrivain', in: Vérène Grieshaber (ed.), *Contemporary Swiss Writing*, London: Institute of Romance Studies/ Interstice, forthcoming.

16 Michael Witt's contention, for example, is that HISTOIRE(S) DU CINÉMA can be traced back to the early 1970s and notably the experience of JUSQU'À LA VICTOIRE and ICI ET AILLEURS. See 'The death(s) of cinema according to Godard', *Screen*, vol. 40, no. 3, Autumn 1999, pp. 331-346 (pp. 336-338). Jonathan Rosenbaum discusses Godard's longstanding dual role as an historically-informed critic and contemporary chronicler in '*Le vrai coupable*: two kinds of criticism in Godard's work', *Screen*, vol. 40, no. 3, Autumn 1999, pp. 316-322.

17 See Witt, 'The death(s) of cinema according to Godard', op. cit..

18 'La vidéo m'a appris à voir le cinéma et à repenser le travail du cinéma d'une autre manière.' See 'L'art à partir de la vie', in: Bergala, *Godard par Godard I*, op. cit., pp. 9-24 (p. 24).

19 Jean-Luc Godard, *Introduction à une véritable histoire du cinéma*, Paris: Éditions Albatros, 1980, p. 15. The experiment failed apparently due to lack of funds, and only seven of the planned ten voyages were completed.

20 The mortal relationship between video and cinema as Cain and Abel was formalised explicitly in SAUVE QUI PEUT (LA VIE).

21 Films sampled in SOFT AND HARD include BROKEN BLOSSOMS, LE MÉPRIS, GONE WITH THE WIND, FRANKENSTEIN, and REAR WINDOW, all of which reappear in HISTOIRE(S) DU CINÉMA.

22 See Witt's Introduction to the 'Godard Dossier', op. cit., pp. 304-305 (p. 305).

23 See 'Godard à Venise': interview with Jean-Luc Godard, *Cinématographe*, vol. 95, December 1983, pp. 3-7 (p. 6).

24 Mercadet and Perrot, 'Beaucoup d'intelligence', op. cit, p. 74.

25 It also featured very heavily in the original video draft of Chapter 4B, LES SIGNES PARMI NOUS, screened at the Institut Français in London in September 1998. See Temple, 'It will be worth it', op. cit..

26 This later becomes Chapter 3A and is, in fact, called LA MONNAIE DE L'ABSOLU. The title LA RÉPONSE DES TÉNÈBRES does feature in the chapter, however, and is in this sense a 'subtitle' or alternative title for 3A.

27 Although Godard tries at length to explain to Daney both exactly what he understands by this term and how crucial a role he assigns it in his project, the clearest discursive expression of 'historical montage', from which the quoted extract derives, is a talk given at the FEMIS the following year. See 'Le montage, la solitude, la liberté', in: Bergala, *Godard par Godard II*, op. cit., pp. 242-249 (p. 242).

28 Ibid..

29 See Temple and Williams, 'Jean-Luc Godard: Images, Words, Histories', op. cit., and Temple, 'Godard, écrivain', op. cit., for an examination of Godard's literary style.

30 See 'Le cinéma n'a pas su remplir son rôle': interview with Jean-Pierre Lavoignat and Christophe d'Yvoire, *Studio*, vol. 156, March 1995, reprinted in Bergala, *Godard par Godard II*, op. cit., pp. 335-343 (p. 336).

31 See Charles Tesson, '"Une machine à montrer l'invisible": Conversation avec Bernard Eisenschitz à propos des HISTOIRE(S) DU CINÉMA', *Cahiers du Cinéma*, vol. 529, 1998, pp. 52-56, where the film historian Bernard Eisenschitz describes the difficult task of locating and checking sources which Godard had employed him to perform (allegedly for legal reasons).

32 See Jean-Luc Godard and Youssef Ishaghpour, 'Archéologie du cinéma et mémoire du siècle', Dialogue I, *Trafic*, no. 29, Spring 1999, pp. 16-35 (p. 22).

33 Ibid., p. 23. We should note in passing that probably the most striking change adopted by Godard in the last-minute re-editing of HISTOIRE(S) DU CINÉMA was indeed the frequent and powerful intercalation of black screen. This rhythmic effect was matched on the soundtrack by stunning moments of silence.

34 Ibid., pp. 17-21.

35 Ibid., pp. 25-26. The comparison with Marker is potentially very rich in terms of their artistic and political itinerary, the thematics of history and memory, technological curiosity and the essay form. See Bellour's discussion of Marker's CD-ROM IMMEMORY in 'The Book, Back and Forth', in: Raymond Bellour, *Qu'est-ce qu'une madeleine?*, Paris: Yves Gevaert Éditions-Centre Georges Pompidou, 1997, pp. 109-154.

36 See, for example, Léon Mercadet and Christian Perrot, 'La télévision fabrique de l'oubli', in: Bergala, *Godard par Godard II*, op. cit., pp. 237-241, where Godard states simply that cinema produced memories while television can only manufacture forgetting (p. 240).

37 See Godard and Ishaghpour, 'Archéologie du cinéma et mémoire du siècle', Dialogue I, op. cit., p. 25.

38 See Jean-Luc Godard and Youssef Ishaghpour, 'Archéologie du cinéma et mémoire du siècle', Dialogue II, *Trafic*, no. 30, Summer 1999, p. 34-53 (p. 53).

39 The meeting between Godard and Furet, best known for his work on the French revolution, took place in Paris in June 1997 and was based around a private screening of
those chapters of HISTOIRE(S) DU CINÉMA then available. See Antoine de Baecque, 'À
la recherche d'une forme cinématographique de l'histoire', Critique, nos. 632-633
(2000), pp. 154-165 (pp. 164-165).

40 See Hayden White 'The modernist event', in: Vivian Sobchack (ed.), The Persistence of
History: Cinema, Television, and the Modern Event, London and New York: Routledge,
1996, pp. 17-38 (p. 22).

41 See Rosenbaum, 'Godard in the '90s', op. cit., pp. 52-53. Godard includes Pound's
own voice in the last stages of Chapter 4B, LES SIGNES PARMI NOUS.

42 See text of JLG/JLG, op. cit., pp. 10-14.

43 See Aumont, Amnésies, op. cit., pp. 10-11.

44 Ibid., p. 13.

45 The voice is taken from the actual recordings of the interviews Truffaut conducted
with Hitchcock in 1967.

46 Auriol's original phrase, 'Cinema is the art of doing pretty things to pretty girls' ('Le
cinéma, c'est l'art de faire de jolies choses à de jolies filles'), is read aloud by Miéville
in 2X50 ANS DE CINÉMA FRANÇAIS and Chapter 3B of HISTOIRE(S) DU CINÉMA, UNE
VAGUE NOUVELLE.

47 See 'La justification par les œuvres', in: Aumont, Amnésies, op. cit., pp. 101-138.

48 For an examination of the literary and filmic notions of the 'essay' in the French tradition, see Michael Temple, 'The Nutty Professor: teaching film with Jean-Luc Godard',
Screen, vol. 40, no. 3, Autumn 1999, pp. 323-330 (pp. 329-330).

49 'Entretien', in: Bergala, Godard par Godard I, op. cit., pp. 215-236 (p. 215).

50 The original reads: 'je ne peins pas l'être, je peins le passage'. This phrase from
Montaigne's epistemological essay is also, interestingly, the epigraph to Élie Faure's
L'esprit des formes.

51 'Godard fait des histoires', in: Bergala, Godard par Godard II, op. cit., p. 163.

52 See Histoire(s) du cinéma, vol. 4, p. 254.

53 Cocteau's phrase, 'Le cinématographe, c'est filmer la mort au travail', is frequently
cited by Godard, both verbally and in his work.

54 This question is addressed in the context of Malraux and the metamorphosis of artistic form in James S. Williams, 'The Signs Amongst Us: Jean-Luc Godard's HISTOIRE(S)
DU CINÉMA', Screen, vol. 40, no. 3, Autumn 1999, pp. 306-315 (pp. 314-315).

55 Speaking of the early achievements of cinema, Méliès stated: 'Mais tout ceci n'est que
l'enfance de l'art'. Quoted in Georges Sadoul, Georges Méliès, Paris: Éditions Seghers,
1962, p. 92.

Notes to 2: Montage, My Beautiful Care, or Histories of the Cinematograph

1 Jean-Luc Godard, 'Godard arrêt sur images: Le cinéaste commente quelques photos
de SOIGNE TA DROITE': interview with Michèle Halberstadt, Première, no. 130, 1988,
pp. 56-59 (p. 59).

2   Lev Kuleshov, 'The Principles of Montage', in: Lev Kuleshov, *Kuleshov on Film*, ed.
    and trans. Ronald Larcac, Berkeley, 1974, pp. 183-195; Jean-Luc Godard, 'Montage,
    mon beau souci', in: Alain Bergala (ed.), *Jean-Luc Godard par Jean-Luc Godard*, vol. 1,
    Paris: Éditions de l'Étoile/Cahiers du Cinéma, 1985, pp. 92-93 (henceforth *Godard par
    Godard I*).
3   François de Malherbe, 'Dessein de quitter une dame qui ne le contentait que de
    promesse', in: François de Malherbe, *Œuvres*, ed. Antoine Adam, Paris, 1971, pp. 21-
    22. Godard has explicitly stated that he felt the need to revisit his earlier text, claiming
    barely to understand it. See 'Godard fait des histoires': interview with Serge Daney,
    Libération, 26th December 1988, pp. 24-27 (reprinted in Alain Bergala (ed.), *Jean-Luc
    Godard par Jean-Luc Godard*, vol. 2, 1984-1998, Paris: Cahiers du Cinéma, 1998, pp. 161-
    173 (p. 173) (henceforth *Godard par Godard II*)). He long planned to give this title to a
    separate self-contained chapter of HISTOIRE(S) DU CINÉMA. Although accorded a
    semi-official role as subtitle to UNE VAGUE NOUVELLE, it recurs across the whole series.
4   For an indication of the implications of a projection of 'montage' back across
    Godard's earlier work, see Alain Bergala, 'Flash-back sur LE MÉPRIS', in: Alain
    Bergala, *Nul mieux que Godard*, Paris: Cahiers du Cinéma, 1999, pp. 15-20.
5   Denis de Rougement, *Penser avec les mains* [1936], Paris: Gallimard, 1972.
6   Godard in 'L'art à partir de la vie: Nouvel entretien avec Jean-Luc Godard par Alain
    Bergala', in: *Godard par Godard I*, pp. 9-24 (p. 14).
7   Jean-Luc Godard, 'Tout ce qui est divisé m'a toujours beaucoup touché', in: *Godard
    par Godard II*, pp. 200-203 (p. 201)).
8   Jean-Luc Godard, *Introduction à une véritable histoire du cinéma*. Paris: Albatros, 1980.
9   Jean-Luc Godard, 'Se vivre, se voir': interview with Claire Devarrieux, in: *Le Monde
    Dimanche (Radio-Télévision)*, 30 March 1980 (reprinted in *Godard par Godard I*, pp. 404-
    407 (p. 405)).
10 Godard, *Introduction à une véritable histoire du cinéma*, op. cit., p. 22.
11 See Daney's introductory comments in 'Godard fait des histoires', op. cit., p. 24. These
    remarks are not reproduced in the version of this interview anthologised in *Godard
    par Godard II*, nor in the translation of the text as 'Godard makes (hi)stories', in: Ray-
    mond Bellour and Mary Lea Bandy (eds.), *Jean-Luc Godard: Son+Image, 1974-1991*,
    New York: MOMA, 1992, pp. 159-167.
12 Jean-Luc Godard, 'Godard fait son cinéma', in: *Le Nouvel Observateur*, no. 1773, 29 Oc-
    tober – 1998, pp. 76-78 (pp. 76-77).
13 Jean-Luc Godard, 'Le montage, la solitude et la liberté', in: *Godard par Godard II*, pp.
    242-248 (pp. 242 and 246-7). This text is the partial transcription of a lecture delivered
    by Godard at the FEMIS on 26 April 1989. Besides here and at numerous points in his
    Montreal lectures, Godard has frequently returned to and rehearsed his ideas on
    montage: Jean-Luc Godard, 'Se vivre, se voir' op. cit.; Jean-Luc Godard, 'Alfred
    Hitchcock est mort': interview with Serge July, in: *Godard par Godard I*, pp. 412-416;
    Jean-Luc Godard, 'Le Briquet de Capitaine Cook': interview with François Albéra
    and Mikhaïl Iampolski, *Les Lettres Françaises*, 19 April 1992, pp. 17-21; Jean-Luc
    Godard, 'À propos de cinéma et d'histoire', in: *Godard par Godard II*, pp. 401-405; and
    the first of his series of five unpublished discussions with Noël Simsolo broadcast in
    the framework of *À voix nue* on Radio France Culture in April 1998.
14 Dziga Vertov, *Kino-Eye: The Writings of Dziga Vertov*, Annette Michelson (ed.), trans.
    Kevin O'Brien, London: Pluto, 1984. Godard and Jean-Pierre Gorin demonstrate ex-

tensive knowledge of Vertovian and Eisensteinian theory in 'Angle and Reality: Godard and Gorin in America', *Sight and Sound*, 42, no.3 (1973), pp. 130-133.

15 STRIKE is referenced through the image of an owl in the first episode of FRANCE/ TOUR/DÉTOUR/DEUX/ENFANTS (an image that recurs, this time in its original form, in TOUTES LES HISTOIRES). THE GENERAL LINE is cited in SCÉNARIO VIDÉO DE SAUVE QUI PEUT (LA VIE) as a point of reference in the inception of SAUVE QUI PEUT (LA VIE).

16 Godard first used this image in an image/text collage entitled 'Là où c'était, je serai. Là où je serai, j'ai déjà été. Là où ça ira, on sera mieux', in: *Cahiers du Cinéma*, nos. 323-324, 1981, pp. 58-59. It recurs in TOUTES LES HISTOIRES and UNE VAGUE NOUVELLE, in the latter case linked to the 'Montage, mon beau souci' title.

17 Cf. Jacques Aumont's contention that Eisenstein's principal contribution is as a *thinker*, indeed one of the most important philosophers of art of the twentieth century. Jacques Aumont, *Montage Eisenstein*, trans. Lee Hildreth, Constance Penley and Andrew Ross, London: BFI, 1987.

18 For Eisenstein's definitions of these terms, see Sergei Eisenstein, '[Rhythm]' and 'Montage 1938', in: Michael Glenny and Richard Taylor (eds.), *S. M. Eisenstein: Selected Works, Volume II: Towards a Theory of Montage*, London: BFI, 1991, pp. 227-258 and pp. 296-326. For an example of Godard's use and discussion of this terminology, see Godard, 'Le Briquet de Capitaine Cook', op. cit., p. 21.

19 Sergei Eisenstein, 'Laocoön', *ibid.*, pp. 109-202 (p. 109).

20 Eisenstein, 'Montage 1938', op. cit., p. 311.

21 Eisenstein, 'Montage 1938', ibid., pp. 310 and 318. Godard refers explicitly to Eisenstein's commentaries on El Greco as a 'monteur' and his paintings as 'montages' in 'Alfred Hitchcock est mort', op. cit., pp. 414-415. The three-day debate on montage (accompanied by projections) between Jacques Rivette, Sylvie Pierre, and Jean Narboni at the Centre Dramatique du Sud-Est in Aix-en-Provence in February 1969 constitutes a further suggestive precursor to Godard's use of the term 'montage'. See 'Montage', *Cahiers du Cinéma*, no. 210, 1969, pp. 17-34.

22 Godard, 'Le montage, la solitude et la liberté', op. cit., p. 248.

23 Godard, *Introduction à une véritable histoire du cinéma*, op. cit., p. 177.

24 Godard, 'Le Briquet de Capitaine Cook', op. cit., p. 19.

25 Tynyanov argued, in terms that resonate across the work of subsequent theorists, that 'the isolation of the material in the photograph leads to the unity of every photograph, to a special dynamic interrelationship of all the objects – or of all the elements of a single object – within the photograph.' See Yuri Tynyanov, 'On the foundations of cinema', in: Herbert Eagle (ed.), *Russian Formalist Film Theory*, Michigan: Slavic Publications, 1981, pp. 81-100 (p. 90).

26 Maurice Merleau-Ponty, 'Le Cinéma et la Nouvelle Psychologie', in: Maurice Merleau-Ponty, *Sens et Non-Sens*. Paris: Nagel, 1966, pp. 85-106 (p. 105). Originally given as a lecture at the IDHEC (the former name of the French national film school) on 13 March 1945.

27 André Malraux, *Esquisse d'une psychologie du cinéma*. Paris: Gallimard, 1946, p. 49. Godard reworked and filmed substantial portions of Malraux's text for HISTOIRE(S) DU CINÉMA, but ultimately did not use the material. See 'Textes pour servir aux HISTOIRE(S) DU CINÉMA', in: *Godard par Godard II*, pp. 183-184.

28 James Monaco perhaps overstates the case when he calls Godard's essay 'one of the most important steps in film theory'. See James Monaco, *How to Read a Film: The Art, Technology, Language, History, and Theory of Film and Media*, Oxford and New York: Oxford University Press, 1981, p. 332.

29 Godard, *Introduction à une véritable histoire du cinéma*, op. cit., p. 175-176.

30 See Jean Cocteau, *Du Cinématographe*, Paris: Pierre Belfond, 1973, and Robert Bresson, *Notes on the Cinematograph* [1975], London: Quartet, 1986.

31 Godard, 'Se vivre, se voir', op. cit., p. 405.

32 Godard, *Introduction à une véritable histoire du cinéma*, op. cit., p. 264.

33 Walter Benjamin, 'The Work of Art in the Age of Mechanical Reproduction', in: Walter Benjamin, *Illuminations*, Hannah Arendt (ed.), London: Fontana, 1973, pp. 211-244 (p. 230); Élie Faure, 'Vocation du cinéma', in: Élie Faure, *Fonction du Cinéma*, Geneva: Gonthier, 1963, pp. 69-91 (pp. 72-73).

34 Jean Painlevé, 'Le cinéma au service de la science', in: Marcel L'Herbier, *Intelligence du Cinématographe*. Paris: Corrêa, 1946, pp. 403-408 (p. 405). For an enthusiastic survey of the early scientific applications of the cinematograph, see Leonard Donaldson, *The Cinematograph and Natural Science: The Achievements and Possibilities of Cinematography as an Aid to Scientific Research*, London: Ganes, 1912.

35 René Clair, *Cinéma d'hier, cinéma d'aujourd'hui*. Paris: Gallimard, 1970, pp. 39-44.

36 Jean Epstein, 'Le Monde fluide de l'écran', in: Pierre Leprohon (ed.), *Jean Epstein*. Paris: Seghers, 1964, pp. 139-140 (p. 140).

37 See Louis Delluc, 'Confidences d'un spectateur', in: Louis Delluc, *Cinéma et Cie*, Paris: Grasset, 1919. Anthologised in L'Herbier, *Intelligence du Cinématographe*, pp. 229-238. Cocteau's *Du Cinématographe* and Clair's *Cinéma d'hier, cinéma d'aujourd'hui* both constantly reiterate the significance of the popular appeal of the cinematograph.

38 Godard, 'Alfred Hitchcock est mort', op. cit., p. 412 and 414.

39 Jean-Luc Godard, 'Le cinéma n'a pas su remplir son rôle': interview with Jean-Pierre Lavoignat and Christophe d'Yvoire, in: *Godard par Godard II*, pp. 335-343 (p. 340).

40 Godard, 'Alfred Hitchcock est mort', op. cit., p. 414.

41 Matthew Teitelbaum (ed.), *Montage and Modern Life 1919-1942*, Cambridge, Mass. and London: MIT Press, 1992. See especially Annette Michelson's essay entitled 'The Wings of Hypothesis: On Montage and the Theory of the Interval' (pp. 61-81).

42 Godard, 'Le Briquet de Capitaine Cook', op. cit., p. 21.

43 Godard to Noël Simsolo, episode one of *À voix nue*.

44 Malraux, *Esquisse d'une psychologie du cinéma*, op. cit., p. 11.

45 This idea was expressed by Guillaume (Jean-Pierre Léaud) in LA CHINOISE and formulated in the terms cited here by Godard in his homage to Henri Langlois at the Cinémathèque in 1966, 'Grâce à Henri Langlois', in: *Godard par Godard I*, pp. 280-283, (p. 282).

46 Godard inserts these words into the mouth of François Reichenbach in one of his fabricated interviews for *Arts* in the 1950s: 'Jean-Luc Godard fait parler François Reichenbach', in: *Godard par Godard I*, pp. 144-146 (p. 144).

47 Godard, *Introduction à une véritable histoire du cinéma*, p. 70. Cf. Sylvia Harvey's reading of film noir as an 'echo chamber' in which the massive displacement to existing systems of values and beliefs is caught and magnified in popular narratives before finding expression elsewhere. Sylvia Harvey, 'Woman's place: the absent family of

film noir', in: E. Ann Kaplan (ed.), *Women in Film Noir*. London: BFI, 1978, pp. 22-34, especially p. 22.

48 Godard in 'La chance de repartir pour un tour': interview with Claude-Jean Philippe, in: *Godard par Godard I*, pp. 407-412, (p. 408)).

49 Godard, *Introduction à une véritable histoire du cinéma*, op. cit., p. 175.

50 'Godard fait des histoires', op. cit., p. 172.

51 I have looked in more detail at this question in 'Qu'était-ce que le cinéma, Jean-Luc Godard? An analysis of the cinema(s) in and around Godard's HISTOIRE(S) DU CINÉMA', in: Elizabeth Ezra and Susan Harris (eds.), *France in Focus: French Cinema and National Identity*, Oxford: Berg, forthcoming 2000.

52 'Godard fait des histoires', op. cit., p. 168. Godard's terminology here engages deliberately with judicial vocabulary, the term 'dossier' invoking the legal sense of a 'case' or 'file' which might be compiled during a police investigation.

53 Godard in 'ABCD...JLG': interview with Olivier Péretié, *Le Nouvel Observateur*, 18 December 1987, pp. 50-52 (p. 52).

54 Godard, *Introduction à une véritable histoire du cinéma*, op. cit., p. 165.

55 Godard, 'Alfred Hitchcock est mort', op. cit., p. 415. Godard employs the term 'démontage' in this sense in *Introduction à une véritable histoire du cinéma*, op. cit., p. 177.

56 Godard, 'À propos de cinéma et d'histoire', op. cit., p. 403.

57 Godard, 'Se vivre, se voir', op. cit., p. 405. Godard's thesis is in place as early as LETTER TO JANE. See 'Enquête sur une image', in: *Godard par Godard I*, pp. 350-362 (pp. 357-358).

58 Godard, 'À propos de cinéma et d'histoire', op. cit., p. 403. The 'Jeromine children' refers to the novel of this title by Ernst Wiechert; 'Narcissus and Goldmund' invokes the Hermann Hesse novel.

59 Bresson, *Notes on the Cinematograph*, op. cit., p. 41. Cf. Godard: 'And that's what cinema is: the rapprochement of things that ought to be brought together, but which aren't predisposed to being so' ('Une boucle bouclée: Nouvel entretien avec Jean-Luc Godard par Alain Bergala', in: *Godard par Godard II*, pp. 9-41 (p. 20)).

60 Godard in 'Le cinéma meurt, vive le cinéma!': interview with Danièle Heymann, *Le Monde*, 30 December 1987, pp. 1 and 10 (p. 10).

61 Godard consistently employs the term rapprochement as a synonym for montage: 'That's what I call montage, simply a rapprochement' (Godard, *Introduction à une véritable histoire du cinéma*, op. cit., p. 22). He refers to the process whereby he composes historical '*études*' in 'Jean-Luc Godard rencontre Régis Debray', in: *Godard par Godard II*, pp. 423-431 (p. 426).

62 The original French reads:
'L'image est une création pure de l'esprit.
Elle ne peut naître d'une comparaison mais du rapprochement de deux réalités plus ou moins éloignées.
Plus les rapports des deux réalités rapprocheés seront lointains et justes, plus l'image sera forte – plus elle aura de puissance émotive et de la réalité poétique.
Deux réalités qui n'ont aucun rapport ne peuvent se rapprocher utilement. Il n'y a pas de création d'image.
Deux réalités contraires ne se rapprochent pas. Elles s'opposent.
On obtient rarement une force de cette opposition.

Une image n'est pas forte parce qu'elle est *brutale* ou *fantastique* – mais parce que l'association des idées est lointaine et juste.'
(Pierre Reverdy, 'L'Image', *Nord-Sud*, no. 13, March 1918 (anthologised in Pierre Reverdy, *Œuvres Complètes*, Paris, 1975, pp. 73-75)). André Breton, we recall, framed his first surrealist manifesto with the opening lines of the poem. It is cited in PASSION, GRANDEUR ET DÉCADENCE D'UN PETIT COMMERCE DE CINÉMA, KING LEAR, one of the television adverts for Marithé et François Girbaud, JLG/JLG: AUTOPORTRAIT DE DÉCEMBRE, and in HISTOIRE(S) DU CINÉMA 4B, LES SIGNES PARMI NOUS.

63 See Gilles Deleuze, *Cinéma 2: L'Image-Temps*, Paris: Éditions de Minuit, 1985, p. 32.

64 Montage is thus extended from cinema and the image to *history*: 'there's the montage, there's a moment of history, there's a moment of cinema' (Godard, 'À propos de cinéma et d'histoire', op. cit., p. 403). The term 'neo-television' is borrowed from Umberto Eco, 'A guide to the Neo-Television of the 1980s', *Framework*, no. 25, 1984, pp. 18-27.

65 For a discussion of art in its role as 'metaphorical bridge' between reality and its representation, see Richard Shiff, 'Art and Life: A Metaphoric Relationship', in: Sheldon Sacks (ed.), *On Metaphor*, London: University of Chicago Press, 1979, pp. 105-120.

66 I.A. Richards, *The Philosophy of Rhetoric*, New York: Oxford University Press, 1936.

67 The suggestive idea of 'stereoscopic vision' as a model for the interpretative challenge of metaphor is borrowed from Paul Ricoeur. See Paul Ricoeur, 'The Metaphorical Process as Cognition, Imagination, and Feeling', *Critical Inquiry*, no. 5, Autumn 1978, pp. 143-159 (p. 154) (reprinted in Sacks, *On Metaphor*, op. cit., pp. 141-157). See, too, Paul Ricoeur, *The Rule of Metaphor: Multi-disciplinary studies of the creation of meaning in language*, trans. Robert Czerny, Kathleen McLaughlin and John Costello, London: Routledge and Kegan Paul, 1978, p. 294.

68 Godard, 'Godard fait son cinéma', op. cit., p. 78.

69 Godard in 'Le Petit Soldat': interview with Frédéric Bonnaud and Serge Kaganski, *Les Inrockuptibles*, 27 November 1996, pp. 22-29 (p. 26).

70 Geoffrey Nowell-Smith, 'Eisenstein on Montage', in: Glenny and Taylor, *S. M. Eisenstein*, op. cit., pp. xiii-xvi (p. xvi).

71 Jean-Luc Godard, 'Malraux, mauvais Français?', *Cahiers du Cinéma*, no. 83, May 1958 (reprinted in *Godard par Godard I*, pp. 127-128 (p. 128)).

Notes to 3: Elizabeth Taylor at Auschwitz: JLG and the Real Object of Montage

1 See 'Godard Makes (Hi)Stories': interview with Serge Daney, in: Raymond Bellour and Mary Lea Bandy (eds.), *Jean-Luc Godard: Son+Image, 1974-1991*, New York: Museum of Modern Art, 1992, pp. 159-168 (p. 165).

2 Gavin Smith, 'Interview: Jean-Luc Godard', *Film Comment*, vol. 32, no. 2, March-April 1996, pp. 31-41 (p. 38).

3 Ibid..

4 Jean Cocteau's hypothetical remark that the lives of Rimbaud and Marshal Pétain might have ended in the same year gives a strange twist to the history of France.

Godard takes the *bon mot* as an allegorical expression of the montage principle: 'You
see a portrait of the young Rimbaud, you see Pétain's portrait in 1948, and you put the
two together, and there you have a story, you have "history". That's cinema' ('Godard
Makes (Hi)Stories', op. cit., p. 160). Meaning resides in extremes of perspective.

5   Jean-Luc Godard, *Godard on Godard*, ed. and trans. Tom Milne, New York: Da Capo
    Press, 1972, p. 181.
6   Gilles Deleuze, *Cinema 2: The Time-Image* [1985], trans. Hugh Tomlinson and Robert
    Galeta, Minneapolis: University of Minnesota Press, 1989, p. 181.
7   Ibid., p. 21.
8   Ibid.
9   Slavoj Žižek, *The Sublime Object of Ideology*, London and New York: Verso, 1994, p. 203.
10 Deleuze, *Cinema 2*, op. cit., p. 20.
11 Smith, 'Interview', op. cit., p. 32.
12 'Godard Makes (Hi)Stories', op. cit., p. 160.
13 Ibid., p. 161.
14 Philippe Dubois, 'Video Thinks What Cinema Creates', in: Bellour and Bandy, *Jean-
    Luc Godard: Son+Image*, op. cit., 169-186 (p. 173).
15 ICI ET AILLEURS, an 'essay film' that reuses footage shot in Palestine as JUSQU'À LA
    VICTOIRE by the Dziga Vertov Group, marks the first appearance of video in Godard's
    work. The ratio of film to video production remains roughly equal in the following
    fifteen years: eleven films to fifteen video tapes. Dubois stresses that Godard's in-
    volvement with video cannot be regarded as a passing phase or period but as 'the
    very site and means of his existential relationship to cinema' (Dubois, 'Video Thinks
    What Cinema Creates', op. cit., p. 169).
16 The blurs, blinks and flickers produced by the superimposition and layering of im-
    ages, sounds, music and text in HISTOIRE(S) DU CINÉMA find a potential and unex-
    pected parallel in the sonic modulations of dub reggae. Dub relies heavily on an
    inventive poetics of the mix: songs rework previous versions, sounds are sampled
    and cut from other sources, tracks drop in and out, rhythms are fragmented and dis-
    torted by prolonged echo effects. The spatial creations of dub correspond, at the level
    of form, method and style, to the effect of 'conceptual vertigo' or cognitive disso-
    nance produced by the radical decomposition of historical time which HISTOIRE(S) DU
    CINÉMA presents in composite images such as Elizabeth Taylor at Auschwitz. The
    quickening pulse which establishes the vital connection between the two serves as
    the medium for attaining the critical condition of sentience which opens theory to
    practice, the mental to the physical, the senses to the intellect, the material to the con-
    ceptual. A detailed study of Godard as a contemporary composer of sound is surely
    waiting to be written.
17 Armond White, 'Double Helix: Jean-Luc Godard', *Film Comment*, vol. 32, no. 2,
    March-April 1996, pp. 26-30 (p. 30).
18 Dubois, 'Video Thinks What Cinema Creates', op. cit., p. 178.
19 Godard often puts himself in the picture as a way to depict graphically the action of
    cinematic vision and the real-time presentation of montage. As Uncle Jean, Jeannot,
    Professor Pluggy, JLG, and finally the all-seeing Master in his library in HISTOIRE(S)
    DU CINÉMA, Godard places himself literally at the centre of the scene of writing in or-
    der to enact the fundamental proposition of his thoery of montage: 'seeing is thinking
    and thinking is seeing, both in one, simultaneously'.

20 Dubois, 'Video Thinks What Cinema Creates', op. cit., p. 178.

21 Nadia C. Seremetakis (ed.), *The Senses Still*: *Perception and Memory as Material Culture in Modernity*, Boulder, San Francisco and Oxford: Westview Press, 1994, p. 129.

22 Dubois, 'Video Thinks What Cinema Creates', op. cit., p. 177.

23 Ibid., p. 181

24 'Godard Makes (Hi)Stories', op. cit., p. 161.

25 James S. Williams, 'The Signs Amongst Us: Jean-Luc Godard's HISTOIRE(S) DU CINÉMA', *Screen*, vol. 40, no. 3, Autumn 1999, pp. 306-315 (p. 313).

26 Ibid..

Notes to 4: '*The Present Never Exists There*': The Temporality of Decision in Godard's Later Film and Video Essays

1   Stanley Cavell, *The World Viewed: Reflections on the Ontology of Film* [1971], enlarged edition, Cambridge, MA: Harvard University Press, 1979, p. 101.

2   Ibid., p. 97.

3   'Le cinéma c'est ça, le présent n'y existe jamais, sauf dans les mauvais films...' (Hervé Guibert, 'Une partie du monde et sa métaphore': interview with Jean-Luc Godard, *Le Monde*, 27 May 1982, p. 19). I would like to thank Michael Temple for help in translating citations from the French.

4   'Le cinéma, quand il est bien fait, c'est d'une puissance directe, totale... Le cinéma, c'est du direct' (Dominique Païni and Guy Scarpetta, 'La curiosité du sujet': interview with Jean-Luc Godard, *Art Press*, Special Issue 4 – 'Godard', December 1984-February 1985, p 14).

5   *The World Viewed*, op cit., p. 226.

6   Ibid., p. 98.

7   'Ce mouvement profond du film qui est la tentative de description d'un ensemble (êtres et choses), puisque l'on ne fait pas de différence entre les deux, et que, pour simplifier, on parle aussi bien des êtres en tant que choses que des choses en tant qu'êtres...' ('Ma démarche en quatre mouvements', in: Alain Bergala (ed.), *Jean-Luc Godard par Jean-Luc Godard*, vol. 1, Paris: Cahiers du Cinéma/Éditions de L'Étoile, 1985, pp. 296-298 (pp. 297-298).

8   'Tout ce qui est divisé m'a toujours beaucoup touché: le documentaire et la fiction' ('Conférence de presse de Jean-Luc Godard (extraits)', *Cahiers du Cinéma*, no. 433, June 1990, pp. 10-11).

9   'J'ai toujours essayé que ce qu'on appelle le documentaire et ce qu'on appelle la fiction soient pour moi les deux aspects d'un même mouvement, et c'est leur liaison qui fait le vrai mouvement' (Jean-Luc Godard, *Introduction à une véritable histoire du cinéma*, Paris: Éditions Albatros, 1977, p. 262).

10 Claude Ollier, *Souvenirs écran*, Paris: Cahiers du Cinéma-Gallimard, 1981, p 126.

11 More fully: 'It was not a story but the (hi)story of this story. Even the pre-(hi)story of this (hi)story'.

12 As formulated in Noël Simsolo, 'Entretien avec Jean-Luc Godard', in: *Jean-Luc Godard: un hommage du Centre Culturel Français et du Museo Nazionale del Cinema de Turin*, Centre Culturel Français de Turin, 1990, pp. 42-43.

13 For a helpful outline of the phases of Godard's career since his first film essay ICI ET AILLEURS, see Philippe Dubois, 'Video thinks what cinema creates: notes on Jean-Luc Godard's work in video and television', in Raymond Bellour and Mary Lea Bandy (eds.), *Jean-Luc Godard: Son+Image, 1974-1991*, New York: Museum of Modern Art, 1992, pp 169-185. It must be noted, however, that my use of the term 'essay' is intended to cover the films made by the Dziga Vertov Group in the late 1960s, the three film essays of the mid-1970s and the two television series following them made in conjunction with Anne-Marie Miéville, and the fifteen or so videotapes and accompanying '*scénarios*' made since then. It is insufficient to say that the essay form is inaugurated by the incorporation of video into film. Rather, what marks out all these works is that they are made *collaboratively*, within the context of a workshop, as Godard refers to Sonimage, the production company he set up with Miéville. Thus, it might also be argued that the feature films from 1980 on, beginning with SAUVE QUI PEUT (LA VIE), could also be covered by the term since each is an '*essai d'investigation cinématographique*', as an intertitle puts it in LES ENFANTS JOUENT À LA RUSSIE.

14 Gilles Deleuze, 'Three questions about SIX FOIS DEUX', in: Bellour and Bandy, op. cit., p. 38.

15 'Si je vais voir un bon film qui s'appelle HÉLAS POUR MOI, mettons d'Oliveira ou de Cassavetes ou de X ou Y, eh bien, si c'est un bon film, je prendrai le "moi" du titre pour moi spectateur' (Samuel Blumenfeld, Christian Fevret and Serge Kaganski, 'L'homme qui en savait trop': interview with Jean-Luc Godard, *Les Inrockuptibles*, no. 49, September 1993, p. 75).

16 'C'est-à-dire que la somme de la description objective et de la description subjective doit amener à la découverte de certaines formes plus générales, doit permettre de dégager, non pas une vérité globale et générale, mais un certain "sentiment d'ensemble"' ('Ma démarche en quatre mouvements', op. cit., p. 297).

17 Cf. Jean-Luc Nancy, 'Finite history', in: *The Birth to Presence*, trans. Brian Holmes, Stanford University Press, 1993, p. 161.

18 'Duras-Godard: un dialogue tendre et passionné', *Magazine littéraire*, no. 278, June 1990, pp. 46-48.

19 Ibid., p. 47.

20 'Ce qui veut dire: "Seul le cinéma a fait ça", mais aussi: le cinéma était bien seul, tellement seul que...' ('Godard fait des histoires': interview with Serge Daney, *Libération*, 26 December 1988, pp. 24-27 (p. 25)).

21 'Je dis c'est la grande histoire parce qu'elle peut *se projeter*. Les autres histoires ne peuvent que se réduire' (ibid., p. 24, emphasis added).

22 'Moi j'avais l'intuition d'abord que le cinéma peut être le seul à la raconter... le film étant le seul qui puisse être raconté dans sa propre langue, dans son propre moyen d'expression... *le film peut se raconter lui-même* autrement que les autres et qu'il n'y avait que dans le visuel qu'il y avait une histoire qui parlait...' (Simsolo, 'Entretien avec Jean-Luc Godard', op. cit., pp. 41-42, emphasis added).

23 'C'est que c'est le film qui pense' ('Duras-Godard: un dialogue tendre et passionné', op. cit., p 46).

24 'Godard fait des histoires', op. cit., p. 26.

25 'Il n'y a aucune invention dans le cinéma. On ne peut que regarder et tâcher de mettre en ordre ce qu'on a vu... si on a pu bien voir' ('Godard à Venise': interview with Jean-Luc Godard, *Cinématographe*, no. 95, December 1983, pp. 3-7 (p. 6)).

26 *The World Viewed*, op. cit., p. xvi.

27 Jean-Luc Godard, interview with Colin MacCabe, in: Colin MacCabe, *Godard: Images, Sounds, Politics*, London: BFI/MacMillan, 1980; pp 132-133.

28 Jacques Derrida, 'Ghost Dance: an interview', *Public*, no. 2, 1989, pp. 61 and 64.

29 As an intertitle in Chapter 1B of HISTOIRE(S) DU CINÉMA puts it, 'DARK VICTORY'. Before and after this intertitle (also a filmtitle), Godard seems to be calling for a return to cinema's 'infancy', to what the Lumière brothers (he claims) named an 'art without a future' or, as he puts it, a 'between yet to be seen'. It seems to be part of his project to reclaim a cinematic present long since displaced, a cinema *inconnu, maudit, oublié*. 'Notre histoire' (a preceding intertitle) consists of the corruption of the cinema (Godard cites the two world wars), culminating in the 'pathetic and inane adult that is television'. (Throughout both television series Godard plays on the phrase 'Il était une fois'. For instance, in part 2A of SIX FOIS DEUX, we see the following sequence of captions: 'Il était une fois. 2 fois il = ils. Ils. S 2 fois = SS.') The 'between yet to be seen' would be a cinema between its beginning and its corruption, between the real and fiction, the mystery between art and technique – oppositions which are treated in HISTOIRE(S) DU CINÉMA as surfaces in search of one other. Or a television between the empirical and the conceptual, between (hi)story and the idea – each episode of SIX FOIS DEUX is split into two such parts: 'neither one nor the other, the proper place of television is between' (part 6A, AVANT ET APRÈS). Godard's voice-over in HISTOIRE(S) DU CINÉMA continues: 'The time has come for life to give back what it has stolen from the cinema'. The footage which begins every second movement of FRANCE/TOUR/DÉTOUR/DEUX/ENFANTS, a young girl (Camille) swivelling a video camera away from us, is shown in the episode of HISTOIRE(S) DU CINÉMA following this one, super-imposed with the words 'L'enfance de l'art'.

30 Guibert, 'Une partie du monde et sa métaphore', op. cit. This is stated explicitly in the voiceover to the fourth movement of FRANCE/TOUR/DÉTOUR/DEUX/ENFANTS: 'Impression/Dictée', between intertitles 'Vérité, Télévision': 'never any silence on TV, no live TV, everything is deferred, life itself is deferred in this way'.

31 Deleuze: 'Godard's questions are always *direct*'; MacCabe: 'almost totally without direct address'. See Gilles Deleuze, 'Three questions about SIX FOIS DEUX', op. cit., p. 35; and MacCabe, *Godard: Images, Sounds, Politics*, op. cit., p. 141. In answer to a question about this from MacCabe, Godard again makes it a question of the before and after: 'The address is provided by the work before the shooting and after the shooting. It's in the *mise-en-scène*. It's to be there for that amount of time', ibid., p. 155.

32 Would this also not be the secret of the answer's resistance to the question that insists on an answer? As the prisoner in part 5A of SIX FOIS DEUX, NOUS TROIS, writes of the need not to submit to the violence of the questions: 'I haven't even got a secret, how shall I manage to have the will to resist.' I have been assisted in translating certain passages from SIX FOIS DEUX by the transcription made by Tom Milne and Gilbert Adair for the BFI, catalogued under the programme's subtitle SUR ET SOUS LA COMMUNICATION.

33 'Je pose continuellement la question. Je me regarde filmer, et on m'entend penser. Bref, ce n'est pas un film, c'est une tentative de film et qui se présente comme telle' ('On doit tout mettre dans un film', in: Bergala, *Godard par Godard I*, op. cit., p. 295).

34 'Ou bien de la philosophie sous forme de musique de chambre' (Claude-Jean Philippe, 'La chance de repartir pour un tour': interview with Jean-Luc Godard, in: Bergala, *Godard par Godard I*, op. cit., pp. 407-412 (p. 411)). The ninth movement of the series is entitled POUVOIR/MUSIQUE. The film made shortly after, SAUVE QUI PEUT (LA VIE), is referred to in its credits as 'a film composed by Jean-Luc Godard', its final section being 'La musique'.

35 'Moi, ce que j'aime bien, c'est deux images ensemble pour qu'il y en ait une troisième, qui n'est pas une image, qui est ce qu'on fait des deux images; exactement ce que fait la justice... enfin, ce qu'est forcé de faire la justice, en présentant l'attaque et la défense, et puis les jurés ou une certaine vérité... Une vérité, c'est fait d'un moment où c'est possible d'être...' (Godard, *Introduction à une véritable histoire du cinéma*, op. cit., p. 261).

36 Alain Badiou, 'Le plus-de-voir', *Art Press*, Godard Special Issue – 'Guide pour HISTOIRE(S) DU CINÉMA', November 1998, p. 86.

37 'Godard, à propos de chaque motif, inventorie avec une audace déroutante le champ des possibles: on dirait qu'il effectue pour chaque plan un très rapide recensement de ses virtualités descriptives et suggestives, avant de s'en tenir à l'une d'elles, puis de l'abandonner, aussitôt qu'indiquée, exactement comme il constitue l'œuvre entière, par approches successives, renouvelées, tournant "autour du pot" et juste au moment où il trouve, la défait, donne même l'impression de s'en désintéresser...' (Ollier, *Souvenirs Écran*, op. cit., pp. 129-130). Ollier is referring in the main to LES CARABINIERS.

38 'À ce que l'autre dit (assertion, proclamation, prône), il répond toujours par ce qu'un *autre* autre dit. Il y a toujours une grande inconnue dans sa pédagogie, c'est que la nature du rapport qu'il entretient avec ses "bons" discours (ceux qu'il défend, le discours maoïste, par exemple) est indécidable' (Serge Daney, 'Le thérrorisé (pédagogie godardienne)', in: *La rampe: Cahier critique 1970-1982*, Paris: Cahiers du Cinéma-Gallimard, 1983, p. 80).

39 'Shakespeare on three screens: Peter Brook interviewed by Geoffrey Reeves', *Sight & Sound*, vol. 34, no. 2, 1965, p. 69. Brook is referring centrally to BANDE À PART.

40 Wallace Stevens, 'A primitive like an orb', in: Holly Stevens (ed.), *The Palm at the End of the Mind: Selected Poems & a Play*, New York: Alfred A. Knopf, 1971, p. 318.

41 'Pour tout dire, je fais participer le spectateur à l'arbitraire de mes choix et à la recherche des lois générales qui pourraient justifier un choix particulier' (Godard, 'On doit tout mettre dans un film', op. cit., p. 295).

42 Stanley Cavell, *A Pitch of Philosophy: Autobiographical Exercises*, Cambridge, MA., Harvard University Press, 1994, pp. 163-164, emphasis added. Resonating a little more with Godard, with his call for a return to cinema's 'infancy', his averment in HISTOIRE(S) DU CINÉMA of 'l'enfance de l'art' (cf. note 29 above), Cavell compares music in this regard with infancy: '(Music, like infancy, marks the permanence of the place of understanding as before what we might call meaning, as if it exists in permanent anticipation of – hence in perpetual dissatisfaction with, even disdain for – what can be said.)', ibid., p. 160.

43 Ibid., pp. 96-97.

44 Ibid., p. 102.
45 Cf. ibid., p. 130.
46 Ibid., p. 101.
47 Ludwig Wittgenstein, *On Certainty*, corrected edition, bilingual, ed. G.E.M. Anscombe and G.H. von Wright, trans. Denis Paul & G.E.M. Anscombe, Oxford: Blackwell, 1974, pp. 18-19.
48 Dubois, 'Video thinks what cinema creates', op. cit., p. 174.
49 Deleuze, 'Three questions about SIX FOIS DEUX', op cit., p. 35.
50 *Le Monde*, 25 Septembre 1975, cited by Dubois, op. cit., p. 170, footnote 2.
51 Gilles Deleuze, *Cinema 2: The Time-Image* [1985], trans. Hugh Tomlinson and Robert Galeta, London: Athlone Press, 1989, p. 154.
52 Ibid., p. 38.
53 *The World Viewed*, op. cit., pp. 134 and 141.
54 Ibid., pp. 155 and 277.
55 Initially in Deleuze, the conjunctive is accentuated at the expense of the predicative (pp. 40-41), but it is a conjunctive which becomes the *constitutive* 'and' of things, the constitutive between-the-two of images (p. 180); and then not a conjunctive 'and' at all but a disjunctive one (p. 248).
56 Godard claims to have had this as an initial intuition in the making of FRANCE/TOUR/DÉTOUR/DEUX/ENFANTS, which in that sense then was a 'laboratory experiment' out of which he 'composed a novel' – the film SAUVE QUI PEUT (LA VIE). See Bergala, *Godard par Godard I*, op. cit., pp. 461-462.
57 'Quelque chose qui correspond sentimentalement aux lois qu'il faut trouver et appliquer pour vivre en société' (Godard, 'Ma démarche en quatre mouvements', op. cit., p. 297).
58 Ibid., p. 298.
59 Deleuze, *Cinema 2*, op. cit., p. 181.
60 Jacques Derrida, 'Videor', in: Raymond Bellour, Catherine David and Christine van Assche (eds.), *Passages de l'image*, Barcelona: Fundació Caixa de Pensions, 1991, p. 176.
61 Païni and Scarpetta, 'La curiosité du sujet', op. cit., p. 14.

Notes to 5: Big Rhythm and the Power of Metamorphosis: Some Models and Precursors for HISTOIRE(S) DU CINÉMA

1 Adapted extract from Maurice Blanchot, 'Le musée, l'art, et le temps', *Critique*, no. 43, December 1950, pp. 195-208, and no. 44, January 1951, pp. 30-42. The original translation (by Beth Archer, in: R. Lewis (ed.), *Malraux: a collection of critical essays*, New Jersey: Prentice Hall, 1964, pp. 147-160) contains some basic errors, which I have corrected in passing. Here is the actual French: 'On semble parfois regretter que les livres de Malraux sur *La psychologie de l'art* n'aient pas reçu une ordonnance plus rigoureuse: on les trouve obscurs, non dans leur langage, qui est clair – et un peu plus que clair, brillant – mais dans leur développement. Malraux lui-même, à la fin de ses essais, semble leur souhaiter une composition plus forte. Peut-être Malraux a-t-il raison, mais ses lecteurs ont sûrement tort. Il est vrai que les idées qu'il développe ont

leurs caprices, elles sont promptes, soudaines, puis elles demeurent sans fin; elles disparaissent et elles reviennent; comme elles s'affirment souvent en des formules qui leur plaisent, elles croient s'y définir, et cet accomplissement leur suffit. Mais le mouvement qui les abandonne, les rappelle; le bonheur, la gloire d'une nouvelle formule les attire à nouveau hors d'elles-mêmes. Ce mouvement – cet apparent désordre – est, à coup sûr, un des côtés importants de ces livres. Les idées n'y perdent pas de leur cohérence; c'est plutôt à leurs contradictions qu'elles échappent, bien que ces contradictions ne cessent de les animer, de les maintenir vivantes. [...] L'excuse de Malraux n'est pas dans la passion qu'il voue à l'art dont il parle, ni même dans l'admiration extraordinaire dont il le fait bénéficier [...] mais dans ce mérite exceptionnel: c'est que les pensées, bien qu'elles tendent, selon leurs exigences propres, à une vue importante et générale de l'art, dans leur dialogue aventuré avec les œuvres, avec les images qu'elles accompagnent, réussissent, sans perdre leur valeur explicative, à s'éclairer d'une lumière qui n'est pas purement intellectuelle, à glisser vers je ne sais quoi de plus ouvert que leur sens, à réaliser, pour elles-mêmes – et pour nous qui sommes destinés à les comprendre – une expérience qui imite celle de l'art plutôt qu'elle n'en rend compte. Ainsi les idées deviennent-elles des thèmes, des motifs, et leur développement peu cohérent, dont on se plaint, exprime, au contraire, leur ordre le plus vrai, qui est de se constituer, de s'éprouver au contact de l'histoire par un mouvement dont la vivacité, le vagabondage apparent nous rendent sensibles la succession historique des œuvres et leur présence simultanée dans le Musée où la culture, aujourd'hui, les rassemble.'

2   *Les voix du silence* comprises four volumes: *Le musée imaginaire*, *Les métamorphoses d'Apollon*, *La création artistique*, and *La monnaie de l'absolu*. It is worth noting that, as with HISTOIRE(S) DU CINÉMA, it was over a considerable period of time that Malraux reworked both the overall construction and internal details of this, his most ambitious work. For example, the best-known and most important tome, *Le musée imaginaire*, experienced a number of transformations, first appearing on its own in 1947, then as part of *La psychologie de l'art* and *Les voix du silence* in the 1950s, and finally alone again in 1965. We should also note in passing that 'La monnaie de l'absolu' is the title of Chapter 3A of HISTOIRE(S) DU CINÉMA, sometimes also known as LA RÉPONSE DES TÉNÈBRES.

3   Alain Cuny (1908-1994) appears directly in several of the sequences specially filmed for HISTOIRE(S) DU CINÉMA (e.g. 2B and 4A). Certain films from his career are heavily sampled, e.g. Marcel Carné's LES VISITEURS DU SOIR and Alain Resnais's L'ANNÉE DERNIÈRE À MARIENBAD.

4   'À ses débuts/il ne sentait/que peu de choses/et il croyait/tout savoir/plus tard/ habité seulement/par le doute, la douleur//l'effroi/devant la mystère/de la vie/ cela se mit à flotter/et maintenant/qu'il sentait tout/il croyait/ne rien savoir//et pourtant/de l'insouciance/à l'inquiétude/de l'enregistrement amoureux/des débuts/à la forme hésitante/mais essentielle/de la fin/c'est/la même force centrale/qui a gouverné/le cinéma//on la suit par dedans/de forme en forme/avec l'ombre/et le rayon/qui rôdent/illuminant ceci/cachant cela//faisant surgir une épaule/un visage/un doigt levé/une fenêtre ouverte/un front/un petit enfant/dans une crèche//ce qui plonge/dans la lumière/est le retentissement/de ce que submerge la nuit/ce que submerge/la nuit/prolonge dans l'invisible/ce qui plonge dans la lumière [...]//le cinéma seul/a vu/que si chacun/est à sa tâche/les masses

s'organisent/seules/suivant un irréprochable/équilbre/que la lumière tombe/où il faut/et néglige/ce qu'il faut/parce qu'il est utile/qu'elle éclaire un point/de la scène/et que l'ombre/peut régner ailleurs//il est seul/à avoir été/toujours présent/ dans tout/ce qu'il regardait/le seul qui ait pu/se permettre de mêler/de la boue/à la lueur des yeux/d'introduire du feu/dans la cendre/de faire briller/dans un linceul/ une rose/ou un bleu pâle/aussi frais/qu'une rose//son humanité/est réellement formidable/elle est fatale/comme la plainte/dévastatrice/comme l'amour// dramatique/comme l'échange/indifférent et continu/entre tout ce qui naît/et tout/ ce qui meurt//en suivant/notre marche à la mort/aux traces de sang/qui la marquent/le cinéma ne pleure pas/sur nous/il ne nous réconforte pas/puisqu'il est/nous-mêmes' (Jean-Luc Godard, *Histoire(s) du cinéma*, 4 vols, Paris: Gallimard-Gaumont, 1998, vol. 4, pp. 96-125). Compare Faure's original in *Histoire de l'art, L'art moderne*, vol. 1, Paris: Denoël, 1987, pp. 97-109.

5   For a discussion of the 'Diderot-Daney' lineage, see Jacques Aumont, 'La justification par les œuvres', *Amnésies: fictions du cinéma d'après Jean-Luc Godard*, Paris: P.O.L, 1999, pp. 101-138. This lineage is literally 'put on screen' both in 2x50 ANS DE CINÉMA FRANÇAIS and episodes 3B and 4A of HISTOIRE(S) DU CINÉMA.

6   See Introduction and 'La curiosité du sujet', *Art Press*, Special Issue 4 – 'Godard', December 1984-February 1985, pp. 4-18 (p. 5).

7   For a discussion of Malraux, Langlois, Godard, see Dominique Païni, 'Un musée pour cinéma créateur d'aura', *Art Press*, no. 221, February 1997, pp. 20-33.

8   This is the abandoned Canadian project (see Chapter 1 above) that became the book of transcriptions entitled *Introduction à une véritable histoire du cinéma*, Paris: Albatros, 1980.

9   'L'identité du cinéma/l'identité/de la nouvelle vague/un soir/nous nous rendîmes/ chez Henri Langlois/et alors/la lumière fut//c'est que, n'est-ce pas/le vrai cinéma/ n'avait même pas pour nos yeux/le visage de madame Arnoux/dans les rêves de Frédéric Moreau/le cinéma, nous le connaissions/par Canudo/par Delluc/mais sans jamais l'avoir vu/il n'avait aucun rapport/avec les films du samedi/ceux du Vox, du Palace, du Miramar/des Variétés/car ces films étaient/pour tout le monde/ /pas pour nous/sauf pour nous/puisque le vrai cinéma/était celui qui ne peut se voir/n'était que celui-là//c'était, c'était/c'était Mary Duncan/n'est-ce pas/Jean George Auriol/mais on ne verrait jamais/la femme au corbeau/et il nous fallut l'aimer/aveuglément/et par cœur/idem/avec les foules d'octobre/et celles de que viva Mexico/n'est-ce pas/Jay Leyda/idem/avec les tramways/de l'aurore//n'est-ce pas/Lotte Eisner/parce qu'oublié déjà/interdit encore/invisible toujours//tel était notre cinéma/et cela m'est resté/et Langlois nous le confirma/c'est le mot exact/que l'image/est d'abord de l'ordre de la rédemption/attention, celle du réel/ nous fûmes donc, éblouis/davantage que le Greco en Italie/que Goya, aussi/en Italie/et que Picasso devant Goya/nous étions, sans passé/et l'homme de l'avenue de Messine/nous fit don de ce passé/métamorphosé au présent/en pleine Indochine/en pleine Algérie/et lorsqu'il projeta l'espoir/pour la première fois/ce n'est pas la guerre d'Espagne qui nous fit sursauter/mais la fraternité des métaphores' (*Histoire(s) du cinéma*, vol. 3 pp. 139-149). An image of Langlois (whose famous eyes will 'close the eyes of oppression', according to the soundtrack) appears in 2x50 ANS DE CINÉMA FRANÇAIS at the end of the 'procession' mentioned above; and

in 3B itself we see a photo of Langlois pasted together with a Lumière cinematograph, thus showing the purity of the curator's intentions and origins.

10 For an account of *L'Espoir* as book and film, see Denis Marion, *Le cinéma selon Malraux*, Paris: Cahiers du Cinéma, 1996.

11 Jules Michelet (1798-1874), author of *Histoire de France* (1838-1851) and *Histoire de la révolution française* (1847-53). The following quotations are taken from the 'Préface à l'*Histoire de France*' cited in Guy Bourdé and Hervé Martin, *Les écoles historiques*, Paris: Seuil, 1983, pp. 130-136.

12 'Cette œuvre laborieuse d'environ quarante ans fut conçue d'un moment, de l'éclair de juillet. Dans ces jours mémorables, une grande lumière se fit, et j'aperçus la France.'

13 'Elle avait des annales, et non point une histoire [...] Le premier je la vis comme une âme et une personne.'

14 See 'Préface à *Cinémamémoire* de Pierre Braunberger', in: Alain Bergala (ed.), *Jean-Luc Godard par Jean-Luc Godard*, vol. 2, 1984-1998, Paris: Cahiers du Cinéma, 1998, p. 208.

15 'Au reste, jusqu'en 1830 [...] aucun des historiens remarquables de cette époque n'avait senti encore le besoin de chercher des faits hors des livres imprimés, aux sources primitives, la plupart inédites alors, aux manuscrits de nos bibliothèques, aux documents de nos archives.'

16 After Bazin, Godard has probably appropriated this tale from Charles Péguy, who wrote a companion-piece to *Clio, dialogue de l'histoire et de l'âme païenne* entitled *Véronique, dialogue de l'histoire et de l'âme charnelle*. There is a great deal more one could say about Péguy and late Godard, but this extract from Péguy's correspondence should give a sense of the potential exchange: 'Clio spends her time looking for traces, vain traces, and then little Veronica, an insignificant Jewess, a kid, gets out her handkerchief and from the face of Jesus takes an eternal trace!' (*Œuvres en prose complètes*, vol. 3, Paris: Gallimard, 1992, p. 1655).

17 'Ainsi ou tout, ou rien. Pour retrouver la vie historique, il faudrait patiemment la suivre en toutes ses voies, toutes ses formes, tous ses éléments. Mais il faudrait aussi, d'une passion plus grande encore, refaire et rétablir le jeu de tout cela, l'action réciproque de ces forces diverses dans un puissant mouvement qui redeviendrait la vie même.'

18 Michelet's original actually reads as follows: 'Son unité n'est pas celle d'une petite pièce en cinq actes, mais (dans un développement souvent immense) l'harmonique identité d'âme [...] C'est le puissant *travail de soi sur soi*, où la France, par son progrès propre, va transformant tous ses éléments bruts [...] La vie a sur elle-même une action de personnel enfantement, qui, de matériaux préexistants, nous crée des choses absolument nouvelles. Du pain, des fruits, que j'ai mangés, je fais du sang rouge et salé qui ne rappelle en rien ces aliments d'où je le tire. Ainsi va la vie historique, ainsi va chaque peuple se faisant, s'engendrant, broyant, amalgamant des éléments, qui y restent sans doute à l'état obscur et confus, mais sont bien peu de chose relativement à ce que fit le long travail de la grande âme.'

19 'Ma vie fut en ce livre, elle a passé en lui. Il a été mon seul événement [...] C'est que l'histoire, dans le progrès du temps, fait l'historien bien plus qu'elle n'est faite par lui. Mon livre m'a créé. C'est moi qui fus son œuvre [...] Si nous nous ressemblons, c'est bien. Les traits qu'il a de moi sont en grande partie ceux que je lui devais, que j'ai tenus de lui.'

20 The last words of 4B, LES SIGNES PARMI NOUS, are: 'que dire/alors/j'étais cet homme'.
   See *Histoire(s) du cinéma*, vol. 4, op. cit., pp. 306-311.

21 See Introduction and 'Le montage, la solitude, la liberté', *Godard par Godard II*, op. cit.,
   pp. 242-248.

22 'Je ne puis désormais plus croire que la peinture, le plus individualiste de tous les
   arts, reste capable, du moins en Europe, de présenter l'image d'une société qui
   évolue, d'un pas de plus en plus sûr, vers des modes anonymes et collectifs de production. Et comme l'expression a toujours été, et ne peut être, que la fille de la production, il faudra bien que nous finissions par prendre notre parti [...] Nous nous
   consolerions aisément de la ruine de la peinture, si nous réussissions à nous
   convaincre que la mystique en formation possède son double expressif, le cinéma,
   dont les débuts ont justement marqué l'apparition des premiers organes communs
   qui la manifestent' (Élie Faure *Fonction du cinéma*, Paris: Denoël/Gonthier, 1953, p.
   48).

23 'Nous tentons de sortir, dans toutes les contrées du monde, d'une forme de civilisation devenue, par excès d'individualisme, impulsive et anarchique, pour entrer dans
   une forme de civilisation plastique, et destinée sans doute à substituer à des études
   analytiques d'états et de crises d'âmes, des poèmes synthétiques de masses et
   d'ensembles en action. J'imagine que l'architecture en sera l'expression principale [...]
   et la cinéplastique, sans doute, en sera l'ornement spirituel le plus unanimement
   recherché, le jeu social le plus utile au développement, dans les foules, du besoin de
   confiance, d'harmonie, de cohésion' (ibid., p. 36).

24 From a speech made to inaugarate the 'Maison de la culture' at Amiens in 1966. See
   André Malraux, *La politique, la culture*, Paris: Gallimard, 1996, p. 329: 'Lorsque les
   hommes sont morts, il ne reste rien de ce qui a été hideux en eux, il ne reste que ce
   qu'ils ont eu de grand quand la transmission est faite par l'art [...] Et si, demain, il ne
   devait rester que des témoignages d'art sur les fours crématoires, il ne resterait rien
   des bourreaux, mais il resterait les martyrs.'

25 'Entre ici/Jean Moulin/avec ton terrible cortège/avec ceux qui sont morts/dans les
   caves/sans avoir parlé/comme toi/et même/ce qui peut être/plus atroce/en ayant
   parlé' (*Histoire(s) du cinéma*, vol. 4, pp. 175-176). For original speech, see 'Transfert des
   cendres de Jean Moulin au Panthéon, 1964', *La politique, la culture*, op. cit., pp. 295-304.

26 'De ses débuts enfantins aux derniers films muets, le cinéma semblait avoir conquis
   des domaines immenses; depuis, qu'a-t-il gagné? Il a perfectionné son éclairage et
   son récit, sa technique: mais dans l'ordre de l'art? J'appelle art, ici, l'expression de
   rapports inconnus et soudain convaincants, entre les êtres, ou entre les êtres et les
   choses.' See *Godard par Godard II*, op. cit., pp. 183-184.

27 'Les masses/aiment le mythe//et le cinéma s'adresse aux masses//mais si le
   mythe/commence à Fantômas/il finit au Christ/qu'entendaient les foules//qui
   écoutaient/prêcher saint Bernard/autre chose que ce qu'il disait/peut-être, sans
   doute//mais comment négliger/ce que nous comprenons/à l'instant où cette voix
   inconnue/s'enfonce/au plus profond de notre cœur?' (*Histoire(s) du cinéma*, vol. 1,
   op. cit., pp. 96-100).

28 See André Malraux, *Le musée imaginaire*, Paris: Gallimard, 1965, p. 13: 'Notre relation
   avec l'art, depuis plus d'un siècle, n'a cessé de s'intellectualiser. Le musée impose une
   mise en question de chacune des expressions du monde qu'il rassemble, une interrogation sur ce qui les rassemble. Au "plaisir de l'œil" la succession, l'apparente contra-

diction des écoles ont ajouté la conscience d'une queste passionnée, d'une recréation de l'univers en face de la Création. Après tout, le musée est un des lieux qui donnent la plus haute idée de l'homme. Mais nos connaissances sont plus étendues que nos musées [...] Là où l'œuvre d'art n'a plus d'autre fonction que d'être œuvre d'art, à une époque où l'exploration artistique du monde se poursuit, la réunion de tant de chefs-d'œuvre, d'où tant de chefs-d'œuvre sont absents, convoque dans l'esprit *tous* les chefs-d'œuvre. Comment ce possible mutilé n'appellerait-il pas tout le possible?'

29 See Malraux, *Les voix du silence*, Paris: Gallimard, 1951, p. 621: 'L'histoire de l'art entière, quand elle est celle du génie, devrait être une histoire de la délivrance: car l'histoire tente de transformer le destin en conscience, et l'art de le transformer en liberté.'

30 See Élie Faure, *L'esprit des formes*, Paris: Gallimard, 1991, p. 27: 'Plus j'avance, plus j'observe, plus je me regarde vivre, moins je conçois qu'il soit possible de considérer l'histoire des peuples et l'histoire de l'esprit autrement que comme une série d'alternances tantôt rapides et tantôt précipitées, de désintégrations par la connaissance et d'intégrations par l'amour. C'est le rythme que Laplace, Lamarck, Spencer surprennent dans l'évolution du drame universel même [...] c'est le rythme du drame chimique où la synthèse et l'analyse s'engendrent alternativement. C'est le rythme du drame physiologique [...] C'est le rythme du drame biologique [...] Ce que nous savons de l'Histoire est encore et sera probablement toujours peu de chose. Peut-être, et sans doute, ne fait-elle que commencer. Mais il faut se résigner à ne rien apprendre d'elle si l'on ne se décide à chercher dans son déroulement une action, confuse à coup sûr, dont on puisse saisir l'aspect quand on la regarde de loin et qu'au lieu de la considérer selon ses soi-disant progrès, ses soi-disant reculs, ses prétendues intentions ou nos prétendus intérêts, on y cherche résolument ce rythme où l'esprit tantôt déterminé par ses événements, tantôt réagissant pour les organiser, ne joue qu'un rôle de régulateur, mais de régulateur unique.'

31 See *Histoire(s) du cinéma*, vol. 4, op. cit., pp. 64-65: 'Une histoire avance vers nous à pas précipités/une autre histoire nous accompagne à pas lents.'

32 See Charles Péguy, *Œuvres en prose complètes*, vol. 3, Paris: Gallimard, 1992, p. 1204: 'Il est indéniable que tout le temps ne passe pas avec la même vitesse et selon le même rythme. Non pas seulement le temps individuel, non pas seulement le temps personnel [...] Mais le temps public même, le temps de tout un peuple, le temps du monde, on est conduit à se demander si le temps public même ne recouvre pas seulement, ne sous-tend pas seulement une durée propre, une durée d'un peuple, une durée du monde.'

33 'La demoiselle de l'enregistrement' is a phrase Godard creatively attributes to Péguy, probably adapting the following sequence from the opening of Péguy's *Véronique, dialogue de l'histoire et de l'âme païenne*: 'I, history, have my story too. I haven't always been this old maid stenographer who makes copies, who makes index cards and recordings all day, who puts them all in boxes [...] I used to sculpt, too. I was allowed to sculpt my discourse, the suppleness and the power of my discourse, according to the contours of the event itself, according to the suppleness and the power of the event's reality. I, too, was a Muse' (*Œuvres en prose complètes*, vol. 3, op. cit., p. 595).

34 See *Œuvres en prose complètes*, vol. 3, op. cit., p. 1152: 'Vous procédez par voie de raccourci, allusion, référence, saisie, étreinte, jeu, nourriture, éclairement, interférence. Correspondance, résonance, analogie, parallélisme. Recreusement. Intelligence, entente.'

Notes to 6: Mortal Beauty

1   Cited in Francis Ponge, *Pour un Malherbe*, Paris: Seuil, 1965, p. 151.
2   Jean-Marie Pontévia, *Tout a peut-être commencé par la beauté*, Bordeaux: William Blake & Co., 1985, p. 19.
3   Robert Graves, *The Greek Myths*, London: Penguin, 1955, pp. 30-31
4   For a detailed analysis of one instance in Chapter 1B when Godard literally 'throws himself' cinematically into videographic existence – the inclusion of a short extract from SOIGNE TA DROITE when, as the Idiot/Prince, he falls head first down an aircraft ramp while being presented with cans of cinefilm – see James S. Williams, 'Beyond the Cinematic Body: human emotion vs. digital technology in Jean-Luc Godard's HISTOIRE(S) DU CINÉMA', in: Scott Brewster, John J. Joughin, David Owen and Richard J. Walker (eds.), *Inhuman Reflections: Thinking the limits of the human*, Manchester: Manchester University Press, 2000, pp. 188-202. Referring to Heidegger's later work on poetry in the context of Merleau-Ponty's theory of embodied perception, Williams argues that Godard's hyperbolic gesture – by which his self-deflating body functions in Chapter 1B as itself a chiastic point of reversal – exemplifies figuration as the chiastic, non-coincident interconnection of seemingly disservered polarities. This is achieved through the 'inward-turning' of the tropology of a poetic language that articulates itself at the limits of the sayable as 'ingathered throw' (*gesammelter Wurf*). [Editors' note]
5   Stated by Godard during his interview in 1989 with Noël Simsolo for Radio France Culture ('À voix nue', *Entretiens d'hier et d'aujourd'hui*, 20 November 1989).

Notes to 7: European Culture and Artistic Resistance in HISTOIRE(S) DU CINÉMA Chapter 3A, LA MONNAIE DE L'ABSOLU

1   'Il y a la culture/qui est de la règle/qui fait partie de la regle/il y a l'exception /qui est de l'art/qui fait partie de l'art/tous disent la règle/cigarettes/ordinateurs/t-shirts/ télévision/tourisme/guerre [...]' (Jean-Luc Godard, *JLG/JLG: Phrases*, Paris: Éditions P.O.L., 1986, pp. 16-17). All translations are my own unless otherwise stated.
2   Here is one such example: 'Art is Dostoevsky, culture was watching my mother read. Later I discovered art in the books that she used to read' ('Une boucle bouclée': interview with Alain Bergala, in: Alain Bergala (ed.), *Jean-Luc Godard par Jean-Luc Godard*, vol. 2 1984-1998, Paris: Cahiers du Cinéma, 1998, pp. 9-41 (pp. 23-24)).
3   'Il est de la règle/que vouloir/la mort de l'exception/non/c'est/non/il est donc de la règle/de l'Europe/de la culture/la règle de l'Europe/de la culture que/d'organiser la mort/de l'art de vivre/qui fleurissait/encore à nos pieds' (Godard, *JLG/JLG*, op. cit., pp. 19-20).
4   'Jean-Luc Godard in Conversation with Colin MacCabe', in: Duncan Petrie (ed.), *Screening Europe: Image and Identity in Contemporary European Cinema*, London: British

Film Institute, 1992, pp. 97-105 (p. 103). In the light of this statement, the commercial selling of HISTOIRE(S) DU CINÉMA, which included interviews with Alain Bergala relayed in retail outlets in France such as FNAC to advertise the handsomely priced product, would appear a major contradiction and spectacular turnaround. Yet Godard has never denied 'democratic' culture its positive, nourishing, pedagogical role. Indeed, from the very beginning of HISTOIRE(S) DU CINÉMA, when he explained his aims for the project to Serge Daney in *Libération* in 1988 ('Godard fait des histoires', 26 December 1988, pp. 24-27), he has harboured the notion of his material being accessible to the public and performing an educative function.

5 See Ien Ang, 'Hegemony-in-Trouble: Nostalgia and the Ideology of the Impossible in European Cinema', in: Petrie (ed.), *Screening Europe: Image and Identity in Contemporary European Cinema*, op. cit., pp. 21-31 (p. 27). Ang argues that the best way for Europe to disentangle itself from its hegemonic past is to become 'post-European', a spirit epitomised by those 'new ethnic' films made in Europe but not from Europe (e.g. Stephen Frears's MY BEAUTIFUL LAUNDERETTE, Po Chih Leong's PING PONG) which 'attempt to come to terms with the complexities of the present without resorting to idealised images of either the past or the future' (p. 30). I will be arguing that Godard adopts a 'trans-European' and 'trans-aesthetic' approach in HISTOIRE(S) DU CINÉMA. For an excellent analysis of PASSION that places the film in its European context while arguing for its postmodern status, see Fredric Jameson's 'High-tech collectives in Late Godard' in: *The Geopolitical Aesthetic: cinema and space in the world system*, London and Bloomington, IN: Indiana University Press, 1992, pp. 158-185.

6 Jacques Aumont, *Amnésies: fictions du cinéma d'après Jean-Luc Godard*, Paris: P.O.L., 1999, p. 115. Aumont refers to the fundamentally documentary nature of these three national cinemas torn between two 'postulations' of fiction, American and Russian.

7 Péguy began *Clio* in 1909, a year after he had refound his faith, and in it he dismisses the new schools of scientific-sociological enquiry. Yet running throughout the text is a profound sense of failure. The problem in writing ancient history, Péguy argues, is that the references are lacking, while for the writer of modern history there are simply too many references. Moreover, if history runs parallel to the event, memory is central to it. Hence, the most delicate problem of aesthetics is essentially a problem of the very organisation of memory.

8 Oswald Spengler, *The Decline of the West* [1923], New York: Alfred A. Knopf, 1962.

9 Denis de Rougemont, *Penser avec les mains*, Paris: Albin Michel, 1936, p. 21. Godard rarely modifies the selected extracts except when he wishes to make the language more clear or accessible. The one important exception to this rule is the following: 'x is a person/a creative element/an incalculable freedom' (*Histoire(s) du cinéma*, vol. 4, p. 61) ('x est une personne/un élément créateur/une liberté incalculable'). The original passage, located just before the end of the text, reads: 'The only value that one can give to the x of the world's equation is that of a person. Yet since a person is a creative act, it introduces every time into the equation an irrational and incalculable element, an element of freedom' (p. 245) ('La personne, telle est la seule valeur qu'on puisse donner à l'x de l'équation du monde. Or, la personne étant un acte créateur, elle introduit à chaque fois dans l'équation un élément irrationnel, incalculable, un élément de liberté'). Godard's dynamic fusion of ideas in this passage, which attributes directly to 'a person' the qualities linked by de Rougemont to an 'an element' and thus itself performs the idea conveyed of creative freedom, is significant for the fact

that it takes place under the letter x, a fact whose importance will become clear shortly when we discuss the chiastic dimensions of Godard's self-reflexive montage.

10 'Rapport d'inactivité', in: Bergala, *Godard par Godard II*, op. cit., pp. 249-51 (p. 251).

11 'Le cinéma est fait pour penser l'impensable', ibid., pp. 294-299 (p. 296). Godard has just explained the complex sequence of association in ALLEMAGNE ANNÉE 90 NEUF ZÉRO where, during discussion of a young girl beheaded during the war, a white rose arrives in the frame to the sounds of a typewriter. This requires historical knowledge of the White Rose Movement founded in Germany in 1942-3 by Hans and Sophie Scholl, who were arrested and killed for distributing typewritten anti-Nazi tracts.

12 'Ce que le genre humain sait, les gouvernements l'ignorent [...] Quand finira le martyre de cette héroïque petite nation?' See 'Pour la Serbie', in: Victor Hugo, *Actes et paroles*, vol. 3: 'Depuis L'exil 1870-1885 "Mes Fils"', Paris: Albin Michel 'L'imprimerie nationale', 1940, pp. 255-58.

13 For an excellent analysis of the political and discursive strategies adopted by Mitterrand and the then Minister for Culture during the GATT talks, including the advocacy of European construction through cultural cohesion and the invocation of a European 'spirit of resistance' and 'consciousness', see Louise Strode, 'France and EU Policy-Making on Visual Culture – New Opportunities for National Identity?', in: Elizabeth Ezra and Sue Harris (eds.), *France in Focus: Film and National Identity*, Berg, forthcoming 2000. Strode argues convincingly that France, although calling for the protection of European cultural identity (vaguely defined) and 'the universal idea of culture', seeks above all to utilise the opportunities of the European Union to bolster its own identity through policy-making on visual culture.

14 See Jacques Derrida, *L'autre cap: mémoires, réponses et responsabilités*, Paris: Éditions de Minuit, 1991. Derrida refers to 'Notes sur la grandeur et décadence de l'Europe' in: Paul Valéry, *Essais quasi politiques. Œuvres*, vol. 1, Paris: Bibliothèque de la Pléiade, Gallimard, 1957, and to 'La crise de l'esprit', ibid., where Valéry asks: 'Will Europe become what it is in reality, that is, a small head of the Asiatic continent? Or else will it remain what it appears to be, that is: the precious part of the terrestial universe, the pearl in the sphere, the brain of a vast body?' (p. 995).

15 See André Malraux, *Les voix du silence*, Paris: Gallimard, 1951, pp. 99-102.

16 See Georges Bataille, *Manet: biographical and critical study*, New York: Skira, 1955, trans. Austryn Wainhouse and James Emmons, p. 103.

17 See Philippe Sollers, 'Il y a des fantômes plein l'écran...': interview with Antoine de Baecque and Serge Toubiana, *Cahiers du Cinéma*, no. 153, 1997, pp. 39-48 (p. 42). Sollers talks of HISTOIRE(s) DU CINÉMA in Heideggerian terms as 'l'*Historial* du cinéma' and emphasises its prophetic and apocalyptic tone, claiming that it is a 'practically funerary monument' (p. 40).

18 Bernard Eisenschitz suggests that the image of Berlin shown is possibly from AS-PHALT. See his account of tracking down references for Godard in HISTOIRE(s) DU CINÉMA and the creative 'errors' and 'ruptures' produced by the video in: '"Une machine à montrer l'invisible": Conversation avec Bernard Eisenschitz à propos des HISTOIRE(s) DU CINÉMA', *Cahiers du Cinéma*, no. 529, 1998, pp. 52-56 (p. 54).

19 Emily Brontë's poem beginning 'The evening passes fast away' includes the words: 'And where thy heart has suffered so/Canst thou desire to dwell?/Alas! the countless links are strong/That bind us to our clay;/The loving spirit lingers long,/And would not pass away – '. The poem, written in 1842-3, was commenced in Brussels a

fortnight before Brontë returned home on account of the death of her aunt and foster mother. Again, in the spirit of LA MONNAIE DE L'ABSOLU, art – resistant and here pugnacious – is linked to a real journey induced by loss and pain.

20 The painting appears to be *Nu Couché Bleu* (1955), although whether this is the original or Godard's own imitation is debatable, since he was not legally allowed by the de Staël family to reproduce any of the artist's paintings. What is perhaps more significant is the fact that the image was painted by de Staël in 1955 just before he killed himself. As such, it can be compared to another image favoured by Godard in HISTOIRE(S) DU CINÉMA, Van Gogh's *Wheatfield with crows*, his very last picture, and also Paul Klee's *Vergesslicher Engel*, a key part of the final sequence of Chapter 1B, drawn in 1939 just before his death in 1940 from a rare debilitating disease called scleroderma. Godard is consistently drawn not only to the late period of artists, but also to traces of the early tragic (e.g. Novalis).

21 The first edition of *Gilles* in 1939 was censored, but the novel was reissued in complete form in 1942. It is a neo-historical, picaresque modernist novel in four parts, covering the years from 1917 to the Spanish Civil War.

22 See Paul de Man, *Allegories of Reading: Figural Language in Rousseau, Nietzsche, Rilke, and Proust*, New Haven: Yale University Press, 1979, p. 53.

23 In *No go the bogeyman: scaring, lulling, and making mock*, London: Chatto and Windus, 1998, Marina Warner has suggested that this image may actually be one of incestuous cannibalism since the buttocks suggest a female youth. If so, the image may not be of Saturn at all but of Kronos incorporating one of his daughters. Warner bases her argument in part on a comparison with another image by Goya used in LA MONNAIE DE L'ABSOLU, the drawing *Saturn devouring his children*.

24 I have explored elsewhere the figure of the chiasmus in terms of the mechanical and inhuman as it operates in Chapter 1B of HISTOIRE(S) DU CINÉMA. See 'Beyond the Cinematic Body: human emotion vs. digital technology in Jean-Luc Godard's HISTOIRE(S) DU CINÉMA', in: Scott Brewster, John J. Joughin, David Owen and Richard J. Walker (eds.), *Inhuman Reflections: Thinking the limits of the human*, Manchester: Manchester University Press, 2000, pp. 188-202.

25 See 'HISTOIRE(S) DU CINÉMA: à propos de cinéma et d'histoire', in: Bergala, *Godard par Godard II*, op. cit., pp. 401-405 (p. 403).

26 See Marie-José Mondzain, 'Histoire et passion', *Art Press*, Godard Special Issue – 'Guide pour HISTOIRE(S) DU CINÉMA', November 1998, pp. 91-98 (pp. 97-98). Mondzain argues that the newly born America transferred its belief in incarnation and resurrection into a new regime, industry, and thus the uniqueness of cinema's initial gesture (notably in the work of Griffith) was soon destroyed by trade. For an extensive study of Godard's changing notion of cinema as pre-eminently a national cinema, see Michael Witt, 'Qu'était-ce que le cinéma, Jean-Luc Godard? An analysis of the cinema(s) at work in and around Godard's HISTOIRE(S) DU CINÉMA', in: Elizabeth Ezra and Susan Harris (eds.), *France in Focus: Film and National Identity*, Oxford: Berg, forthcoming 2000.

27 In 'Résistance de l'art', in: Bergala, *Godard par Godard II*, op. cit., pp. 443-446, an interview that originally appeared in November 1997 in *Le Monde de l'éducation*, Godard talks of his long interest in the period of the Occupation and the Resistance and argues that ROME, OPEN CITY was a film of resistance because of its value of resurrection.

Godard does not, however, consider here the question of resistance in cinema as it informs his own film practice and particularly HISTOIRE(S) DU CINÉMA.

28 'Une boucle bouclée', in: Bergala, *Godard par Godard II*, op. cit., p. 18: '"L'État, c'est la *pensée qui forme*." Moi, je crois plus à une forme qui pense [...] C'est la forme qui pense, au cinéma. Dans le mauvais cinéma, c'est la pensée qui forme.'

29 De Rougemont, *Penser avec les mains*, op. cit., p. 243.

30 See 'Le bon plaisir de Jean-Luc Godard', in: Bergala, *Godard par Godard II*, op. cit., pp. 305-322 (p. 318).

31 For an excellent analysis of the changes affecting nation-state sovereignty in the new, 'Greater Europe', see Zygmunt Bauman, *A Life in Fragments: essays in postmodern morality*, Oxford: Blackwell, 1995, in particular 'Europe of Nations, Europe of Tribes' (pp. 243-256). Bauman argues that the Wall offered an effective barrier to the spread of the privilege called 'Europe' (p. 245), but that now, with the idea of a supra-state and all-European institutions and agencies, what is left of the traditional sovereignty of nation-states (and especially of their contractual obligations toward their subjects) appears very easy, too easy, to hold and uphold, i.e. 'a prize with no penalty attached; a right without duties, taking without giving, pleasure without responsibility' (p. 248). Bauman signals the dangers today of an 'endless fissiparousness of nationalisms' with ever new regional, linguistic and denominational differences being picked up by ever new prospective elites as distinctive identities powerful enough to justify a separate state, or quasi-state, formation' (p. 250). The forces of ethnicity (in Serbia, for instance) 'are once more set loose, untamed and unanchored, free-floating and uncontrolled' (p. 247), and states have become now 'no more than transit stations in travel of goods and money administered by multi-national (i.e. non-national, trans-national) executives'.

32 See Jeffrey Skoller, 'Reinventing Time, Or The continuing Adventures of Lemmy Caution in Godard's GERMANY YEAR 90 NINE ZERO', *Film Quarterly*, vol. 3, no. 3, 1999, pp. 35-42, where Skoller argues that Godard is interested in the space between the shots that holds them apart such that there is no chain of interlinked images to form a whole. The interstice is a form of thought, a virtuality that exists between non-linking images. According to Skoller, ALLEMAGNE ANNÉE 90 NEUF ZÉRO creates a distinction between knowledge and thought since thinking is defined by the virtual or what is unthought, and to think is to experiment and to create (p. 42).

33 Jürgen Habermas, *The Past as Future* (Interviews with Michael Haller), London and Lincoln, NE: University of Nebraska Press, 1994, p. 71. According to Habermas, world history has offered a unified Europe a 'second chance', and 'Europe must use one of its strengths, namely its potential for self-criticism, its power of self-transformation, in order to relativise itself far more radically *vis-à-vis* the others, the strangers, the misunderstood. That's the opposite of Eurocentrism' (p. 96).

34 See 'Jean-Luc Godard rencontre Régis Debray', in: Bergala, *Godard par Godard II*, op. cit., pp. 423-431, where Godard claims that art has disappeared and that Picasso represented the end of one of the chapters of man's artistic creation as conceived by Malraux (p. 423).

35 See Régis Debray, *Le code et le glaive: après l'Europe, la nation?*, Paris: Albin Michel, 1999, p. 103. The book is part of a new series called Fondation Marc-Bloch which advocates the State and Nation as the only proper framework for democracy and the continuation of the Republic. Interestingly, Debray also considers the case of Péguy and Hugo,

referring to the latter's introduction to the guide of the 1867 Exposition Universelle entitled 'Paris', where Hugo talks fancifully of Paris as being in the twentieth century the capital of a new nation Europe eventually to be called simply Humanity (p. 72).

36 'Si une image, regardée à part, exprime nettement quelque chose, si elle comporte une interprétation, elle ne se transformera pas au contact d'autres images. Les autres images n'auront aucun pouvoir sur elle, et elle n'aura aucun pouvoir sur les autres images. Ni action, ni réaction' (Robert Bresson, *Notes sur le cinématographe* [1975], Paris: Folio, 1995, p. 23). It goes without saying that for Godard there is never a single image but rather relations of images, and the movement between them. See Chapter 2 of this collection for Michael Witt's extensive analysis of Godard's terms of reference for montage.

37 See Bergala, 'Une boucle bouclée', op. cit., p. 35.

38 For a fine discussion of the Kantian sublime in the context of history, see Jean-François Lyotard, 'The sign of history', in: Andrew Benjamin (ed.), *The Lyotard reader*, Oxford: Blackwell, 1989, pp. 393-411.

39 See Gilles Deleuze, *Cinéma 2: L'image-temps*, Paris: Minuit, 1995, pp. 234-235. Deleuze talks of Godardian montage as operating 'between two actions, two affections, two perceptions, two visual images, two sound images, between sound and the visual: to show the indiscernible, i.e. the border' (p. 235).

40 See Raymond Bellour, *L'entre-images: photo, cinéma, vidéo*, Paris: La Différence, 1990, pp. 330-7. Bellour refers to Godard's use of video as a '*passeuse*' which offers an intermediate vision, an 'intermedial' language.

41 See Kaja Silverman and Harun Farocki, *Speaking about Godard*, New York: NYU Press, 1998, p. 184. They also declare that in PASSION Godard uses the trope of analogy but only to renounce it: 'there is nothing sublime about similarity; it is not the point where contraries meet, but the site of their disappearance' (p. 185). I will argue differently that in HISTOIRE(S) DU CINÉMA analogies of the human form are pursued, maintained and even prioritised.

42 See Jacques Rancière, 'La sainte et l'héritière: À propos des HISTOIRE(S) DU CINÉMA', *Cahiers du Cinéma*, no. 536, 1999, pp. 58-61, where Rancière laments Godard's sacred belief in the image and its original vocation of presence (destroyed by the 'original sin' of nineteenth-century artifice and fiction). He describes Godard ironically as 'le plus rigoureux des iconodules'.

43 Chapter 1A of HISTOIRE(S) DU CINÉMA (TOUTES LES HISTOIRES), NOUVELLE VAGUE and ALLEMAGNE ANNÉE 90 NEUF ZÉRO are all punctuated by the slow, deep murmurings and mounting crescendos of Hindemith's symphony *Mathis der Maler* (Mathis the painter) (1933-4), notably the opening moments of the second and third movements, 'Grablegung' and 'Versuchung des heiligen Antonius'. Inspired by the life of Matthias Grünewald and in particular his *Isenheim Altarpiece*, the symphony is linked in theme and style to Hindemith's later opera of the same name, in which an artist leads a rebellion against authority. Its ultimate message is one of faith in art rather than politics, and as such the music expresses exactly the type of artistic resistance currently cultivated by Godard. It is worth noting that performances of the opera were banned in Germany by the Nazis, a fate that also befell Hindemith's other spiritual, Christian works such as the 1923 song cycle *Das Marienleben* (The life of Mary).

44 Godard: 'ô quelle merveille que de regarder ce qu'on ne voit pas/ô doux miracle de nos yeux aveugles'; Bernanos: 'ô merveille, qu'on puisse ainsi faire présent de ce

qu'on ne possède pas soi-même, ô doux miracle de nos mains vides!' (Georges Bernanos, *Journal d'un curé de campagne* [1936], Paris: Pocket, 1994, p. 200).

45 See Jean-Luc Godard and Youssef Ishaghpour, 'Archéologie du cinéma et mémoire du siècle', Dialogue I, *Trafic*, no. 29, Spring 1999, pp. 16-35 (p. 31).

46 Sollers, 'Il y a des fantômes plein l'écran...', op. cit., p. 48.

47 Rancière, 'La sainte et l'héritière', op. cit., p. 61.

48 See 'Godard peintre' in: Jacques Aumont, *L'œil interminable: Cinéma et peinture* , Paris: Séguier, 1989, pp. 223-247 (p. 242). Aumont places Godard in the context of Classicism where the body 'expresses' and is the privileged site of feeling, of 'passion'. Compare this with Angela Dalle Vacche's analysis of Godard's collage method in the much earlier PIERROT LE FOU, which argues that the film is animated by a logocentric impulse, and, more generally, that Godard's cinema tends towards abstraction and is actually iconophobic. Dalle Vacche claims specifically that Godard's use of collage and its ability to thrive on the boundary between word and image (thus creating semiotic permutation) marks an attempt to overcome the pain of sexual difference. See Angela Dalle Vacche, *Cinema and Painting: how art is used in film*, London: Athlone, 1996, pp. 107-134. What Aumont and Della Vacche do not disagree on, however, is the primary importance for Godard of the image's capacity to create and disclose feelings and emotions.

49 See Jean-François Lyotard, *Discours, figure*, Paris: Klincksieck, 1985, pp. 11-18. For Lyotard, the function of art (as opposed to the ego) is to lift repression and reverse it: 'the forms forbid the fulfilment of desire, they prevent it from hallucinating itself and discharging itself into the lure of carrying the contents into effect, simply because these forms do not let us stay ignorant of themselves' (p. 355). And: 'Fantasy makes opposition out of difference; the poetic remakes difference out of *that* opposition' (p. 357). It could surely be argued that the rich, poetic montage of HISTOIRE(S) DU CINÉMA, which freely connects resurrected traces of the recorded past, epitomises Lyotard's notion of art as difference and the lifting of repression.

50 A point of comparison in this regard might be Jean Louis Schefer's notion of the 'enigmatic', 'paradoxical body', which he opposes to doxical figuration in western painting produced by perspectival and volumatic space. Godard has a similar suspicion of perspective and his perception of the body is equally attached to the elements of time and memory. Yet Godard's presentation of the body in LA MONNAIE DE L'ABSOLU is from a specifically Christian perspective, whereas Schefer's is that of the pagan body which Christianity combats (Schefer is drawn to those films precisely which figure unformed, deformed or freakish bodies). See Paul Smith (ed.), *The Enigmatic Body: Essays on the Arts by Jean Louis Schefer*, trans. Paul Smith, Cambridge: Cambridge University Press, 1995, in particular 'The Plague' (pp. 37-53) (on Uccello's *Deluge*) and 'Cinema' (pp. 108-138).

51 See Terry Eagleton, *The Ideology of the Aesthetic*, Oxford: Blackwell, 1990, p. 357. Much could be said of the resemblances in style between HISTOIRE(S) DU CINÉMA and the Adorno of *Minima moralia*, including the method of intensive fragmentation and the use of epigrammatic *aperçus*.

52 Theodor Adorno, *Minima moralia*, London, 1974, p. 247.

Notes to 8: The Evidence and Uncertainty of Silent Film in
HISTOIRE(S) DU CINEMA

1 '[L]es masses/aiment le mythe/et le cinéma/s'adresse/aux masses/mais si le
mythe/commence à Fantômas/il finit au Christ/qu'entendaient les foules/qui
écoutaient/prêcher saint Bernard/autre chose que ce qu'il disait/peut-être, sans
doute/mais comment négliger/ce que nous comprenons/à l'instant où cette voix
inconnue/s'enfonce/au plus profound/de notre cœur' (Jean-Luc Godard, *Histoire(s)
du cinéma*, Paris: Gallimard-Gaumont, 1998 (4 vols), vol. 1, pp. 96-100; all quotations
from the video rely on the book version unless otherwise indicated). I would like to
thank the Celeste Bartos International Film Study Center at The Museum of Modern
Art in New York (John Harris and Sally Berger), and Electronic Arts Intermix in New
York for their help with my research. Thanks also to Janet Bergstrom for the film reference and to James S. Williams for translation help (and a key film reference).

2 Quoted in Raymond Bellour, '(Not Just An Other Film-maker)', in: Raymond Bellour
and Mary Lea Bandy (eds.), *Jean-Luc Godard: Son+Image, 1974-1991*, New York: Museum of Modern Art, 1992, pp. 221.

3 André Malraux, *Esquisse d'une psychologie du cinéma*, Paris: Gallimard, 1946. The full
text by Malraux reads as follows: 'Le cinéma s'adresse aux masses, et les masses
aiment le mythe, en bien et en mal. La guerre suffirait à nous le montrer, si nous
voulions l'oublier: le stratège de café est un personnage moins répandu que "celui
qui sait de source sûre que l'ennemi coupe les mains des enfants". Le journalisme, des
fausses nouvelles aux feuilletons, ne ment que par mythes. Le mythe commence à
Fantômas, mais il finit au Christ. Les foules sont loin de préférer toujours ce qu'il y a
de meilleur en elles; pourtant elles le reconnaissent souvent. Qu'entendaient celles
qui écoutaient prêcher saint Bernard? Autre chose que ce qu'il disait? Peut-être; sans
doute. Mais comment négliger ce qu'elles comprenaient à l'instant où cette voix
inconnue s'enfonçait au plus profond de leur cœur?'

4 A direct reference to the film appears in 'Dialogue entre Jean-Luc Godard et Serge
Daney', *Cahiers du Cinéma*, no. 513, May 1997, pp. 49-55 (p. 50). A more elliptical remark about the film can be found in Godard's interview in 1989 with Noël Simsolo
for Radio France Culture ('À voix nue', *Entretiens d'hier et d'aujourd'hui*, 20 November
1989).

5 Both ERREUR TRAGIQUE and the first three episodes of FANTÔMAS appear in 1913, but
ERREUR TRAGIQUE's premiere was in January and the first episode of FANTÔMAS was
in May. For a complete filmography of Feuillade, see Francis Lacassin, *Maître des lions
et des vampires: Louis Feuillade*, Paris: Pierre Bordas et fils, 1995.

6 Interview with Simsolo, op. cit..

7 Henri Bergson, *Creative Evolution*, trans. Arthur Mitchell, Mineola, N.Y.: Dover Publications, 1998, pp. 304-308.

8 The passage from the film is as follows: 'est-ce que tu as deux mains/demande
l'aveugle/mais ce n'est pas en regardant/que je m'en assure/oui/pourquoi faire
confiance à mes yeux/si j'en suis à douter/oui/pourquoi n'est-ce pas mes yeux/que
je vais vérifier/en regardant/si je vois mes deux mains' (*Histoire(s) du cinéma*, vol. 1,
p. 140). The passage from Wittgenstein can be found in Ludwig Wittgenstein, *On Cer-*

tainty, G.E.M. Anscombe and G.H. von Wright (eds.), trans. Denis Paul and G.E.M. Anscombe, New York: Harper Torchbooks, 1969, pp. 18-19.

9 G.E. Moore, 'Proof of an External World', in: *Philosophical Papers*, New York: Collier Books, 1962, p. 133.

10 Ibid., p. 143.

11 Ibid., p. 147.

12 Ibid., p. 148.

13 Wittgenstein, *On Certainty*, op. cit., p. 3.

14 Ibid., p. 4.

15 Ludwig Wittgenstein, *Philosophical Investigations*, third edition, trans. G.E.M. Anscombe, New York: MacMillan, 1958, p. 5.

16 Ibid., p. 32.

17 For a detailed discussion of the performative qualities of speech, see John R. Searle, *Speech Acts: An Essay in the Philosophy of Language*, Cambridge: Cambridge University Press, 1969.

18 My reading of this passage by Godard is indebted to Judith Butler's discussion of the illusion of matter/sex/body as a fixed entity in *Bodies That Matter: On the Discursive Limits of 'Sex'*, New York: Routledge, 1993.

19 'Voilà, le cinéma est là pour faire de la métaphysique. C'est d'ailleurs ce qu'il fait mais on ne le voit pas ou alors ceux qui en font ne le disent pas. Le cinéma est quelque chose d'extrêmement physique de par son invention mécanique. C'est fait pour s'évader, et s'évader c'est de la métaphysique' ('J'ai toujours pensé que le cinéma était un instrument de pensée', *Cahiers du Cinéma*, no. 490, April 1995, p. 71).

20 My understanding of how the gaps or interstices in film and narrative function is deeply indebted to Hélène Cixous's discussion of the uncanny in the article, 'Fiction and Its Phantoms: A Reading of Freud's *Das Unheimliche* ("The Uncanny")', *New Literary History*, vol. 7, no. 3 (1976), pp. 525-548. The 'uncanny' is for Cixous 'a composite that infiltrates the interstices of the narrative and points to gaps we need to explain' (p. 16). Gilles Deleuze also points to the 'interstices' and 'gaps' throughout his discussion of Godard in *Cinema 2: The Time-Image* [1985], trans. Hugh Tomlinson and Robert Galeta, Minneapolis: University of Minnesota Press, 1989, esp. p. 179.

21 *Histoire(s) du cinéma*, vol. 1, op. cit., p. 81.

22 The full quotation does not appear in the text of *Histoire(s) du cinéma* as published, but sounds as follows: 'Histoires du cinéma, avec un "s"; toutes les histoires qu'il y aurait, qu'il y aura, qu'il y aurait, qu'il y a eu... qu'il y a eu'.

23 'Ne va pas montrer/tous les côtés des choses/garde, toi/une marge/d'indéfini' (*Histoire(s) du cinéma* vol. 1, op. cit., pp. 15-17).

24 The passage as it appears in *Histoire(s) du cinéma*, vol. 1, op. cit., pp. 259-266 is as follows: 'les poètes/sont ceux des mortels qui/chantant gravement/ressentent la trace des dieux enfuis/restent sur cette trace/et tracent ainsi aux mortels/leurs frères/le chemin du revirement/mais qui/des mortels/est capable de déceler/une telle trace/ il appartient aux traces/d'être souvent inapparentes/et elles sont toujours/le legs d'une assignation/à peine pressentie/être poète/en temps/de détresse/c'est alors/ chantant/être attentif/à la trace/des dieux enfuis/voilà pourquoi/au temps de la nuit du monde/le poète dit le sacré'. The original text from Heidegger reads as follows: 'Poets are the mortals who, singing earnestly of the wine god, sense the trace of the fugitive gods, stay on the gods' tracks, and so trace for their kindred mortals the

way toward the turning. The ether, however, in which alone the gods are gods, is their godhead. The element of this ether, that within which even the godhead itself is still present, is the holy. The element of the ether for the coming of the fugitive gods, the holy, is the track of the fugitive gods. But who has the power to sense, to trace such a track? Traces are often inconspicuous, and are always the legacy of a directive that is barely divined. To be a poet in a destitute time means: to attend, singing, to the trace of the fugitive gods. This is why the poet in the time of the world's night utters the holy' ('What are Poets For?', in: Martin Heidegger, *Poetry, Language, Thought*, trans. Albert Hofstadter, New York: Harper, 1971, p. 94).

25 Ibid., p. 96.

26 Ibid., p. 92.

27 Ibid., p. 108.

28 Deleuze, *Cinema 2*, op. cit., p. 179.

29 Ibid., p. 180.

30 For a detailed description of how these 'shock' cuts work in Feuillade, see my articles, 'The Innovators 1910-1920: Detailing the Impossible', *Sight & Sound*, April 1999, pp. 28-30, and 'Zones of Anxiety: Movement, Musidora, and the Crime Serials of Louis Feuillade', *Velvet Light Trap*, vol. 37, Spring 1996, pp. 37-50.

31 Deleuze, *Cinema 2*, op. cit., p. 182.

32 The original French reads: 'Singulière fortune où le but se déplace,/Et, n'étant nulle part, peut être n'importe où!'. Both the French and English versions appear in Charles Baudelaire, *The Flowers of Evil and Paris Spleen*, trans. William H. Crosby, Brockport: BOA Editions, 1991, pp. 252-253

33 Deleuze, *Cinema 2*, op. cit., p. 60.

34 Martin Heidegger, 'Conversations on a Country Path', *Discourse on Thinking* (a translation of *Gelassenheit*), trans. John M. Anderson and E. Hans Freund, New York: Harper, 1966, p. 61.

35 Ibid., pp. 88-89.

36 Ibid., p. 75.

37 Douglas Hofstadter, *Gödel, Escher, Bach: An Eternal Golden Braid*, Toronto: Basic Books, 1980, p. 127.

38 For an example, see M.C. Escher, 'Day and Night', ibid., p. 252.

39 Ellen Draper, 'An Alternative to Godard's Metaphysics: Cinematic Presence in Miéville's LE LIVRE DE MARIE', in: Maryel Locke and Charles Warren (eds.), HAIL MARY: *Women and the Sacred in Film*, Carbondale: Southern Illinois Press, 1994, p. 69.

40 Trinh T. Minh-ha, 'Film as Translation' (with Scott MacDonald), in: *Framer Framed*, New York: Routledge, 1992, p. 122.

41 See especially, *Camera Obscura*, vols. 8-9-10 (Fall 1982). The introduction is reprinted in Bellour and Bandy, *Son+Image*, op. cit., along with Laura Mulvey's article, 'The Hole and the Zero: the Janus Face of the Feminine in Godard' (pp. 75-88). The collection, HAIL MARY: *Women and the Sacred in Film*, provides an interesting range of perspectives on Godard, some more explicitly feminist than others.

42 Butler, *Bodies That Matter*, op. cit., p. 10.

43 Trinh T. Minh-ha, *Woman/Native/Other: Writing Postcoloniality and Feminism*, Bloomington: Indiana University Press, p. 90.

44 Gilles Deleuze, 'Three questions about SIX FOIS DEUX', in: Bellour and Bandy, *Son+Image*, op. cit., p. 41.

Notes to 9: The Crisis of Cinema in the Age of New World Memory: The Baroque performance of KING LEAR

1   Gilles Deleuze, *The Fold: Leibniz and the Baroque*, trans. Tom Conley, Minneapolis: University of Minnesota Press, 1993, p. 27.
2   Ibid., 110.
3   Jean-Luc Godard, *For Ever Mozart*, Paris: P.O.L., 1996, p. 28.
4   Jean-Luc Godard, *Histoire(s) du cinéma*, 4 vols, Paris: Gallimard-Gaumont, 1998, vol. 4, pp. 36-38.
5   Ibid., p. 47.
6   Cited by Raymond Bellour, 'The Book, Back and Forth', in: Christine van Assche (ed.), *Qu'est-ce qu'une madeleine?* Paris: Yves Gevaert/Centre Georges Pompidou, 1997, p. 147.
7   See Katherine Dieckmann, 'Godard in his Fifth Period', in: David Sterritt (ed.), *Jean-Luc Godard: Interviews*, Jackson: University of Mississippi Press, 1998, p. 172.
8   Ibid..
9   David Impastato, 'Godard's LEAR... Why Is It So Bad?', *Shakespeare Bulletin*, vol. 12, no. 3 (Summer 1994), p. 38.
10 Jean-Luc Godard, *Histoire(s) du cinéma*, vol. 3, op. cit., 1998, p. 51.
11 Gavin Smith, 'Jean-Luc Godard', in Sterritt, *Jean-Luc Godard: Interviews*, op. cit., p. 188.
12 Godard, *Histoire(s) du cinéma*, vol. 3, op. cit., p. 155.
13 All quotations from KING LEAR are from *The Riverside Shakespeare*, Boston, 1974, ed. G. Blakemore Evans.
14 I develop this point in 'Getting Stoned: Psychoanalysis and the Epistemology of Tragedy in Shakespeare', in: *Drama Trauma: Specters of Race and Sexuality in Performance, Video, and Art*, London and New York: Routledge, 1997, pp. 31-56.
15 Smith, 'Jean-Luc Godard', op. cit., p. 193.
16 The certain uncertainty of projection is discussed toward the end of KING LEAR when Professor Pluggy teaches the *New York Times* interviewer about the architectonics of cinema where 'chairs are facing the the same space: voice projected all over here: this is our invention: same space, dark: here they know to look at' – even while the destruction of perspective no longer permits them to know exactly what that 'what' signifies.
17 It is almost as if William Shakespeare, Jr. the Fifth is haunted by the crisis of *socius* that Jacques Derrida analyses in 'No apocalypse, not now: à toute vitesse, sept missives, sept missiles', in: *Psyché, Inventions de l'autre*, Paris: Galilée, 1987, pp. 363-86.
18 Godard, *Histoire(s) du cinéma*, vol. 4, op. cit., p. 262.
19 'Everyone occupies this position', suggests Kaja Silverman when suggesting that the similar condition of 'betweenness' in PASSION means that 'to be human is to reside within the interval'. See Kaja Silverman and Harun Farocki, *Speaking About Godard*, New York and London: New York University Press, 1998, p. 188.
20 In this regard, the effect of the Godardian sound event is curiously similar to that of Jean Laplanche's 'enigmatic signifier' through which the primal trauma of enigmatic shock is replayed in art and life to the extent that 'the signifier may be *designified*, or lose what it signifies, without thereby losing the power to signify to'. See Jean

Laplanche, *New Foundations for Psychoanalysis*, trans. David Macey, Oxford: Basil Blackwell, 1989, p. 45.

21 Smith, 'Jean-Luc Godard', op. cit., p. 190.

22 Pierre Lévy, *Cyberculture: Rapport au Conseil de l'Europe dans le cadre du projet 'Nouvelles technologies: coopération culturelle et communication'*, Paris: Odile Jacob, 1997, p. 179.

23 Smith, 'Jean-Luc Godard', op. cit., p. 190.

24 In *Speaking About Godard*, op. cit., pp. 141-145, Farocki and Silverman engage in a provocative exchange about the impact of Godard's editing in front of double video monitors.

25 Jean-Louis Baudry, 'The Apparatus: Metapsychological Approaches to the Impression of Reality in the Cinema', in: Phillip Rosen (ed.), *Narrative, Apparatus, Ideology*, New York: Columbia University Press, 1986, p. 307.

26 Ibid., 316.

27 For the sake of foregrounding the effect of these lines at the outset of the twenty-first century, I cite Harun Farocki's citation of this line with its prescient diacritical effect which identifies the machine on which I write, as well as that which ushered in the first generation of digital graphics.

28 Silverman and Farocki, *Speaking About Godard*, op. cit., p. 142.

29 The National Association of Scholars and the National Alumni Forum are conservative American lobbying organisations whose academic members decry, among other evils, the teaching of Shakespeare in relation to the politics of race, class and gender, not to mention the philosophy of poststructuralism.

30 Gilles Deleuze, *Logique du sens*, Paris: Minuit, 1977, pp. 138-139.

31 Gilles Deleuze, *Cinema 2: The Time-Image* [1985], trans. Hugh Tomlinson and Robert Galeta, Minneapolis: University of Minnesota Press, 1989, p. 131. Deleuze refers here to paragraph 57 of *La Monadologie*, Paris: Aubin, 1983, p. 173.

32 Ibid., p. 180. For a more extensive discussion of the cinematic implications of Deleuzian 'incompossibility', see my reading of PROSPERO'S BOOKS, 'You Are How You Read: Baroque Chao-errancy in Greenaway and Deleuze', *Iris*, no. 23, Spring 1997, pp. 87-107.

33 Deleuze, *Cinema 2: The Time-Image*, op. cit., p. 181.

34 Ibid., p. 183.

35 Ibid., p. 188.

36 Ibid., p. 224.

Notes to 10: The Power of Language: Notes on PUISSANCE DE LA PAROLE, LE DERNIER MOT and ON S'EST DÉFILÉ

1 This chapter brings together two previously published works by Jean-Louis Leutrat which the editors have freely adapted for the collection: *Jean-Luc Godard, un cinéaste mallarméen*, Paris: Schena-Didier Érudition, 1998, and 'Un besoin de distance', *Vertigo* (French), no. 18 (1999), pp. 124-128.

2 See 'Jean-Luc Godard: Des traces au cinéma': interview with Michel Ciment and Stéphane Goudet, *Positif*, no. 456, February 1999, pp. 50-57 (p. 55).

3 'Je m'en vais ou je m'en vas, car l'un et l'autre est ou sont français... et se dit, ou se disent.' One might add that Godard is also fond of quoting or paraphrasing the affirmation by Antoine de Rivarol (author of *Discours sur l'universalité de la langue française* (1784)) of the 'incorruptibility' of French syntax.

4 'Parce que c'est elles qui font souffrir, ou ce sont elles, car l'un et l'autre est ou sont français, et se dit ou se disent.'

5 'Tout le mystère est là: établir les identités secrètes par un deux à deux qui ronge et use les objets, au nom d'une centrale pureté.' See Stéphane Mallarmé, *Propos sur la poésie*, Monaco: Éditions du Rocher, 1946, p. 174. (All translations are by the editors with the exception of those of Mallarmé's 'Le nénuphar blanc' taken from the Penguin *Selected Verse* edition.)

6 'L'image est une création pure de l'esprit, elle ne peut naître d'une comparaison, mais du rapprochement de deux réalités [...] Une image n'est pas forte parce qu'elle est brutale ou fantastique, mais parce que l'association des idées est lointaine est juste' (Pierre Reverdy, *Le gant de crin* [1927], Paris: Flammarion, 1968, p. 30).

7 Edgar Allan Poe, 'The Power of Words' [1845], in: *The Complete Works of Edgar Allan Poe: Tales*, New York: Avenel Books, 1981, pp. 514-516 (p. 516).

8 See *Histoire(s) du Cinéma*, Paris: Gallimard-Gaumont, 1998, vol. 4, p. 42. The original phrase can be found in Denis de Rougemont, *Penser avec les mains*, Paris: Albin Michel, 1936, p. 146.

9 'J'avais beaucoup ramé, d'un grand geste net assoupi, les yeux au dedans fixés sur l'entier oubli d'aller, comme l'heure coulait alentour. Tant d'immobilité paressait que frôlé d'un bruit inerte où fila jusqu'à moitié la yole, je ne vérifiai l'arrêt qu'à l'étincellement stable d'initiales sur les avirons mis à nu, ce qui me rappela à mon identité mondaine. Qu'arrivait-il, où étais-je?' ('Le nénuphar blanc', *Divagations*, Paris: Gallimard, 1976, p. 91).

10 Paul Bénichou, *Selon Mallarmé*, Paris: Gallimard, 1995, p. 19.

11 Bertrand Marchal, *La religion de Mallarmé*, Paris: José Corti, 1988, p. 443.

12 See Michel Chion, *L'audio-vision*, Paris: Nathan, 1990, and Michel Chion, *Le son*, Paris: Nathan, 1998.

13 Jean Paulhan, *Les fleurs de Tarbes* in: *Œuvres complètes*, vol. 3, Paris: Cercle du livre précieux, 1967, p. 82.

Notes to 11: Investigation of a Mystery: Cinema and the Sacred in HÉLAS POUR MOI

1 My thanks to Philippe Wuppermann for his incisive remarks and support.

2 According to Giraudoux, writing in 1929, 37 different versions of the myth had been produced prior to his play. In an article in *Le Monde* (7 September 1993) at the time of the film's release, 'Amphitryon 39-93'. Jean-Michel Frodon claims that Godard's film is the 39th version.

3 Quoted from the screenplay written during shooting, available for consultation at the BIFI (Bibliothèque du Film et de l'Image) in Paris. Henceforth I shall refer to this document as 'Screenplay'.

4   'Reportage is generally worthwhile only if it's combined with fiction, but fiction is
     only interesting if it can be backed up by documentary evidence' ('Entretien – Les Ca-
     hiers rencontrent Godard après ses quatre premiers films', in: Alain Bergala (ed.),
     Jean-Luc Godard par Jean-Luc Godard, vol. 1, 1950-1984, Paris: Cahiers du Cinéma, 1985,
     pp. 215-236 (p. 232)).

5   To cite just a few of the reviews: 'There's no point in attempting to understand what
     he is saying, since you cannot make anything of the entangled and confused dia-
     logue. Not that you care anyway, since you soon stop trying to follow. There's little
     hope that anyone will stay awake', M. Stouvenot, Le Journal du Dimanche, 5 September
     1993; 'The only question the director doesn't ask and which he clearly doesn't care
     about is: "Is there still an audience for Godard's films?"', Le Journal du dimanche, 12th
     September 1993; 'And so, not surprisingly, the film is a shambles. It exaggerates and
     irritates', F. Julien, VSD, 9-15 September 1993; 'An attempt to express the inexpress-
     ible with images, it is both arrogant and poignant. However, you need a lot of belief
     and stamina to avoid losing the thread!', A.C., Les Échos, 8 September 1993; 'HÉLAS
     POUR MOI is an irritable, grumpy film in a foul mood', G. Lefort and O. Seguret,
     Libération, 8 September 1993; 'A garrulous film and a wall of silence: far from the vi-
     sionary Godard we were hoping for and expecting', S. Chemineau, La Tribune Des
     Fossés, 8 September 1993.

6   'HÉLAS POUR MOI is a film [...] born a little early, like a premature baby, because in the
     cinema one simply cannot wait [...] You get the finance in order to shoot, not to wait
     for things to happen in their own time', M.N. Tranchant, 'Jean-Luc Godard: "Je viens
     d'ailleurs"': interview in Le Figaro, 30 August 1993.

7   'I wanted to go further but that was an unrealisable dream. The film does not carry its
     logic through to the end but it manages to say something. A few traces and hints re-
     main [...] you feel that something is unfinished', ibid..

8   Thierry Jousse, 'La loi de la gravitation': interview with Jean-Luc Godard, in: Alain
     Bergala (ed.), Jean-Luc Godard par Jean-Luc Godard, vol. 2, 1984-1998, Paris: Cahiers du
     Cinéma, 1998, pp. 272-285 (p. 272). (This interview originally appeared in Cahiers du
     Cinéma, no. 472, October 1993.)

9   Godard, quoted in Vincent Remy, 'L'Épître aux Gascons', Télérama, 8 August 1993.

10   Jean-Luc Godard, 'Fragments du discours d'un amoureux des mots', ibid..

11   Here I follow the analytical categories espoused by Godard in his article 'Montage
     mon beau souci', in: Bergala (ed.), Godard par Godard I, op. cit., pp. 92-94.

12   Jean-Luc Godard, Introduction à une véritable histoire du cinéma, Paris: Éd. Albatros,
     1980, p. 69.

13   Pascal Bonitzer, 'Dieu, Godard, le zapping', in Trafic, no. 8, Autumn 1993, p. 10.

14   Though Klimt's investigation begins with the start of the film, the character of Klimt,
     played by Bernard Verley, was added by Godard 'two months after shooting':
     'Godard stopped the film and reworked his entire story. That was when he called me
     in and explained to me that the film was a complete failure [...] Therefore, after much
     thought, Godard decided to change the structure of the film and add a character,
     called Abraham Klimt, who in reality acts as the director's double and helps us to un-
     derstand the non-finite nature of the film. It's as if the role of Klimt introduces another
     film within the film. Klimt is a publisher who has received an unfinished manuscript
     concerning an appearance of God. He is making enquiries to find out what really
     happened. He returns to the places on the edge of Lake Geneva where the story took

place and tries to find out what guise God assumed' (Bernard Verley, 'Mon tournage avec Godard', *L'Événement du Jeudi*, 2 September 1993).

15 Vernet argues that these features particularly involve the spectator in the auditorium, whom he sees as playing a pivotal role in the story: see M. Vernet, 'Le regard à la caméra', *Iris*, no. 82 (1983); 'Figures de l'absence 2: La voix-off', *Iris*, no. 85 (1985); 'Le personnage de film', *Iris*, no. 87 (1986); and *Figures de l'absence*, Paris: Éd. de l'Étoile, 1988.

16 Jousse, 'La loi de la gravitation', op. cit., p. 272.

17 Close-up of Simon plus two 'full-screen' quotations (unattributed) from Faulkner: 'The past is never dead/It hasn't even yet passed'.

18 See Jousse, 'La loi de la gravitation', op. cit..

19 Ibid., p. 276.

20 Interview with Noël Simsolo on 'À voix nue', Radio France Culture, April 1998, un-published transcription, p. 8-9.

21 Alain Bergala, 'HÉLAS POUR MOI, ou du présent comme passé légèrement corrigé,' *Cinémathèque*, no. 5, Spring 1994, pp. 19-27 (pp. 25-26).

22 See Jean-Luc Godard and Youssef Ishaghpour, 'Archéologie du cinéma et mémoire du siècle', Dialogue I, *Trafic*, no. 29, Spring 1999, p. 16-35 (p. 22). The original phrase from Wilde is: 'The one duty we owe to history is to rewrite it' ('The Critic as Artist').

23 Bergala, *Godard par Godard II*, op. cit., p. 312.

24 Georges Bataille, *Œuvres complètes*, vol. 1, Paris: Gallimard, 1976, p. 560. This defini-tion of the sacred is closely linked to the Greek concept of truth, '*aletheia*'.

25 Jousse, 'La loi de la gravitation', op. cit., p. 272.

26 For a detailed study of this type of film, see A. Ayfre and H. Agel, *Le cinéma et le sacré*, Paris: Éds. du Cerf, 1953, especially 'L'ascèse liturgique' (pp. 21-53), and 'Couleur du quotidien' (pp. 75-90). See also Paul Schrader, *Transcendental Style in Film: Ozu, Bresson, Dreyer*, New York: Da Capo Paperbacks, 1972.

27 See especially C.T. Dreyer's ORDET.

28 Dreyer himself directed VAMPYR in 1932. See also the fruitful remarks by Marc Vernet on the horror film: 'L'en-deçà ou le regard caméra', in: Vernet, *Figures de l'absence*, op. cit., pp. 29-58 and 43-53.

29 In HÉLAS POUR MOI several sequences take place in the video shop, notably the se-quence where Benjamin summarises the horror films for the 'mother of the little girl'.

30 In I CONFESS, the priest bound to the oath of confidentiality cannot divulge the iden-tity of the murderer who has confessed to him. He is considered guilty right up until the ending when the murderer's wife denounces her husband. This extract is quoted in HÉLAS POUR MOI. The inter-title 'la loi du silence' (the law of silence), which ap-pears in HÉLAS POUR MOI on several occasions, is the French title of Hitchcock's film.

31 This citation, apparently not from St. Paul and therefore attributed to him 'by mis-take', also appears in KING LEAR and HISTOIRE(S) DU CINÉMA, where the word 'resur-rection' sometimes replaces 'redemption'.

32 'I'm not a believer, it's not a film about religion' (Godard to S. Thepot, *La Croix*, 1 Sep-tember 1993).

33 Jean-Luc Godard on HISTOIRE(S) DU CINÉMA, in: 'J'ai fait une échographie': interview with P. Murat and J.C. Loiseau, *Télérama*, 11 November 1998, p. 38.

34 Martine Joly, *L'image et les signes: approche sémiologique de l'image fixe*, Paris: Éd. Na-than, 1994, p. 58.

35 Youssef Ishaghpour, 'Jean-Luc Godard cinéaste de la vie moderne: Le poétique dans l'historique', unpublished paper delivered at the Cerisy conference in 1998, 'Godard et le métier d'artiste'.
36 Ibid..

Notes on Contributors

Jacques Aumont teaches film aesthetics at the University of Paris III-Sorbonne Nouvelle. He is also editor of *Iris* and *Cinémathèque*. His published works include *L'œil interminable* (Séguier, 1989), *Du visage au cinéma* (L'Étoile, 1992), *L'image* (Nathan, 1990), VAMPYR *de Carl-Th. Dreyer* (Yellow Now, 1993), *À quoi pensent les films* (Séguier, 1995), *De l'esthéthique au présent* (De Boeck et Larcier, 1998), and *Amnésies: Fictions du cinéma d'après Jean-Luc Godard* (P.O.L., 1999).

Vicki Callahan is a visiting lecturer at University of California-Irvine and University of California-Los Angeles. She has a book forthcoming from Wayne State University Press entitled *Zones of Anxiety: Mapping Disorder and Difference in the Crime Serials of Louis Feuillade*. She is also currently co-editing an anthology of feminist theory, history, and visual culture.

Jonathan Dronsfield is a Leverhulme Fellow in Philosophy at the Centre for Modern European Philosophy, Middlesex University. He is currently researching accountability and justification in modern French philosophy. He is also a film-maker.

Lætitia Fieschi-Vivet is a postgraduate student at Birkbeck College London and is writing a Ph.D. on the sacred in Godard's later work.

Jean-Louis Leutrat teaches film at the University of Paris III-Sorbonne Nouvelle where he is also President. His published works include *Julien Gracq* (Éditions Universitaires, 1967), *Le western, archéologie d'un genre* (Presses Universitaires de France, 1987), *Des traces qui nous ressemblent* (Comp'Act, 1990), *Le cinéma en perspective: une histoire* (Nathan, 1992), and *Jean-Luc Godard, un cinéaste mallarméen* (Schena-Didier Érudition, 1998).

Timothy Murray is Professor of English and Director of Graduate Studies in Film and Video at Cornell University. His publications include *Like a Film: Ideological Fantasy on Screen and Canvas* (Routledge, 1993), *Drama Trauma: Specters of Race and Sexuality in Performance, Video and Art* (Routledge, 1997), and he has edited *Mimesis, Masochism, and Mime: The Politics of Theatricality* *in Contemporary French Thought* (Michigan UP, 1997). He is the curator of the international exhibition 'Contact Zones: The Art of CD-ROM', and is currently completing a book on digital aesthetics and baroque theory.

Michael Temple teaches French at Birkbeck College London. He is the author of *The Name of the Poet: Onomastics and Anonymity in the Works of Stéphane Mallarmé* (Exeter UP, 1995), and editor of *Meetings with Mallarmé in Contemporary French Culture* (Exeter UP, 1998). He is currently writing a book on Jean Vigo for Manchester University Press and is co-editing *The French Cinema Book* for the British Film Institute.

James S. Williams teaches French and comparative literature at the University of Kent at Canterbury. He is the author of *The Erotics of Passage: Pleasure, Politics, and Form in the Later Work of Marguerite Duras* (St Martin's Press/Liverpool UP, 1997), *Critical Guide to Camus's* La peste (Grant and Cutler, 2000), editor of *Revisioning Duras: Film, Race, Sex* (Liverpool UP, 2000) and co-editor of *Gay Signatures: Gay and Lesbian Theory, Fiction, and Film in France, 1945-1995* (Berg, 1998). He is currently writing a book on the films of Jean Cocteau for Manchester University Press, and co-editing for Berg a volume entitled *Gender and French Cinema*.

Michael Witt teaches French and Film at the University of Surrey Roehampton. He is the author of a doctoral thesis entitled 'On Communication: The Work of Anne-Marie Miéville and Jean-Luc Godard as Sonimage from 1973-1979'. In 1999 he edited a dossier of texts on HISTOIRE(S) DU CINÉMA for *Screen*, and his essays on late Godard have appeared in books and journals in France, Australia and the UK. He is currently co-editing *The French Cinema Book* for the British Film Institute.

Alan Wright teaches film studies at the University of Canterbury in Christchurch, New Zealand. He has published articles in *Wide Angle, Journal of Composition Studies* and *Disclosure*, and is currently researching the essay film and questions of nation and cinema.

Index